W9-CHF-628

# THE PASSIONATE ATTACHMENT

*By* GEORGE W. BALL

The Discipline of Power

Diplomacy for a Crowded World

Global Companies:
The Political Economy of World Business (ed.)

The Past Has Another Pattern

Error and Betrayal in Lebanon

*By* DOUGLAS B. BALL

Financial Failure and Confederate Defeat

# The Passionate Attachment

AMERICA'S INVOLVEMENT WITH ISRAEL, 1947 TO THE PRESENT

GEORGE W. BALL

AND

DOUGLAS B. BALL

W · W · NORTON & COMPANY

NEW YORK LONDON

Printed in the United States of America.

The text of this book is composed in Times Roman,
with the display set in Times Roman.
Composition and manufacturing by the Haddon Craftsmen, Inc.
Book design by Jacques Chazaud.

Library of Congress Cataloging-in-Publication Data

Ball, George W.
The passionate attachment : America's involvement with Israel 1947 to the present / George W. Ball with Douglas B. Ball.
p. cm.
Includes index.
1. United States—Foreign relations—Israel. 2. Israel—Foreign relations—United States. 3. United States—Foreign relations—1945- 4. Military assistance, American—Israel.
I. Ball, Douglas B. II. Title.
E183.8.I7B35 1992
327.73056—dc20 90-37033

ISBN 0-393-02933-6

W. W. Norton & Company, Inc., 500 Fifth Avenue, New York, N.Y. 10110
W. W. Norton & Company Ltd., 10 Coptic Street, London WC1A 1PU

1 2 3 4 5 6 7 8 9 0

To Ruth M. Ball
with love from one author (her husband)
and the other author (her son).

# CONTENTS

## PART II



## PART III



## PART IV



## PART V

# Foreword

The title of this book, as many readers will recognize, is a phrase used by George Washington in his farewell address in 1796. Washington counseled the new nation that in shaping its international relations, it should abjure any "passionate attachment" to, or "inveterate hatred" of, any other nation. Instead, it should "cultivate peace and harmony with all."

Washington uttered that warning because a vocal faction of Americans was exhibiting what he regarded as an excessive and potentially dangerous enthusiasm for revolutionary France, while another faction was favoring Britain with equal fervor. This sharp cleavage of sentiment had already led foreign interests to seek to manipulate American opinion and Washington feared that France might embroil the fledgling United States in a disastrous war.

Washington's fears were well grounded. Two years later, in 1798, three American diplomats arrived in Paris seeking to restore the United States' once friendly relations with France. Ignored, insulted, and pressured to pay large bribes to the Directors and their corrupt foreign minister, Talleyrand, one member of the American delegation, John Marshall, the future Chief Justice, was enraged. His anger knew no bounds when the insolent agents of Talleyrand (styled Messrs. "W, X, Y, Z") told Marshall that France could not care less about America's diplomatic representations.

> Perhaps you believe that in returning and exposing to your countrymen the unreasonableness of the demands of this government, you will unite

> them in their resistance to those demands. You are mistaken: you ought to know that the diplomatic skill of France and the means she possesses in your country are sufficient to enable her, with the French party in America, to throw the blame which will attend the rupture of the negotiations on the federalists . . . and you may assure yourselves that this will be done.[1]

Confronted by an intransigent regime that openly boasted that it had more power in the United States than America's own government, Marshall put the French claim to the test. He prepared in Paris a report of these transactions and dispatched it to President Adams at Philadelphia.

The publication of Marshall's papers proved the French wrong: the Democratic-Republicans, led by Jefferson, were utterly discredited as the tools of a corrupt, arrogant, and bellicose foreign power. In late 1798, they suffered a catastrophic electoral defeat, after which America and France drifted into an undeclared war.

Today that incident is far more than an historical footnote; it is a tract for the times. Washington's cautionary language is as apposite to America's emotional involvement in the prolonged Arab-Israeli conflict as it was to our ancestors' divisive entanglement in Anglo-French rivalry. Just as in Washington's day a powerful American faction was attached to France, today an even more powerful faction is passionately attached to Israel, producing a variety of evils. Such a passionate attachment, in Washington's words, results in

> —"Sympathy for the favorite nation, facilitating the illusion of an imaginary common interest in cases where no real common interest exists; it also, by infusing into one the enmities of the other, betrays the former into a participation in the quarrels and wars of the latter without adequate inducement or justification";
>
> —"It leads also to concessions to the favorite nation of privileges denied to others, which is apt . . . to injure the nation making the concessions . . . by exciting jealousy, ill will, and disposition to retaliate in the parties from whom equal privileges are withheld";
>
> —"It gives to . . . citizens (who devote themselves to the favorite nation) facility . . . to tamper with domestic factions, to practice the arts of seduction, to mislead public opinion, to influence or awe the public councils!"
>
> And finally, those
>
> —" . . . who may resist the intrigues of the favorite, are liable to become suspected and odious, while its tools and dupes usurp the applause and confidence of the people to surrender their interests."[2]

A passionate attachment to foreign interests even more intense than those that worried George Washington is now distorting United States relations with Israel and the Arab nations and people, diminishing our nation's authority and preventing it from effective action. Only by heeding George

Washington's sage advice will America be able to prevent further episodes in a seemingly endless war between Israel and the Arabs that might culminate in irrevocable catastrophe for both Arabs and Israelis.

After four decades of intermittent fighting, a vast flood of sophisticated arms is continuing to inundate the arena of conflict. Vicious hatred between Arabs and Jews has attained a new height of intensity. A darkening sense of injustice is inflaming the Arab spirit, and the moral standards of thousands of young Israelis are being corroded by their participation, or acquiescence, in the brutal mistreatment of Palestinians.

Despite the fact that the combination of these ugly developments gives renewed urgency to George Washington's plea, most of our statesmen still prefer politics to reality. Bored and wearied by their country's diplomatic passivity, the American people grow daily more cynical and resigned to the continuance of Arab-Israeli carnage as a permanent blight on the Middle East.

It has become abundantly clear that our country's passionate attachment to Israel encourages an automatic process in which actions and counteractions generate a dynamic energy that propels the participants toward unconscionable positions. Amid the rhetorical din of charge and countercharge, moderate voices on either side have a hard time making themselves heard.

Our purpose in this book is to analyze how the current situation came about and how it might be corrected, leaving the final assessment of responsibility to future historians.

The creation of Israel was distinguished by the valor and perseverance of its founders, and is remembered as a tremendously inspiring achievement. Every epic event deserves its own saga; some of the world's most brilliant writers, novelists, and historians have dramatically and lyrically retold the story of the building of Israel. They have recounted it both as a self-contained tale and as one more chapter in a long chronicle of pathos and grandeur that illuminates the tragic history of the Jewish people.

Yet historians should not be content with only half the story; the displacement of vast numbers of people is a heartbreaking tragedy for the dislocated. For Americans to understand the full meaning of the problems not only faced, but caused, by Israel, it is essential that we comprehend these epochal events both as they appeared to the Zionist pioneers and to the displaced Arab *indigenes*.

There are those who may feel that this book contains an excessive number of incidents critical of Israel and its leaders; that is because those incidents have inspired much ingenious and basically counterproductive mythmaking. Although the myths may have provided Israel with some short-term tactical advantages, they may also, if not critically examined, prejudice the Israeli cause and in the long run impede the attainment of enduring peace in the Middle East.

At the heart of the problem is the Jews' sense of insecurity and the Arabs' feeling of injustice and dispossession.

The Israelis never dare forget that there are more than a few Arab leaders still calling for Israel's destruction and that most Arabs would be happy to see Israel disappear. They are aware that the Arab population in the Middle East exceeds the Jewish population of Israel by over forty to one and that a single defeat could mean Israel's extinction.

The Arabs' anger and fear spring largely from frustration based on constant defeat that results from the superior fighting abilities of an Israel that lives on the cutting edge of modern technology and draws freely on America's almost unlimited resources. The inability of the Arabs to translate their numerical dominance and greater economic resources into military victory contributes to an unhealthy state of bitterness and hopelessness.[3]

Meanwhile, several Arab countries have tried to move from hereditary monarchies to some more modern form of polity, but, in a typical Third World pattern, have seen power preempted by military adventurers, who are thoughtlessly hailed by their followers as "military heroes." Because the Arab people have had almost no experience with democracy and some Arab countries lack the middle class needed to support democratic government, the military has represented the only unifying institution in many Middle Eastern societies where the pace of change has been shockingly uneven.

These conditioning factors, the fears they breed and the deep emotions they arouse on both sides, partially explain why the combatants have found increasing difficulty in making peace. But that by itself is by no means the only key to their failure to resolve the problem; that failure also results from America's infatuation with one side and distaste for the other.

---

This book was completed in April 1992. Since that time, the Israeli election has produced political changes which, it is claimed, will speed up the pending negotiations and lead to an ultimate settlement of the problems of the Occupied Territories.

By substituting what is asserted to be Rabin's pragmatism for Shamir's ideological rigidity, the election has lifted the hearts of every American wishing an end of the frustrating Middle East conflict. Yet, before we become too elated, we should squarely face the realities documented by four decades of experience. Those decades have been cluttered by Israeli commitments made and ignored in the interests of its leaders' relentless expansionism.

What, if anything, can experience tell us about Rabin's current promises?

First, by the end of nine months his government will achieve an agreement granting autonomy for the Palestinians in the Occupied Territories. This is not the first time such a promise has been made. Negotiations for autonomy were also contemplated by the agreed Framework for Peace that was part of the Camp David Accords, but differences between the parties as to the content of autonomy were so wide that the Israelis and Palestinians never reached the point of actual negotiations.

Rabin's second promise is that Israel will create no new "political" colonies in the Occupied Territories but will continue to build such new settlements as its government deems necessary for "security reasons." Let us remember that during a previous interlude in power Labor governments built a large number of settlements which they justified as needed for "security reasons," but which Israel's military authorities scornfully dismissed as weakening rather than strengthening Israel's defense against invasion.

Even if effectively carried out, Rabin's new promises would not secure tranquillity for the area, since they deal at most with only a limited aspect of the Arab-Israeli struggle. Rabin intends to exclude East Jerusalem from any autonomy negotiations, despite the fact that the United States regards it as a particularly sensitive part of the West Bank; he has said nothing about returning the Golan Heights to Syria (Israel's only serious potential enemy), although Israel has installed guns on those heights capable of bombarding Syria's capital of Damascus; nor, finally, has he even mentioned the removal of Israeli surrogate forces from south Lebanon.

In appraising the chances for progress toward peace, Americans must finally consider the attitude of Rabin himself, who has assumed personal charge of the negotiations. When as Defense Minister four years ago he was assigned responsibility for maintaining order in the Occupied Territories, he instructed his troops that: "the first priority was to use force, might, beatings." Then he added cynically, "No demonstrators have died from being thwacked on the head" (see chapter nine). That is scarcely the attitude of one who will negotiate with compassion and understanding. Nor, according to Henry Kissinger, is Rabin likely to display those qualities when negotiations actually begin; Kissinger, who dealt with him repeatedly, assessed the bargaining tactics of Rabin as follows:

> Yitzhak [Rabin] had many extraordinary qualities, but the gift of human relations was not one of them. If he had been handed the entire "United States Strategic Air Command" as a free gift he would have (a) affected the attitude that at last Israel was getting its due, and (b) found some technical shortcoming in the airplanes that made his accepting them a reluctant concession to us. [Quoted from chapter four]

Thus, while hoping for an end to Middle East turmoil, we should not rule out the chance that the forthcoming discussions may at best be merely a partial success—one more deception in a seemingly endless series of abortive peacemaking efforts.

# Acknowledgments

This book has had a long parturition. It would never have been completed without the generous assistance of many people who do not necessarily concur in all of its conclusions.

We particularly thank Barbara Wendell Kerr, who through long nights of labor turned the tangled rain forest of our prose into an English garden, cleaning away the undergrowth so light could shine on the subject.

Throughout the effort we have relied persistently on Merle Thorpe, Jr., who has long dedicated his time, effort, and resources to promote a sensible view of the United States relations with Israel. We have also been continually encouraged and instructed by Lucius D. Battle, who was for many years president of the Middle East Institute, and by Donald Neff, who has written with brilliance and incisiveness of Israel's wars. During our early work on the book, Yoma Ullman was a great source of help and encouragement.

We have drawn needed enlightenment on recondite problems of international law from Professors W. Thomas and Sally Mallison.

We have also relied heavily on the advice of two members of the Princeton faculty, Professors L. Carl Brown and Richard Ullman. Both have not only provided wise counsel but have identified and recruited graduate students whom we retained for research. Among those students, we would particularly mention Rodney J. Fabrycky, Erik G. Yesson, Molly Greene, Jens Heycke, and Marion Katz. If we have failed to note all who helped, it is not that any disappointed us, but that the group is too numerous for specific thanks.

Finally, we thank Karen Vasudeva for her patience, assiduity, and splendid judgment in turning our often illegible manuscript into readable text through the instrumentality of a word processor. No one could have more clearly discerned the essence of our often clouded ideas.

# List of Maps and Tables

## Maps



## Tables

# PART I

CHAPTER ONE

# The Creation of Israel and Its War of Independence

ZIONISM HAS BEEN an active movement for roughly a century—and Zionism's gifted adherents have told and retold its story again and again. This book will concentrate on the relations of the United States with the nation that Zionism brought into being.

The practical process that ultimately produced that nation began immediately after World War I, when statesmen of the victorious powers set about rearranging the rickety political furniture left behind when the Ottoman Empire disintegrated. They almost at once confronted hard and sensitive decisions.

Among the first was the choice whether the League of Nations' Palestinian Mandate should be awarded to Britain or the United States. That the British had major reservations about undertaking it was indicated by a comment of Lord Cecil at a meeting of the Eastern Committee of the British War Cabinet: "there is not going to be any great catch about [the governance of Palestine] because we shall simply keep the peace between the Arabs and the Jews. We're not going to get anything out of it." To that he added, with extraordinary prescience, "Whoever goes there will have a poor time . . . " but "If the Americans are put into Palestine they will get into the most awful confusion."[1]

As everyone expected, the Versailles Conference awarded the Palestinian Mandate to Britain. The British accepted with some reluctance, well knowing that, as Lord Balfour put it in an exceptionally candid memorandum, "so far as Palestine is concerned, the powers have made no statement of fact which is not admittedly wrong, and no declaration of policy which, at least in the letter, they have not always intended to violate."[2]

Britain conducted its mandate for twenty-eight years. Then, when both its will and physical resources had been drained by two wars in two generations, it found the continuance of its colonial role too irksome and unrewarding. So the British government gave notice in May 1947 that it intended to abandon the mandate in one year. That forced America to assume much of the responsibility, and, as Lord Cecil had predicted, the United States did indeed get "into the most awful confusion."

Britain's decision to leave put the burden on the United Nations and the other leading powers to determine who should govern Palestine after the British departed. There were two practical solutions: either to partition the mandate and thereby create two nations; or to maintain the unity of the land, which, under democratic rules, meant giving control to the Arab majority. It was far from an easy choice. When the British had offered partition in 1937, the Arabs had indignantly rejected it; when the British backtracked and favored a unitary state in 1939, the Zionists cannonaded them with abuse.

Then in 1947 the United Nations Special Committee on Palestine (known as UNSCOP) proposed, against the better judgment of many of its members, that the Palestine Mandate be divided between a Jewish and an Arab state.[3] To secure a favorable General Assembly vote for such a plan, President Harry Truman engaged in active lobbying for the Zionist cause.[4] Eventually, the votes of at least Haiti and the Philippines were secured by the unauthorized intervention of private American citizens.[5]

Although Truman subsequently sought to justify his action on the ground that Britain's promised departure would leave a vacuum in Palestine and that his foreign policy advisers had urged him to recognize the new Jewish government promptly, the influence of domestic pressures cannot be totally excluded. Running for a second term, Truman was in deep political trouble. The Gallup Poll in early 1948, when the campaign began, showed Truman with 44.5 percent of the vote and Dewey with 49.5 percent; the Roper Poll showed Dewey with 52.2 percent of the vote against Truman's 37.1 percent. Even in 1947, Truman knew he would need every vote he could get and that the Jewish American population could very well turn the balance. In his memoirs, he commented that "The Department of State's specialists on the Near East were, almost without exception, unfriendly to the idea of a Jewish State."[6] That comment was certainly accurate; the experienced diplomat William Phillips, who had served in 1946 as an American member of the twelve-man Anglo-American Committee of Inquiry on Palestine, joined in producing a report; ten of the committee were against a Jewish state. George Kennan, then director of the State Department's Policy Planning Staff, strongly opposed it, as, finally, did the Secretary of State, George C. Marshall, who eloquently urged the President against partition.

But, on White House instructions, the United States delegation to the

United Nations ignored these opposing views, and in November 1947, nine months after Britain made the decision to withdraw its mandate, Resolution 181(II) of the United Nations General Assembly gave legitimacy to Israel.[7]

The United Nations acknowledged the need for economic union between the two partition states if they were to be economically viable, and that Israel and its Arab neighbors must have peaceful relations with each other if they were not to be permanently dependent on handouts from other nations—even though no one could then have come near predicting the amount of money those handouts would ultimately require.[8]

At the time of UNSCOP's report, Palestine was inhabited by 1,350,000 Arabs and 650,000 Jews; thus the Arabs constituted approximately two thirds of the population. The partition solution provided that the Jews, who occupied less than 6 percent of the lands in the mandate, should receive 56 percent of the mandated territory for a Jewish state, while the Arabs, who then occupied 94 percent of the land, should be allotted only 44 percent.

As might have been anticipated, the Arabs unanimously rejected what they regarded as a grotesquely skewed misallocation. They challenged the power of the United Nations to dispose of Arab-inhabited lands without the consent of the population and further contended that a two-thirds majority should decide the fate of the entire country. In addition, they rejected as unfair a scheme of distribution which involved ejecting the Palestinians from lands long held by their families for the benefit of a numerically smaller population of Jews, most of whose members were newcomers.

Both Arabs and Jews agreed that the boundaries as drawn were unworkable. As delineated by UNSCOP, these boundaries would have given the Jews access to their properties along the Jordan Valley only through a tiny passageway southwest of Nazareth, while the Arabs would hold equally tiny corridors connecting their holdings in West Galilee or Gaza with the West Bank. The city of Jaffa would become an Arab exclave in the middle of the Jewish coastal plain; Jerusalem would remain a pocket of Jewish settlers completely surrounded by Arabs in an internationalized city.

To the Arabs, the whole procedure seemed a callous manifestation of colonialist maneuvering by the great powers. By manipulating the United Nations, the powers were seeking to divide the country under an impracticable formula highly prejudicial to the Palestinians.

The year 1948 confronted Washington with a harsh reality. The Truman administration had opted for partition only to realize late in the day that such a choice might produce a dangerous explosion.[9] Faced with the obvious danger of disorder and even war in Palestine which the scheduled departure of the British in May seemed to portend, Truman strove to find some means of heading off the bloodshed. Thus, on February 19 he told Secretary Marshall to present an interim Trusteeship proposal and to disregard political considerations. In conformity with Marshall's instructions, on March 24, 1948, Warren Austin, the U.S. delegate to the United Nations, urged that, without prejudice to a final settlement,[10] the Security Council should hold in abeyance, by means of a temporary Trusteeship, the General Assembly's partition resolution of November 29, 1947.

That policy prevailed until May 12, when Truman met with several of his aides. It was just three days before Israel's creation—and, more important, just six months prior to the American presidential election. Although his closest political adviser, Clark Clifford, urged the President to recognize the Jewish state, Secretary of State George Marshall echoed the President's early comments about not permitting domestic politics to interfere in foreign policy. Under Secretary of State Robert Lovett expressed the same view.

Taking account of the activities of the United States in late 1947, Kermit Roosevelt bitterly concluded that

> The process by which Zionist Jews have been able to promote American support for the partition of Palestine demonstrates the vital need of a foreign policy based on national rather than partisan interests. A Palestine Zionist . . . may dismiss the Russian threat to the United States from his consideration, but an American may not, even if he is a Zionist. . . . Only when the national interests of the United States, in their highest terms, take precedence over all other considerations, can a logical, farseeing foreign policy be evolved. No American political leader has the right to compromise American interests to gain partisan votes. . . . The present course of world crisis will increasingly force upon Americans the realization that their national interests and those of the proposed Jewish state in Palestine are going to conflict. It is to be hoped that American Zionists and non-Zionists alike will come to grips with the realities of the problem.[11]

In the end, domestic politics almost certainly made the difference. In 1947 Truman himself admitted in a memorandum to David Niles, "We could have settled this Palestine thing if U.S. politics had been kept out of it. Terror and [Rabbi Hillel] Silver are the contributing causes of some, if not all, of our troubles."[12]

So, when David Ben-Gurion announced the founding of the State of Israel on May 14, 1948, the United States competed with the Soviet Union to be the first nation to extend de facto recognition, and immediately thereafter Clifford asked the Jewish leaders what else they wanted. They asked for de jure recognition, a $100 million loan to Israel, and an end to the arms embargo in the Middle East in their favor. On October 28, before the election, Truman delivered an address affirming that "Israel must be large enough, free enough, and strong enough to make its people self-supporting and secure."[13] Truman won the election with 75 percent of the Jewish vote; on January 19, 1949, he announced the $100 million loan, and on January 31, recognized Israel de jure.[14]

Israel's supporters contend that the Jews came to Israel with an idealistic vision of the country they wished to build, and that the early Zionist settlers tried to live peacefully with the native Palestinians and the neighboring Arab states. But their intentions were thwarted when the armies of five Arab states invaded Israel. In the course of the war that followed, Arab leaders ordered the native Palestinians to depart. The result, which Chaim Weizmann, Israel's first president, interpreted as a "miraculous cleansing of the land," left the Israelis free to take over and develop the whole land of Israel without a large, obstructionist Arab minority.

This self-seeking, mythologized version of history came by constant repetition to acquire the authority of received truth and for many years escaped critical dissection. But, with fresh scholarship inspired by the delayed publication of censored memoirs and the opening of Israeli government archives, historians are finally obtaining an accurate picture of what really happened.

## The Failure to Observe the Partition Resolution

The boundaries proposed by the partition resolution were totally impracticable for each side, and there is now strong evidence that the Israelis never intended to live under them. As explained by the late Israeli scholar and publisher Simha Flapan, "acceptance of the U.N. Partition Resolution was an example of Zionist pragmatism *par excellence.* It was a tactical acceptance, a vital step in the right direction—a springboard for *expansion* when circumstances proved more *judicious.*"[15]

In view of what subsequently occurred, one should skeptically dismiss the assertion that the Israelis had been happily living at peace with the local Palestinians until their "War of Independence." Moreover, the claim that peace broke down only after May 15, 1948, when armies from the surrounding Arab nations crossed the frontiers of the mandate, is open to serious question. In fact, fierce communal fighting between Arabs and Jews had commenced five months before, in December 1947, soon after the UN Partition Resolution; and by May 15, when the Arab armies entered the mandate (and thus turned the communal fighting into an international war), roughly 200,000 Palestinians had already fled the country. Meanwhile Israeli forces had used those months (December 1947–May 1948) to conquer and secure control of substantial territory in the area assigned to the Jewish side.

Though it has been argued that during those five months both military forces kept largely within the areas assigned by the Partition Plan to their respective sides, Israeli troops were already involved in various campaigns, particularly along the Jerusalem road, that definitely involved the conquest of territory allotted to the Arabs.[16] As a result, though the Jews claimed pro forma to desire a truce, their ambitions and military superiority clearly indicated expansionist intentions.[17]

Following a pattern that was later to become habitual, the Israelis began preparations for the conflict long before the Arab side made any organized effort. In November 1947, six months before the Arab national armies arrived on the scene, the Jewish leaders had drawn up several plans. One of them, operation Plan D (or Plan Dalet), was designed to rearrange local demography and to give Israel an additional 10 percent of the mandate's land area beyond that assigned to it by the Partition Plan.[18]

## The Israeli Version and the Informed American View

Meanwhile, Israeli diplomats in Washington were painting a far different picture. Their story was that Arab armies had invaded Palestine even before the British left and that the fledgling Jewish state was in mortal peril. The United States, they argued, should promptly end its arms embargo in Israel's favor, and the United Nations Security Council should condemn the Arab states as aggressors and vote arms sanctions against them. When proof was requested to support those accusations, none was forthcoming.[19]

Though Israel's alarmist account was accepted without challenge by large elements of the sympathetic Jewish American community, America's diplomats were not deceived; they knew from the beginning that the Arabs were certain losers in their war with Israel. Every source confirmed the overwhelming military superiority of the Israelis over their Arab opponents. A British minister advised the American ambassador that well-trained and armed Israeli forces outnumbered the similarly trained and armed Arab forces by about four to one, and that they were certain to win the first phase of the fighting.[20] Harold Beeley, a British representative at the United Nations (specializing in Palestinian affairs), reported to the State Department official responsible for the Middle East, Loy Henderson, that the Israeli forces were markedly superior and that it was their plan to exploit that advantage in an effort to expand beyond the territory allotted to them in the November 19, 1947, UN Assembly Resolution.[21]

In addition to cable accounts then being received from America's missions in the Middle East, Secretary of State George C. Marshall drew upon his long military experience by issuing a circular that bluntly analyzed the Arab armies' deficiencies. Iraq, the circular noted, was so politically unstable that it could deploy few troops. Egypt was short of key equipment and, in view of a police strike, needed its army at home. Syria lacked weapons and, in the three years since the French had left, had done nothing to organize its armed forces. Neither Lebanon nor Saudi Arabia had real armies, the Saudi Arabian forces consisting only of primitive tribal levies. Even the best of the Arab forces, the Trans-Jordanian Army (the Arab Legion), was crippled by the absence of its British officers.[22] Finally, quarrels between the Hashemites, the Saudis, and the Syrians would—Marshall correctly predicted—make effective coordination impossible.

In sum, the circular stated, the Arab states would probably confine their operations to the areas allocated to the Arab side and would be of little help in fighting the Israelis.[23] That analysis was confirmed by Ambassador S.

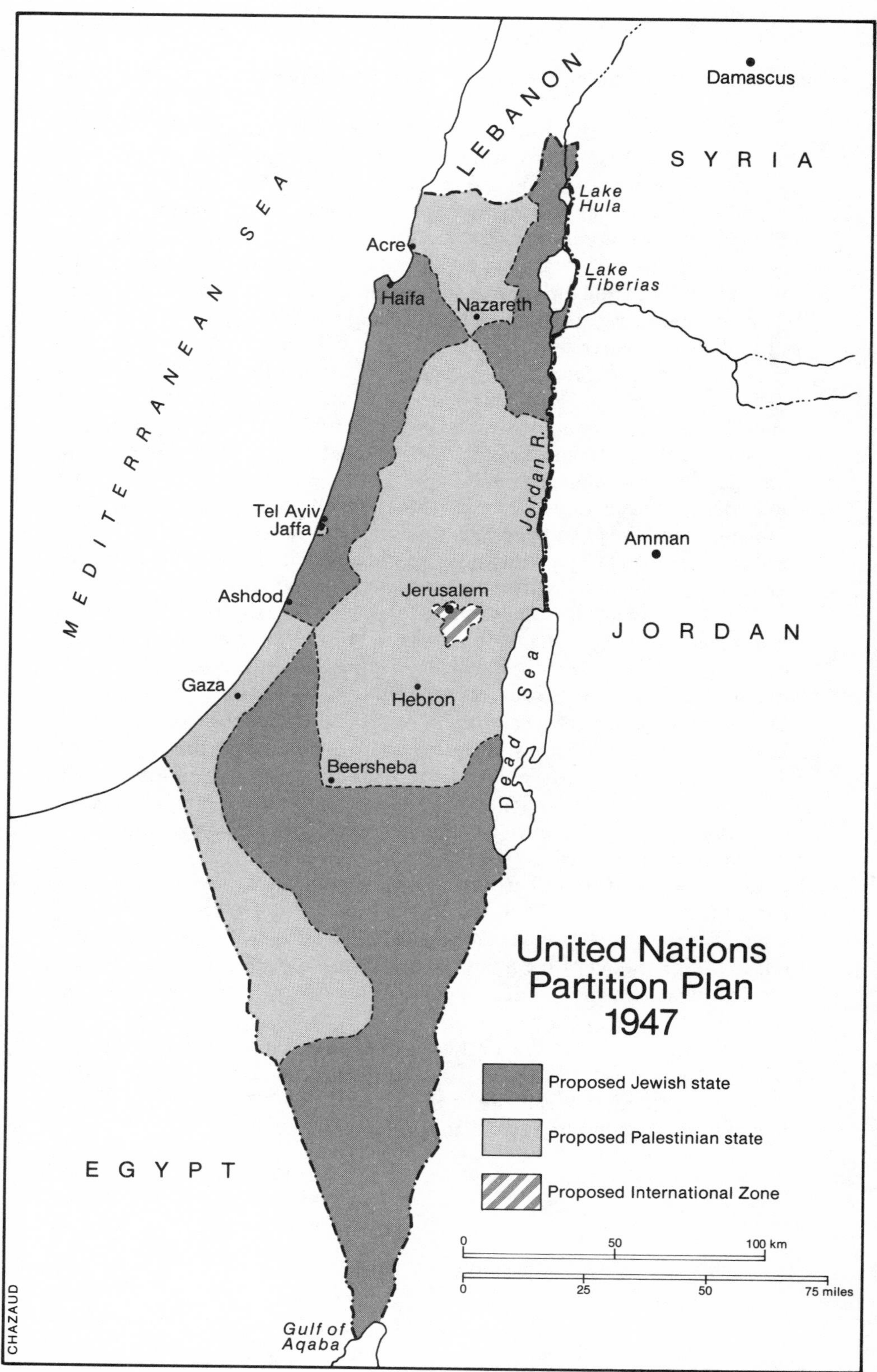
LEBANON
Damascus
SYRIA
Lake Hula
Lake Tiberias
MEDITERRANEAN SEA
Acre
Haifa
Nazareth
Jordan R.
Tel Aviv
Jaffa
Amman
Ashdod
Jerusalem
JORDAN
Gaza
Hebron
Dead Sea
Beersheba
United Nations Partition Plan 1947
Proposed Jewish state
Proposed Palestinian state
Proposed International Zone
EGYPT
0
50
100 km
0
25
50
75 miles
Gulf of Aqaba
CHAZAUD

Pinckney Tuck in Egypt, who reported that Egypt had less than 22,000 regulars.[24]

Although an American-imposed UN arms embargo no doubt caused problems for the Arab side, it only partly explained the Israeli victory. The central reason was that during and immediately after World War II most of the Arabs had been, or still were, preoccupied with winning their independence from their colonial masters and establishing new governments; thus they could devote only marginal attention to the impending Palestinian-Israeli contest. Syria and Lebanon had become independent only in 1945 and 1943 respectively. Egypt still had British troops occupying the Suez Canal. Iraq and, to a greater degree, Jordan remained very much under British tutelage. Nor did any of the Arab regimes bordering the mandate territory then favor the creation of an independent Palestinian state; each had its own designs on the territory, and assumed it was entitled to some of the spoils.

Such was the Arab confusion that as late as May 1, 1948, the Egyptian Army was still searching for road maps of Palestine so as to have at least a vague idea of where to go in case Cairo decided to intervene.[25] The Iraqi commander appointed to mastermind this adventure resigned on May 13 to avoid the role of scapegoat for the impending defeat. He foresaw that "the absence of agreement on a precise plan can only lead to disaster."

Once the Arab armies finally entered Palestine on May 14, 1948, a cease-fire, adopted by the UN Security Council on May 22, enabled Israel to utilize the truce period June 11–July 9, 1948, to replenish its equipment with weapons procured from diverse sources around the world. By contrast, because of a British military embargo, the Iraqis, Egyptians, and Trans-Jordanians remained short of arms. Still, subsequent analysis has shown that the Arabs' defeat was primarily due to political and social, rather than military or technical problems.[26] The cease-fire, which had so benefited the Israelis, ended on July 9, 1948. Fighting resumed for another nine days until, once more under pressure from the United States, another armistice went into effect on July 18, 1948. That in turn lasted until October 15, when the fighting again resumed until January 8, 1949. As Flapan put it, "After the first cease-fire, the Israeli army was able to confront and defeat each Arab army separately, while the rest kept out of the fight." As a result, the Arabs lost ground on all sides and Israel emerged with 21 percent more territory than had been assigned to it by the UN Partition Plan.

Even after the January armistice, the Israelis continued their attacks, seizing Jordanian-occupied parts of the Negev on March 6–10, 1949.[27] Though the fighting in this phase of the war had finally ended, it had engendered hatreds and ambitions guaranteeing future hostilities.

## Conflicting Objectives on the Arab Side

Not only did the Arab side suffer from fundamental differences between two blocs (the Hashemites of Iraq and Trans-Jordan formed one bloc; Egypt, Syria, and Saudi Arabia the other), but King Abdullah, the ruler of Trans-Jordan and the nominal commander of the Arab armies, had a hidden agenda of his own. Far from being committed to the destruction of Israel (as, apparently, were other Arab leaders), he had for years dreamed obsessively of constructing a Greater Syria, which would comprise Syria, Trans-Jordan, Lebanon, and at least the Arab part of Palestine. Allied with Hashemite Iraq, that "Greater Syria" would constitute the dominant Arab nation, especially as it would be supported by the British.[28]

Thus, rather than fighting the Zionists, he hoped to use Jewish financial and technological assistance to achieve his own program, and he did, in fact, succeed in persuading the Jewish Agency, the precursor of the Israeli government, to pay him a regular subsidy. He also reached a secret understanding with the Jewish Agency that he would be allowed to control the part of Palestine intended for an Arab state; in return, he would not interfere with the establishment of the Jewish state. Yet he in no way shared Israeli ambitions; in fact, had his "Greater Syria" been created, there is nothing to indicate that he would not have aspired ultimately to take control of the Jewish part of Palestine.

Abdullah's private ambitions and the other major splits in the Arab ranks were well known to Zionist leaders and to the U.S. government.[29] Still, because of—rather than in spite of—their suspicion of Abdullah, the Arab leaders appointed him commander of the invading Arab forces. This tactical decision was taken in the hope that by entrusting Abdullah with overall responsibility, the Arabs would deflect him from making a separate deal with Israel and compel him to commit his battle-trained Legion, the best available Arab army, to a unified Arab cause.

In addition, according to Simha Flapan, Abdullah's nomination showed that the Arab states were under few illusions as to the outcome of the war:

> They sent less than half their forces against the Israelis—what the Arab chiefs of staff viewed as absolutely minimal for an effective war against Israel. And although Abdullah was overall commander, they never revealed to him the size, composition, or strategic plans of the invading armies. Furthermore, they tried until the last moment to prevent the invasion. They knew they could not defeat the Jewish state. Had the situation been otherwise, they would never have left the "honor of victory" in Abdullah's hands.[30]

In addition, it should be noted that King Abdullah, being more interested in seizing the contiguous parts of Palestine for himself and thus preventing the creation of a Palestinian state, shaped his operational plans with that object in view rather than seeking the destruction of Israel. Thus, the clashes of the Israeli and Jordanian forces were practically confined to those areas assigned to the aborted Palestinian state in November 1947.[31]

## The Deir Yassin Massacre

Among the threats spread by the advancing Israeli army was that the inhabitants had better flee or their village would become another Deir Yassin.

Deir Yassin was a small Arab village just outside Jerusalem. It had stayed out of the struggle and, wishing to be neutral, its inhabitants had entered into a mutual nonaggression pact with the neighboring Jews. They had also agreed not to harbor those attacking the Israelis.[32]

Yet the village was almost the first to suffer the horror of Plan Dalet, which went into effect on April 1, 1948. It called for the destruction and evacuation of twenty villages in order to purge the land of Palestinian inhabitants by gaining "control of areas given to us by the UN in addition to areas occupied by us which were outside these borders."

As an important part of this plan, Prime Minister David Ben-Gurion decreed that the rural areas around cities be destroyed so that the Arab urban economy would collapse, compelling the Arabs to leave in search of employment and sustenance elsewhere. He also decreed that Arab attacks were to be answered by the systematic laying waste of Arab farm areas, and by rendering the Arab villages uninhabitable, thus driving their populations away permanently.[33]

On April 2, 1948, General Israel Galili, head of the Haganah (later the Israeli Defense Force) General Staff, announced a plan for a concentrated offensive involving "operations of conquest and occupation" intended, among other things, to "cleanse" the area of Arab inhabitants.[34] Zionist forces would conduct a holding operation while they simultaneously "softened up" the Palestinians and, through terror, undermined the morale of the civilian population.

The massacre at Deir Yassin began on April 9, 1948, five weeks before the British Mandate on the State of Israel was ended or the Arab armies ventured into Palestine. It was the work primarily of Menachem Begin's Irgun Zvai Leumi, assisted by Yitzhak Shamir's Stern Gang (Lehi), both anti-British and anti-Arab groups active in committing terrorist acts.

Irregular forces from those two organizations blew up houses and killed by gun or knife practically the entire population of the village. When, with help from Haganah (the regular Israeli armed forces) in Jerusalem, the assailants had silenced all resistance, the remaining civilians were seized and ordered into the square, where they were lined up against the wall and gunned down. Others were killed when their homes were dynamited.[35]

A Swiss Red Cross representative, Jacques de Ruynier, led the first party to reach the site, arriving before the terrorists had finished their work. He found 150 bodies thrown into a cistern and another 40 to 50 at one side. He counted in all 254 dead, including 145 women, of whom 35 were pregnant.[36]

The other surviving women and children were stripped, and with their hands above their heads, paraded in three open trucks up and down King George V Avenue in Jewish Jerusalem, where spectators spat on them and stoned them.[37]

### *Propaganda Use of the Massacre*

There is no way that Menachem Begin, as head of the Irgun, can avoid responsibility for the sanguinary event. Yet in his memoirs *The Revolt,* he takes refuge behind a claim of military necessity. He represents this attack on a practically defenseless village as a great triumph of Jewish arms, while ignoring the massacre of noncombatants.

Indeed, Begin sent the following message to his Irgun troops, in which the word "conquest" appears three times:

> Accept my congratulations on this splendid act of conquest. Convey my regards to all the commanders and soldiers. We shake your hands. We are all proud of the excellent leadership and the fighting spirit in this great attack. We stand to attention in memory of the slain. We lovingly shake the hands of the wounded. Tell the soldiers: you have made history in Israel with your attack and your conquest. Continue thus until victory. As in Deir Yassin, so everywhere, we will attack and smite the enemy. God, God, Thou hast chosen us for conquest.[38]

## The Palestinian Flight and an Exclusively Jewish Israel

The Jewish plan for an exclusively Jewish state, free of the inconvenient presence of native peoples, was scarcely new. Theodor Herzl had laid out the framework for such a system in 1898, when he sought a charter from the Ottoman Sultan, Abdul Hamid II, for the Jewish Colonial Society, a precursor of the Jewish Colonial Trust established in 1899. One of the provisions of that abortive charter gave the Society the power to deport the natives, and Herzl sought such powers whether the new Jewish homeland was to be in Argentina, Kenya, Cyprus, or Palestine. The Jewish Land Trust incorporated this doctrine in its rules, which designated all its properties exclusively for Jewish use and even prohibited the employment by the Jewish tenants of non-Jews, thereby forcing such persons to seek employment abroad.[39]

Israel's victory in the 1947–48 War would not have fulfilled its purpose had the Palestinian population remained in place after the defeat of the Arab armies, since the Zionist doctrine of exclusivism, plus their commitment to democracy, required that the Jews achieve a preponderate majority.

Palestinian flight was speeded by the close interreaction of Jews and Arabs and the growing communal warfare between the two peoples. While there were certainly Arab attacks as well as Jewish ones, the evidence strongly suggests that after November 1947, it was the Jews who were on the strategic offensive and the Arabs' efforts were increasingly reactive.

Well before the Arab armies had arrived, at least 200,000 Palestinians had fled, primarily to Lebanon. By the end of the war, the refugee numbers had swollen to 780,000. From the Zionist viewpoint, it was essential not only for the Palestinians to depart but for the Israelis to avoid giving the impression that their forces had forcibly ejected them. Expulsion would have given a legal basis for the Palestinians' right to return, and would have strengthened the Palestinian claims for compensation for the £110 million of property seized or destroyed.

With this in mind, Israel's protagonists in America devised an elaborate cover story to cast the blame onto the victims. The Palestinians had fled, the story contended, not because the Israeli Army had forcibly removed them but because Arab leaders had repeatedly broadcast instructions calling on the Palestinians to leave. The reason behind these instructions—so the story ran—was that, even though the Jewish leaders were urging the Arabs to stay, the Arabs wished them to leave so as to make way for advancing Arab armies.

This self-serving account was incorporated in mimeographed pamphlets disseminated widely throughout the American Jewish community and was, in time, expanded into a book by Joseph Schechtman.[40] That book was accepted as gospel by most Jews in America and its arguments even now resurface in letters to the editor. For a long period the story remained unchallenged; then, in 1958, a Palestinian scholar, Walid Khalidi, concluded after detailed examination that the Schechtman account had distorted the facts. Two years later, after reviewing all relevant evidence, an Irish journalist, Erskine Childers, reaffirmed the same conclusion.

Both Childers and Khalidi found that the principal spur to Palestinian flight had been fear, engendered by a terror campaign fostered by the Israeli Army. Word was spread that the inhabitants had better get out quickly or their village would be decimated and the inhabitants killed. Christopher Hitchens summarizes the evidence in this matter and shows that Israeli propagandists have exploited the unfortunate fact that it is harder to refute false propaganda than it is to disseminate it.[41]

Lurid accounts of the Deir Yassin Massacre were extensively used to frighten the Palestinians into flight.

Following this atrocity, the Haganah and the Irgun launched massive surprise attacks on towns and villages, using mortars, rockets—and a homemade contraption called a *Davidka,* which very inaccurately tossed 60 pounds of TNT some 300 yards into densely populated areas.[42] Panic was intensified by broadcasts in Arabic from clandestine Zionist radio stations and by loudspeakers mounted on armored cars warning of the possible spread of cholera and typhus. They also announced that "innocent people" would pay the price for the Palestinians' use of violent tactics against the Jews.[43]

To illustrate the sophisticated level of the psychological warfare, a British journalist, David Hirst, Middle East correspondent for *The Manchester Guardian,* quotes an Israeli reserve officer as writing that

> As barrel bombs rolled down the street an uncontrolled panic swept through all Arab quarters, the Israelis brought up jeeps with loud speakers which broadcast recorded "horror sounds." These included shrieks, wails, and anguished moans of Arab women, the wail of sirens and the clang of fire alarm bells, interrupted by a sepulchral voice calling out in Arabic: "Save yourself, all ye faithful: the Jews are using poison gas and atomic weapons. Run for your lives in the name of Allah."[44]

The magnitude of the induced flight was remarkable. In 1930, when Jews formed only 17 percent of the population, Ben-Gurion had said that the Jews "must root themselves in this land and become a self-ruling nation."[45] When the war ended in early 1949, the Zionists (who had been allotted 56 percent of the mandate area) had now occupied 77 percent of it. Out of 1,300,000 Arab inhabitants they had displaced nearly 780,000. They now had sole control of entire cities and hundreds of villages.[46]

### *New Evidence on the Massacre*

At long last, forty years after the Deir Yassin incident, in 1988, new contemporary evidence came to light that conclusively disproved the Schechtman version of the Palestinian flight. This new information consisted partially of an IDF Intelligence Branch Report dated June 30, 1948, entitled "The Arab Exodus from Palestine in the Period 1/12/47 to 1/6/48."[47]

The report was disclosed by the Israeli historian Benny Morris (diplomatic correspondent of *The Jerusalem Post*) and published in the January 1986 issue of *Middle Eastern Studies.*[48] He later expanded this article into a book, *The Birth of the Palestinian Refugee Problem, 1947–1949* (1987) in which he included additional materials drawn from the British and American archives.

Morris's article demolishes the official Israeli explanation of the Palestinian exodus. The story that emerges is that up to June 1, 1948 (the period covered by the report), most of the 300,000–400,000 Palestinians who left their homes did so when attacked by the Irgun and the Lehi (Stern Gang).

The bulk of the exodus was not caused by orders and commands from Arab leaders; the report limited their effect to "5 percent of the villages evacuated"—primarily in cases where local Arab commanders gave orders to evacuate "either out of a desire to turn the village into a base for attack on the Jews or fear that the village could turn into an 'anti-Arab' fifth column."

By June 1948 the depopulation of some 250 villages and several towns resulted from the following factors:

—At least 55 percent of the total exodus was caused by Israeli Army operations and their influence. In addition, the report noted that "psychological factors also affected the rate of emigration."

—The operations of the Irgun and Stern Gang directly caused an additional 15 percent of the migration, and the report credits the "special effect of the massacre at Deir Yassin."

—10 percent of the refugees were induced to flee by the "general fear" resulting from "a crisis of confidence" at the Arab ability to stand up to Jewish arms.

—Another 8 to 10 percent stemmed from "local factors," such as the breakdown of Arab-Jewish peace negotiations in specific localities.

—Another 2 percent resulted from "whispering" operations, involving "friendly advice" by Jewish liaison officers to Arabs to quit their villages.

—The last 2 percent was attributed to orders of expulsion by the Haganah. (Morris says that this last figure is closer to 5 percent.)[49] Morris notes that "the report makes no mention of any blanket orders issued to Arab radio stations or through other means, to the Palestinians to evacuate their homes and villages. . . . " He then states that

> the Intelligence Branch report . . . goes out of its way to stress that the exodus was contrary to the political-strategic desires of both the Arab Higher Committee and the governments of the neighboring Arab states. These, according to the report, struggled against the exodus—threatening, cajoling, imposing punishments, all to no avail. There was no stemming the panic borne tide.

Morris's conclusions are that "the Report . . . thoroughly undermines the traditional official Israeli 'explanation' of a mass flight ordered or 'invited' by the Arab leadership for political strategic reasons."[50]

### *Further Corroborating Evidence*

More confirmatory information has recently surfaced. Tom Segev recounts from Yitzhak Rabin's memoirs how and why 50,000 Arab inhabitants who had remained in their homes at Ramlah and Lydda (Lod) were forced out of the country. When asked as to their fate, Ben-Gurion waved his hands in a gesture signaling that they should be expelled. Israeli troops under the command of Generals Allon and Rabin drove the Palestinians down the Beth Horan Road, firing shots to speed them on their way.[51]

—An Israeli named Yetzhak, then more than eighty years old, served as the Jerusalem commander of the Haganah's intelligence service. His book recounting his experiences was originally held up by official censors, but has now been published. That book strongly denies the claim that attacks on Deir Yassin by the Irgun and the Stern Gang occurred "because the village was the center of resistance."[52]

—An Israeli historian named Yitzhaqi described a familiar pattern of occupation of an Arab village, saying that in the first months of the "War of Independence" Haganah and Palmach groups carried out dozens of such operations: " . . . the method adopted being to raid an enemy village and blow up as many houses as possible in it. In the course of these operations many old people, women and children, were killed wherever there was resistance."[53]

—Another Israeli writer, Uri Avnery, stated: "The impact of this carnage on the Arab population of Palestine was immense and accelerated the flight of villagers in other areas of the country."[54]

Finally, we have the words of the late Israeli leader Yigal Allon, who wrote that "To clean the inner Galilee" quickly, "we tried to use a tactic which took advantage of an impression created by the fall of Safed and the [Arab] defeat in the area which was cleaned by Operation Metateh—a tactic which worked miraculously well."[55]

## The Lausanne Conference: The United States Begins Its Departure from Principle

Driving out the Palestinians by fear or force was Israel's first step in fulfilling its doctrine of exclusivism. To consolidate its objective of a nation run by Jews and only for Jews (a goal widely accepted then and now by all but a few fringe groups on the left), the Israeli government had next to prevent the Palestinians from returning home or claiming compensation.

But the evolution of international mores had by then declared illegal the forced exile of a conquered people. It was inevitable that the United Nations General Assembly Resolution 194 of December 11, 1948, should call for the repatriation of the refugees who had been driven out by force or fear. As a price for obtaining full membership in the United Nations in 1949, Israel's ambassador, Abba Eban, had given assurances that Israel would faithfully adhere to the UN Charter and to the resolutions of the relevant UN bodies.

The magnitude and nature of the restraints assumed by the Israelis to gain UN membership were given practical effect when the UN General Assembly established the Palestine Conciliation Commission to meet at Lausanne, Switzerland, with a mission of tying up the loose ends of the 1948–49 War. To head the U.S. delegation, the United States sent Mark Ethridge, the respected publisher of the *Louisville Courier-Journal.* The American government's need to prepare for the Lausanne Conference required it to take stock of the relevant international principles that should govern a settlement, if it were to last. These principles required peace and the recognition of Israel's legitimacy; the right of peoples to self-determination; prohibition against the acquisition of territory by force; and the right of the Palestinian refugees to return home or be compensated and resettled.

The instructions given Mark Ethridge were a mere codification of these principles, with the sole exception that, primarily in response to British policy, the United States opposed extending the right of self-determination to the Palestinians. Instead, it favored the transfer of Arab Palestine to Trans-Jordan. The British did not wish to reward the Mufti of Jerusalem, who had allied himself against them during World War II, while Egypt and Saudi Arabia objected to the Jordanian annexation of the West Bank and Jerusalem because it limited their own territorial ambitions. The Israelis encouraged Jordan's pretensions in order to keep the Arab Legion passive, while complaining to the United States about the Jordanian annexation and denying its validity. Ironically, Israel was the only party at that time favoring an independent Arab Palestine, since it hoped to convert Palestine into a vassal state it might later annex. Today, the constant clamor regarding the alleged dangers to a powerful Israel of an independent Palestinian state seem all the more exaggerated in the light of this earlier confidence.[56]

The conference was faced with formidable problems. There were, by U.S. estimates, approximately 780,000 Palestinian refugees, not all in the camps, while the Arabs remaining in Israel numbered under 100,000. By then American officials clearly knew that the Israelis had, by fear or compulsion, forced the refugees from their homes. The United States hoped, however, at least to reunite families and induce the Israelis to repatriate approximately 400,000 Palestinians. The American delegation was also under orders to compel Israel to disgorge most, if not all, of its ill-gotten territorial gains acquired during that recent war.[57]

The authors had originally assumed that this conference collapsed because of the Arabs' intransigence and refusal to negotiate directly with Israel. But an examination of the Americans' diplomatic correspondence of the period has demonstrated conclusively that Israel was the party that undercut America's peacemaking efforts and that the Americans unwisely acquiesced in that result.

### *Conflicting Tactics of Israel and the Arabs*

Israel's tactical plan for achieving its goals at the conference, as the American delegation soon discovered, was to try to inveigle the Arab states, one by one, into signing peace treaties, while bullying each in turn into making further territorial concessions. Then, after the treaties were signed, the Israelis planned to put the refugee negotiations on permanent hold.

To thwart Israel's plan, the Arab governments instructed their delegates not to negotiate with Israel except in the presence of the Palestinian Conciliation Commission and to secure a satisfactory settlement of the refugee problem before entering into a peace treaty with Israel. Thus, if the Israelis wanted peace, they would have to make a fair provision for the refugees. But, as that would interfere with Israeli exclusivism and hopes for expansion, Israel preferred to let this opportunity lapse.[58] The negotiations that followed offered a preview of the undignified arguing over procedural points that was to darken hopes for peace during the next forty years.

### *The Refugee Settlement Problem*

On May 3, 1949, the director general of the Foreign Ministry, Dr. Walter Eytan, who headed the Israeli delegation, recited for Mark Ethridge Israel's predetermined policy line. Israel, he said, had had nothing to do with the flight of the Arabs, and, since the Arabs' attack on Israel was the real and only cause of the present situation, Israel accepted no responsibility for the refugee population.[59]

Under firm pressure from Ethridge, Eytan grudgingly conceded that if Israel wanted peace, it would have to help solve the refugee problem. But from both a social and practical viewpoint, Eytan argued, Israel would find it utterly impossible to accept the return of any of the refugees.[60]

When asked for Israel's specific proposals, Eytan announced the following:

First, it would accept the reunion of families. But since the Arabs held a spacious view of what constituted a family, Israel would insist on defining that concept. In any case, large-scale international aid would have to be forthcoming before Israel took anyone back.

Second, the Israelis would pay compensation only for lands owned and cultivated by Arab farmers. Israel would pay nothing for urban properties or rural lands not in active cultivation. Nor would it make payments to individuals, but only to a common fund to be used for refugee resettlement.[61]

On May 25 and 26, Dr. Eytan further clarified Israel's position. He claimed that a great deal of Palestinian property had been destroyed during the war, and that "if an Arab expects to return to house, trade, or field the illusion should be dispelled."[62] For social and primarily security reasons, the Israeli government reserved the right to determine where any returning Palestinians might live.

On the same day that Ethridge reported these uncompromising positions to Washington, Dr. Eytan met with the Palestine Conciliation commission in Lausanne. The stalemate in the negotiations between Israel and the Arabs could, he asserted, be broken only by an "imaginative broad plan" for resettling the refugees, which would include international financing for the project. Ethridge observed to Eytan that his proposal lifted the responsibility for solving this problem from the shoulders of the Arabs and Israelis and placed it on the United States. Eytan replied that, though Ethridge had stated the proposition somewhat crudely, that was indeed what he was suggesting. Ethridge answered that the United States was not prepared to assume unconditional responsibility.

*First,* Ethridge said, the American government must be satisfied that Israel would take its full share of refugees and give ironclad assurances regarding the Arabs' civil rights. Israel must pay full and fair compensation to those who did not return, and also fully compensate those who returned to Israel but recovered less than all of their homes, farms, and business properties. Unless such a settlement were a part of a comprehensive peace, the President could not expect Congress to furnish the necessary funding.

*Second,* the Arabs had to agree that their governments would receive the refugees who did not return to Israel.

*Third,* any plan adopted had to be acceptable to the United Nations; it was clear that the members of that body would not approve any plan if Israel and the Arabs evaded their responsibilities and did not make peace.[63]

Any hope of further progress on this subject terminated on June 10, when Eytan informed Ethridge that because of bellicose rumblings emanating from Cairo, the Israelis would not admit any more Arabs, who would be classified as enemy aliens in the event of war.[64]

### *Territorial Troubles*

Just as the United States failed to make progress with the refugee issue, it was also frustrated by the territorial negotiations.

Mark Ethridge had been specifically ordered to secure the reversal of a substantial part of the Israeli conquests in 1948–49. In particular, this involved the areas around Lydda and Ramlah, in Galilee, and other Arab-inhabited areas.

Israel, Eytan indicated, was prepared to accept the truce lines with Lebanon and Syria which were co-terminous with the international boundary. But he then went on to demand that a clause be inserted into each treaty calling for territorial adjustments. When a startled Ethridge asked what Eytan meant by this, he was told that Israel's development plans called for the acquisition of Lebanese and Syrian territory (that is currently occupied by Israel), with a view to exploiting their water resources for Israeli use. Eytan was evasive when queried as to the compensation those nations would receive, leaving the strong impression that Israel did not expect to furnish any.[65]

Eytan also claimed for Israel the whole of the West Bank, asserting that to award the area to Jordan would be to reward its alleged aggression during the late war. Since Moshe Sharett, the Israeli foreign minister, had been negotiating with King Abdullah scarcely two weeks before on the basis that Jordan would retain the West Bank, the blatant duplicity of this policy line seemed self-evident.[66]

### *U.S. Reactions to Israeli Recalcitrance*

Israel's territorial claims and its positions on the refugees were a direct challenge to the United States that ought to have been met promptly. Instead, the flaccid manner in which Washington responded became a stylized practice: to take a strong, principled position, then retreat from principle in the face of Israeli opposition.

That does not mean, however, that American diplomats, who were well aware of Israel's delinquencies, supported this practice. On May 24, 1949, the future Secretary of State, Dean Rusk, drew up a memorandum for Acting Secretary of State James Webb. The Rusk memorandum reviewed the information furnished by Ethridge and ended with this paragraph:

> If the Govt. of Israel continues to reject the basic principles set for the Res. of the GA of Dec. 11, 1948 and the friendly advice offered by the US Govt. for the sole purpose of facilitating a genuine peace in Palestine, the US Govt. will regretfully be forced to the conclusion that a revision of its attitude toward Israel has become unavoidable.[67]

Three days later, on May 27, Webb forwarded this memorandum to the White House, pointing out Israel's lack of cooperation. As he succinctly put it:

> Our representations on these two questions have thus far met with no success with the Israeli Government. Israeli officials have, in fact, informed our representatives . . . that they intend to bring about a change in the position of the United States Govt. on the above points, *through means available to them in the United States*. There are also indications that the Israelis are prepared to use the implied threat of force to obtain the additional territory which they desire in Palestine.[68] (Italics added)

In light of the Israelis' claimed ability to manipulate the U.S. government and their announced intention to pursue a course of territorial aggrandizement, Webb strongly urged President Truman to make it unambiguously clear that if they continued to ignore the United States' advice, their American aid would be cut off.

Such a statement, Webb advised, must be accompanied by actions designed to convince Israel to change its policy. The Israelis should be told that, in addition to a negative attitude toward all future requests, the United States would refuse to send technical advisers or provide training for Israeli officials, and would withhold approval of the unallocated $49 million balance of the $100 million Export-Import Bank loan.

Webb ended his memorandum by acknowledging that disciplinary action against Israel would arouse resistance among American Jews, and he urged the President to consult with his political advisers so that the State Department could act with his full backing. Webb also urged speed, since unless there was progress, the Lausanne Conference might break up on May 30.[69]

The next day, May 28, 1949, Truman sent a letter to Prime Minister Ben-Gurion, pointing out that he was seriously disturbed by Israel's uncompromising attitude, both as regards the refugee and territorial questions. He alluded to Eytan's expansionist remarks to Ethridge, and reiterated the U.S. government's position that Israel would have to compensate for its acquisition of any territories above and beyond the November 29, 1947, lines by exchanging territory originally granted for a Jewish state.

The President then asserted that a solution to the refugee problem was an indispensable requisite to real peace. The U.S. government was annoyed that its remonstrations had made such a small impression on the Government of Israel. America's support for Israel was based on principles that were now being violated.

The letter concluded that if the State of Israel persevered in its present course, there would be a rupture in the negotiations of the Palestine Conciliation Commission. In that event, "The United States Government would regretfully be forced to the conclusion that a revision of its attitude toward Israel has become unavoidable."[70]

Prime Minister Ben-Gurion's and Foreign Minister Sharett's initial response was reported to Washington on May 29 by the American ambassador. Although the Israeli leaders conceded that the United States was entitled to "have a say," they were determined to pursue their own policies unaided by the advice or opinions of others. The prime minister told Ambassador James G. McDonald that neither the United States nor the United Nations had acted vigorously to enforce the November 29 Resolution, nor to prevent what he styled the "aggression" of Syria, Egypt, Lebanon, and Iraq,[71] while Israel had conducted a "successful war of defense." Therefore, to return to the November 29 boundaries was out of the question for security and other reasons.

The prime minister had further contended that in light of the unfriendly Arab attitude, the readmission of the refugees to Israel would simply augment the number of enemy aliens. He concluded by inquiring whether the United States was prepared to defend Israel in the event of renewed hostilities. Ben-Gurion's express views can be summarized in three points: (1) that the Americans should mind their own business; (2) that the Arabs were to blame for everything; and (3) that Israel was entitled to American protection regardless of the policies it pursued.[72]

After reviewing McDonald's reporting telegrams, Mark Ethridge was annoyed by the ambassador's cabled reports and noted: "I regret McDonald is apparently refraining from using his influence with Israeli Government [*sic*] to underline the President's and Department's approved position regarding Palestine as set forth in Deptel 682 May 24. We need all the help we can get, particularly in Tel Aviv."[73]

Ethridge's concern over McDonald's anti-Arab and pro-Israeli bias was amply confirmed when, on June 11, McDonald reported that the Israeli press was unanimous that the United States had no moral or legal right for its "demands" and that such demands must be "resisted."[74]

*Israel's Reply*

On June 8, 1949, the Government of Israel forwarded a lengthy, formal reply to President Truman's message. In keeping with its established story, it predictably sought to place all blame on the Arabs and to deny any responsibility for its own conduct.

First, the Israeli government took both sides of the territorial expansion case. It claimed the right to seize added territory because of its "defensive war." It then proclaimed Resolution 181(II) inoperative and claimed that as Resolution 194 had not specified any boundaries, Israel could take what it pleased.

Since Ben-Gurion had labeled the refugees "aggressors," Israel regarded their flight as solely their own fault. And as Israel did not find it convenient for its own purposes to take back the refugees, it would not do so. As for Resolution 194, it said only that the refugees might return when Israel found it convenient, and Ben-Gurion implied that there would never be such a time. In any case, as the United Nations had admitted Israel to membership, that constituted complete UN acceptance of Israel's position.[75,76]

One can understand why such evasions and misrepresentations were put forward by the Israelis. It is more difficult to understand why President Truman let them get away with it without so much as a rebuke. Others, however, were made of sterner stuff.

In commenting on this Israeli reply to the State Department, Ethridge refuted the Israeli-inspired canard of Arab obstructionism by asserting that "if there is to be any assessment of blame for a stalemate at Lausanne, Israel must accept primary responsibility." The key to getting the logjam broken was, he observed, a definitive Israeli commitment to readmit some of the refugees. But Israel had "refused to indicate either publicly or privately how many refugees she is willing to take back and under what conditions." Israel was thus in direct violation of the General Assembly Resolution, and he dismissed out of hand Israel's claim that it should be exempted from accountability for the refugees on the grounds of internal security, economic inability, or possible Arab attacks. "Aside from her general responsibility for refugees, she [Israel] has particular responsibility for those who have been driven out by terrorism, repression and forcible ejection."

In Ethridge's view, the claim that Israel had no ambitions or aggressive plans was a complete fabrication. He repeated that during a conference at Tiberius on April 20, 1948, Prime Minister Ben-Gurion had stated that Israel wanted the entire western shore of the Dead Sea. Moshe Sharett, the Israel foreign minister, had told the Palestine Conciliation Commission at their first meeting that the Israeli government insisted, for security reasons, on the strip from Haifa to Tel Aviv being widened to the Samarian Hills. Ethridge further pointed out that Israel had taken over many villages in the Tulkarm area and had also seized new territory by force around Jerusalem.

Ethridge found Israel's attitude toward the refugees to be particularly reprehensible for a country that purported to be based on moral principles. In the long run, he insisted, Israel's security rested on the quality of its relations with its neighbors. It could have no true security until there was peace in the Middle East. Ethridge ended his commentary by noting that

> There has never been a time in the life of the commission when a generous and a farsighted attitude on the part of the Jews would not have unlocked peace. . . . As an advocate of the new state I hope they come on it eventually. Otherwise there will be no peace in the Middle East, no security for Israel and no possibility of lifting the economic blockade with which she must remain a remittance-man nation.[77]

President Truman is reported to have read Ethridge's telegram and been particularly impressed with his prescient comments, which succinctly describe Israel's position today.

## THE SIGNIFICANCE OF THE FAILURE AT LAUSANNE

Given Ethridge's views (which were shared by practically everyone in the State Department) it is obvious in retrospect that the United States, for domestic political considerations, allowed a key opportunity for securing peace in the Middle East to lapse. Israel was then very vulnerable, and Ethridge's cable—as well as those from American diplomats in Arab capitals—made it clear the Arabs were reluctantly prepared to accept Israel if it would take back half the refugees. But America refused to act.

Since it left key problems unsettled, the failure of the Lausanne negotiations and the dissolution of the Conciliation Commission assured the persistence of Israel's endless war. The American government now had to decide whether future United States efforts at peacemaking would ever be more than pro forma.

An event shortly thereafter reinforced the probability of a negative answer. Confronted by the Israeli answer of June 8 and Ethridge's report that the Lausanne Conference had collapsed, future U.S. Ambassador George McGhee, then in charge of refugee problems, drafted a memorandum for Secretary of State Dean Acheson, who was to meet with President Truman. Heading the list of recommendations to compel a change in Israel's position was a proposal for holding up the $49 million residue of the $100 million Export-Import Bank loan until Israel had properly addressed the refugee question.

On June 10, Ambassador McGhee repeated that proposal, and on being advised that it had been approved by the President, McGhee invited the

Israeli ambassador, a former colleague at Queens College Oxford, to lunch at the Metropolitan Club. There McGhee tactfully advised him of the department's decision.

The ambassador's response was to look McGhee in the eye and tell him that he could not get away with this maneuver since the ambassador could, through his own White House contacts, assure him that the decision would be overruled. Sure enough, an hour after McGhee returned from lunch, he received a message from David Niles at the White House informing him that the President had officially disassociated himself from the plan he had earlier approved.[78]

After this experience, the administration abandoned any further effort to secure peace based on the principles enunciated in Ethridge's instructions. Instead, as James Webb put it, the United States "will seek a basis of settlement among the parties." This, in practice, translated to mean that because America lacked the political will to put pressure on the Israelis, it would follow the procedure of first finding out what was acceptable to Israel, then attempting to sell it to the Arabs.[79]

CHAPTER TWO

# The Eisenhower Administration Halts the Retreat

THE TRUMAN ADMINISTRATION had inaugurated a pattern of enunciating principled positions on Middle East questions, then backing away under pressure. Dwight Eisenhower's accession to the presidency on January 20, 1953, provided a new opportunity to advance a Middle East peace. Because he had been elected by a landslide, in the face of overwhelming Jewish support for Adlai Stevenson, the general was under no obligation to the Zionists and was therefore largely immune to the domestic forces that had heavily influenced Harry Truman.

With the Cold War approaching its apex, Eisenhower's Secretary of State, John Foster Dulles, sought to encircle the Soviet adversary with a *cordon sanitaire* of alliances. Such a strategy would, in his view, be reinforced by an immediate Arab-Israeli peace, and he thought the time was propitious for a renewed effort.

Israel was in a particularly vulnerable stage: a vast influx of Jewish refugees was pouring in from the Arab states, and the country urgently needed further financing to accommodate them. Circumstances were combining to provide America with a tailormade opportunity to exercise its leverage with Israel.

The Eisenhower administration managed successfully in two incidents: one involved an Israeli effort to divert the waters of the Jordan; the other concerned Israel's refusal to evacuate the Sinai in 1957. In both cases Eisenhower resisted the increasingly powerful compulsions of America's passionate attachment and forced Israel to comply with principle. Until 1992, these were the last occasions on which America acted incisively toward Israel. Unfortunately, these actions were not part of a pattern, nor was the administration able or willing to follow up its successes by securing a comprehensive peace.

## The Jordan River Diversion

Among the loose ends left over after the Israeli "War of Independence" was a dispute over the control of bits and pieces of Palestinian territory near the Palestinian village of Banat Ya'qub, then occupied by Syrian troops. The United Nations Representative, Dr. Ralph Bunche, worked out a truce agreement which provided that those lands would be evacuated by Syrian forces, but only after Israel had agreed to let the Arab inhabitants continue to farm them. Israel also agreed that it would not occupy those areas, but would leave them as part of a neutral zone.

Yet no sooner had the Syrian troops withdrawn than the Israelis drove the Arab farmers from their lands, and moved in Israeli settlers. When the Syrians opened fire to expel the settlers, Israel complained that the truce had been violated and asserted a right to occupy the areas. The United Nations Truce Observers on the spot cited Israel for violating the agreement and put the responsibility for the disturbances that followed flatly on Israel. The United Nations team was not, however, aware that Israel planned to use Banat Ya'qub for a major water diversion project that would move the waters of the Jordan Valley to central Israel and the North Negev. Nonetheless, consistent with their almost religious faith in the tactical effectiveness of a fait accompli, the Israelis sought to "create new facts" that would thwart UN opposition. They therefore began working under searchlights on a twenty-four-hour-a-day basis to speed the project.

Meanwhile, the Israelis contrived to conceal their plans; they omitted any appropriation for the project in their published budget and did not mention it to the Americans working with them on water projects. However, American intelligence penetrated this smoke screen. President Eisenhower and Secretary Dulles concluded that Israel had deliberately deceived them; it showed no intention of keeping an earlier promise to cooperate in an American-sponsored regional water-usage plan.

To signal its displeasure, the U.S. government withheld $26 million under the Mutual Security Act and suspended economic aid until Israel agreed to cooperate with the United Nations observers. President Eisenhower further instructed the Treasury to prepare a presidential order stripping the tax-deductible status from contributions made by Jewish Americans to such Zionist organizations as the United Jewish Appeal (UJA). Yet, because of a misplaced desire to save Israeli feelings, the administration refrained from making any public announcement of these actions, and Israel chose to interpret this restraint as a sign of weakness. So, convinced that the U.S. government would give way in the end, Israel continued work on the project.

Indeed, the Israelis might have ignored America's protests indefinitely had not Force 101, consisting of three hundred Israeli commandos led by Ariel Sharon, launched a devastating seven-hour raid on the West Bank village of Kibya, on the night of October 14–15, 1953, killing fifty-three Palestinian civilians. According to a UN report, the Israeli forces drove the Palestinians into their homes, then blew them up.

Here again—as was to happen so often in the future—America was subjected to a mirage of untruths and bureaucratic obfuscation. Although Force 101 was clearly a governmental operation, the Government of Israel resorted to a dodge it would use in 1985 in the Pollard affair when, caught in another compromising situation, it attempted to disown the raid on the pettifogging ground that it had not been approved by the prime minister's Defense Committee. In addition, Israeli spokesmen promoted the story that exasperated settlers had merely retaliated for raids made against them by West Bank Palestinians. Even some members of the Israeli Cabinet warned that that cover story was too blatant a prevarication to be accepted, and they were swiftly proved right. Far from being deceived, the United States condemned the raid and for the first time publicly disclosed that it had already suspended construction funds for Israel's water supply.

This revelation prompted spokesmen for organized committees of Jewish Americans to protest about "unwarranted duress." Hadassah, a Jewish charitable organization, denounced the aid cutoff as "an attempt to coerce a friendly government to surrender what it believes to be its legitimate rights in the peaceful development of its own resources."[1] An attaché at the Israeli Embassy hoped to divert attention from the water controversy by making a widely advertised speech claiming that the Kibya raid was in response to Jordanian aggression. (He neglected to mention that Israel had been condemned by the UN Truce Observers for border incidents ninety-five times as compared with sixty border violations by Jordan. Moreover, most of the Jordanian incidents had involved unarmed persons trying to infiltrate back to their homes.)[2]

U.S. public outrage was echoed by pro-Israeli congressmen, and by David Ben-Gurion, who accused the administration's advisers of anti-Semitism. "There are many," he said, "and they are powerful, who believe religiously that we ought to be the eternal wanderer because of something that happened two thousand years ago in this very country." It was a thinly veiled reference to the well-known Presbyterianism of John Foster Dulles.[3]

Still Eisenhower did not budge. Since money was running out in Jerusalem, Israel's representatives notified President Eisenhower on October 19 that Israel had ceased work on its water diversion project and would cooperate with the Security Council's efforts to solve the Jordan River Development problem.

Though that event clearly showed that the withholding of aid could produce Israel's compliance, the Israelis interpreted the fact that America had restored aid within hours after compliance as proving that by sufficient pressure they could get the results they wanted. In the end, they carried out their project in modified form.[4]

## The Suez Affair Begins

Eisenhower's second challenge came in connection with the Suez incident.

On February 28, 1955, Premier Gamal Abdel Nasser made a speech full of warnings against such Israeli actions as a particularly bloody raid on the Gaza Strip in alleged retaliation for raids made from Gaza. Nasser was already annoyed with the United States because it had denied his request for arms a few months earlier. Now he again requested permission for Egypt to buy arms, but received no immediate reply.

Subsequently, on September 4, 1955, Deputy Premier Gamal Salem announced that Egypt had received a proposal from the Soviet Union for an arms sale which it would feel compelled to accept if the West did not honor outstanding arms orders. When the Department of State treated this notice as an idle threat, Nasser, highly annoyed, announced on September 27 that Egypt had concluded a cotton-for-arms barter agreement with Czechoslovakia. The deal included arms worth $200 million and involved MiG planes, tanks, artillery, small arms, and even submarines.

Israel promptly renewed its arms appeal to Britain, France, and the United States jointly, and asked for a treaty guaranteeing Israeli security. But the Western powers had no intention of becoming co-belligerents in Israel's favor. In any case, they knew that the training, armaments, and morale of Israel's armed forces remained far superior to those of the Arabs; if hostilities broke out, Israel would surely win.

In a speech on August 26, 1955, to the Council on Foreign Relations in New York, Secretary Dulles outlined the possible terms of an equitable Middle East peace.

He asserted that the problem of the refugees was not insoluble. Recognizing that Israel alone could not assume all the financial burdens involved, the President would recommend to Congress "substantial participation" in an international loan that would provide funding to compensate, resettle, or repatriate the refugees. And it would help develop various irrigation projects, which would at least provide arable lands for some of the dispossessed. The Secretary of State also added:

> President Eisenhower has authorized me to say . . . he would recommend that the United States join in formal treaty engagements to prevent or thwart any effort by either side to alter by force the boundaries between Israel and its Arab neighbors. I hope that . . . it would be sponsored by the United Nations.

> By such collective security measures, the area would be relieved of the acute fears which both sides now profess. . . .
> If there is to be a guarantee of borders, it would be normal that there would be prior agreement upon what the borders are. . . .
> The task of drawing permanent boundaries is admittedly one of difficulty.[5]

Because that speech contained a reference to possible boundary revision, it provoked Israeli protests, which led Dulles to make the American position more explicit. He therefore replied to Israeli *démarches* for American aid and territorial guarantees that, while guarantees were possible, he did not propose to accept Israel solely on its own terms. If Messrs. Sharett and Ben-Gurion wanted American diplomatic, political, and military aid, they would have to demonstrate their peaceful intentions by helping to solve the prickly problems over refugees and boundaries. President Eisenhower confirmed that position on November 9 by a formal statement from his hospital bed in Denver, where he was convalescing after a heart attack.

## The Suez Adventure

One of the key events in the diplomatic maneuvering that preceded the denouement at Suez was the request by President Nasser for help in funding the $1.3 billion Aswan Dam that Egypt needed for irrigation and for power. Although Dulles had indicated that the United States might undertake a small portion of the funding, on July 16, 1956, the Senate Appropriations Committee, under pressure from Israel's American friends, explicitly prohibited the use of any Mutual Security Program funds for the dam. On July 19 the State Department released a statement critically appraising Egypt's international credit. In response, Nasser nationalized the Suez Canal Company on July 26, 1956, in order, he said, to obtain funds for the dam.

The action then shifted to Paris, where the French (who blamed Nasser for their troubles in Algeria) had broken the Tripartite Declaration by selling jet aircraft and other military equipment to Israel. That encouraged the Israelis to connive with the French and British on an adventure designed to seize the Canal and bring about the overthrow of Nasser.

On October 29, 1956, the Israelis moved up the timetable, informing President Eisenhower that they intended to eliminate Egyptian guerrilla bases in the Sinai Peninsula. Their actual plans called for the seizure of Gaza and the whole of the Sinai, which they intended to keep—if they could.

On November 1 the French and British invaded Egypt, having vetoed Security Council resolutions offered by the United States ordering them to halt their invasion and directing Israel to return behind the truce lines. Although Eisenhower found it painful to turn the United Nations against his two World War II allies, he was furious with their leaders for keeping him in the dark.

He was particularly upset when he found that Israel had conspired with France and Britain to plan a united attack. Eisenhower in fury told Dulles: "Foster, you tell 'em, goddamn it, we're going to apply sanctions, we're going to the United Nations, we're going to do everything that there is so we can stop this thing." He later explained: "We just told the Israelis it was absolutely indefensible and that if they expect our support in the Middle East and in maintaining their position, they had to behave. . . . We went to town right away and began to give them hell."[6]

Suddenly, on November 6, Eden capitulated. A few hours later France followed suit. Eisenhower's forthright policy had triumphed. He was reelected that same day with 58 percent of the vote.[7]

Only Israel held out. Pleased with the success of his aggressive move, Ben-Gurion dug in his heels.[8] Although Israel agreed to a cease-fire, it refused to remove its troops from the whole of the Sinai; it wanted to keep Sharm el-Sheikh and the Gaza Strip. As Ben-Gurion stated, "The armistice agreement with Egypt is dead and buried and cannot be restored to life. In consequence, the armistice lines between Israel and Egypt have no more validity. On no account will Israel agree to the stationing of a foreign force, no matter how designed, in her territory, or in any territories occupied by her."[9] Even when faced with a General Assembly resolution on February 2, 1957, demanding Israel's withdrawal, Ben-Gurion refused.

That was the final straw; Eisenhower's patience had been tested and exhausted. On February 11 he wrote a strong note to Ben-Gurion demanding Israel's withdrawal, only to have Ben-Gurion refuse once again.

Jewish American organizations tried hard to generate congressional resistance to Eisenhower's position. On February 1, Senator William Knowland, the Republican minority leader, protested to Dulles against the administration's stand. Knowland agreed that the policy might be right in theory, but pointed out to Dulles the domestic political implications and threatened to revolt. Dulles answered Knowland by noting, "We cannot have all our policies made in Jerusalem," and he justified the American position on the following grounds:

> First, sanctions would be necessary to compel Israel's withdrawal and a withdrawal was needed to maintain the American position among the Arabs. . . .
> [Second] I am aware how almost impossible it is in this country to carry out a foreign policy not approved by the Jews. Marshall and Forrestal learned that. I am going to try to have one.
> That does not mean I am anti-Jewish, but I believe in what George Washington said in his Farewell Address that an emotional attachment to another country should not interfere.[10]

On February 20, Eisenhower called a meeting of the congressional leadership. When the lawmakers, ever sensitive to the pro-Israeli lobby, refused to help, Eisenhower resorted to television that same night.[11]

Eisenhower did more than talk. He issued an ultimatum to Ben-Gurion to pull Israel's forces back to the Israeli border. He also laid plans with Dulles that, if the Israelis did not comply, the United States would cut off the flow of all aid to Israel, including not only development assistance but technical assistance and shipments of agricultural products under Public Law 480. He would also delay the disbursement of an already arranged Export-Import Bank loan and terminate all forms of military assistance, including those in the pipeline. He canceled export licenses for the shipment of munitions or other military goods. Finally, he ordered Secretary of the Treasury George Humphrey to draft a change in U.S. tax regulations so that the Jewish American organization benefactors would no longer be entitled to a federal income tax deduction for contributions that benefited Israel.

In spite of further efforts by Israel's supporters to deflect White House pressure from the Jewish state, Eisenhower did not cave in; so, as the Israeli government began to run out of money, Ben-Gurion, on March 5, 1957, grudgingly capitulated. On March 16, Israel withdrew from almost all the territory it had occupied in the Suez offensive.[12]

Its decision to withdraw was further stimulated by Washington's open support for a resolution in the United Nations that not only threatened sanctions but called for the installation of a United Nations peacekeeping force (UNEF) along the Israeli-Egyptian border.[13] In addition, it provided the assurance of "innocent passage" for Israeli shipping in the Gulf of Aqaba.

Eisenhower's incisive actions made it clear that in planning a military campaign to overthrow Nasser, the Israelis had erred in assuming that the United States would modestly avert its eyes. As President Eisenhower explained to Rabbi Hillel Silver of the Zionist Organization of America, he intended to conduct foreign policy without regard to domestic political considerations—to which the rabbi pointedly responded: "You can get reelected without a single Jewish vote."

Eisenhower did free the Sinai of Israeli troops, but he did not follow up that success by seeking a comprehensive peace—for two possible reasons: first, Dulles was gravely ill and finally died; second, Eisenhower was obsessed with excluding the Soviets from the Middle East and would not, therefore, risk their reinvolvement by asking the Security Council to propose a comprehensive settlement.

The Eisenhower administration failed to realize that a Middle East peace was indispensable to minimize Soviet influence, nor did it take account of the fact that its concentration on the Soviet menace only weakened America's Middle East objectives. The Arab countries resented the Eisenhower Doctrine's basic implication that the United States played an essential role in the Middle East; the Arabs believed that they could best maintain their independence by strengthening their own governments.

The other obstacle faced by Eisenhower was Nasser's nationalistic determination to pursue his own aims without foreign guidance or control. When

America responded to Nasser's assertive independence by seeking allies among the conservative monarchies opposing him, it hopelessly alienated the Egyptians.

In retrospect, it seems evident that Eisenhower's desire to exclude the Soviet Union from the Middle East could succeed only if Israel first made peace with its neighbors. So long as the hostilities continued, Nasser and the radical states would not dare abandon their Soviet bloc connections, nor would they acquiesce in plans directed against their Moscow patron.

By early 1960, the Eisenhower administration had become thoroughly frustrated with the Middle East, and was ready to wash its hands of it. That passivity resulted from the mutually contradictory positions of the two sides, with each insisting that it would conclude peace only on its own terms. The Israelis would yield none of the territory they had seized from 1948–56 and would not take back any—or only a few—of the 1 million Arab refugees. Nor would they pay anything like fair compensation for the £110 million of Arab property they had seized.

The Arabs demanded that Israel return to the boundaries laid down in the 1947 resolution and that those Arabs who had lived in the areas remaining under Israeli rule either must be allowed to return to their homes or be compensated for their lost property if they chose not to do so. Neither side was willing to give an inch.

Alarmed at the flow of Soviet arms to Iraq and the United Arab Republic, Prime Minister Ben-Gurion insisted that Israel should receive equivalent assistance from the West. But President Eisenhower was opposed to having America become "a major supplier" for anyone in the Middle East; he preferred to let others play that role.[14]

Moreover, Jewish pressure encouraged the U.S. Congress to adopt an increasingly anti-Nasser line. As a result, Congress denied Public Law 480 food grants[15] to Egypt and brought America further into the Israel/Egypt controversy by quarreling with Egypt about the Arab boycott and the denial by Egypt of the use of the Suez Canal to Israeli ships or neutral shipping carrying Israeli goods.

Thus, despite his principled stand in 1956–57, President Eisenhower left the Middle East still at war, with Soviet influence mounting among the Arab states. Although he missed the opportunity to use the leverage he gained by freeing the Sinai to achieve a basic, comprehensive Middle East settlement, Eisenhower deserves great credit for being the last president for thirty years to stand up to the pressures and importunings of the Israeli government and its American supporters. By so doing, he demonstrated conclusively that if it chose to, an American government could effectively influence even such a powerful Israeli leader as Ben-Gurion. That demonstration should have laid to rest the myth that America lacks the capacity to influence Israel.

Unhappily, the administrations that followed Eisenhower's were either too weak, too absorbed by other affairs, or too sensitive to domestic pressures to do anything constructive about peace in the Middle East. They succeeded only in accelerating the American retreat from principle.

CHAPTER THREE

# Kennedy Largely Holds to Principle; Johnson Increases the Momentum of the Retreat

EISENHOWER HAD DEMONSTRATED how a strong President could damn the torpedoes and shape American policy toward the Middle East strictly in accordance with UN resolutions and established international law. But his successor, John F. Kennedy, had been elected by only a plurality, and although he agreed intellectually with Eisenhower, he did not possess the same degree of political self-confidence. To be sure, he wanted to steer a principled course and establish better relations with the Arabs. He did not share Dulles's view that neutrality in the Cold War was immoral and he understood why the Arabs must distance themselves to some degree from the United States.[1] Accordingly, he sent a letter to all the Arab chiefs of state early in his administration assuring them that the United States not only supported Arab self-determination, but his administration was prepared to offer assistance in settling the refugee question.[2]

## THE KENNEDY ADMINISTRATION

Kennedy tried to pursue a simple formula for peace. If he could persuade Israel to compensate or repatriate a substantial number of Palestinians, most of whom were still living in rapidly deteriorating refugee camps, the Arab countries might then be encouraged to resettle the remaining refugees. So he commissioned Joseph E. Johnson, president of the Carnegie Endowment for

International Peace, to prepare a detailed report calling for Arab refugees to choose either to return to their homes in Israel or to be compensated by Israel and resettled in the Arab countries or elsewhere.

Well before Johnson's report was formally announced, the Government of Israel urged the American Jewish community to work assiduously to block American pressure on Israel to repatriate refugees. In the fall of 1962, Ben-Gurion conveyed his own views in a letter to the Israeli ambassador in Washington, intended to be circulated among Jewish American leaders, in which he stated: "Israel will regard this plan as a more serious danger to her existence than all the threats of the Arab dictators and Kings, than all the Arab armies, than all of Nasser's missiles and his Soviet MIGs. . . . Israel will fight against this implementation down to the last man."[3]

Nor were the Arabs much more enthusiastic. Since the plan had made no mention of the territorial questions, they denounced it as a pro-Israel ploy to smooth over the Arab-Israeli conflict by an unacceptable compromise on the Palestinian refugee problem.

Ben-Gurion's obsessive objective was to acquire advanced weapons systems. Eisenhower had earlier denied Ben-Gurion's request for an early warning system and Hawk ground-to-air missiles[4] on the grounds that these would stimulate the arms race and drive the Egyptians to seek similar weapons from the Russians. Kennedy was as yet untested on the issue.

Thus when Ben-Gurion visited New York on May 20, 1961, and presented the standard Israeli demands for guarantees and arms sales, Kennedy stalled, assuring the Israeli prime minister that Middle East policy was under close examination. In August 1962 that reassessment produced an agreement to supply Hawk missiles for "strictly defensive" purposes.

Nor was that Kennedy's only gesture toward Israel; he also proposed joint meetings with Israel's military experts to discuss its security concerns,[5] which quickly enabled the Israelis to present their shopping lists.[6] In fact, Israeli propaganda hailed the talks as a first step toward a tacit U.S. alliance with Israel.

Yet, at the outset, Kennedy refused the Israelis' demand for a security guarantee. In a December 1962 meeting at Palm Beach, he explained to the Israeli foreign minister, Golda Meir, that the United States had global interests, and if it were to exert any influence in the Arab Middle East, it needed to cultivate good relations with all nations. Realizing Golda Meir's disappointment, Kennedy then did exactly what he had thus far resisted doing: He promised that the United States would come to Israel's aid if it were attacked.

That commitment was repeated in October 1963 in a message to Prime Minister Levi Eshkol, who had succeeded Ben-Gurion, in which Kennedy justified the commitment by commenting that it would relieve Israel's sense of insecurity. Kennedy hoped that, freed from fear of an Arab attack, Israel would drop its plans for a nuclear arsenal. As we now know, that was a vain hope. Israel had no intention of giving up its nuclear ambitions.

However Kennedy would have succeeded in his relations with Israel must remain one of the many intriguing questions for which his assassination precludes any answer.

## The Johnson Administration

There could have been no sharper contrast in personality and manner than between John F. Kennedy and Lyndon B. Johnson. Johnson was a man of notable acumen in domestic politics, well aware of the critical Jewish role in Democratic Party concerns. But his views on foreign policy were haphazard; he had no background in the field. Besides, after 1965, he was distracted by the mounting disaster of Vietnam.

Johnson set back the chances for an Arab-Israeli solution by failing to restrict the flow of armaments into the Middle East. Like Kennedy, Johnson acted on the fallacious theory that Israel would take a more flexible view toward refugees and boundaries if its arms were superior to those of all its Arab neighbors combined. As events later demonstrated, this was a thoroughly wrong-headed policy—indeed a catastrophe—because it fostered the acceleration of the arms race, and also gave the Israelis every incentive to be intransigent with the Arabs. If the Israelis saw themselves as behind in the arms race, they would refuse to negotiate from "weakness"; if they were sure they were ahead, they would see no need to grant the Arabs even the most trifling concessions.[7]

The Israelis were proved right in their assumption that Johnson would be more friendly than Kennedy. Although in the fiscal year 1964 (the last under President Kennedy) aid to Israel had amounted to only $40 million, under President Johnson it rose in the fiscal year 1965 to $71 million, and in fiscal 1966 to $130 million.

Johnson also expanded the purposes for which Israel could use its aid funds. Under President Kennedy, all the fiscal 1964 money had been earmarked for economic purposes; in 1965, 20 percent ($14 million), and in 1966, 71 percent ($91.3 million) was provided explicitly as military aid. Thus, while Kennedy had sold Israel only $21.5 million of solely defensive Hawk missiles, Johnson, during the years 1965–66, provided Israel with offensive weapons in the form of 250 modified M-14 tanks and 48 A-1 Skyhawk attack aircraft.

Far from assuaging Israel's territorial ambitions, President Johnson's arms aid bolstered Israel's temptation to pursue a preemptive strategy. It greatly strengthened the hands of men like Shimon Peres and Moshe Dayan, as well as Likud members who not only favored a tough stance vis-à-vis the surrounding Arab states, but who wished to pursue the territorial acquisition program laid out by Walter Eytan in 1949. As a result, from 1960 through 1965, the Israelis spent no less than 11.3 percent of their GNP for arms, largely purchased cash-and-carry from France. At the same time, Israel contended that U.S. aid in 1964 and 1965 constituted an American seal of approval for its expansionist policies.

The result was unhealthy for American interests, particularly since the Israelis soon began using the economic largesse America provided on concessionary terms to pay for their French arms. When the administration tried to investigate these transactions, it met with obstruction and evasion.[8]

Tensions were heightened by a July 14, 1966, Israeli raid against Syria, made ostensibly in retaliation for guerrilla raids originating in that country. Although some military targets were hit, the chief Israeli assault was directed against the Syrian dams in the Banias Valley, which prevented waters from flowing into the Jordan Valley. Thus, the "retaliation" was actually part of Israel's declared program for securing access to Syrian water resources. Still, except for official American warnings from Secretary Rusk, America's preoccupation with Vietnam and its displeasure with Syria's radical regime deflected it from more than pro forma attempts to discourage these Israeli activities.

Far more serious was the November 13, 1966, raid on Es-Samu, a town in the West Bank, which, according to the UN Truce teams, resulted in the deaths of fifteen Jordanian soldiers and three civilians, and left thirty-seven Jordanian soldiers and seventeen civilians wounded.[9] This precipitated riots (November 14–25), which were instigated by the Palestinians and soon took on an anti-Hashemite tone. Rioting resumed in December. By May 14, 1967, when Syrian and then Egyptian troops were massed along their respective borders with Israel, Jordan found itself in a hazardous situation.

King Hussein of Jordan knew perfectly well that the Arabs could not win a war with Israel. However, on succeeding his grandfather, Abdullah, in 1952, he found himself bound to Egypt and Syria by a treaty that required Jordan's intervention if either were attacked. Because public opinion backed this course, Hussein felt he had to stand by Syria and Egypt, or risk becoming an outcast at home and isolated in the Arab world.

If Israel ever managed to dispose of both Syria and Egypt it might well turn on Jordan, using any one of several plausible pretexts. Even were that fate avoided, Israel might reduce Jordan to the level of an Israeli protectorate. For all these reasons, win or lose, Hussein felt Jordan would be better off to join a war against Israel as part of the Arab community.[10]

## The Background to the Six-Day War

In April 1967, Syria, hoping to challenge Nasser's leadership status in the Arab world, dispatched trained guerrillas to carry out harassing raids against Israel. Israel then assembled a considerable force on the Syrian border and threatened dire retaliation if the Syrians persisted in their reckless activities. Belatedly realizing that Israel was in earnest, the Syrians appealed to the Soviet Union for protection and demanded Egyptian support under the November 1966 defense treaty.

Despite his admitted military weakness, Nasser rushed in with a demonstration of support for Syria that brought only humiliation for himself, defeat for the other Arabs, and disaster for the Palestinians. To reassert his wavering leadership against the Syrian challenge, Nasser put his forces on the alert on May 14, and by May 20, 58,000 Egyptian troops were in the Sinai.

To counter Syrian claims that he was hiding behind the United Nations Emergency Force (UNEF), Nasser asked Secretary General U Thant to withdraw that force from the Egyptian-Israeli truce lines. Since Israel had not agreed to this force being stationed on both sides of the border (and therefore its consent was not required before those troops were pulled out), U Thant had no choice but to agree to Nasser's demand. At the same time, Syria announced it had assembled 12,000 men (a mere 20 percent of its army) on the Israeli border, a provocative but ineffectual act.

Worse followed. On May 21, Nasser called up the Egyptian reserves (100,000 strong) and noisily put the Egyptian economy on a war footing. The next day he announced his intention to blockade the Straits of Tiran at the lower end of the Gulf of Aqaba, although it had been agreed after 1957 that this was an international waterway and Egypt had no justification for closing that area. On May 24–25, the Egyptian Navy closed the Straits to Israeli shipping and laid mines. (On May 30 came the reluctant adherence of Jordan to the Egyptian-Syrian defense pact.)

Despite his own and his allies' manifest lack of preparedness, Nasser had not only provided the Israelis with a plausible *casus belli* but had incited them to mobilize a force of 230,000 reservists ready for combat. Made nervous by his own brinksmanship, Nasser sent out a whole series of messages on May 28 stating that he had no intention of attacking Israel. But he canceled out the effect of these pronouncements by a speech the next day to Egypt's National Assembly in which he loudly claimed Soviet support. How Nasser expected to get out of this vise of his own making is difficult to imagine; he had sent his best corps miles away to interfere in the Yemen civil war and he had only about 200,000 Arab soldiers available to oppose 280,000 vastly superior Israelis. Perhaps he was hoping his Soviet friends would build a bridge for him at the United Nations over which he could escape and still save face. If so, his enemies were determined to give him no such opportunity.[11]

The Johnson administration knew that Israel enjoyed an overwhelming superiority over its Arab neighbors. In assessing the military balance in the Middle East in 1966, the Joint Chiefs of Staff held that, in spite of Jerusalem's loudly vocalized alarm, Israeli superiority was actually increasing.[12] America had provided Israel with the F-4 Phantom, which was infinitely better than any of the Soviet MiGs acquired by the Arabs.[13]

Confronted by an Arab-provoked crisis, Secretary of State Rusk warned the President that the United States had two options: it could either "let the Israelis decide how best to protect their own national interests [or, what Rusk thought preferable] . . . undertake effective efforts to mediate the crisis while keeping both sides firmly in hand." Any "preemptive action" by Israel would, he observed, seriously embarrass the United States. On the other hand, in view of the United States' position of world leadership, the American people would do what had to be done, especially if "the fault is on the other side and there is no alternative." Thus, "the question of responsibility for the initiation of hostilities is a major problem for us."[14]

The Johnson administration's response to Rusk's advice was greatly influenced by the events of the preceding decade. Many people felt that Nasser had been guilty of monumental ingratitude toward America. After President Eisenhower had rescued him from the British, French, and Israelis in the Suez affair, 1956–57, Nasser had shown jarring independence in the years that followed. Contrary to the assurances given President Kennedy, he had involved Egypt in the Yemen civil war, and had attacked those Arab states deemed friendly to the United States. The senior author, then the Under Secretary of State, remembers having to fight hard with Congress every year to continue our Food-for-Peace aid to Egypt so that the United States could maintain some kind of leverage in Cairo. Few, either at the State Department, the White House, or on Capitol Hill would have been sorry to see Nasser humiliated or even overthrown. In addition, elements in the Pentagon saw a potential Arab-Israeli war as a heaven-sent opportunity not only to test American vs. Soviet weapons under combat conditions, but also to destroy Soviet influence in the Arab world by demonstrating that nation's inability to protect its Middle East clients.

The President decided to pursue both of Rusk's options. Although America ostensibly tried to find a peaceful solution (its efforts were, in truth, sadly lethargic), the Israelis were given to understand that the U.S. government had no great objection to their taking matters into their own hands. President Johnson made that very clear; he merely warned Israeli Prime Minister Levi Eshkol that Israel should not be seen as the party initiating hostilities.[15]

American tolerance for Israel's belligerent stance was reinforced by the Central Intelligence Agency, which reported on May 24 that the Israelis could defeat any single Arab country, or all of them in combination, in not more than a week. (In fact, it took only six days.) When interviewed for the Johnson Library, Nicholas de B. Katzenbach, then the Under Secretary of State, pointed out that, based on the information furnished them, the cabinet and sub-cabinet officers were so sure of an Israeli victory that they made absolutely no contingency plans for either a prolonged contest or the even more unlikely possibility of an Israeli defeat. Claims that Israel was the David to the Arab Goliath were mythmaking for the ill-informed American public.

The United States' rationalization for not interfering to prevent an Arab-Israeli war might be summarized as follows:

First, by allowing the armies of the Soviets' Arab protégés to be destroyed, the West would nullify three or four years of Soviet effort and induce the radical Arabs to perceive the Soviet Union as an ineffectual protector. It might even persuade the Arabs to turn for help to the United States in order to get their territory back; in any event it would strengthen the hand of the United States throughout the Middle East.

Second, by destroying the equipment the Soviet Union had sent to the Middle East, Israel would not only humiliate Moscow and its Arab allies but would relax its pressure for further American arms, which America was finding unduly expensive.

Third, there were those (especially in the Congress) who hoped that the radical Arab regimes, humiliated and deprived of military support, would be overthrown by their disgruntled armies and peoples. Nasser had narrowly avoided being deposed in 1956 and, were he subjected to a second crushing military defeat in 1967, America would certainly see the last of him.

Fourth, the war opened the possibility for a definitive solution to the Arab-Israeli struggle. A third smashing Israeli victory within nineteen years would dispel the Arab illusion that Israel could be eliminated. Because the United States alone had influence in Jerusalem, the Arabs would have to kowtow to the United States in order to get their territory back. We would, therefore, be able to impose an Israeli-style peace that would end this problem once and for all.

The political parts of this analysis proved lamentably inaccurate. Thirty-five years later, it is now easy to see that the Arabs had more staying power than the administration thought, and that Israel would refuse to return any but a small portion of its captured territory.[16]

## The 1967 War—An Easy Israeli Victory

The senior author resigned in October 1966 as the Under Secretary of State (now called the Deputy Secretary) and therefore was not in the government at the time of the 1967 War. The authors have had to rely on published sources in the discussion that follows.

That war has kept historians busy disputing which side had the greater responsibility for starting it. Without probing too thoroughly, we can safely make two statements. Nasser certainly provoked it, and the casual American brushoff, "The Arabs asked for what they got," is partially apposite. Yet, many Israeli leaders welcomed its occurrence as a plausible pretext for achieving their territorial goals. Moreover, the fact that the Israelis opened the war with Egypt without a prior ultimatum was fully consistent with their tactical doctrine of a preemptive offensive—an understandable but hardly laudable reflex of a nervous nation surrounded by enemies. It wished to exploit the factor of surprise for which its army was specially equipped.

So, early on the morning of June 5, as reported by the UN observers, Israel attacked the Egyptian forces and airfields. While Israel at the time denied this claim, Prime Minister Begin would later clarify the question when, in a speech on August 8, 1982, before the National Defense College in Jerusalem, he classified the 1967 conflict not as a "war of necessity" but as a "war of choice. . . . Nasser did not attack us. We decided to attack him."[17]

Leaving aside the origin of the conflict, there is no doubt that, as American military experts had predicted, the Israelis quickly subdued the Arab armies, destroyed or captured their equipment, and humiliated their governments—all in six days. Only by deft maneuvering did Nasser avoid being overthrown.

Israel had occupied the Sinai Peninsula all the way to the Suez Canal, had wrested the Golan Heights from Syria, had seized the Gaza Strip, captured the West Bank from Jordan, and had speedily conquered and promptly annexed the Arab part of Jerusalem, along with substantial outlying areas.

## *The Attack on the* Liberty

During the war, Israel attacked the U.S.S. *Liberty*. The *Liberty* was an American intelligence-gathering vessel, then cruising in international waters near Egypt and reading the radio transmissions of both sides. It flew the American flag and was painted in U.S. Navy colors, complete with number and name.

On the fourth day of the war, with both Jordan and Egypt routed, the Israelis turned their attention to Syria, the original cause of all this trouble. Guns mounted on the Golan Heights had subjected Galilee to sporadic bombardment for years and the Israelis had every intention of capturing those Heights before hostilities were over. Meanwhile, the United Nations had adopted a cease-fire resolution and they feared there might not be enough time to accomplish this objective without, as it were, going into overtime.

The *Liberty*'s presence and function were known to Israel's leaders. They presumably thought it vital that the *Liberty* be prevented from informing Washington of their intentions to violate any cease-fire before they had completed their occupation of the Golan. Their solution was brutal and direct. Israeli aircraft determined the exact location of the ship and undertook a combined air-naval attack. Apprised of Israel's plans from various sources, the U.S. Navy Department faced a delicate problem. Due regard for the lives of America's naval personnel should have impelled the Navy to urge the State Department to warn off Israel in no uncertain terms; meanwhile, the Navy should have alerted the *Liberty* to its danger and dispatched ships or planes for its protection. But none of these actions was taken in time.

There has, for years, been a continuing argument about this tragic lapse. Some say that a warning to Israel might have exposed U.S. sources of secret intelligence. Whatever the motive, the President or one of his aides took the decision to risk the ship and its crew, and merely ordered them, without explanation, to steam west at top speed. Unhappily, that notice was too little and taken too late. Israeli ships and planes attacked, killing 34 American sailors, wounding 75, and leaving 821 rocket and machine-gun holes in the *Liberty*. It was only when the Israelis were preparing to board the ship that American planes belatedly appeared from the west and forced them to retire.

The sequel was unedifying. The administration tried vigorously to downplay the whole matter. Although it silenced the crew, casualties to the sailors and damage to the ship could not possibly be concealed. Thus, an elaborate charade was performed. The United States complained pro forma to Israel, which reacted by blaming the victims. The ship, they rejoined, had not been clearly marked but looked like an Arab ship—which was definitely untrue. Nor did the Israelis even pretend that they had queried the American Embassy in Tel Aviv regarding the status of the well-marked ship. In the end, the Israelis tendered a reluctant and graceless apology; indemnities for the victims and damaged ship were both parsimonious and slow in coming. The sordid affair has still not been erased from the history books; an organization of devoted survivors has kept the cause alive over the years by publishing a newsletter and holding well-advertised meetings.

Yet the ultimate lesson of the *Liberty* attack had far more effect on policy in Israel than America. Israel's leaders concluded that nothing they might do would offend the Americans to the point of reprisal. If America's leaders did not have the courage to punish Israel for the blatant murder of American citizens,[18] it seemed clear that their American friends would let them get away with almost anything.

*Problems Resulting from the 1967 War*

Not unnaturally, the Israelis greeted their military success in the 1967 War as a great victory, but on balance it created more problems than it solved. It left Israel with military control over an additional 900,000 Arabs (1.75 million now), which made it an empire. And, as we now know, the discontented subjects of the new empire, the Palestinians, would presently become a major colonialist headache. Even in the short term, the situation left a new mess; the truce was necessarily impermanent, and simple prudence might have impelled the Israelis to find a durable and definitive solution.[19]

On June 21, two days after the UN General Assembly special session had convened to consider settlement terms, Israeli Foreign Minister Abba Eban and two of his colleagues met with Secretary Dean Rusk. Eban outlined the Israeli demands for the restoration of the original international boundaries between the old Palestine Mandate and Egypt and Syria, respectively; this idea obviously contemplated Israel's annexation of the Gaza Strip. In the context of a peace treaty, he said, Israel envisaged "only such changes which security considerations in the south and the unimpaired free flow of the Jordan headwaters in the north necessitated."[20]

This seemingly bland formulation indicated an Israeli interest in annexing the eastern coast of the Sinai Peninsula and that portion of Syrian territory through which water flowed into the Jordan Valley. The Israeli Cabinet was not yet prepared to make any pronouncement regarding the West Bank. In fact, it was divided over whether to seek a deal with King Hussein or try to develop some form of association between the West Bank and Israel that would involve limited autonomy for the West Bank and economic union between them.

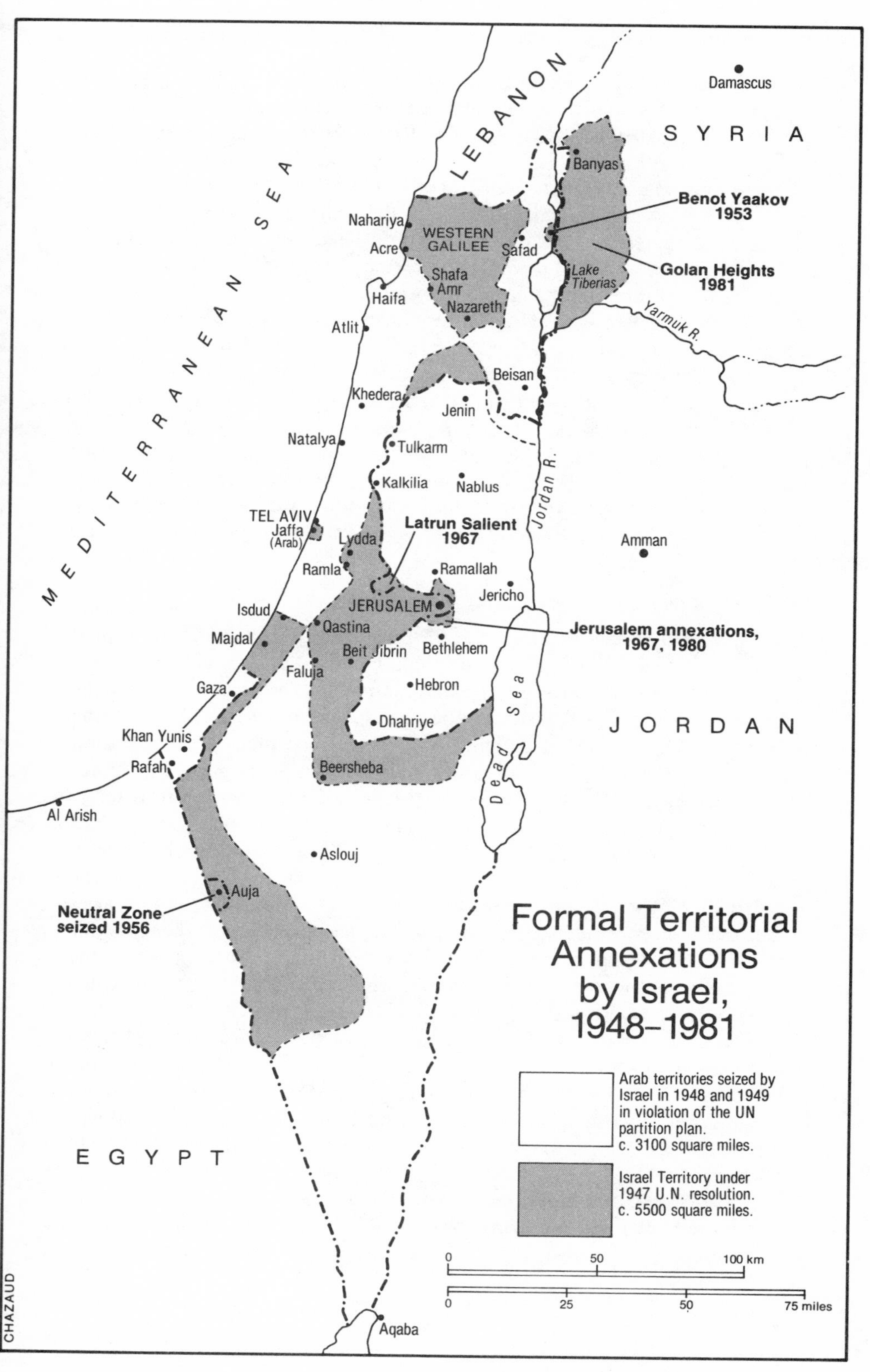

Formal Territorial Annexations by Israel, 1948–1981
MEDITERRANEAN SEA
LEBANON
SYRIA
JORDAN
EGYPT
Damascus
Banyas
Benot Yaakov 1953
Golan Heights 1981
Lake Tiberias
Yarmuk R.
Nahariya
WESTERN GALILEE
Acre
Safad
Shafa Amr
Haifa
Nazareth
Atlit
Beisan
Khedera
Jenin
Natalya
Tulkarm
Kalkilia
Nablus
Jordan R.
TEL AVIV
Jaffa (Arab)
Lydda
Latrun Salient 1967
Amman
Ramla
Ramallah
Jericho
JERUSALEM
Isdud
Qastina
Jerusalem annexations, 1967, 1980
Majdal
Beit Jibrin
Bethlehem
Faluja
Gaza
Hebron
Dead Sea
Dhahriye
Khan Yunis
Rafah
Beersheba
Al Arish
Aslouj
Auja
Neutral Zone seized 1956
Aqaba
Arab territories seized by Israel in 1948 and 1949 in violation of the UN partition plan. c. 3100 square miles.
Israel Territory under 1947 U.N. resolution. c. 5500 square miles.
0
50
100 km
0
25
50
75 miles
CHAZAUD

On the fate of the Palestinians, Secretary Rusk spoke briefly and to the point: "There is a constitutional precedent for letting people themselves decide." He also reminded the Israelis that King Hussein had considerable staying powers and was not to be written off. Finally, he warned that Israel's enemies might use the Israeli seizure of Jerusalem to stir up anti-Semitism.

No settlement was achieved between the belligerents. Nor did the United Nations take action. After three weeks of futile debate in the General Assembly, the matter was held over for the regular September session of both the General Assembly and the Security Council.

In advance of that session, the Americans handed Israel's representatives another draft resolution, framed with the Soviets in mind, only to have Israeli Foreign Ministry officials tell the American ambassador, Walworth Barbour, that such a proposal would put America on a collision course with Israel. Both Secretary Rusk and President Johnson were annoyed at Israel's peremptory attitude toward the United States, which was, after all, providing the wherewithal for Israel's economic, military, and diplomatic activities. Once again, however, America's domestic politics prohibited the use of that leverage to induce a more cooperative mood on Israel's part.

### *The Khartoum Declaration*

As was to happen so often, the Arabs chose this particularly inauspicious moment to make a dramatic gesture that from both a public relations and a practical viewpoint proved extremely damaging to them. When the Arab League assembled in Khartoum on August 29–September 1, 1967, its members found themselves in violent disagreement. To please the more radical leaders and in return for subsidies provided by the Arab oil-producing countries, Nasser and Hussein agreed to the passage of a resolution calling for "liquidating the consequences of Israeli aggression" and what became known as the Three No's—"no negotiations, no recognition and no peace with Israel."

In spite of this negative language, Israel, for at least a brief period after the June war, continued to affirm its willingness to exchange the lands it had seized for peace. Thus, when in June 1968 the senior author, in his capacity as U.S. ambassador to the United Nations, visited Jerusalem, Prime Minister Eshkol commissioned him to tell King Hussein, with whom he would be lunching the next day, that in exchange for peace Israel would be prepared to give back to Jordan "substantially all of the territory" (i.e., less Jerusalem) it had seized in the 1967 War. But Hussein did not respond favorably. He was presumably constrained by the Khartoum Declaration and his treaty commitments with Egypt. Moreover, he dared not cede the Islamic holy city of Jerusalem to Israel.

Given the Arabs' public refusal to make peace, a stalemate was inevitable. When the United Nations assembled in New York, the atmosphere progressively deteriorated. On October 24, the Egyptians sank the Israeli destroyer

*Elath.* In retaliation, the Israelis destroyed two oil refineries in Port Suez. That in turn gave Egypt leverage to extract offensive arms from the Soviet Union.

### *Negotiations at the Waldorf-Astoria*

The American ambassador to the United Nations, Arthur Goldberg, was selected to conduct the negotiations to resolve the 1967 War. Although an accomplished labor mediator and a former Supreme Court justice, Goldberg was known to be pro-Zionist and was therefore mistrusted by the Arabs. Thus, he undertook that task in a strained atmosphere.

Goldberg met with King Hussein on November 3, and assured him that the U.S. government believed that, while America "could not guarantee that everything would be returned by Israel, some territorial adjustments would be required. There must be a withdrawal to recognized and secure frontiers for all countries which were not the old armistice lines." Goldberg also noted that there must be a mutuality in adjustments.[21] For example, if Jordan made an adjustment in the Latrun Salient, a bulge of Jordanian territory lying midway on the highway between Tel Aviv and Jerusalem, then "there ought to be some compensatory adjustment for it."

Then, on November 6, Secretary Rusk assured King Hussein during a visit to Washington that the United States did not approve of Israeli retention of the West Bank, saying, "the United States was prepared to support the return of a substantial part of the West Bank to Jordan with boundary adjustments, and would use its influence to obtain compensation for Jordan for any territory it was required to give up." Finally, on November 8, Hussein met with President Johnson who, according to Hussein, repeated the same U.S. assurances. When asked how soon the Israeli withdrawal might take place, the President reportedly answered, "Six months."

On November 10, King Hussein again met with Arthur Goldberg and said he was "extremely pleased" and "extremely satisfied" with the assurances he received in Washington. When Hussein asked Goldberg if Israel agreed with the U.S. position, Goldberg responded: "Don't worry. They're on board."[22]

Meanwhile, on November 7 the United States offered a draft resolution on a peace settlement in the UN Security Council. Egypt's foreign minister, Mahmoud Riad, with whom Goldberg had been negotiating, criticized the U.S. draft and declared: "This is nothing more than an Israeli draft under a U.S. name." It called merely for "withdrawal of armed forces from occupied territory." It did not mention Israel or contain any time frame or indicate which occupied territories—whether those acquired in 1948 or 1967. On November 15, Goldberg met with officials from Iraq, Lebanon, and Morocco and assured them "that the United States did not conceive of any substantial redrawing of the map."[23]

Because the Arabs did not trust Goldberg, he followed the practice of first talking directly with the Israelis; then an American official would walk to the Jordanian suite and convey the latest Israeli position. After that, the Jordanians would present an Arab view which the same official would take back to Goldberg, who in turn would discuss it with the Israelis.

In retrospect, the United States delegation was, at best, maladroit in telling Israel that it would not be required to withdraw from any of the territories captured in the 1967 War until all negotiations had been completed. The U.S. officials fatuously assumed that once the resolution was passed, only technical and brief negotiations would be needed.

Although the Arabs took this assumption for granted, it did not happen that way. They failed to realize that the Israelis were past masters at exploiting so-called "constructive ambiguities" and wanted a chance to negotiate all aspects of the withdrawal. Trained in their own school of diplomacy, they insisted on fuzzy language so that they could then start haggling from scratch as though no resolution had ever been adopted. However, similarly experienced in bazaar practices, the Arab leaders quickly realized that they would be negotiating from weakness if they began their discussions while the Israelis still occupied their territory. They therefore insisted on including spelled-out terms in the resolution, but Israel, passively backed by the Americans, objected.

At that point, Lord Caradon, the British UN representative, came up with a compromise draft that was accepted by the exhausted representatives on both sides. His draft, which became Resolution 242, dated November 22, 1967, reads as follows:

> THE SECURITY COUNCIL,
>
> EXPRESSING its continuing concern with the grave situation in the Middle East,
>
> EMPHASIZING the inadmissibility of the acquisition of territory by war and the need to work for a just and lasting peace in which every state in the area can live in security,
>
> EMPHASIZING FURTHER that all member states in their acceptance of the Charter of the United Nations have undertaken a commitment to act in accordance with Article 2 of the Charter.
>
> 1. AFFIRMS that the fulfillment of Charter principles requires the establishment of a just and lasting peace in the Middle East which should include the application of both the following principles: (i) Withdrawal of Israeli armed forces from territories occupied in the recent conflict: (ii) Termination of all claims or states of belligerency and respect for an acknowledgment of the sovereignty, territorial integrity and political independence of every state in the area and their right to live in peace within secure and recognized boundaries free from threats of acts of force.
>
> 2. AFFIRMS FURTHER the necessity (a) for guaranteeing freedom of navigation through international waterways in the area: (b) for achieving a just

settlement of the refugee problem; (c) for guaranteeing the territorial inviolability and political independence of every state in the area, through measures including the establishment of demilitarized zones;

3. REQUESTS the Secretary General to designate a special representative to proceed to the Middle East to establish and maintain contacts with the states concerned in order to promote agreement and assist efforts to achieve a peaceful and accepted settlement in accordance with the provisions and principles in this resolution;

4. REQUESTS the Secretary General to report to the Security Council on the progress of the efforts of the special representative as soon as possible.

The resolution as finally approved followed Caradon's proposal, with two exceptions:

First, while neither the Soviets nor the Arabs made any specific objection to President Johnson's proposed clause "to limit the wasteful, destructive arms race in the area," this idea was dropped from the resolution—thereby leaving the way clear for unrestricted arms competition in the area.[24]

Second—and a cause for endless problems in the future—America failed to insist on the British and Soviet demand to include the definite article "the" in the clause calling for the return of "territories occupied in the recent conflict."[25] By deleting the definitive article before "territories occupied," the American delegation secured Arab approval by an ambiguity that amounted to deception. As noted above, Hussein and other Arab leaders had been given to understand that they would be able either to recover all their territory or be compensated for any minor border rectifications on which Israel insisted.

Practically everyone else, including the British government speaking through Lord Caradon, thought that even without a definite article in the English text (it *was* included in the French and Spanish versions), the resolution would require the Israelis to evacuate all, or practically all, of the territories, with only minor adjustments.[26]

But even though the Israelis secured the ambiguous phrasing that would enable them to engage in an incessant filibuster for the next quarter century, they still found the resolution unsatisfactory because the preamble (borrowed from the basic principles of the UN Charter) asserted "the inadmissibility of the acquisition of territory by war," which, they contended, contradicted the assurance of "secure and recognized boundaries."[27]

If Israel found fault with Resolution 242, the Arabs were equally dissatisfied by the United States' insistence that the Palestinians be referred to only as "refugees." Israel did not wish to acknowledge the existence of another people with a claim to the land it occupied, and the United States government, having long opposed an independent Arab Palestinian state, joined Israel and Jordan in implicitly denying that there was such a thing as Palestinian nationalism, a Palestinian people, or that Palestinians had any right to choose their future government.

As part of Resolution 242, Secretary-General U Thant was given authority to appoint a United Nations special representative to conduct peace talks, and he assigned an experienced Swedish diplomat, Gunnar Jarring, to the task. Though nothing substantive came of his efforts, Jarring did obtain a document signed by Abba Eban acknowleding Israeli acceptance of Resolution 242.[28]

While negotiations were still going forward in the United Nations, the military arm of the PLO had taken up positions in Jordan and was using them as a launching base for raids against Israel.[29] Contrary to the explicit objections of the State Department, the Israelis decided to launch a punitive attack on the Jordanian town of Karameh in March 1968. But the Israelis met with such determined resistance, chiefly from the Jordanian Army,[30] that they were compelled to withdraw with serious casualties and without achieving their objectives. Frustrated, the Israelis then attacked and destroyed the East Ghor irrigation canal, also contrary to the wishes of the American government.

Almost automatically, the U.S. government limited its reaction to a pro forma gesture of disapprobation. It held up the delivery of certain arms for a few weeks, then grudgingly delivered them. In succeeding years that ritualistic formula would become almost automatic.

## The Six-Day War and the Contradiction in Zionist Objectives

The American handling of the events leading up to the 1967 War and its aftermath encouraged the Zionist leaders to rely on a set of objectives that were fundamentally contradictory.

The Jewish state that they had always contemplated must, they insisted,

1. be independent of any other power;
2. be a state exclusively for Jews, managed by Jews, and for the benefit of Jews; and
3. be based on democratic principles; in other words, it must be a nation for the people and ruled by the people through the machinery of equal suffrage.

Prior to the War of Independence, many Jewish Israelis recognized that to achieve the first two objectives while complying with the third meant that Israel must reduce the preexisting Arab majority.

Had these been Israel's sole objectives, the Jewish leaders might have been able to achieve peace with their neighbors. But they complicated their future when, as a final objective, they adopted expansionism on the grounds that the presumed ingathering of Jews on a worldwide basis would require a larger territory than that secured up to 1949. Were Israel to expand in the crowded Middle East, it would find itself in control of an increasing number of disaffected Arabs. To maintain its exclusivism, it would either have to reduce the power of the Arab population by economic and political discrimination or outright expulsion, both of which are the negation of a true Western-style democracy.

This contradiction in Israeli policies might have shown itself immediately after what the Israelis call their War of Independence had Israeli arms not driven from the country by fear or force roughly 780,000 Palestinians. But after the 1967 War they were not so lucky. That conflict extended Israel's dominion to include the large and growing population of Palestinians in Jerusalem, the West Bank and Gaza, and Syrian Druse on the Golan Heights. And this time the local Arabs did not oblige Israel by fleeing; instead, they elected to stay in their homes, even under a regime of rigorous repression.

Thus the 1967 War brought the Israeli face to face with the inherent contradictions in their policies. They could expel the Palestinians in the Occupied Territories or rule them under a discriminatory regime in violation of generally accepted human rights standards, but only if they were prepared to forgo their pretension to be regarded as a democratic state. Or they could grant the Palestinians equal citizenship and thus nullify their even more fervently held objective of exclusivism.

The Israelis, however, still sought to pursue both options at once: an Athenian democracy for the Jews, and second-class citizenship, or even feudal servitude, for everyone else. This stance has not only undercut their proud claim to democracy but, as they are now gradually discovering, it has incited a permanent struggle with the whole Arab world. All but the hard-line politicians who control the current Israeli government now sadly recognize that so long as Israel retains the Occupied Areas and discriminates against the resident Arabs, the frightened and angered Arab communities that surround them will never make peace. Indeed, so long as America continues to pursue Johnson's policy of maintaining Israeli military superiority and thus encouraging those elements in Israel pressing for territorial expansion, a noxious cloud of endless war will inevitably befoul the Israeli atmosphere.

## The Results of Johnson's Middle East Policies

In sum, the Johnson administration, motivated by what at the time seemed acceptable objectives, took several actions concerning the Arab-Israeli conflict that have seriously complicated any effort to reach final settlement.

First, the administration put America in the position of being Israel's principal arms supplier and sole unqualified backer.

Second, by assuring the Israelis that the United States would always provide them with a military edge over the Arabs, Johnson guaranteed the escalation of an arms race—which cannot benefit Israel, the United States, or the Arab states. Only the arms merchants profit, while the area will continue near the poverty threshold.

Third, by refusing to follow the advice of his aides that America make its delivery of nuclear-capable F-4 Phantoms conditional on Israel's signing the Nuclear Non-Proliferation Treaty, Johnson gave the Israelis the impression that America had no fundamental objection to Israel's nuclear's program.[32]

Fourth, by permitting a cover-up of Israel's attack on the *Liberty,* President Johnson told the Israelis in effect that nothing they did would induce American politicians to refuse their bidding. From that time forth, the Israelis began to act as if they had an inalienable right to American aid and backing.

Those are merely some of the ways in which the Johnson administration impeded an ultimate settlement. In addition, a strong case can be made that it tragically erred by permitting the injection of deliberate ambiguity into Resolution 242.

Finally, by permitting the overrunning of the Occupied Territories and not forcing a withdrawal, Johnson's administration unwittingly laid the basis not only for Israeli overconfidence but for future wars and now the *Intifada.*

CHAPTER FOUR

# The Retreat Accelerates Under Nixon

LIKE PRESIDENT EISENHOWER, with whom he had served as Vice President in 1953–61, Richard M. Nixon was under no obligation to the friends of Israel. Most of the American Jewish community had strongly backed Hubert Humphrey in 1968.[1] As Henry Kissinger noted in his memoirs: "The President was convinced that most leaders of the Jewish community had opposed him throughout his political career. . . . He delighted in telling associates and visitors that the 'Jewish lobby' had no effect on him."[2]

As a conservative from California, Nixon tended to equate American liberals with Jews who opposed the Vietnam War. He thus wrote in his own memoirs:

> What [the Israelis] must realize is that these people . . . will give Israel a lot of lip service, but they are peace at any price people. . . . He [Nixon] does not want to see Israel go down the drain and makes an absolute commitment that he will see to it that Israel always has "an edge." On the other hand, he must carry with him . . . the 60 percent of the American people who are . . . the silent majority, and who must be depended upon in the event that we have to take a strong stand against Soviet expansionism in the Mideast. . . .[3]

But when he found himself unable to mobilize the silent majority to his satisfaction, Nixon felt forced to try to propitiate the pro-Israeli forces; in the end he became a more bountiful friend of Israel than any previous chief executive.

To understand Nixon's passivity toward the Middle East during the early years of his administration, one must realize that to begin with, he was almost wholly preoccupied by the war in Vietnam, the opening of a door to China, and the beginnings of detente with the Soviet Union. With so many diverse interests at stake, Nixon was reluctant to jeopardize his whole program by inviting a bruising political fight with Israel's supporters.[4] Therefore, most of the time he spent on the Middle East was devoted to managing crises and maintaining the status quo.

A secondary factor was the adverse reaction to the trips of his special envoy to the Middle East, former Governor William Scranton. After making a pre-inaugural swing through the region in late 1968, Scranton concluded that U.S. policy should be more "evenhanded." Though that remark brought a storm of protest from Israel, which considered anything other than staunch support as criticism, Nixon did nothing beyond having his press secretary point out that "Scranton remarks [are] not Nixon remarks."

As Nixon confessed in his memoirs:

> One of the main problems I faced . . . was the unyielding and shortsighted pro-Israeli attitude in large and influential segments of the American Jewish community, Congress, the media and in intellectual and cultural circles. In the quarter century since the end of World War II this attitude had become so deeply ingrained that many saw the corollary of not being pro-Israel as being anti-Israeli, or even anti-Semitic. I tried unsuccessfully to convince them that this was not the case.[5]

Moreover, both he and his National Security Adviser, Henry Kissinger, looked on the Middle East primarily as an element of the East-West struggle. Neither thought of it as merely a local fracas in which America and the Soviet Union had become tangentially involved.[6]

## The War of Attrition

During the early Nixon years there were two outbreaks of warfare between the Arabs and Israelis.

The first was the so-called "War of Attrition" (1969–70), in which the Egyptians sought to put pressure on Israel and the United States to carry out Resolution 242. In the end, however, the only results were heavy casualties on both sides, especially among the Egyptians, ruinous expense, and—most ominous—the first direct clash between Soviet personnel and the Israeli Defense Forces (IDF).

The war arose from a combination of three factors: the humiliation of the Arabs in the 1967 War; the overweening self-confidence of the Israelis, who had blocked any peace settlement that would not accord them extensive annexations; and the inherent temptation of propinquity between IDF and Egyptian forces positioned a few yards from each other just across the Suez Canal.

Thus, late in 1968, the Egyptian Army began shelling IDF troops with monotonous regularity. In response, Israel not only fired back but built a fortified defense—the Bar-Lev Line—across the east bank of the Suez Canal. To minimize casualties from Egyptian fire, Israel chose to escalate the fighting by resorting to massive bombing raids. That air offensive was extended to deep penetrations of Egyptian air space until, by the end of the year, Defense Minister Moshe Dayan was able to claim that Israel had destroyed twenty-four missile sites, an estimated one third of Egypt's front-line combat planes, and had left Egypt's air defense system virtually in ruins. Meanwhile, Israel's pilots pointedly emphasized their air superiority by using sonic booms to smash windows in Cairo.

Kissinger's attitude was personally favorable to Israel, but he wanted the United States to play a waiting game. He based his strategy on the assumption that by failing to secure a return of land for the Arabs, the Soviets would exhaust the Arabs' patience. America could then step in and force the Arabs to accept a peace satisfactory to Israel. Since Nixon considered that Kissinger's Jewish background disqualified him for deep involvement in Middle Eastern matters, he at first gave Secretary of State William Rogers primacy in that region.[7]

On December 9, 1969, Secretary of State Rogers—evidently without Nixon's approval—tried to break the cycle of war before the Soviets intervened to extricate the Egyptians from the developing mess. Abruptly repudiating Kissinger's waiting policy, he offered the so-called "Rogers Plan," which was immediately accepted by Jordan and, with qualifications, by Egypt. Its key points were a requirement for direct negotiations, a renewed truce to pave the way for negotiations,[8] and a settlement based on Resolution 242 that would deny the legality of acquiring territory by force.

As might have been expected, the Israelis gave the Rogers speech a cool reception. The following day, the Israeli Cabinet rejected "all outside efforts to prescribe boundaries," while Golda Meir (then prime minister) said that Rogers was "moralizing" and that "the major powers could not make peace on behalf of others."[9] But those reactions were not decisive factors, since Kissinger and Nixon had already sent word to Mrs. Meir that the Rogers Plan did not have the President's backing and that the Americans would make no effort to follow it up.[10]

Apart from this foray there were few occasions when the War of Attrition produced much direct bargaining between Washington and Jerusalem, although one incident might be noted. Nixon was disturbed by the realization that the Arabs were becoming ever more attached to the Soviet Union while the Kremlin was sending word through Ambassador Anatoly Dobrynin that it would support a cease-fire along the Canal. So, disregarding Kissinger's advice, Nixon decided that the United States should move once again, as had been suggested by Governor Scranton in 1969, toward a policy of "even-handedness."

However, when Kissinger mentioned a possible cease-fire while giving a message to Yitzhak Rabin (then the Israeli ambassador to Washington) that the Nixon administration was limiting deliveries in 1970 to eight Phantoms and twenty Skyhawks, Rabin responded in a manner that Kissinger described as follows:

> Yitzhak had many extraordinary qualities, but the gift of human relations was not one of them. If he had been handed the entire "United States Strategic Air Command" as a free gift he would have (a) affected the attitude that at last Israel was getting its due, and (b) found some technical shortcoming in the airplanes that made his accepting them a reluctant concession to us.[11]

Rabin was not responding simply on his own; he was reflecting his instructions from Prime Minister Golda Meir, who had already complained to Nixon about the rumored military reductions. In her message, Mrs. Meir touched on the usual points. She enlarged on the dangers to Israel from Arab military power and her sense of "abandonment." Then she reverted to a patented Israeli ploy: if Israel did not get all it wanted, desperate public opinion would compel it to take some irrational action. And "one can't overstate the seriousness of the situation that will result." It was a familiar refrain.

Though Nixon's reference to a cease-fire evoked from Rabin a less than enthusiastic response, that was not the end of it. After consultations in Jerusalem, Rabin brought an answer from the Israeli Cabinet: Israel would agree to a cease-fire only if America guaranteed the cessation of all military activity, the *doubling* of Nixon's offer to replace its military equipment, and a public announcement that the President would maintain Israeli air strength and its military superiority.

As Kissinger put it, "I was now being directly exposed for the first time to Israeli negotiating tactics. In the combination of single-minded persistence and convoluted tactics the Israelis preserve in the interlocutor only those last vestiges of sanity and coherence needed to sign the final document."[12]

Meanwhile Israel was being paid back for its deep penetration raids into Egypt. Those raids had led Nasser to appeal to the Soviet Union for aid. Accordingly, in January 1970, after a Soviet warning to Nixon which the administration scornfully dismissed because of a faulty Israeli intelligence analysis of Russian capabilities and intentions, the Soviet Union provided Nasser with an effective air defense system. By March 17, 1970, Soviet troops in Egypt were equipped with an array of advanced weapons, including SA-2s. Simultaneously, it was announced on March 17 that 1,500 Soviet technicians and a quantity of SAM-3 missiles—weapons that the Soviets had not even granted to North Vietnam—had arrived in Egypt. By April 24, a month later, the number of Soviet technicians had reached 10,000 and Soviet pilots were flying Egyptian planes in combat.[13]

That unsettling development was exacerbated when on June 4 eighty-five senators sent a petition to Rogers demanding that Washington supply Israel with 125 additional fighter planes. It was a demand that could only escalate the arms race and the hostilities.

The direct intervention by Soviet fighting personnel led Rogers to put forward his so-called "Plan B," which proposed that the cease-fire be restored for ninety days, that the parties reaffirm Resolution 242 in all its provisions, and that they also agree to resume negotiations under the auspices of Ambassador Jarring.

On June 23, Nasser announced his acceptance; two days later, Jordan followed suit. But Prime Minister Golda Meir held out for "clarifications." Those "clarifications" included a demand that the United States obtain an agreement from Egypt and the Soviet Union to refrain "from changing the military *status quo* by emplacing SAMs west of the Suez Canal," and that the United States commit itself to supply aid to Israel "in all that concerns the maintenance of her security and balance of forces in the region."

On July 23 and for two weeks following, there was an exchange of correspondence between President Nixon and Golda Meir about the exact meaning of the American offer. As usual, the United States undercut its own proposal: America, Nixon assured Mrs. Meir, would not compel Israel to accept the Arab interpretation of Resolution 242 in developing guidelines for the revived Jarring Mission. It was a reckless statement, since that resolution had been interpreted by the Johnson administration as requiring that, in exchange for peace, Israel must yield practically all of the Occupied Territories.

Nonetheless, despite Jerusalem's pettifogging, the prospect of fighting the Soviets directly had already produced a prompt result—three days after the Soviet presence in Egypt became public knowledge, Israel on March 22 began modifying its tactics and by April 13 had stopped its deep penetration raids.[14]

In the end, in spite of the continued forward movement of Soviet air defenses, a troubled cease-fire went into effect on August 7. Almost immediately, however, Ambassador Rabin complained that five Israeli Phantoms had been shot down over Egyptian territory by Soviet missiles, apparently newly emplaced in violation of the cease-fire arrangements. Still, even if the Russians were cheating, why were the Israeli planes flying over the western bank of the Suez Canal after the truce was supposed to be in effect? But as both Moscow and the Egyptians rejected the complaint filed with them by the U.S. government, the Israelis, on September 6, announced that they would not attend any of the meetings under Jarring's auspices. They had never wanted negotiations under UN auspices, and the truce violations provided them with a plausible pretext for avoiding discussions that might force them to abandon their territorial ambitions.

## INTRA-ARAB PROBLEMS—THE JORDANIAN CRISIS, JUNE TO SEPTEMBER 1970

During the summer of 1970 while the War of Attrition was winding down, affairs in Jordan were reaching a crisis. The PLO had not only built up a large private army for incursions into Israel, but was also involved in attempts to assassinate King Hussein. Finally, on September 5, Dr. George Habash's extremist Palestinian group, the PFLP, hijacked three airliners (British, Swiss, and American) and brought them to a small airfield northeast of Amman, where over three hundred passengers were held hostage before the planes were destroyed.

The situation rapidly disintegrated. The Jordanian forces were weary of Palestinian provocations and loudly demanded that the King unleash them against their foes. Left to its own devices, the Royal Army could readily crush the guerrillas. But if the Iraqis or the Syrians intervened, matters could become serious. In that case, the Israelis would almost certainly take action. That, in Kissinger's words, would force the United States, as "everyone agreed," to "stand aside, but block Soviet retaliation against Israel."[15]

On September 20–21, the Nixon administration decided that in an emergency, the Israelis were to be encouraged to mount air strikes against an impending Syrian invasion of northern Jordan. The Israelis then advised the Americans that, in their opinion, air strikes might not be enough; actual ground intervention would be needed. In fact the Israelis did, as a precaution, mass troops on the Golan Heights that could flank any Syrian force which might invade Jordan.

The Israelis were not eager to rush into war with Syria, and they demanded constant reassurances. They also made clear that they were prepared to intervene only because they could not tolerate a Syrian-dominated radical regime in Amman.

Not, however, until September 21 did the United States give the green light to an Israeli ground operation in Jordan, and then only on condition that King Hussein agree. The King agreed to Israeli air strikes, but he unequivocally opposed Israeli ground operations.

In the end, thanks to the courage and skill of the Jordanian soldiers, coupled with dissension in Damascus, Syria withdrew the armored forces it had dispatched to aid the guerrillas, and, lacking their help, the guerrillas were crushed.

The crisis was over. Nonetheless, the backers of Israel have ever since used the incident to prove that Israel is not only prepared to make great sacrifices to protect the United States' interests in preventing the extension of Soviet power through its Syrian surrogate, but is also capable of projecting its power beyond its own borders and therefore of serving American diplomatic and military purposes in the Middle East.

What this analysis overlooks is that in threatening to intervene, Israel was not serving American interests out of pure altruism; Syria was one of Israel's most dangerous enemies. Thus, in blocking Syria, it was pursuing its own agenda as well. In any case, the American aid subsequently bestowed on Israel more than compensated for any expenses incurred by it due to its mobilization.

## The Sadat Era Begins, 1970–73

Although the elimination of Nasser had always been an objective of Israeli policy, the government in Jerusalem was caught unprepared by Nasser's death on September 28, 1970, which may have been hastened by the strain created by the crisis in Jordan. Nasser's successor, General Anwar el-Sadat, was not widely known outside his own country and the experts at first assumed that he would produce no brilliant initiatives.

Both Sadat and the Israelis continued along their different courses. Then Sadat began to signal that he wished to shift patrons; he preferred the United States to Russia. While this was what Kissinger had hoped for, he either failed to analyze Sadat's motives correctly when Sadat purged Soviet supporters from the Egyptian government in May 1971, or he felt Sadat's position was so weak that nothing need be done for him. Our government apparently failed to realize that Sadat's political position was such that he had to recover Egyptian territory speedily or risk being overthrown.

Sadat approached American representatives in Cairo and drafted, with their aid, a peace proposal that he had been led to believe would meet with America's acceptance. Yet once again, Washington showed no will of its own and, at Israel's behest, brusquely rejected the Sadat proposal. Embarrassed, Sadat concluded in May 1971 that under those circumstances he had no choice but to maintain his relationship with the USSR and signed a friendship treaty with the Soviets.

Considering that Egypt had already been disappointed in its dealings with the Soviet Union, he did not take that step happily. There had been no recovery of Egyptian territory; Moscow was unwilling to provide the arms Egypt needed to undertake that job; nor would it assist Egypt in building its own arms industry.[16] The Soviets had no interest in the destruction of Israel, and they wished to avoid a direct confrontation with the United States.

When, therefore, at the Moscow Conference in May 1972, Gromyko and Kissinger agreed on nothing more than a bland repetition of Resolution 242 (with specific emphasis on border rectifications), Sadat concluded that the Soviet Union had totally reneged on its promises to recover Egypt's seized territories. He therefore expelled his Soviet advisers, and in February 1973 sent a private emissary to Kissinger to discuss a United States-brokered deal.

During the last half of 1972 President Nixon was largely concerned with the lengthening shadows of Watergate and was anxious that his reelection should not be further impeded by a war in the Middle East. Kissinger was preoccupied with "back channel" negotiations between himself and Soviet Ambassador Dobrynin. Once Nixon had been reelected overwhelmingly, he again came face to face with the perennial Middle East Catch-22. Not trusting Israel, the Arabs would not make peace until Israel agreed to return their territory, while the Israelis persisted in the illusion that they could both keep the conquered territory and have peace.

During her visit to the United States in early 1973, Prime Minister Golda Meir stated that the Arabs had no military option, and told Secretary Kissinger that the longer the status quo could be maintained, the greater the likelihood that Israel could retain all the seized territories. Her chief objective was to persuade America to keep feeding Israel's military machine so she could carry out her annexation program. These plans met with neither rejection nor disapprobation at the White House.

In its arms-aid negotiations in 1973, Israel had exploited Jewish Americans' political pressures on Congress so effectively that by March 1, 1973, not only did President Nixon agree to new airplane deliveries but he even approved plans for co-production of aircraft in Israel. That was accomplished through a secret agreement which, however, found its way into *The New York Times.*[17]

## The Yom Kippur War

A less preoccupied American government should have anticipated adverse Arab reactions to these developments. But, convinced of Israeli military superiority and the unlikelihood of an Arab assault—an intelligence finding carefully fostered by the Israelis—Secretary Kissinger's first reaction to the news of the Egyptian attack on October 6, 1973 (Yom Kippur, the holiest day in the Jewish calendar), was that there must be some kind of misunderstanding.

In retrospect, it seems clear that although the Egyptians had been planning this move for some time, they lacked confidence in the outcome of their attack, and thus had made no preparation for an exploitation drive into the Sinai. Their ambition was simply to crack the frozen attitudes in Washington and Jerusalem and to appease the Egyptian people by providing some small military success that would cancel out the humiliation of 1967. Sadat had been facing serious internal unrest and he had, at the last minute, frustrated a *coup d'état* supported by the Soviets.[18] Few had expected the Egyptian forces to cross the Canal so swiftly or to occupy its entire east bank.

The 1973 War differed from earlier conflicts in that Egypt and Syria had managed to stage a strategic surprise.[19] The Mossad (Israeli Secret Service) had apparently failed to warn the government that Sadat had completely reorganized the Egyptian Army. The Egyptian high command had compensated for its weaknesses in armor-maneuverability and trained combat pilots by the massive deployment of infantry equipped with anti-tank weapons and protected by ground-to-air missiles.

While Israel had long contemplated the possibility of a major Egyptian crossing of the Canal, it had apparently assumed that unless Egypt could neutralize the Israeli Air Force, the Egyptians would not embark on a new war before 1975. What the Israelis did not anticipate was that the Russians would help Egypt create one of the densest missile walls in the world. In addition, to prevent the Israeli Air Force from striking deep into Egypt, the Soviets supplied the Egyptians with SCUD surface-to-surface missiles with a 180-mile range.

It was the delivery of the first SCUD in April 1973 that finally decided Sadat to move his forces across the Canal, at which point, as earlier agreed with President Assad of Syria, Syrian forces would simultaneously attack on Israel's northern border. Neither Israeli intelligence services (on which the United States was depending) nor the Israeli government's reaction to the warnings its intelligence had given it proved adequate. Israel interpreted the Arab armies' movements to the front as yet another Arab bluff to force it into an expensive mobilization. By the time the threat of war became clear, the politicians in Jerusalem were caught in a political quandary as to whether they should attempt yet another preemptive attack of their own (with all the odium it would entail) or passively await the action of the enemy, in the hope that the political gains might offset the negative military factors. During October 6–8, 1973, the Israelis lost fifty aircraft and hundreds of tanks. Only on October 9 did they launch a counterattack, stabilize their line, and thereafter prevent any further Egyptian territorial gains during the sixteen remaining days of the war.

### *Disregard of the UN Cease-Fire*

As they had done in 1948–49 and 1967, and were to do again in 1982, the Israelis disregarded the United Nations' cease-fire order of October 22, 1973, in order to achieve their war goals. Not satisfied with a delay secured by the Americans, which allowed them to launch a counterattack across the Canal, they tried to complete the encirclement of the Egyptian Third Army and starve it into submission. That effort continued until after the United States had obtained a more forceful resolution from the UN Security Council demanding that the parties abide by the cease-fire. The United States had also threatened that if the Israelis did not relax their constricting grip, America would itself open the siege lines and feed the Egyptian troops.

During and after the truce resolution, the Israelis demanded more truce-related concessions and threatened an adverse publicity campaign against the U.S. government for joining with the Soviet Union in dictating truce terms to Israel. And, as always, the United States meekly suppressed its indignation, and attempted to mollify Israel by delivering the additional planes and tanks requested.

## Step-by-Step Diplomacy, 1973–75

After the truce, the Israelis stopped repeating Golda Meir's boastful claim that they had "never had it so good."[20] The psychological shock had been substantial. Israel's casualties had been heavy; its dreams of an endless expansion of empire had been given a rude jolt. The revelation that Arabs could indeed fight bravely and efficiently proved deeply upsetting.

As Secretary Kissinger himself pointed out, the United States then saw a wider range of options for peace in the Middle East than did Israel. As Golda Meir put it to Kissinger, "You're saying we have to accept the judgment of the U.S. . . . we have to accept your judgment? Even on our own affairs? On what is best for us?" Kissinger retorted: "We all have to accept the judgment of other nations."[21]

In trying to work out the initial stage of the disengagement, in October 1973, Kissinger confronted an Israeli government that faced an election in December. This conjunction of events was bound to make his job difficult since the Labor government, for electoral reasons, would find it politically necessary to resist American pressure. On November 7 he produced, with Egypt's concurrence, a six-point program calculated to get the worst problems immediately behind them.[22] That same evening, the Assistant Secretary of State for Middle Eastern Affairs, Joseph Sisco, and a National Security staff member, Harold Saunders, arrived in Jerusalem to inform the Israelis that Egypt had accepted what was largely an Israeli draft, only to find that Israel was unable to take yes for an answer. Golda Meir subjected the Americans to hours of grueling harangue before getting the program approved by her own cabinet, and even then only after she had complained about a provision that called for UN control of the supply routes to the Third Army.

## The Geneva Conference, 1973

The U.S. government agreed only reluctantly to United Nations Resolution 338 and its call for a Geneva Conference. Given his determination to exclude the Soviet Union from the Middle East, Secretary Kissinger viewed the conference as an occasion for limiting the Soviets to an essentially ceremonial role in peacemaking. After the initial meeting, he hoped to shunt them aside while the United States engaged in separate negotiations with the warring powers.[23]

Israel compounded his difficulties by insisting on an explicit proviso declaring that once the conference had gone into session, Israel might veto further members—for instance, the PLO. In response to Golda Meir's obstinate resistance, Nixon wrote:

> I want to say to you in all solemnity that if Israel now fails to take a favorable position to participate in the conference on the basis of the letter that we have worked out, this will not be understood either in the United States or in the world and I will not be able to justify the support which I have consistently rendered in our mutual interests to your government.[24]

But that was only a ritual threat.

## The Reaction of Syria

During Kissinger's visit to Syria on December 15, 1973, he found President Hafez Assad, the ruler of Syria since 1970 and head of the Ba'ath Socialist Party, quite uninterested in the Geneva Conference; it would, Assad correctly predicted, accomplish little, and he informed the Secretary that whether Syria would ever participate would depend on his answers to three questions:

1. Did the United States agree with Syria that Syria should not give up any of its territory?
2. Did the United States agree that there could be no solution unless the Palestinian problem was solved?
3. Was the United States going to Geneva with an objective consonant with those points, or only to engage in the usual obfuscations before breaking up the conference without having achieved anything?

These cogent questions presented Kissinger with a difficult dilemma, which he tried to finesse. If he told the Syrians they should not yield any territory, that would infuriate Israel. If he agreed that the Palestinians were the core of the problem, the Israelis would be even angrier. Yet, if he backed Israel's annexation of the Golan and denied the Palestinians a role, the Arabs would torpedo Kissinger's plans. Kissinger, therefore, gave Assad vague assurances and hoped for the best.

Kissinger's dealings with the Israelis on December 17 were even more discouraging. With an election looming in a fortnight, Golda Meir wanted to protect herself against the Likud bloc. So she not only resisted the idea of any withdrawal but tried to force Secretary Kissinger to agree that the Palestinians were not even to be mentioned at the conference, and that United Nations participation would be limited solely to convening the conference.

## The Egyptian-Israeli Disengagement

When Kissinger began his disengagement negotiations, Sadat primarily wished to clear the Israelis off all Egyptian territory. However, he had no objection to considering a wider peace so long as it would not be regarded as a betrayal of the Arab cause.

The Israelis, on the other hand, had more spacious ambitions. Without promising to return Egyptian territory, they demanded that the blockade at the mouth of the Red Sea be lifted; that the Straits of Tiran be opened; that Israeli ships be allowed to use the Suez Canal; and that the Egyptians issue a declaration of nonbelligerency. The Egyptians refused to do any of these things until they got their territory back.

Through General Mordechai Gur, the Israelis had already disclosed their proposed withdrawal lines in Geneva, yet they now came up with much harder terms. Obviously the Egyptians were in no mood to accept less than what they had first been offered.

Ultimately, thanks to Sadat's flexibility and Kissinger's resourcefulness, the Israelis came round, and on January 18, 1987, an agreement was signed at Kilometer 101 in Egypt, thereby bringing an end to the first phase of negotiations.

## The Consequences of the Oil Embargo

At this point a new weapon was brought into play in the Middle East wars—an embargo by the oil-producing states against the West.

All during the Sinai I negotiations, the American government was facing the damaging economic dislocations caused by the price increases for Arab oil precipitated by the 1973 War. The Arabs had for years been talking casually about their possible use of oil as a "weapon" against the United States; but it had required a war to bring it about. In America, long gas lines created rage and panic—an atmosphere conducive to anti-Arab posturing. Some regarded the Organization of Petroleum Exporting Countries (OPEC) action as vindictive, while others saw it in populist terms as the malevolent exploitation of a monopoly position. Few, in or out of the government, had the temerity to point out the obvious causal connection between Israel's actions, America's active and tacit support for them, and the consequent Arab resentments that precipitated the oil crisis.

Otherwise sensible people expressed extremist views. Some academics endorsed the theory that if the Arabs persisted in their vindictive pricing policies, the consuming nations were entitled to seize the oil fields by force. The senior author recalls having a public debate with Professor Robert W. Tucker of Johns Hopkins University, who had advocated such a view in *Commen-*

*tary,* a magazine published by the American Jewish Committee.[25] The senior author suggested that Tucker had propounded an essentially anarchistic theory. Translated into domestic terms, it implied that "if my wife feels the butcher is overcharging, I am entitled not only to beat him up but to seize his meat supplies."

Yet, with the shortages creating national hysteria, such ideas were fashionable. Indeed, an article in the March 1979 *Harper's* by "Miles Ignotus,"[26] written in response to the panic caused by the fall of the Shah of Iran, conveyed the same message. In both cases, there was an orgy of racist and insulting comments that compared the Gulf oil states to the Barbary pirates, which further alienated the Arab nations from the United States and vice versa.

After the arrangement with Egypt, Kissinger then shuttled between Jerusalem and Damascus. The Arabs were not about to lift the oil embargo until the United States had worked out an Israeli-Syrian agreement. Yet the Israelis adamantly refused to negotiate until Syria had liberated its Israeli prisoners. Kissinger proposed that the Syrians furnish the Israelis with the number and names of the prisoners, and in turn the Israelis would provide a counterproposal for disengagement. After both sides accepted, the negotiations could begin.

Kissinger found that he had considerably underestimated Israel's intransigence. Given the provisions of the Geneva Conventions, Israel quite properly regarded the submission of the list of names not as a quid pro quo concession, but its rightful due. But then the Israeli Cabinet debated whether there should be any negotiations at all. Though Assad demanded that Israel yield at least half the Golan Heights, the Israelis offered to return only one third of the 200-square-mile salient they had driven into Syrian territory during October; they would then keep one third of the area and make the rest a United Nations demilitarized zone. Israel demanded that the Syrians pull their air defenses and artillery back to Damascus or even beyond it. Since Assad would not sign an agreement unless Syria gained something for its sacrifices, the Israeli bargaining position proved a major obstacle to Kissinger's plans.

Nor were matters made easier by Israel's insistence that any territories they evacuated should fall under UN administration and remain depopulated. Syria suspected that the Israelis wanted the area depopulated so that Israel might take it over at a later date.

The negotiations eventually degenerated into a struggle for possession of the former provincial capital of the Golan Heights, Quneitra, a deserted market town with a population once estimated at anywhere between 20,000 to 50,000 people. At the end of the 1967 War when the town was evacuated by the Syrian forces, the Israeli military drove out the civilian population in the last hours before the truce. Contrary to the claims made by Kissinger,[27] the city in 1974 was still largely intact. But, before evacuating it, the Israelis systematically rendered it uninhabitable.[28]

Although the Syrians had a realistic view of the negotiations, the same could not be said of the Israelis. They expressed themselves as put upon, isolated, unappreciated, and overly dependent on American promises. This led them to seek incessant reassurances. They disagreed with Kissinger's contention that the United States could induce the Arabs to be reasonable only if it could procure Israel's cooperation.

At that tense moment, the Israelis launched a retaliatory raid into Lebanon. This in turn prompted a Palestinian guerrilla attack on the Israeli town of Ma'alot where a large number of hostages were seized. By the end of this affair, three guerrillas and sixteen schoolchildren had been killed; sixty other persons were wounded. Any prospects for exploring the possibility of a Syrian-Israeli peace died along with the victims.

In the end, the Israelis accepted a plan (which Kissinger had worked out with the Syrians) simply because they were tired of the constant tensions. After thirty-one days of shuttling by the American Secretary of State, the disengagement phase was completed when both sides signed an agreement on May 18, 1974.

## The Ford-Kissinger Period, 1974–77

Shortly after Kissinger achieved the Syrian disengagement, the rhythm of diplomacy had been broken by the forced resignation of Nixon in August 1974. His successor, Gerald Ford, was well disposed toward Israel, but his inexperience in foreign policy compelled him to lean heavily on his inherited Secretary of State.

After the disengagement deal and the change of president, Kissinger had felt it necessary to decide with whom he should next negotiate. There were sound reasons for talking with the Jordanians, if only to prevent King Hussein from being shut out of the peace negotiations. King Hussein feared—and with good reason—that unless he recovered some occupied territory from Israel, the Arabs would, as had been foreshadowed at the November 1973 conference at Algiers, finally deprive him of the right to represent the West Bank in any negotiation. Thus Hussein foresaw that if the Israelis wished to avoid an independent PLO state, they would have to negotiate with him while he was still able to function effectively. Unfortunately, neither the United States nor Israel realized what the Algiers conference portended, or the damage it would do to America's and Israel's respective peace plans.

Kissinger conveyed the King's message to the Israelis on January 20, 1974, while Nixon was still President, but did not press it. In view of Israel's almost total preoccupation with the domestic politics of cabinet making following its December elections, and the heightened influence of the national religious parties, no Israeli politician aspiring to cabinet office would commit himself. Thus, one more opportunity was lost.

Having achieved the first step of separating the armies, Kissinger now had several options vis-à-vis Syria and Egypt. He could nibble at the problem of peace by his step-by-step method or he could try for a comprehensive settlement. The latter choice meant tackling the Palestinian issue with no assurance of success, and the likelihood of incurring the wrath of both sides. Why risk a highly dubious undertaking that might well result in failure, particularly as the Israeli government was obviously in no position to make the hard decisions a comprehensive peace would require? The government had passed under the control of a triumvirate, and the only issue on which its members were unanimous was that nothing could be done about the West Bank before Israel had another election.

Later in 1974, as Hussein had foretold, the Arabs abruptly changed the ground rules. On October 28 at an Arab conference at Rabat, the Arabs decreed that the PLO was the "sole legitimate representative of the Palestinian people." That act deprived Hussein of any authority to negotiate on behalf of the inhabitants of the West Bank. In spite of American efforts to induce Sadat to intervene on the King's behalf, Sadat joined the Syrians and Saudis to force through this resolution. The King's ultimate decision, on July 31, 1988, to cede to the PLO any Jordanian claims to speak for the Palestinians of the West Bank was the inevitable consequence of these events.

### *Egypt and Israel, Sinai II*

The second phase of negotiations between Israel and Egypt opened with Sadat concentrating primarily on recovering the oil fields in the Sinai at Abu Rudeis and Ras Sudr, as well as the Mitla and Gidi passes. However, despite their tactical anxiety to split Egypt from Syria, the Israelis were unwilling to yield the oil wells or mountain passes to Egypt. Instead, they proposed that Egypt renounce belligerency and sign a long-term agreement leaving Israel in possession of a large stretch of Egyptian territory. This far-fetched Israeli proposition was basically a maneuver designed to assure that Israel would still occupy the Sinai after the Arab oil weapon ceased to be effective. Then Israel could annex the bulk of the Sinai with impunity.[29] Having been alerted to this by revealing reports in the Israeli newspapers, the Syrians and Soviets set about to short-circuit Israel's plans.[30]

Once Israel had rejected Kissinger's efforts, the Secretary returned to Washington where President Ford, in a formal interview, blamed Prime Minister Rabin for a lack of flexibility. The President and Secretary of State then repeated the ritual announcement of a threatened policy reassessment regarding America's relations with Israel.

On April 1, 1975, Kissinger carried out that "reassessment" by consulting with various personalities in the American foreign policy establishment (known in press circles as "the familiar suspects"). The senior author, who was present, recommended that Kissinger abandon his step-by-step approach and concentrate America's diplomatic resources on the search for a comprehensive agreement in which the United States and the Soviet Union would work out the guidelines for a settlement that could then be negotiated at Geneva. He contended (and was supported in this by some others at the meeting) that the Soviet Union could no longer be ignored, and that in furthering the Israeli policy of trying to create divisions among the Arabs, Kissinger would simply make a settlement more difficult. Practically all of those present favored a revived Geneva Conference and an American peace plan; the Palestinian question, they told the Secretary, must be confronted head-on.

The Ford administration was, however, not eager to undertake a difficult, and potentially unsuccessful, negotiation or to make a major commitment of America's prestige and effort. It preferred something better calculated to show quick results—something that would involve less expenditure of America's political capital, even though the idea might be exceedingly costly in financial terms. No doubt part of its calculation reflected a revised assessment of the evolving situation.

Included in that assessment was evidence that, having gained domestic prestige by standing up to the Americans three months earlier, Rabin was now prepared to accept more reasonable truce lines and to recognize that the Egyptians could not yet make peace. Yet he was emphatic that if the Americans wanted peace badly enough, they must agree to the following conditions:

*First,* the United States would deploy military personnel as a buffer between the Egyptian and Israeli forces, thereby preventing future hostilities.

*Second,* the United States would furnish Israel with a $2 billion aid package; it would also abandon attempts for an interim agreement along the Jordan-Israeli front.

*Third,* the United States would agree not to support anything more than "cosmetic" changes in the Golan Heights borders.

In addition, Rabin requested a clear commitment that America would assist Israel in case the USSR intervened in a future war and would do all in its power to interdict any such occurrence.

Given these demands, Rabin's package represented, in effect, nothing less than an effort to euchre the United States into agreeing to the Israeli annexation of Gaza, Jerusalem, the West Bank, the Golan and, possibly, parts of the Sinai. That would, at a minimum, give neither Jordan nor Syria the slightest incentive to make peace. Yet Kissinger went along with the Israeli demands.

The second phase of Kissinger's shuttle diplomacy, Sinai II, involved another long negotiation that was concluded on September 4, 1975. Its conclusion stirred up little American enthusiasm. Nor were the Israelis happy, though they exacted still more side agreements that were to prove highly deleterious to future peace efforts.

Among those were three secret U.S. protocols with Israel and one with Egypt that interpreted Sinai II and promised future actions. In those protocols, the United States gave assurances to Israel concerning military assistance, oil supplies, and economic aid. The agreements also promised to support Israel against the Soviet Union, as well as a vague commitment to provide a "positive response" to Israeli requests for more F-16 aircraft and Pershing missiles, with conventional warheads. The United States further agreed that the next negotiation with Egypt or Jordan would focus on a peace treaty.

Those commitments effectively abrogated the suspension of arms aid initiated during the policy "reassessment" in April 1975. When one adds up the guarantees of aid and Israel's oil supply, the cost of the agreements involved an increase of roughly $4 billion, or 200 percent above the 1975 levels, just for the three following years and confined only to aid. As such, these transactions strongly resembled a none-too-subtle system of extortion.[31]

### *Agreement Not to Talk to the PLO*

The most important side agreement was Kissinger's pledge not to talk with the PLO until it agreed to accept Resolution 242 and Israel's right to exist within secure and recognized boundaries. The United States also agreed to coordinate its strategy at Geneva with Israel and to keep all negotiations on a bilateral basis. Acceptance of Israel's demands effectively made the United States a party to Israel's scheme to exploit divisions among the Arabs and prevent any united Arab front—a plan certain to impede the achievement of a comprehensive settlement.

Kissinger made some effort to cancel out the negative aspects of these agreements by speaking to the Arab representatives at the United Nations in New York on September 29, 1975. He said, disarmingly, that the United States was prepared to work for a Syrian-Israeli second step if that were wanted. The United States, he said, would also consider ways of working for an overall settlement, including how the "legitimate interests of the Palestinian people" could be met. He had, of course, rejected advice to do just that earlier in the year.

During the Syrian negotiations, Secretary Kissinger had promised Israel that in the event of further negotiations over the Golan Heights, any further territorial adjustments would be merely "cosmetic." In making this promise, Kissinger was not alone. The 1991 negotiations brought to light a letter from President Ford promising Israel that the United States would give primary consideration to Israel's military interests on the Golan Heights. Since Israel declared the area to be nonnegotiable on military grounds, this in effect constituted an American promise that Israel would be backed in its insistence on annexing the area. This would help explain America's curious conduct in voting for a resolution opposing Israel's formal annexation of the area in December 1981, and then vetoing a follow-up resolution on January 20, 1982, when world opinion would be less focused on the question.

As events developed, nothing further was done about the Middle East before Ford and Kissinger left office on January 20, 1977.

CHAPTER FIVE

# Carter Tries But Fails to Slow the Retreat from Principle

THE CARTER ADMINISTRATION took office under circumstances that differed widely from those of its predecessor. It was untouched by scandal and enjoyed considerable diplomatic opportunities for progress in the Middle East. Carter's background as a born-again Baptist predisposed him to take an interest in the Holy Land. Although he had visited Israel briefly in 1973, he had little direct knowledge of the region.

His Secretary of State, Cyrus Vance, a distinguished lawyer with considerable government experience, had served as Lyndon Johnson's Deputy Secretary of Defense, had participated in the Paris talks on Vietnam in 1968 and had worked on the Cyprus question in 1967. A principled pragmatist, he was known for his directness and integrity. A steady and patient negotiator, he had shown a capacity for inspiring confidence in his listeners.

Carter's National Security Adviser, Zbigniew Brzezinski, though widely different in background and temperament, largely agreed with Vance about the Arab-Israeli conflict. Both men took the Palestinian issue seriously and favored a comprehensive settlement.

## INITIAL DISCUSSIONS WITH RABIN

During the first months of his administration, Carter and his top advisers saw the indispensable need for Israel to evacuate most of the Occupied Areas as the price for peace and, unlike his predecessors, Carter properly saw the Arab-Israeli struggle primarily as a regional contest, only peripherally connected with the Cold War. Carter's intention was to reconvene the Geneva Conference at the end of 1977 with a view to seeking a comprehensive settlement, and he sent Secretary Vance to the Middle East on February 14 to sound out the prospects for that conference. Vance conferred with Prime Minister Rabin, who acknowledged that Israel was militarily far stronger than it had been two years earlier. Nonetheless, he still asked for additional military assistance to enable Israel to "negotiate from strength."

The auspices for a serious negotiation were far from bright, particularly after Foreign Minister Yigal Allon told Vance that no matter what the PLO agreed to, Israel would never, under any circumstance, negotiate with it. A further meeting followed in March 1977, when Rabin visited Washington at Carter's invitation. That conversation was, if anything, more discouraging.

The only positive result from Carter's first diplomatic effort was the development of three principles: (1) that the negotiators must seek a true peace; (2) that they must precisely delineate borders; and (3) that they must deal effectively with the Palestinian question. For, as the President reiterated on March 16, "There has to be a homeland provided for the Palestinian refugees who have suffered for many, many years."[1]

## The Whole Direction Changes with the Accession of Begin

But these preparatory discussions with Rabin in no way prepared the Carter administration for the drastic change in Israeli politics that took place when Menachem Begin became prime minister.

Although Begin had been involved in Israeli politics all his mature life, he had never been seriously considered as a future prime minister, first, because the Labor Party seemed invincible, and second, because he had a dubious background. During the British Mandate he had led a notorious terrorist group, the Irgun Zvai Leumi, which, in the words of the late editor Simha Flapan, "established the pattern of terrorism adopted 30 years later by Al-Fatah [the Palestinian terrorist group headed by Yasser Arafat]."[2]

Even a partial list of Begin's Irgun operations was sensational:

—It engineered the 1948 massacre at Deir Yassin, killing 244 Arab men, women, and children.

—It masterminded the bombing of the King David Hotel in Jerusalem on July 24, 1946, that killed 103 persons and wounded 29, including Arabs, Jews, and British personnel.

—It captured two British sergeants, and threatened to kill them if some of Begin's captured men under sentence of execution were not released.

> When the British did not comply, the Irgun hung both men and booby-trapped their bodies.[3] Of the hangings, Begin later commented that "it was a cruel deed to hang two sergeants, but it was inescapable. . . . We repaid our enemy in kind . . . I think that by what we did we must have saved the lives of several dozen men of the underground [because the British then commuted death sentences on Jewish terrorists]."[4]

Begin's biographer, Eric Silver, has explained that Begin's announced strategy was that of all terrorists: to humiliate the rulers and thus prove that their power is not omnipotent. And he quotes Begin as follows:

> The very existence of the underground . . . must in the end undermine the prestige of a colonial regime that lives by the legend of its omnipotence. . . . Every attack which it fails to prevent is a blow at its standing. Even if the attack does not succeed, it makes a dent in that prestige, and that dent widens into a crack which is extended with every succeeding attack.[5]

It seems unlikely that President Carter was fully aware of Menachem Begin's background, for the Israeli government obviously downplayed his terrorist past. Even had Carter known it, Begin was now prime minister of Israel and Carter had no option but to deal with him. He therefore invited Begin to visit the United States.

Though Carter did not realize it, Begin's election threw into discard the basic concept of Resolution 242: the exchange of territory for peace. Although that resolution had been accepted by the Israeli government in power at the time it was adopted, Begin had resigned his ministry in the National Unity Government rather than accept it, and his views had not changed since.

On its side, the Carter administration made an unhappy error when Vice President Walter Mondale, in an address on June 17, 1977 before the World Affairs Council of Northern California, included a statement that emasculated any American effort to conduct self-respecting relations with Israel:

> We do not intend [he declared] to use our military aid as pressure on Israel. If we have differences over military aid—and we have some—it will be on military grounds or economic grounds, but not on political grounds. If we have differences over diplomatic strategy—and that could happen—we will work this out on a political level. We will not alter our commitment to Israel's military security.[6]

Since this pledge was soon expanded to include economic as well as military aid by the Carter administration and the Congress, the United States unilaterally discarded practically all of its leverage with Jerusalem.

Prior to Begin's arrival on July 19, 1977, Vance insisted that the discussions should be focused on Begin's interpretation of UN Resolution 242 and also on the delicate subject of Jewish settlements in the Occupied Territories, which had been neglected by Carter's predecessors since 1967. So long as the Israelis continued to build settlements and implicitly rejected Israel's previous acceptance of Resolution 242, Begin could not honestly claim that he was going to Geneva without preconditions or to bargain in good faith.

By the same token, the American public had to realize that the Arabs were not asserting "preconditions" simply because they insisted on the original interpretation of 242. Furthermore, the Arabs had to come forward with their own peace offers in order to expose Begin as an obstructionist.[7] Secretary of Defense Harold Brown, alluding to America's past inabilities to nail down Begin, cynically noted: "We have him just where he wants us."[8]

On June 28, 1977, the State Department (rather than President Carter) released its formal interpretation of Resolution 242.

> Within the terms of Resolution 242, in return for this kind of peace, Israel clearly should withdraw from occupied territories. We consider that this Resolution means withdrawal from all three fronts in the Middle East dispute—that is, Sinai, Golan, West Bank and Gaza—the exact borders and security arrangements being agreed in the negotiations.
> Further, these negotiations must start without any preconditions from any side. This means, no territories, including the West Bank, are automatically excluded from the items to be negotiated. To automatically exclude any territory strikes us as contradictory to the principle of negotiations without preconditions.[9]

The Carter administration hoped to secure from Begin an admission that Resolution 242's terms were binding on Israel, which would put a crimp in his plans. Moreover, the Americans wished to prevent Israeli demands that the negotiations be free from what they styled "preconditions;" otherwise, the Americans would enable Israel not only to disregard Resolution 242's binding provisions but to tie up any conference with endless discussions on every imaginable question. So long as Israel was determined to return only what it pleased and the United States refused to impose sanctions on Israel's misconduct, or to allow others to do so, Israel would not have the slightest incentive to negotiate in good faith. It was a lesson President Carter was to learn the hard way in his negotiations at Camp David.[10]

State Department experts advised the President that Begin believed the Jewish state should comprise all the land lying between the Jordan River and the Mediterranean, and that the Israelis had a right to settle anywhere in that territory. Begin also opposed active U.S. intervention in any Arab-Israeli negotiations. He viewed the United States role as limited to getting the parties together at a conference; after that, the Israelis would wing it alone.

In opening his talks with Begin on July 19, President Carter reiterated his commitment to a comprehensive peace settlement. Begin, anticipating Carter's demand that Israel return captured lands for peace, attacked the very idea of returning to the 1967 borders.[11]

Contrary to the fears of the State Department, Begin said that Israel was indeed ready to negotiate on the basis of UN Resolutions 242 and 338. He offered in detail a proposal for convening a Geneva Conference, with an opening session followed by the establishment of "mixed commissions" which would negotiate peace treaties with the several Arab states. Only when the peace treaties were ready for signature would the Geneva Conference be reconvened. If this plan proved unacceptable, Israel was ready for negotiations through "proximity talks," relying on the good offices of the United States.

Carter then warned Begin that the new settlements in Israeli-occupied territory were jeopardizing any prospect for negotiations, but stopped short of restating the position he had taken with Rabin that they were illegal. Carter also told Begin that Rabin had agreed to the participation of PLO representatives as a part of the Jordanian delegation.

Begin rejected the idea that any member of the PLO could participate. Palestinians could be part of a Jordanian delegation and Israel would not inspect their credentials too closely, but none could be a member of, or associated with, the PLO. Begin then repeated the right-wing Israeli claim that the Palestinians already had a state of their own—Jordan—an assertion the American officials left unchallenged. Carter closed the meeting by asking the Israelis to stop overflying Saudi Arabian territory.[12] Begin merely promised to look into the matter.

Later the same day, Begin and his delegation met with Secretary of State Vance, who immediately launched into a discussion of the points raised in Begin's proposal for a Geneva Conference. He inquired if Begin had any objections to a joint Arab delegation. When Begin replied that it was illogical, Vance proposed that the Arab joint delegation appear for the initial session of the Geneva Conference, after which negotiations would take place on a bilateral basis. Begin agreed to consider this possibility.

Secretary Vance then turned to the five key bargaining points on which the administration had agreed. The first concerned the need for a comprehensive settlement. Begin heartily agreed with this, but insisted that the goal should be a collection of individual "peace treaties" between Israel and its Arab neighbors. Similarly, Begin had no objection to the administration's points, which called for UN Resolutions 242 and 338 to be used as the basis of negotiation. A true peace in his view would make nonbelligerency statements redundant.

However, problems arose when Vance suggested that Israel should withdraw to mutually agreed and recognized borders on all fronts under Resolutions 242 and 338, but phased over years and with external security guarantees. Begin dismissed the idea of permanent guarantees by stating that "in the old world there is no guarantee that can guarantee a guarantee."[13]

Although Begin said he had already told Carter of his views concerning borders, Vance, ignorant of that conversation or mistaking the meaning of what he had heard, assumed an acceptance of his position, whereas Begin had already rejected it. It was not the last time that the Americans failed to secure an explicit statement from the prime minister as to his position, or to make sure that both sides were in real agreement.

When Secretary Vance, in making his fourth point, put forward the idea of a demilitarized "Palestinian entity" with provisions for economic and social relations with Israel, Begin stated that they could only agree to disagree. He promised to present this idea to his cabinet, but assured Vance that it would not be adopted. A Palestinian state, he claimed, would be a "mortal danger"—a Soviet base with planes, Soviet generals, and "other undesirable paraphernalia."

Vance's fifth point proposed that the West Bank might for a period be held under a Trusteeship, with Israel one of the trustees along with Jordan. At some point the Trusteeship would be ended and a plebiscite held to ascertain the views of the people who lived in the area. The United States, Vance assured Begin, favored a link between the Palestinian entity and Jordan. The Secretary, however, failed to get Begin to explain how he could possibly hope to achieve peace when he offered terms that no Arab leader could accept and still survive.

Finally, after a dinner with Carter on the evening of July 19, Begin, having been advised of Rabin's unsuccessful meeting, sought to end his visit on a more positive note. He assured Carter that he supported peace efforts and was trying to arrange direct talks with Sadat. He also handed Carter a long document enumerating all the strategic benefits that the United States gained from its relationship with Israel.

Begin told Carter that the United States should not use the phrase "minor adjustment" when discussing a territorial settlement with the Arabs. Whether the Syrians would agree or not, Israel intended to stay permanently in the Golan Heights, nor would Begin tolerate "foreign sovereignty" over the West Bank, Gaza Strip, or Jerusalem. He would, however, back "substantial withdrawal" from the Sinai Peninsula.

On July 20, the two groups met again to summarize their findings. Since Carter had not been sufficiently alert to Begin's territorial comments the night before, and since he also assumed that Begin had accepted his principle of withdrawal on all fronts, he could not understand why Begin had contradicted Vance on this point. Carter believed there had been trouble only with regard to a Palestinian state—the point that Begin had declared nonnegotiable.[14]

Carter thought that if only the Arab and Israeli leaders would get together, they would like one another and soon come to an agreement. It was the typically optimistic American view that was to lead directly to his ultimate disillusionment following Camp David in 1978.

Any goodwill that his visit might have generated was dissipated by Begin's actions on his return home. Carter had asked him to stop building new settlements and Begin had promised that he would not establish any new settlements without notice or cause any new settlers to be moved into the

Occupied Areas other than into previously existing settlements. But Begin got around the letter of this agreement by legalizing three existing settlements that had no legal status.

Carter understandably felt that he had been double-crossed, particularly because he had just approved a significant arms-sales package for Israel that allowed Israel for the first time to use American funds to build its own tanks.[15]

Begin's visit exposed the latent weakness of the administration's position: it thought it was dealing with a rational, Western-style man rather than a devious Byzantine ideologue. Confronted with such an unfamiliar antagonist, the Americans failed to insist on a reconciliation of the contradictions between Begin's expressed willingness to adhere to Resolutions 242 and 338 and his announced intention never to withdraw from the West Bank, the Golan Heights, or the Gaza Strip. Unlike the Labor Party government, Begin did not argue "security" considerations; he straightforwardly asserted religious and historical claims to the whole area as part of ancient Israel.

After further ruminations in Jerusalem, Begin dispatched a message to Vance on July 25, confirming his adherence to Resolution 242; but, though that resolution might be interpreted to apply to each front, he did not interpret it as requiring withdrawal on all fronts. He also objected to any reference to the PLO in the formulations being considered by the Americans.[16]

Then, on July 30, Begin wrote directly to Carter requesting rather peremptorily that Vance, before his forthcoming trip to the Middle East, should be specifically instructed not to talk to the Arabs about the 1967 lines with "minor modifications." If he did, Begin asserted, there would be nothing left to negotiate about. Begin also reiterated his opposition to the State Department's fourth and fifth points.

Carter was quite properly piqued that Begin should tell an American President how he should formulate Vance's negotiating position. Carter's negative view of Begin's impertinence was reinforced by a respectful and conciliatory July 28, 1977, message from the PLO suggesting a willingness to make peace with Israel provided that the United States agreed to an independent Palestinian "state, unit, entity" with some links to Jordan.

Recognizing that Israel and the Arabs held diametrically opposite positions on the key question of Palestinian representation, Carter spent two months trying to square the circle. In dispatching Vance to the Middle East, he instructed him to try to persuade the parties to accept his five principles, or, if they did not, "We need enough public support so that we—along with the USSR—can marshal world opinion against the recalcitrant nations." Furthermore, Vance was to try to obtain agreement on the composition of delegations and a pledge from the PLO that it subscribed to Resolutions 242 and 338 as a prerequisite for participation in the conference. Carter's letter also instructed Vance to keep the Soviet Union fully informed, with a view to securing its aid.

By proposing that there should be agreement on the composition of the

Arab delegation or delegations, the United States was, in effect, giving Israel a veto over who should represent its antagonists in negotiations—a hitherto unheard-of precedent.[17]

That letter represented the first of several important shifts in the President's position. He now saw the Geneva Conference as the forum for critical negotiations rather than serving merely as a ceremonial umbrella. In view of the Soviets' standing in the Arab world, Carter realized that he would have to work out a joint position with the USSR as to what constituted a fair settlement and then coordinate America's actions with those of the Soviets.

In Egypt, Vance discovered that Sadat, though increasingly impatient, was still reassured by the U.S. government's peace efforts and its determination to see to it that Arab territory was returned with "only minor modifications." In giving Sadat such assurances, Vance specifically ignored Begin's admonitions to Carter.

Sadat had no objection to minor border rectifications so long as they were not at Egypt's expense. He wanted the Soviet Union role at Geneva kept to a bare minimum, enough to allow the Soviets to save face, but nothing more.

Sadat went on to warn Vance, in a vein reflecting the conclusions reached by Mark Ethridge more than thirty years before, that Egypt and Israel were incapable of reaching an agreement because there was too much distrust and dislike between them. Therefore, if anything were to be achieved, the United States must be a very active interlocutor in the peace process. Finally, Sadat handed Vance a draft peace treaty between Egypt and Israel, and suggested that Vance procure from the Israelis, Syrians, and Jordanians similar drafts.

Vance's trip to Jerusalem was almost wholly negative. He discovered that Israeli reaction to his communicating with the PLO was even more sour than he had predicted.[18] Begin made it clear that because of Vance's contacts with the PLO, the Israelis regarded their commitments under the Kissinger memorandum of 1975 as a dead letter; however, they still expected the United States to honor its obligations on a nonreciprocal basis. For itself, the Begin government would not attend any conference at which recognized PLO representatives were present. Thus Israel construed U.S. efforts to secure PLO adherence to Resolutions 242 and 338 and also to secure its recognition of Israel's right to exist to be totally irrelevant. Begin also summarily vetoed a united Arab delegation at Geneva, thereby concurring with Sadat's stance.

Begin thought Sadat's idea of a peace treaty a good one, since he believed that a peace treaty automatically entitled the powers signing it to full diplomatic relations.[19] Begin then made a startling proposal to Vance. He suggested offering "our Arab neighbors in Judea, Samaria and Gaza full cultural autonomy" and "a choice of Israeli citizenship with full voting rights."[20]

When Vance got home and analyzed what he had heard, he found little to be cheerful about. With the exception of Anwar Sadat, he knew all the Arab states wanted a united delegation, if for no other purpose than to ensure that the Egyptians did not make a separate peace with Israel. Sadat and Begin were already in essential agreement that each country had to have its own delegation at Geneva and be free to pursue its own policies.

Sadat still gave no sign that he was prepared to make a separate peace; he was interested in a general settlement that would provide a cover for his negotiations with Israel. Nonetheless, the trend of events was clearly heading in the direction of a bilateral rather than comprehensive settlement.

At this point, American-Israeli relations were becoming frayed. The Americans were annoyed that, in spite of America's objections, the Israelis were pushing on with their settlements program in the Occupied Areas. They were also alarmed because they detected the Israelis' intention to intervene in southern Lebanon, which would deprive the Americans of their credibility in the Arab world. The administration spent August and September of 1977 bickering with the Israelis over all these topics.

There were other reasons during 1977 and 1978 why American-Israeli relations cooled even further. When Carter tried to please the Israelis by offering a security agreement, Begin rebuffed it, saying that Israel would be contributing far more of value to the United States than would America to Israel. Since aid to Israel was mounting into the billions year by year, Begin's view did not accord with that of the White House or State Department.

## Working Toward Geneva

Besides the settlements and the later improper use of American arms, other evidence began to accumulate that the Israelis were not keeping faith with the United States. As the administration continued to work toward a Geneva Conference, the Israelis became increasingly less enthusiastic about the project.

Meanwhile, the U.S. government approached the Soviet Union to act as co-Chairman of the conference with a view to hammering out a joint position on the conference agenda and the principles it would be asked to enforce.[21] On September 9, 1977, the Soviets replied in such moderate tones that Assistant Secretary Alfred L. Atherton, Jr., was ordered to pursue these conversations with Soviet Representative Mikhail Sytenko.

Further negotiations between Gromyko and Carter on one level and Atherton and Sytenko at the working level led to the adoption of an essentially American position, with the addition of one phrase concerning the "legitimate rights" of the Palestinians—which the Soviet representatives, and perhaps even the Carter administration, accepted as meaning some form of self-determination for the Palestinians.

On October 1, 1977, President Carter authorized the formal publication of the U.S.-Soviet communiqué announcing their agreement. This communiqué read in part:

> The United States and the Soviet Union believe that, within the framework of a comprehensive settlement of the Middle East problem, all spe-

> cific questions of the settlement should be resolved, including such key issues as withdrawal of Israeli Armed Forces from territories occupied in the 1967 conflict; the resolution of the Palestinian question, including insuring the legitimate rights of the Palestinian people; termination of the state of war and establishment of normal peaceful relations on the mutual recognition of the principles of sovereignty, territorial integrity and political independence.[22]

Unhappily, the publication of that communiqué at that time was a gaffe; Congress had not been informed, nor had sufficient spade work been done to prepare American opinion for such a major move. In keeping with their own convictions, President Carter and Secretary Vance had felt that the intrinsic merits of their well-digested plans would commend them to the American public.[23] But they greatly underestimated the ferocity of the pro-Israeli lobby, whose opposition to the communiqué was loud and prolonged. Ultra-conservatives and anti-Soviet elements fiercely denounced the proposed conference as being both pro-PLO and a capitulation to Moscow. Israel, they complained, should not be pressed too hard on the important Palestinian issue. Previously convinced by Kissinger's fallacy that somehow or other America should and could freeze the Soviet Union out of the picture, many objected to the prominence now given to it, despite its close relations with Syria.

Instead of launching an information program and seeking public support for its policies, the administration, on October 5, repudiated its agreement with the Soviet Union by joining in declaring with Israel that "acceptance of the joint U.S.-U.S.S.R. statement of October 1, 1977, by the parties is not a prerequisite for the reconvening and conduct of the Geneva Conference."[24] That action definitively doomed the administration's hope of a comprehensive settlement.

Anwar Sadat's initial reaction to the October 1 communiqué was one of delight. He assumed that the Syrians, now under heavy pressure from Moscow, would have to be cooperative. Moreover, the statement's polite genuflection toward the Palestinians would enable Egypt to negotiate with Israel without fear of isolation in the Arab world. He could now, he thought, carry on direct negotiations with Israel unaided by either the Geneva Conference or the United States.

Sadat, as events later made clear, was primarily interested in a bilateral deal with Israel, and was developing greater and greater doubts about the necessity for a comprehensive settlement. But there is no evidence (outside that furnished by the Israelis) that the Soviet-American declaration inspired Sadat's trip to Jerusalem, or led him to change his policies.[25]

## Geneva Abandoned; Private Egyptian-Israeli Talks

Having reconnoitered the ground for a satisfactory Egyptian-Israeli negotiation, Sadat announced his willingness to go anywhere for peace and even to talk to the Israelis in their Knesset in Jerusalem. Indeed, the Egyptian leader hinted strongly that the United States should induce Begin to invite him to Jerusalem. On November 15, Begin sent such an invitation to Sadat through the Americans. On November 19, Sadat arrived in Jerusalem . . . to great fanfare, being the first Arab head of state to set foot in Israel, and the next day he gave an historic speech before the Knesset.

These developments short-circuited the Geneva Conference. The Israelis and the Egyptians had opposed it, and, now that they had succeeded in talking directly to each other, the conference seemed unnecessary.

The United States faced some drastic rethinking. Although President Carter remained committed to a comprehensive settlement, that now seemed a mirage. Sadat needed a fig leaf to cover Egypt's withdrawal from the war against Israel, and if the United States helped him to reach that goal, a peace treaty covering the Palestinian problem and other major contentions between the Israelis and the Arabs would be shoved into the distant future.

Such a settlement also had attractions for the Israelis, since a bilateral deal between Cairo and Jerusalem would relieve Israel of the danger of a two-front war and, by softening the pressure on Israel, save it from having to confront the Palestinian issue.

Events quickly demonstrated that the United States needed to oversee negotiations between Israel and Egypt if they were to encompass more than a simple bilateral arrangement affecting only the Sinai. To avoid that outcome, Sadat urged Vance to try to persuade the Israelis to agree that as part of the deal with Egypt, Israel would withdraw from the Occupied Territories and take some positive action about the Palestinian problem. Begin took only one day to reject that proposal; the Israelis, he maintained, intended to keep the West Bank as an integral part of Israel. Begin told Vance that when he was in Washington later that week, he would present his ideas on "home rule" for the Palestinians to Carter.

### *The Palestinian Problem Surfaces*

Vance's fear that Begin contemplated his "home rule" proposal for the Palestinians as a permanent solution was confirmed when Carter and Begin met in Washington on December 16. Begin presented a "plan" which he admitted did not have the sanction of the Israeli Cabinet. In that twenty-one-point document, Begin spelled out the powers of the new Arab Administrative Council. Besides failing to state by whose authority this body was being established, the document severely circumscribed its powers. Begin insisted that no effort be made at this time to settle the sovereignty of these areas.

Unlike the West Bank, the Sinai had little value for Israel except for its oil fields. Thus, it was not surprising that Begin was prepared to withdraw to the old international border with Egypt in phases over three to five years, during which Egyptian sovereignty would be restored to the Sinai and diplomatic relations established. But Begin contended that Israeli settlers should still be able to live in the Sinai with Israeli and UN forces to protect them. However, Begin misconstrued Carter's response that Sadat would be glad to hear about Begin's willingness to withdraw to the international frontier; he interpreted those words as an Egyptian approval of Begin's plan to maintain Israeli settlers on Egyptian territory.

In the light of subsequent events, some of the ideas Begin advanced were sheer shadowboxing. He countered Carter's objections to the Israeli West Bank settlements by agreeing to allow Arabs in the Occupied Areas to acquire land in Israel, then promptly limited this to only those Arabs who became Israeli citizens. Of course, he well knew that Arabs then resident in Israel were incapable of acquiring any land, except from other Arabs (the rest of the land being owned directly or indirectly by the Israeli state).

President Carter asked Begin the obvious questions. He pointed out that Begin's plan made no reference to withdrawal from the Occupied Territories, nor did it deal with the great mass of Palestinians living outside the territories. Were they to be allowed to return? If so, when and where? And if the question of sovereignty were left open indefinitely, how did Begin propose that it should be ultimately resolved?

Begin's response was that Resolution 242 did not require Israel to withdraw from the West Bank and Gaza. When Brzezinski questioned him on this point, Begin replied that Israeli sovereignty would not go beyond the 1967 lines. But, in view of the almost daily Israeli seizures of West Bank land and water, Brzezinski then inquired as to who would have the power under this new arrangement to expropriate land. Though Begin claimed that the Administrative Council would have that power, he quickly hedged with the proviso that the Council could exercise only such powers as the Israeli Military Government conceded to it, and those powers were subject to unilateral curtailment by the Military Governor in the interests of Israel's security and "public order."

Thus it was quite obvious that the Council would have no real powers, and the Palestinians would formally continue to be nonresident citizens of Jordan. As a result, though effectively under Israeli rule, they would derive no protection from Israeli law—such as it was.

Carter's impression was that Begin's proposals were simply a device for keeping the territory and avoiding a fair solution to the Palestinian problem—and he was clearly correct. Though acceptance of such a plan would be politically catastrophic for Sadat, Begin still asked Carter's public support for his proposals and wondered why Carter did not consider them a fair basis for negotiations.

Brzezinski did not bother to conceal from the Israeli premier his view that the proposals were no more than a variant on the Homeland Scheme employed by South Africa. He openly referred to the Arab Administrative Council as presiding over a "Basutoland."

In sum, though it seemed quite possible to work out an agreement between Israel and Sadat over the Sinai, the administration saw little chance of achieving any progress with the other Arab problems, which Sadat sorely needed to avoid total ostracism by the rest of the Arab world.

That was confirmed when Carter telephoned Sadat in December 1977. Though Sadat adamantly opposed the continuation of Israeli settlements on Egyptian territory, he was even more disturbed by Begin's evident failure to consider any limitation on what he suggested as an interim administration. Fully aware of the Israeli proclivity for claiming "security" as a justification for its annexationist program, Sadat opposed having responsibility for security in East Jerusalem and for the West Bank to remain with Israel.

On December 17, Carter met again with Begin to review what they had discussed and to advise him of Sadat's reactions. Begin briskly launched into an extended recitation of the prominent Americans who favored his proposals. Administration officials were shocked when Begin quoted Senator Henry Jackson of Washington as saying that the American people would support his (Begin's) proposals—an insult to diplomatic tradition and unacceptable meddling in domestic American politics.[26]

Unwilling to challenge his visitor on this issue, Carter merely pointed out to Begin that

> the determination of whether this [Begin's proposal] appears as an empty proposal, or one full of meaning, will depend on how much autonomy or self-rule is being offered. This needs to be defined. If you have a military governor, and if the population is allowed self-rule just as long as it behaves, but the military governor can restore Israeli control whenever he wants then this has no meaning.[27]

Carter dismissed any critical comment implied by that statement, then erred unwittingly in telling Begin that his proposals were a "fair basis for negotiations." Begin heard only what he wanted to hear and ignored all qualifications and negative implications. Had Carter been either more cynical, more experienced, or less of a southern gentleman, he would never have given Begin the slightest encouragement that could be quoted (and was, again and again) as supporting the Begin proposal.[28]

## Direct Israeli-Egyptian Negotiations

On December 25, Menachem Begin, accompanied by Moshe Dayan, Ezer Weizman, and Attorney General Aaron Barak, arrived in Ismailiya on the

Suez Canal to negotiate with President Sadat and his advisers. Although Begin had assumed that Sadat was amenable to his proposals, he soon discovered his error. He promptly attributed that circumstance to Sadat's advisers, and requested that Sadat carry on the discussions without them.

During the conversation, Begin detected Sadat's possible interest in making a separate peace—which encouraged him to be as difficult as possible regarding anything except strictly Egyptian issues. Begin was excited by the thought that he might make a separate deal with Egypt that would exclude the hard Palestinian issues. Thus he dug in and waited until the conference broke up.

President Carter flew to Riyadh on January 3, 1978, for talks with King Khalid of Saudi Arabia. Because he regarded the Saudis as a major support for American interests in the area, he agreed to sell them F-15 interceptor aircraft. That automatically triggered a loud outburst from Israel's congressional claque, which opposed all arms sales to the Arabs as a potential danger to Israel. This knee-jerk reaction greatly complicated the President's task in the coming months.

Nor did Carter's "Aswan Declaration" on January 4 advance matters. He spelled out the need for true peace, called for Israeli withdrawal from the Occupied Areas with appropriate security arrangements, expressed hope for the normalization of relations between the warring parties, and proposed a resolution of the Palestinian problem through self-determination.

That statesmanlike pronouncement enraged the Israelis, and they promptly expressed their scorn for both Carter and Sadat by ordering the establishment of four new settlements in the Sinai Peninsula. Begin showed no visible concern that this action violated a promise made to Carter by Israel's Foreign Minister Dayan on September 19, 1977, that Israel would establish only six new settlements over the next year, all within existing "military camps."

Within days, the Israelis had violated that assurance by establishing a new site at Maale Adumim, which Begin tried to excuse by claiming it was merely an extension of an old settlement nearby. Now Begin devised a new excuse for the three additional settlements. When Carter remonstrated sharply, saying that the foreign minister had made it quite clear that there were to be no new settlements before September 18, 1978, Begin blandly maintained that that promise extended only until the end of the year 1977; therefore he was entitled to set up more settlements starting in 1978.

For the moment, however, Carter had effectively made his point; Begin established no more settlements during 1978, although the Gush Emunim extremists did set up an "archeological site" at Shiloh on January 23, 1978, which Begin refused to recognize and which thus remained unofficial.

That experience with Begin's legalistic quibbling was a prelude to many more incidents of the sort; consequently Carter might have been wiser to recognize immediately that Begin's oral assurances were unreliable. The prime minister should have been required to write out all his promises in precise detail, but Carter made the understandable error of assuming that Begin and he followed the same code.

Although the Begin-Sadat talks had foundered on the rock of Israeli obduracy, Begin assured Vance on January 16 that he and Sadat had come close to an agreement at Ismailiya. The Egyptian failure to sign a treaty, he explained, was due entirely to the opposition of Sadat's associates. Begin then selectively quoted from the record of his December talks with Carter to imply that Carter had endorsed his proposals, which, of course, was far from the truth. Begin told Vance that the Israeli settlements involved matters of principle (which they indeed did, since they were clearly illegal under international law); thus, he contended, they must remain in the Sinai and should be protected by Israeli forces. The United States, Begin argued, should respect Israeli principles even though they directly collided with the Geneva Conventions.

Begin's complaints were redolent of self-pity and wounded feelings. He reiterated to Vance that Carter had endorsed his position; why wouldn't he make a public statement that it was a fair basis for negotiation? Moreover, he wished Carter to make a statement that the settlements were legal. But inasmuch as the State Department Legal Adviser had unequivocally declared all the settlements to be illegal, Vance refused to budge.

Nor was Vance's displeasure assuaged when Dayan asserted that if Sadat would not allow the Israeli settlers to stay, the Israelis would have to demand significant readjustments in the Egyptian-Israeli border so that the settlements could remain part of the sovereign territory of Israel. If Begin had held fast to such an absurdity, it would, of course, have assured the prompt collapse of the talks.

To add to the sour mood, on the afternoon of January 18, the members of the Egyptian delegation in Jerusalem informed Vance that Sadat, having concluded, rightly, that Begin preferred land to peace, had recalled them. Only a telephone call from Carter prevented Sadat from breaking off the military committee meetings with Weizman as well.[29]

President Carter's reaction was to invite Anwar Sadat on January 23 to come to Camp David for private talks. He hoped to create a situation in which the United States could come forward with its own proposal, which Sadat, by prearrangement, would accept. Carter would then be free to devote his energies solely to the intractable Menachem Begin. During their Camp David meeting on February 4, 1978, Carter and Sadat both recognized the power of Israel's American lobby, the American Israel Public Affairs Committee (AIPAC) and the need to tailor their plans to try to offset that lobby's influence with Congress. Sadat told Carter that when he made his famous trip to Jerusalem, he had hoped to convince AIPAC that he was an Arab who truly favored peace and deserved their support.[30]

Following that February 4 meeting, rules for the negotiations were revised: Egypt would not again pull out of talks with the Israelis, but would instead put forward an Egyptian proposal with respect to the West Bank and Gaza, which, Sadat assumed, Begin would reject. Then, while criticizing some aspects of it, the United States would accept it with modifications. That would put the burden on Begin. Meanwhile, with Sadat's support, the American government would keep hammering away at Begin regarding his interpretation of Resolution 242 and his settlement programs—two issues that U.S. public opinion might support.

Though the plan was multipolar and focused on a comprehensive settlement, consciously or unconsciously, Carter and Sadat were drifting toward a bilateral Egyptian-Israeli deal. Such a deal, as the administration well knew, would play directly into Israel's central strategy toward the Arabs: *Divide and conquer.* Offsetting that, however, was the enormous potential value of an Egyptian-Israeli treaty; especially as it appeared to be the one possible breakthrough toward peace.

On February 16, 1978, Israeli Foreign Minister Moshe Dayan arrived for talks with Carter and Vance. Vance told Dayan that the Americans wanted a statement that would be acceptable to King Hussein. Without support from some other Arab, Sadat would be awkwardly isolated.

Dayan replied brusquely that though Israel wanted peace with Egypt and approved U.S. efforts to facilitate face-to-face talks, Israel would not yield on the issue of Resolution 242. Israel would not withdraw on all fronts; the West Bank would never be evacuated. Other parties could propose whatever they wished; Israel was there to stay. Israel would keep its military positions, its settlements, and its right to establish new Jewish settlements. He admitted that that position was inconsistent with both the commonly understood meaning of Resolution 242 and the position taken by preceding Israeli governments, but it was the Begin government's position, and that was final.

Because the Israeli government interpreted the refusal of Vance and Carter to make a public issue of Israel's position as tacit consent for its policies, the Carter administration reaped both Israeli contempt for its pusillanimous posture and Arab outrage that a nation with ample means should not only fail to assert its position but show no intention of ever doing so.

The Carter administration's continuing criticism of Israeli policies, while approving the sale of aircraft to Saudi Arabia, resulted in the resignation of Mark Segal, who served as the White House liaison with the Jewish American community.[31] That caused repercussions both in the Jewish community and in Israeli government circles, and no doubt induced President Carter to try to placate Begin by accepting Israel's autonomy proposal with a five-year limitation. Then Carter again undermined his own bargaining position by intimating to Defense Minister Weizman that America might not object to a continued Israeli occupation after the five-year period.[32]

When he next met with Begin on March 22, Carter acknowledged that peace between Egypt and Israel would have to precede any comprehensive settlement. Yet, even that limited goal was blocked by Begin's intransigence.

Though Carter had not insisted either on a complete Israeli withdrawal or a fully independent Palestinian state, Begin still used these issues as an excuse for his own refusal to withdraw.

The United States position, as outlined by Carter, consisted of four points:

—America supported Begin's self-rule proposal for the West Bank and Gaza, but only as a transitional measure, and it stipulated that, during the transition period, authority must be derived from an Arab-Israeli agreement, not from an Israeli military government.
—Carter agreed to defer the sovereignty question in accordance with Israel's wishes.
—Meanwhile, the West Bank and Gaza should be demilitarized, with Israel's forces withdrawing into encampments.
—Although the Israelis would be given an effective veto over security-related issues, there would be no new settlements nor any expansion of existing settlements.

Unhappily, as Carter pointed out to Begin, the Israelis were showing no flexibility. Begin had refused to stop settlements activity in the West Bank; refused to give up his settlements in the Sinai; would not allow the Sinai settlements to be put under UN or Egyptian protection; and would not agree to withdraw from the West Bank even if Israel could retain military outposts. Finally, Begin refused to recognize that Resolution 242 applied to all fronts. He would not allow the Palestinians the right to choose their own government at the end of the interim period. Begin's only response to this summation was to protest that Carter was putting an unfairly negative connotation on his proposals.[33]

## The Road to Camp David

As spring advanced, the scenario that Carter and Sadat had worked out in February fell apart because of domestic political considerations that Carter could not ignore. The President had to avoid any impression that he was negotiating on Sadat's behalf or that he was in any way colluding with the Egyptian president. His critics carped that he seemed more interested in the Palestinian question than Sadat was.

Moreover, immersed in details, Carter had not resolved the key elements necessary for a real settlement. While he and Vance talked about a plebiscite for the Palestinians at the end of a five-year period, they caved in to Begin's resistance by striking from the alternatives a bona fide Palestinian state. All that the Palestinians were offered was a choice of joining either Israel or Jordan.

Although impartial observers had definitely reported that the West Bank

Palestinians loathed Israel and did not wish to return to Jordanian rule, Begin remained adamant, insisting on retaining the territories and dismissing the wishes of the Arab inhabitants as irrelevant.

As a final impediment to peace, Carter faced difficulties with the Senate. He was seeking the ratification of the Panama Treaty, the normalization of relations with China, and the ratification of the SALT II Treaty. Since he needed the support of senators who rejected some or all of these proposals, he could not afford to alienate everyone simultaneously.

It was not good political weather. Egypt's proposals proved not particularly useful; the battle over aircraft sales to Saudi Arabia cut deeply into the President's political capital; and Prime Minister Begin's belated responses were strongly negative.

That summer, William Quandt, a Carter NSC adviser, summarized in a memorandum to the President the answers to the question: What concessions had Begin given the United States? He answered as follows:

—Begin had offered President Carter a vigorous defense of his "self-rule" proposal; has repeated the litany that everything is negotiable and there are no preconditions; and vaguely agreed to submit suggestions about the West Bank's status after the five-year interim period.

—Begin was smugly satisfied that his proposals were fully adequate and persisted in that assumption, even though the Americans had repeatedly told him they were not. Begin, moreover, showed absolutely no interest in exploring any of the alternatives that the Americans laid before him.

Quandt also painted a vivid picture of how far the United States had already gone in its retreat from principle. Though Quandt's memorandum should have been a clear warning to Carter and his successors, they did not heed it.

## The Beginnings of Camp David

With all parties—the Americans, Egyptians, and Israelis—now thoroughly frustrated, President Carter decided to invite both the Israel premier and the Egyptian president to the United States for talks under his auspices.[34] In spite of the failure at Ismailiya, he continued to believe that if Begin and Sadat got to know each other better, they could work with one another. He may also have concluded that routine diplomacy had created a bureaucratic swamp that engulfed any sensible proposals; a new environment was needed.

Both Vance and Brzezinski strongly urged Carter to focus the conference on the Palestinian issue. Carter, however, instinctively felt that Sadat would, in the end, abandon the Palestinians in favor of recovering his own territory, while any linkage between those two issues might jeopardize the accomplishment of even a limited settlement.[35]

Sadat's dilemma was clear enough: he could get a bilateral deal that would restore Egypt's territories, but only at the cost of forfeiting Egypt's leadership position in the Arab world.

The Israelis who arrived at Camp David were untroubled by any such fundamental choice. Faithful to their own entrenched habits, they put aside strategic worries and saw the negotiation in tactical terms. They envisaged it as a way to achieve a prime Israeli objective, notably to detach the strongest and most dangerous military power from the Arab coalition. If that could be managed, they could impose terms on the other Arab nations, retaining all the territories conquered in the north and east.[36]

## The Camp David Negotiations

The negotiations that took place from September 5 to September 17, 1978, at Camp David were, in many ways, a recapitulation of what had occurred the preceding year. To maintain so far as possible his position in the Arab world, Sadat wished for some visible linkage between an Egyptian treaty and the Occupied Areas. Caught in an uneasy truce, and with a slumping economy, Sadat needed a diplomatic success to divert the peoples' minds. He had, at the very least, to return to Cairo with the assurance of a regained Sinai.

By this time, Begin had thoroughly polished his negotiating script. The West Bank and Gaza Strip were historically parts of Israel—they belonged to it by legal right, not merely by conquest. In 1948, the Egyptians and Jordanians had improperly occupied territories that were not theirs, and they were not entitled to regain them. Moreover, Begin felt free of the compulsion that beset Sadat; he had no political need to return home with a treaty. So long as he maintained control over the Occupied Territories, he was, in his own view, no worse off than he had been before.

What upset Sadat's calculations was the shocking degree to which America had abandoned principle; when Sadat expected American support, it was not forthcoming. Facing congressional elections in November 1978, President Carter was eager not to be perceived as an ally of Egypt against Israel. Still, after all the effort he had invested, he, like Sadat, emphatically needed to show results, even if only a bilateral deal between Begin and Sadat.[37]

The fears of Carter's advisers regarding the outcome of the negotiations soon became a reality. Contrary to the American President's optimistic expectations, Anwar Sadat and Menachem Begin not only differed on the terms of a treaty, but their personal antipathy became so evident that the Israeli delegation warned Secretary Vance that he should try to keep the two men apart as much as possible. Begin's sanctimonious rigidity infuriated Sadat, while Begin came to feel that his only prudent course was to find a means of breaking up the conference without taking the blame for that denouement.

By the fifth day, the Israelis openly admitted that they would make no concessions regarding the West Bank and Gaza, but would be content to conclude a restricted land-for-peace deal with Egypt. Their tactics were obviously to make just enough concessions to prevent Carter from exploding in anger. In the end, what blocked the road to success was Begin's adamant insistence on maintaining the Israeli settlements in the Sinai.

On September 15, President Sadat precipitated a crisis by threatening to leave. That threat was averted only when Carter made a heartfelt personal appeal. Carter also quietly warned Sadat that his departure would mean an end to the United States–Egyptian relationship, which, given the alienation of Moscow, would be a death blow to Sadat's regime.

Meanwhile, the more sensible members of the Israeli delegation were busily trying to soften their chief's position. Ezer Weizman approached Secretary Vance with a proposal to compensate Israel for giving up airfields in the Sinai: the United States would pay Israel $3 billion to build new bases in the Negev. Although President Carter expressed his aversion to the idea of "buying" peace, the air base question was so important to Begin that only an American agreement to this trade-off persuaded the Israeli prime minister to drop his objections.

Begin's continued defiance over the Sinai settlements caused Dayan to telephone Ariel Sharon (the agriculture minister) in Jerusalem. Sharon, a Begin intimate, then called Camp David to tell Begin that if abandoning the Sinai settlements was essential to arranging a peace with Egypt, that sacrifice had to be made.[38]

In the end, the Egyptians and Israelis signed an agreement that could be deemed not only a success for the Egyptians but a major tactical achievement for Israel. Egypt recovered the Sinai, Israel's air bases and settlements were to be dismantled, and the settlers withdrawn. The Egyptians were to be no worse off territorially than they had been at the beginning of 1948.

## The Effects of the Camp David Accords

Like many medicines, the accords had various side effects. The treaty diminished Egypt's claim to traditional leadership of the Arab world—a role it had enjoyed for thirty years. Nor did the treaty come to grips with the Palestinian issue, which was key to an overall settlement.

The document merely referred in general language to "the legitimate rights of the Palestinian people" and the right of the Palestinians to choose their own form of government. It lacked any Israeli declaration of intention to relinquish the Occupied Areas or any explanation as to what would happen at the end of the five-year transition autonomy period for which the agreement provided. It said nothing about Jerusalem, the settlements on the West Bank, Gaza, or the Golan Heights. All the Egyptians received from America were vague promises of U.S. aid and also a commitment, later subjected to considerable controversy, that Israel would not establish any more settlements in the West Bank and Gaza Strip during negotiations between Israel and Egypt regarding the five-year transition government.

Israel emerged as the hands-down winner. At little cost, it had achieved what it had unsuccessfully sought thirty years before: a separate peace with Egypt. Moreover, the canny Begin so structured the agreement that the Israeli Knesset, not he, would order the dismantlement of the Sinai settlements.

Begin could further congratulate himself that he had not been forced to concede that Resolution 242 applied to any front other than Egypt. He had also been allowed to flout the statement in Resolution 242 prohibiting "the acquisition of territory by war." Although he had promised "full autonomy" for the Palestinians for the five-year interim period, he had drained that term of any substantive meaning. Instead of abolishing the military government, he had agreed only to "withdraw" it, which merely meant that it would no longer be located in the West Bank yet could be reactivated at any time to assert control over any Palestinian "self-governing authority."

President Carter had the modest satisfaction of having induced one Arab nation and the Israelis to make peace with one another. But it was not a success which did him much good at election time, and its deficiencies soon began to haunt him.

Experience quickly proved that Carter had erred in not securing on the spot a letter from Begin guaranteeing that no more settlements would be established in the Occupied Areas until the end of the five-year autonomy period. The consequences of that oversight came to light on Monday, September 18, when Begin sent Carter what purported to be the promised letter. But instead of stating what the two men had agreed on, it merely restated verbatim an earlier draft that Carter had rejected. Efforts to get Begin to agree to a complicated finesse drafted by Foreign Minister Dayan failed.[39]

Though Begin had conceded nothing, he could not leave his victory alone. He proclaimed that he would never agree to let the Arabs veto where Israelis could settle; the Jews, he said, had as much right to settle in Hebron as Tel Aviv.[40]

During the next six months, until Israel and Egypt signed a formal treaty of peace in March 1979, Menachem Begin continued to demonstrate his genius for tactical obfuscation. Begin well knew that President Carter's position depended on his showing progress on the Arab-Israeli front; and after February 1979, when the Shah was overthrown in Iran and the American Embassy was seized, he carefully exploited Carter's preoccupation with the hostages. Begin also patiently stalled the negotiations with Egypt until early 1980; he knew full well that in an election year, Carter would find it particularly inexpedient to have a run-in with Israel.

## The Egyptian-Israeli Autonomy Negotiations, 1978–81

Under the Camp David Accords and the subsequent treaty, it was provided that Egypt, Israel, and Jordan, together with the representatives of the Palestine people, were to negotiate an autonomy agreement. But not having been represented at Camp David, the Jordanians and Palestinians complained that their views had been completely ignored, and asserted that they were not bound by arrangements entered into by others without their consent. Thus, the only parties prepared to negotiate on the basis of the Camp David Accords were the Egyptians and the Israelis, and they could agree on almost nothing—not even on the meaning of the words "full autonomy." Prime Minister Begin considered that "full autonomy" was limited to cultural and religious matters and had no serious political meaning; he planned at the end of the five-year period to annex the entire area, with the assent of the "inhabitants," i.e., the Jewish settlers. For their part, the Egyptians found themselves in a hopeless position. They had no authority from anyone to represent the Palestinians and, even if they could reach an understanding with Israel, there was no guarantee that the Palestinians would abide by any agreement made under these conditions. Thus it was inevitable that the talks should break down.

What these ill-fated negotiations should have taught the United States was the futility of trying to negotiate over whether to hold elections in the Occupied Territories. Such elections could obviously be held any time that Israel permitted them to take place. Negotiations on this point were simply a dodge to avoid relevant discussions that ought to have taken place. What was needed was an end to the various military occupations; agreement on self-determination for the former Egyptian and Jordanian territories that had once been part of the Palestinian Mandate; and some constructive thinking about the fate of the Palestinian people. Despite this lesson, the U.S. government (as will be seen in Chapter 7) once more launched into negotiations about elections. And not surprisingly, when confronted by a decision about whether such talks would actually take place, the Israeli government collapsed.

## Israel's Lebanese Adventure of 1978

In the spring of 1978 world attention was diverted from the Israeli-Egyptian problems when, on March 14–21, Israel moved a large force into Lebanon. On March 15, the Israelis announced that to thwart the continuation of Palestinian raids from southern Lebanon, they had established a 6–9-kilometer-wide "security belt." Though Prime Minister Begin claimed that they had no intention of permanently occupying Lebanese territory, he emphasized that Israel would not withdraw until "an agreement" had been concluded that would prevent the PLO from once again occupying positions in that area.[41]

On March 19, the United Nations Security Council adopted a formal resolution (by a vote of 12 to 0)[42] calling on Israel to withdraw from southern Lebanon.

When Israel did not move as the Security Council directed, President Carter demanded its withdrawal. The Israelis claimed that they had already removed both their men and their American equipment.

Unfortunately for the Israelis, American satellite technology permitted the administration to verify that, like earlier Israeli denials, this was a patent lie. Accordingly, Carter sent Ambassador Richard Viets with a message to Begin demanding their evacuation within twenty-four hours or there would be an aid cutoff. He found Begin at home, and after he had shown Begin the satellite pictures, Begin poured himself two stiff drinks. Then he said, "Mr. Viets, you win."[43]

In 1976 Congress had amended the 1952 Arms Export Control Act to require the President to report to Congress any breach of a law that restricted countries receiving arms from the United States to use them "solely for internal security and for legitimate self-defense." On April 5, 1978, Secretary Vance had advised Congress that Israel "might" have violated that law while invading Lebanon. This declaration was practically meaningless, however, since the Secretary stated that no penalty was planned for the alleged infraction because Israel had given assurances that it would withdraw from Lebanon.

Vance proved wrong on two counts. Israel did not withdraw, and Congressman Benjamin S. Rosenthal, Democrat of New York, attacked Vance's action because it "contradicts prior policy followed consistently by previous Administrations that when Israel responded to PLO raids that came out of Lebanon," they were "legitimate acts of self-defense." Chiming in, Menachem Begin, in a letter dated April 6, formally declared that Israeli military actions in southern Lebanon were "acts of legitimate self-defense."[44]

On April 7, another official American statement charged Israel with illegally using American-supplied cluster bombs (CBUs) in the Lebanon invasion.[45] The United States had been supplying these bombs to Israel ever since the early 1970s, on the express Israeli assurance that they would be used only for defensive purposes against fortified military targets and only if Israel were attacked by more than one country. The Israelis had now admitted employing the weapon in violation of their agreement and Israel had apologized.[46]

On April 12, the Carter administration requested new and more stringent restrictions on the use of cluster bombs, including a prohibition on their use unless approved by a politically responsible superior.[47] On April 20, Defense Minister Ezer Weizman conceded that Israeli planes had indeed dropped U.S.-supplied cluster bombs during the March invasion, but denied any knowledge of the American law that prohibited their use.[48]

In any case, when the Israelis withdrew from Lebanon (other than their "security zone"), they made no effort to obtain a written agreement with Lebanon, Syria, or the PLO binding those parties to refrain from further raids. Instead, they turned over all their posts to a mercenary militia unit headed by Major Sa'ad Haddad. Although Israel was under obligation to transfer all the areas it had occupied in Lebanon to the UNIFIL forces, the Israelis replied evasively that since they had never occupied the Christian enclaves in southern Lebanon, the areas were not Israel's to turn over. Moreover, they contended, the UN Resolution on the subject had said only that the area was to be turned over to Lebanese control, and Major Haddad and his associates were indisputably Lebanese.

After a sharp correspondence with Secretary General Kurt Waldheim, matters simmered until the summer of 1981, when PLO operations against Israel reached such a level that the United States felt impelled to intervene. By arranging an agreement between the PLO and Israel, the American negotiator, Philip Habib, had secured both sides' commitment to keep the peace along the Lebanese frontier. This arrangement (except for instances when Israeli soldiers—who were not supposed to be in Lebanon—had been killed by land mines or in ambushes) was scrupulously observed by the PLO until Israel's invasion of Lebanon in June 1982.[49]

CHAPTER SIX

# The Retreat Turns into a Rout Under the Reagan Administration

BECAUSE THE COLD WAR supplied the coordinates by which Ronald Reagan charted all aspects of foreign policy, he warmly embraced the doctrine that Israel was an important U.S. "strategic asset," a bastion blocking the encroachment of Soviet power into the Middle East. He had expressed the view during his 1980 campaign that Israel was "perhaps the only remaining strategic asset in the region on which the United States can truly rely . . . her facilities and air fields could provide a secure point of access if required in . . . emergency."

Earlier, in August 1979, he had referred to "Israel's geopolitical importance as a stabilizing force, as a deterrent to radical hegemony and as a military offset to the Soviet Union," and, he added, "only by full appreciation of the critical role the State of Israel plays in our strategic calculus can we build the foundation for thwarting Moscow's designs on territories and resources vital to our security and our national well being."[1]

In spite of the fact that Israel had become a state through self-determination, Reagan opposed the extension of that right to the Palestinians. In addition, he explicitly adopted Israel's position toward the Camp David peace process; he would, he said, "continue to support the process as long as Israel sees utility in it."[2] Finally, he announced that he would use the full panoply of U.S. influence to "insure that the PLO has no voice or role as a participant in future peace negotiations with Israel." Reagan was thus clearly the most partisan of Israel's supporters, just when in 1981 Israel's Arab neighbors seemed prepared to make peace with Israel.[3]

According to political wisdom, the best time to launch major diplomatic initiatives is during an administration's first-term honeymoon. Because Reagan's first Secretary of State, Alexander Haig, believed even more passionately than his chief in Israel's role as a potential American surrogate in defending the Middle East against Moscow's ambitions,[4] Haig promptly visited the Middle East. His primary mission was not to make peace, but to persuade both the Arabs and Israelis to join in a "strategic consensus"—directed against the Soviet Union.

Fired by both conviction and expediency, the Israelis emphasized the immediacy of the Soviet menace to the region. By contrast, the Arabs made clear that for them Israel was of far greater immediate concern.

Secretary of Defense Caspar Weinberger did not share Haig's view of Israel's utility. He thought that Turkey, Egypt, and Saudi Arabia would be more useful than Israel in blocking Soviet Middle East ambitions. Ronald Reagan was not, however, deterred by Weinberger's skepticism; his unrequited love for Israel led him to grant the Israelis more financial assistance than had all of his predecessors put together.

By October 1, 1980, just shortly before the election, total U.S. aid to Israel had aggregated over $18 billion (almost equally divided between loans and grants). Under the Reagan administration, aggregate aid by January 20, 1989, had increased to roughly $46 billion. During its tenure, the Reagan administration gave over $27 billion to Israel—or one third more than all the aid provided from 1948 until 1980, of which approximately $23 billion was in grants.[5]

Like Johnson and Nixon before him, Reagan felt that his assistance to Israel entitled his administration to Jewish American support on every issue. Once, when such support was not forthcoming, Secretary of the Interior James Watt lectured the Israeli ambassador, threatening diminished aid if Israel did not whip its local partisans into line.[6] Nonetheless, despite lukewarm Jewish support and halfhearted Israeli cooperation, Reagan, like Johnson and Nixon before him, continued to shower benefits on Israel.

Although the Reagan administration was singularly ill-equipped to play a mediating role in the Arab-Israeli dispute, its difficulties were magnified by Likud Party domination of the Israeli government throughout most of Reagan's tenure. To be sure, Labor Party governments had not necessarily proved easy to deal with, but they had still shown a semblance of flexibility; Menachem Begin, Yitzhak Shamir, and the Likud bloc, on the contrary, were driven by Zionist revisionism, which rejected any territorial compromise as heresy.

## The AWACs Controversy

Reagan received early instruction as to the extent of Israeli clout during the AWACs affair. His problems with the airborne warning and control airplanes (AWACs) first began when he revived one of Carter's proposals to sell the Saudis five AWACs that would alert them to approaching enemy (presumably Iranian) aircraft.

Despite White House staff anxiety over possible congressional opposition, Reagan announced the planned sale on March 6, 1981. Initially, the Israeli military expressed no opposition to the deal, simply stating their intention to shoot down any AWAC that ventured near their territory. But in America, AIPAC seized this opportunity to demonstrate its political muscle;[7] it mobilized pro-Israeli congressional members so effectively that on October 14, the House voted 301 to 111 to reject the sale. Finally, on October 28, Reagan persuaded the Senate to refrain from blocking the $8.5 billion sale by a narrow vote of 48 to 52.

That paper-thin victory taught Reagan that even his popularity could barely overcome AIPAC disapproval. Thereafter, Reagan from partiality and Congress from expediency would never again cross swords with the AIPAC lobby. In the words of Professor Cheryl A. Rubenberg, professor of international relations at Florida International University, "thereafter how a Senator voted on this issue became the most important factor in the lobby's determination of an individual's 'friendship' toward Israel. Those who were labeled 'unfriendly' faced serious problems at reelection."[8]

## Israeli Provocation and America's Response

Following this incident, relations between the United States and Israel settled into a rigid pattern—a kind of choreographed ballet. By the end of Reagan's first term, that ritualized pattern had become a political fact that critically distorted policy. This is how it worked.

In response to a real or contrived Arab provocation,[9] Israel would embark on certain military actions that tested the limits of international tolerance. The U.S. government might then express disapproval, and even suggest that Israel stop whatever it was doing. That homily was often accompanied by a condemnatory resolution passed by the UN Security Council, largely to placate the Arabs.

Israel—and its American partisans—responded with loud indignation to America's mild disapprobation. Yet, almost before these objections could be raised, the President (or the Secretary of State) neutralized America's cautionary words by asserting categorically:

(1) that Israel is America's "ally";
(2) that America gives the highest priority to Israel's security;
(3) that the U.S. government will never pressure Israel to comply with its wishes. Such unilateral diplomatic disarmament, not evident in our relations with any other country, has become a conditioned reflex.[10]

Unmollified, the Israeli government would respond by asserting:

(1) that it acted for vital reasons of national security, of which it was the best, indeed the only, judge;
(2) that it was only seeking to advance the United States' own interests; or
(3) that it never perpetrated the alleged offense.

Meanwhile, the Israeli government would challenge the good faith of any critical Jewish Americans. Jewish Americans, it would declare, must give unquestioning loyalty because they choose to live in America instead of joining their fellow Jews on the Middle East barricades.

Finally, if, as occasionally happened, the Israeli government should comply even partially with America's requests, it would couple that acquiescence with demands for more aid or special favors. Then, when the President granted such demands, Congress, on its own, would frequently raise the amount requested by the White House. The President would promptly approve the bill as passed.

If the U.S. government reluctantly concluded—as it did occasionally—that an Israeli action endangered international peace, offended world opinion, or harmed major American interests, it might threaten to withhold—or even actually temporarily withhold—military aid or some political concession.

AIPAC would then express such intense outrage that Congress would hasten to release the withheld equipment—thus validating the comment of I. L. Kenen (founder of AIPAC) that his organization was established "to lobby the Congress to tell the President to overrule the State Department."[11]

At this point the President would fold his tent and leave the field without further resistance. He would have restored the withheld aid and provided Israel with a substantial financial or political "peace offering," after which he or the Secretary of State would terminate the incident by the soothing proclamation that American-Israeli ties were now stronger than ever.[12]

## The Reagan Administration Ardently Embraces Israel

In dealing with both the Arabs and the Israelis, prior administrations had laid claim to impartiality, but from the beginning Reagan wore his heart on his sleeve. Early on, at a press conference on February 2, 1981, Reagan was asked whether the implantation of Israeli settlements in the Occupied Territories was legal. He replied, "I disagreed when the previous administration referred to them [Israel's West Bank settlements] as illegal. They're not illegal."[13] He thereby bluntly overruled the 1979 opinions of the State Department Legal Adviser and Resolutions 468, 469, 471, and 605 of the UN Security Council.

That left the State Department trying to save face by putting out pro forma statements which finessed the legality question and simply stated that the settlements were "not helpful" because they "interfered with the peace process." Secretary Haig, in fact, encouraged the Israelis to pursue their settlements plans and opposed legislation that would have prevented Israel from using America's aid for the construction of new settlements. Thus encouraged, the Begin regime quickly increased the number of settlers in the Occupied Areas from 3,000 when Begin assumed office in 1977 to 40,000 when he retired in 1983.[14]

Reagan passively assisted Begin and Shamir to build settlements in an effort to "create new facts" and thus block peace except on their own terms. He also effectively gave Israel a right of veto over American policy on arms sales. In one case, for example, he reversed Carter's decision to prohibit Israel from selling to Ecuador advanced Kfir aircraft with American-made engines. President Carter had wished to discourage an arms race in Latin America that would drain those poor nations of desperately needed resources.[15] Reagan's reasoning? "There is a feeling that it is not a bad thing to have Israel able to turn to its own resources for foreign exchange."[16] In other words, the United States encouraged Israel to enter the Third World international arms market, in competition with American producers, as a means of improving its balance of payments.

## Israel Bombs the Osirak Reactor

Reagan was quite mistaken in thinking that his benevolence would persuade Israel to behave more discreetly. On the contrary, freed from fear of American restraint, the Israeli Air Force on June 7, 1981, used eight American-supplied F-16 fighter bombers, escorted by six F-15s, to destroy completely the Osirak nuclear reactor near Baghdad. In justifying their action, the Israelis claimed that the Iraqis were about to manufacture nuclear weapons at that facility and asserted the right to attack any country which they deemed a threat to their security.

That raid violated Israel's truce agreements with Iraq in 1948 and 1973, whereby each party renounced hostile actions against the other;[17] it also contravened the Arms Export Control Acts of 1952 and 1976, under which Israel had agreed that its use of American weapons would be limited to "legitimate self-defense" or UN collective security purposes.

By hindsight, we now know that Iraq has been steadily working toward the construction of building nuclear weapons in violation of its commitments under the Non-Proliferation Treaty.

Viewing the issue against the background of the Gulf War and its revelations, many may now look back on Israel's raid on the Osirak reactor as a wise and prophetic action. Had the IDF not destroyed that reactor in 1981, Saddam Hussein might well have been able to use nuclear weapons in the Gulf War.

There is a hard core of plausibility in this argument. Its basic flaw, however, is that Israel was in a dubious moral-political position to destroy Iraq's effort to build a nuclear capability since it had itself already built a substantial arsenal of nuclear weapons—as confirmed by the defector Vanunu.

Such a judgmental question is not an easy one for Americans to resolve, particularly since their government had never made any serious representations to Israel about its nuclear arsenal or firmly insisted that it sign the Nuclear Non-Proliferation Treaty.

Israel contends that it was necessary for it to destroy the Osirak reactor in its own defense. Self-defense, it argues, should override larger questions of international principle. Besides, some Israelis point out, the attack did not serve merely the purpose of Israel's self-defense, but reinforced the security of other members of the international community.

Although the self-defense argument is an understandable Israeli position, it nevertheless seems hard to square with America's stated objective of building a new world order based on established international principles.

No doubt Israel would be far less likely to use its nuclear weapons for aggressive purposes than would the bloodthirsty Saddam Hussein, but that is purely a subjective judgment. It cannot stand the test of Kant's Categorical Imperative which holds, roughly speaking, that one can test the ethical quality of an action only by considering the probable consequences were it to be universalized. Would Israel's attack on Iraq's nuclear facility have justified an attack by Iraq on Israel's elaborate facilities at Dimona?

Besides, how true is the thesis of Israel's passivity? Israel has never shown much reluctance to use force; indeed, as we have shown in Map 2, it acquired by war more than half the territory it now controls.

Some contend that Israel may have built its nuclear facilities only to deter aggression from its near neighbors, but that argument would be stronger did not Israel constantly deny its possession of a nuclear arsenal.

The other element of deterrence is a belief by Israel's antagonists that it would really utilize nuclear weapons if threatened by critical attack. No one can answer that question with total assurance. During the Yom Kippur War in October 1973, reports reached the American government that Israel was indeed prepared to use its nuclear arsenal. Panic-stricken by its initial reverses at the hands of the Arabs, and before the army had even set foot on Israeli soil, the Israeli government ordered the arming of parts of its nuclear arsenal and the emplacement of nuclear warheads on its Jericho missiles.[18] Most Americans assume that, in contrast with Saddam Hussein, Israel would not use its nuclear weapons for territorial conquest, but that does not mean it would refrain from using them were its national existence to be seriously threatened.

There is an additional possibility, of course, which some have considered: perhaps Israel's nuclear arsenal is not for use against the Arabs but as a means to bring pressure on the United States to come to its rescue if it were seriously imperiled. Suppose Israel were about to be overrun, it could say to America, "If you do not intervene immediately and effectively, we shall use our nuclear arsenal." That would put any American government in a no-win position. To violate its nuclear taboo could set in train forces that might not be containable; yet it could not idly stand by while Israel was destroyed.

In view of the international uproar, not to mention his statutory obligations, Secretary of State Haig could scarcely ignore the raid; so he did the next best thing. He announced on June 10, 1981, that the administration was delaying delivery of four F-16 aircraft while it examined whether the raid had violated the 1952 Mutual Defense Assistance Agreement, as amended in 1976. Then, on June 11, President Reagan neutralized even that small gesture by informing the Israeli ambassador that the United States did not "anticipate any change" or "fundamental reevaluation" in its relationship with Israel.

In spite of these reassuring words and his own inclinations, Haig was still required by statute to report the incident to Congress. Although conceding that there had probably been "a substantial violation" of American law, he asserted that Congress would have to "consider the contention of Israel that this action was necessary for its defense because the reactor was intended to produce atomic bombs and would become operational very soon . . . "[19]

What the Secretary's statement meant, translated from the original "Haig-speak," was that Israel could attack any nation it pleased by autocratically claiming that the act was in "self-defense." Since that would give Israel *carte blanche* to commit aggression, all governments except those of the United States and Israel denounced that doctrine.

When questioned as to why the administration had not followed the required procedure of investigating and rendering a decision, Secretary Haig replied, "There has never been one in the past, and we did not feel it was necessary on this occasion. It's just that simple."

The bombing of the Iraqi reactor caused such a furor at the time that the Arab ambassadors forced the President to receive them *en masse* on June 11. So, even as Haig was defending Israel's raid to Congress, Reagan told the Arabs that he regretted this incident and doubted the propriety of the Israeli government's actions.[20]

Reagan's effort to propitiate the Arabs was undermined by *Maariv,* a leading Israeli newspaper, which reported on June 15 that American officials (reputedly including American Ambassador Samuel W. Lewis) had been furnishing American intelligence to Israel on the Iraqi reactor. Charges of American complicity in the raid received further confirmation on June 18, when the Nuclear Regulatory Commission (NRC) announced that it had informed Israel regarding the capabilities of 1,000-kilo bombs to destroy a reactor. Following that embarrassing disclosure, the White House, State, and Defense departments hastened to disassociate themselves from the NRC. Copying Israeli tactics, administration spokesmen denounced the NRC aid as a rogue operation for which no one was accountable.[21]

## The End of a Tawdry Affair

The administration might well have ended its delay in shipments in mid-July, had not the Israelis inopportunely chosen July 17–18 to use American-supplied planes to bomb an apartment house in Beirut, killing over three hundred persons and wounding eight hundred. Israel justified that mass killing on the ground that the bombs were aimed at an alleged PLO headquarters, but the Mossad had failed to discover that the small PLO office had moved out two days earlier, leaving only the civilian residents of the apartment house to endure the carnage. Prime Minister Begin instinctively blamed the victims: the PLO leaders should never have hidden themselves among the civil population; the Lebanese were delinquent for allowing the PLO in their midst.[22]

As it was, America's further delay in delivering military equipment lasted only four weeks. On August 17, the Secretary announced that the President had decided to resume shipment of F-16s and F-15s to Israel. Haig made a token defense of America's ten-week postponement, commenting that the delay had "accomplished a great deal" because "it certainly was a clear manifestation of the discomfort that we felt at the time of the raid on the Iraqi reactor." Haig regretted that the Israelis had not been "happy with the suspension," but he hastened to add that the administration did not "see any change in our long-standing relationship" with Israel.

Haig had, however, overestimated Israeli tolerance for these efforts to placate UN and Arab opinion. Because Haig had not publicly apologized to Israel, the Israeli ambassador to the United States, Ephraim Evron, read him an Israeli government telegram complaining that America's withholding of the weapons had been "unhelpful and unjust." Then, preempting the ritual of reassurance normally played by American spokesmen, he announced that the resumption of shipments would make "the traditional close bonds of friendship between Israel and the United States deeper and even stronger."[23]

No sooner had these unpleasant incidents blown over than President Reagan and Prime Minister Begin, after two days of talks, concluded an agreement on September 10 calling for closer strategic ties involving military cooperation just short of a military alliance. As Secretary Haig put it, there would be "joint military exercises, probably naval; some stockpiling of American supplies in Israel, probably medical; and some strategic planning focusing on Soviet threats to the Middle East region." Details were to be worked out in subsequent negotiations.

The timing of that announcement suited both parties. President Reagan, then in the middle of the AWACs brouhaha with Congress, welcomed the chance to demonstrate his friendship for Israel. Prime Minister Begin wanted to counter Jewish American apprehensions that "Begin's policies are hurting support for Israel in the United States," a view confirmed by 53 percent of Jewish Americans in a September 14 Gallup Poll.

While in Washington, Begin could happily tell reporters that "this is the warmest atmosphere I have ever enjoyed." Nor was that just hyperbole, for in greeting Begin in Washington, President Reagan assured him that "the security of Israel is the principal objective of this Administration and that we regard Israel as an ally" in the search for regional stability.[24]

On November 30, the United States and Israel issued a joint communiqué detailing their "strategic cooperation against threats to the Middle East caused by the Soviet Union or Soviet-controlled forces from outside the region." But, in spite of that brave language, the agreement clearly fell short of what Israeli Defense Minister Ariel Sharon wanted. It did not commit the United States to come to Israel's aid in the event of an Arab attack; it only mentioned a Soviet threat; and it made no provision for U.S. military maneuvers nor for the stockpiling of arms and munitions on Israeli soil, which could be appropriated by Israel for its own use in case of war without requiring any increase in the official aid level. In fact, Sharon was so disappointed that he nearly canceled his trip to the United States.

If the agreement left the Israelis unhappy, it made the Arabs furious. At the Arab summit meeting in Benghazi on September 18 to 20, the hard-line nations of Libya, Syria, Algeria, and South Yemen had suggested a similar relationship with the Soviet Union.[25] Now, in December, the Syrian foreign minister, Abdel Halim Khaddam, told America's envoy, Philip Habib, that the United States' usefulness as a mediator was finished because of America's alliance with Israel. America, he said, was no longer a neutral, but merely a satellite of an enemy state.[26]

## Israel Annexes the Golan Heights

As the year 1981 drew to a close, President Reagan flew to London to attend the Big Seven economic summit conference. Simultaneously, the long-deferred crisis over the trade union organization Solidarity, in Poland, reached a climax when General Wojiech Jaruzelski staged a coup on December 13.

With Reagan thus preoccupied, Prime Minister Begin saw a golden chance to rush through the Knesset a series of laws that annexed the Golan Heights. The annexation decision was made in an emergency cabinet meeting that very morning. Appearing before the Knesset in a wheelchair (he had just been released from the hospital with a broken hip), Begin said he had decided to carry out his long-standing intention of annexing the Golan because of a recent escalation of "extremist positions" by Syria. Though the Knesset passed the measure by a vote of 63 to 17, a large number of Labor Party members abstained not because they opposed annexation, but because they disagreed with Begin's methods.

In an emotional address to the Knesset, Begin admitted that he had acted without consulting the United States, but he insisted that "No one will dictate our lives to us, not even the United States. . . . No power will succeed in pushing us back to those borders of bloodshed and provocation." Subsequently, American spokesmen denied what was widely rumored and generally believed in the State Department, that the action was deliberately timed to exploit the diversion of America's attention by the Polish crisis.[27]

World opinion universally condemned the Israeli move, and at the Security Council meeting on December 17, even the United States joined in a unanimous vote for a Syrian resolution that called the Israeli annexation of the Golan "illegal, null and void" and "without legal effect," and threatened "appropriate measures" if Israel did not reverse its decision.

Yet, on January 5, 1982, when the Council met to consider "appropriate measures" if Israel did not rescind its annexation action, the United States threatened to veto any proposed follow-up resolution. It was another demonstration of what by then was an iron law: America might vote to express displeasure at some Israeli action, but would still refuse to allow any enforcement measures. The clear lesson for Israel was that it could safely ignore the Security Council.

In his December 17 news conference, President Reagan admitted that he had been "caught by surprise" by the Golan Heights action. Then he cheerfully noted that, "other than a few hour's interruption the peace process is going forward." He did not bother to explain (probably because he saw no connection between these events) how the so-called "peace process" was ever to produce any effective result without Syrian agreement.

## The United States Temporarily Suspends the Agreement

Despite the President's conciliatory statement, the United States, on December 18, suspended its recently concluded strategic accord with Israel because of the Golan Heights annexations. The State Department expressed particular disappointment that Israel's action had occurred so soon after the agreement had been concluded and during the crisis in Poland. The "spirit" of the strategic accord, the State Department declared, "obligated each party to take into consideration in its decisions the implication for the broad policy concerns of the other," and "we do not believe that that spirit was upheld" by Israel's Golan move.

The administration had suspended the agreement, officials stated, for two reasons:

—to notify Israel that the United States could not passively accept unilateral Israeli moves that damaged America's Middle Eastern relations; and

—to deter Israel from invading southern Lebanon.

The reaction to that statement might have been expected. The still hopeful Arabs expressed qualified satisfaction; Prime Minister Begin was enraged.

Summoning U.S. Ambassador Lewis to his Jerusalem residence, Begin delivered a forty-minute harangue. Later, to underscore Lewis's humiliation, Begin's secretary read a transcript of this lecture to the Israeli press.

Begin complained to Lewis that the suspension of the strategic accord was the third time that Israel had been "punished" in six months, the earlier occasions being the Baghdad and Beirut bombings. Both Israeli actions had been in "self-defense," he claimed. He then told Lewis that

> You don't have the right, from a moral prospective to preach to us regarding civilian loss of life. We have read the history of World War II and we know what happened to civilians when you took action against an enemy. We have also read the history of the Vietnam war and your phrase "bodycount." . . . Are we a vassal state? A banana republic? Are we fourteen-year-old boys, that if they don't behave they will have their knuckles smacked? . . . The people of Israel has lived for 3,700 years without a memorandum of understanding with America and it will continue to live without it for another 3,700 years.[28]

Begin claimed bitterly that not only had the Saudi Arabian AWACs sale been ratified against Israel's wishes, but the ratification had been "accompanied by an ugly anti-Semitic campaign. First we heard the slogan 'Begin or Reagan,' and then it followed that anyone who opposed the deal . . . was not loyal to the United States . . . afterward we heard the slogan 'we will not let the Jews determine the foreign policy of the United States.' " The Greek Americans had regularly influenced U.S. policy toward Turkey, Begin said, and he saw no reason why the American Jewish community should be frightened into silence. So, regardless of American views, the Golan Heights annexation would remain in effect.

Begin then added that if the Israelis had notified the United States in advance of the annexation, the United States would have prevented it. Thus, Israel's silence had resulted from a sensitive concern for the feelings of a friend, because, said Begin, "the truth is we did not want to embarrass you." Begin was particularly irate because Secretary of State Haig had linked the restoration of the strategic agreement to Israeli flexibility in the peace negotiations and its continuance of restraint in Lebanon.[29]

## The Origins of Israel's Lebanese Invasion

Such restraint was speedily abandoned. Although on December 20 Secretary Haig took a new line, warning against creating an "atmosphere in which blank checks are available for the leadership in Israel," in the next five months he openly supported Israel's scheme to take over Lebanon.[30]

As noted, Israel's forays into Lebanon had long worried the State Department. Ambassador Philip Habib had successfully concluded an agreement in

July 1981 between Israel and the PLO that resulted in comparative tranquility on Israel's northern frontier. In spite of Israeli mutterings about violations, no Israeli town had been attacked—although some of its soldiers, surreptitiously in Lebanon, had been killed or injured by mines.

Israel, however, had held territorial and political ambitions in Lebanon long before the PLO leaders had been driven out of Jordan and found Lebanese refuge. Moreover, the Israeli believed that the PLO was responsible for the disorders in the West Bank and Gaza. Israeli strategists saw a Lebanese campaign as combining the accomplishment of Israeli goals vis-à-vis that nation together with the "decapitation" of the PLO leadership and the destruction of its comparatively feeble military power.[31]

Moreover, according to an Israeli scholar, Yehoshua Porath, far from showing delight, the Begin government was annoyed that in late 1981 and early 1982 the PLO observed the cease-fire arranged by Ambassador Habib. If the PLO could achieve such discipline, it might become respectable and thus force Israel into serious political negotiations, As a result, Porath wrote,

> the Government's hope is that the stricken PLO, lacking a logistic and territorial base, will return to its earlier terrorism. . . . In this way, the PLO will lose part of the political legitimacy that it has gained and will mobilize the large majority of the Israeli nation in hatred and disgust against it, undercutting the danger that . . . the Palestinians . . . might become a legitimate negotiating partner for future political accommodation.[32]

## Israel's First Objective in Invading Lebanon: Destruction of the PLO's Leaders

Those Israelis who wished at all costs to evade negotiations wanted to destroy the PLO as a political force. They hoped that the Palestinians, deprived of their leaders, would let Israel have its way. Palestinian "autonomy" could be restricted to street cleaning and garbage collection, while the Palestinian claim to "self-determination" was ignored. Thus the Begin administration's ambition was to assure that "they [the PLO] are dead people politically."[33]

Other hard-line elements, including Defense Minister General Ariel Sharon, were still angling for a Deir Yassin-type massacre by which the Maronite Phalange (the private gangster army of the Gemayel family) would spread sufficient terror through the Palestinian refugee camps of Lebanon to create a panic-stricken flight to Syria.[34] "Quiet on the West Bank," said General Sharon, required "the destruction of the PLO in Lebanon."[35]

As Yoel Marcus wrote in *Ha'aretz:*

> behind the official excuse of "we shall not tolerate shelling or terrorist actions" lies a strategic view which holds that the physical annihilation of

> the PLO has to be achieved. That is, not only must its fingers and hands in the West Bank be amputated (as is now being done with an iron fist), but its heart and head in Beirut must be dealt with. As Israel does not want the PLO as a partner for talks or as an interlocutor for any solution in the West Bank, the supporters of confrontation with the PLO hold that the logical continuation of the struggle with the PLO in the occupied territories is in Lebanon.[36]

The key elements of this grand design were elaborated during repeated visits between members of the Israeli government and Bashir Gemayel. Bashir was the son of a prominent Maronite Christian leader, Pierre Gemayel, an admirer of Hitler, who had founded a private army with an attached political party, named the Phalange in honor of General Franco and patterned on Hitler's Brown Shirts.[37] So Israel invaded Lebanon with the thought, as then Foreign Minister (subsequently Prime Minister) Shamir put it, that "the defense of the West Bank starts in West Beirut."[38]

## Israel's Second Objective—To Install an Obedient Maronite Government in Lebanon

Israel's first objective was to be secured by its second: the installation of a minority Maronite Christian government to rule over a Lebanese protectorate which would conclude a separate peace with Israel. As early as May 24, 1948, the patriarch, David Ben-Gurion, had written in his diary: "the weak link in the Arab coalition is Lebanon. Moslem rule is artificial and easy to undermine. A Christian state must be established whose southern border will be the Litani. We shall sign a treaty with it." Then, on June 11, three weeks later, he wrote: "in the Galilee, the main enemy is [*sic*] Lebanon and Syria and our aim is to hit Beirut and to rouse the Christians [to revolt]. . . . "[39]

Six years later, Ben-Gurion was still advocating this strategic scheme. On February 27, 1954, Prime Minister Moshe Sharett described in his own diary Ben-Gurion's frantic advocacy of that objective: "This is the time [Ben-Gurion said] to push Lebanon, that is the Maronites in that country, to proclaim a Christian state. . . . He began to enumerate the historical justification for a restricted Christian Lebanon. If such a development were to take place, the Christian powers would not dare oppose it!" Sharett, who himself opposed the plan, then injected the comment that, "if we were to push and encourage it on our own we would get ourselves into an adventure that will place shame on us."

Nevertheless, proponents of the scheme continued to agitate for it, and contacts were made with key Lebanese factions. Then, on May 16, Ben-Gurion further outlined his scheme at a meeting where Moshe Dayan was present. Again, as recorded by Prime Minister Sharett, Dayan said:

> the only thing that's necessary is to find an officer, even just a major. We should either win his heart or buy him with money, to make him agree to declare himself the saviour of the Maronite population. Then the Israeli army will enter Lebanon, will occupy the necessary territory, and will create a Christian regime which will ally itself with Israel. The territory from the Litani southward will be totally annexed to Israel and everything will be all right.

Earlier, on May 15, Prime Minister Sharett's diary notes that "the Chief of Staff supports a plan to hire a [Lebanese] officer who will agree to serve as a puppet so that the Israeli army may appear as responding to his appeal to liberate Lebanon from its Moslem oppressors. This will, of course, be a crazy adventure. . . ."[40]

During the Suez episode in 1956, Ben-Gurion's plan for Lebanon had been put on hold, but it was revived after the Yom Kippur War of 1973, and by 1982 the Israelis had obtained their puppet Maronite officer—Major Sa'ad Haddad.

There were further ramifications. Geopolitical ambitions were not Israel's sole motivation for crossing the Lebanese border; Israel also coveted the water supply of southern Lebanon. In 1949, as noted, Walter Eytan had advanced a claim to that area as a necessary part of Israel's development schemes. Now, in 1982, with the Sea of Galilee drying up and renewable fresh water supplies approaching exhaustion, some Israelis were eager to exploit Lebanon's political turbulence to divert the waters of the Litani and other rivers to Israel.

## Israel's Grand Design for Lebanon

The grand design concocted between Israeli strategists and Bashir Gemayel's Phalange consisted of four major steps:

1. The IDF would invade Lebanon and link up with the Phalange; then the Phalange, aided by the IDF's presence, would overawe the Lebanese Parliament and coerce it into electing Bashir as president.
2. After establishing a government friendly to Israel, Bashir would sign a formal treaty of peace.
3. A new government would accord Israel full diplomatic relations. This would also advance Israel's strategic plan by letting it impose peace on one Arab neighbor at a time, and would virtually permit Israel to annex the region south of the Litani River.
4. Once the new Lebanese government were in place, Israel would assist it to expel the Palestinians and Syrians from Lebanon and extend Bashir Gemayel's control throughout what was left of the country.

Israeli leaders[41] knew that timing was of the essence. Lebanon was required to elect a new president by August 23, 1982, and the IDF had to be in Beirut before that.

## Exchanges Between Begin and Haig

In October 1981, Prime Minister Begin wrote to Secretary of State Haig laying the groundwork for an Israeli intervention in Lebanon. Haig answered Begin's note with an ambiguous response: "if you move, you move alone. Unless there is a major, internationally recognized provocation, the United States will not support such an action." Deciphered, this meant that Israel was told to get itself a plausible pretext if it wanted American support.

With this in view, Begin dispatched Israel's Director of Israeli Military Intelligence to Haig on February 3, 1982, to advise him, in Haig's words, that Israel was preparing to invade Lebanon "from the Israeli border to the southern suburbs of Beirut," with its target "the PLO infrastructure," adding that "the Syrians would be avoided if possible."[42]

Because Israel's problem was to find, or create, an "internationally recognized provocation" to satisfy Haig's conditions, it bombed suspected PLO positions in Lebanon on April 21, killing twenty-three persons in ostensible retaliation for the death of an Israeli officer killed by a land mine on Lebanese territory. Then, on May 9, following the attack on a bus in Jerusalem, Begin formally denounced the cease-fire agreement, and the Israeli Air Force bombarded what were alleged to be PLO headquarters, killing eleven and wounding fifty-six, very few of whom were in any way connected with the PLO.[43] Such provocations achieved their purpose of goading the PLO to respond by firing one hundred Katyusha rockets into Israel. On May 15, the Israeli Army Chief of Staff, General Rafael Eitan, confirmed that thirty thousand troops were massed along the Lebanese border.

General Sharon came to Washington in late May 1982 and detailed his program, much to the dismay of State Department officials who (except for Haig) knew nothing of these plans and did not find such *realpolitik* attractive. Haig delivered a speech on May 26 soliciting public support for Sharon's attack on Syria and the PLO by declaring:

> The time has come to take considered action in support of both Lebanon's territorial integrity within its internationally recognized borders and a strong central government capable of promoting a free, open, democratic and traditionally pluralistic society.

How "free" Lebanon would have been under a minority Maronite dictatorship, backed by Israel, can only be conjectured; the final result was bad enough.

Haig tried to rationalize a policy of inactivity by contending that there was nothing the United States could do to stop Israel. In truth, Haig lacked the will to use America's leverage and was content to sit back, give Israel its head, and thereafter hover over it like a protecting angel.

Later, when faced with overwhelming evidence of an imminent Israeli attack, Haig wrote Begin on May 28, 1982, that he "hoped there was no ambiguity on the extent of our concern about possible future Israeli military actions in Lebanon . . . [which] regardless of size, could have consequences none of us could foresee."[44]

Once again Begin replied in stylized indignation:

> Mr. Secretary, my dear friend, the man has not yet been born who will ever obtain from me consent to let Jews be killed by a bloodthirsty enemy and allow those who are responsible for the shedding of this blood to enjoy immunity.[45]

On reading these words, Haig later wrote that he "understood that the United States would probably not be able to stop Israel from attacking."[46] Nevertheless, considerable evidence suggests that Haig never really wanted to deter the Begin government from carrying out Sharon's "grand design," since he was basically sympathetic. In the words of two well-known Israeli journalists, Ze'ev Schiff and Ehud Ya'ari, "Israel could not have asked for a better spokesman for its cause than Secretary of State Alexander Haig. Washington—unsolicited it seemed—was going to do its part by protecting Israel's political flank, giving Menachem Begin good reason to feel that he was standing on solid ground."[47]

## Israel's Lebanese Adventure

Israel's initial raids on Lebanon were no more than noises off stage—mere curtain-raisers for the long-awaited main event. On June 4, 1982, a terrorist group obligingly furnished Israel with at least a shadowy *casus belli* by shooting in the head an Israeli envoy posted in London. It did not matter that British government investigators announced that the attack was not the work of the PLO, but of a radical group headed by Abu Nidal, who was under sentence of death by Arafat. That distinction made no impression on Prime Minister Begin, or on General Eitan, who said: "Abu Nidal, Abu Shmidal, we have to strike at the PLO."[48] This implied what Begin and his colleagues had long believed: Palestinian resistance groups were fungible; they were, according to Moshe Arens (then Israel's ambassador to Washington and later minister of defense and foreign relations), "all of the same Mafia-type octopus that works out of Lebanon."

To throw the Syrians off balance, Begin asked Haig to convey to Damascus assurances that the PLO was Israel's only target and that the IDF would not attack Syrian forces unless they attacked first. Although Haig gave every sign of knowing that Sharon planned to attack Syria's troops in Lebanon, he promptly forwarded that message and thus made the United States a party to deception when the IDF did attack the Syrians without even the pretense of a provocation.[49] Thus, as Ze'ev Schiff has noted:

> A more resolute American response would have strengthened moderate elements in the cabinet and would have prevented the two-month shelling of Beirut. Israel cabinet ministers who were against extending the war to Beirut said they could not oppose the plans as long as Washington did not come out against them. "I cannot show myself to be less of a patriot than the Americans," one Minister said. Later, when the Israeli government was considering plans to enter West Beirut, the same Minister said: "The Americans have got Israel into a mess. They have got us to climb up a high tree and now it's a hell of a job climbing down again."[50]

Once the IDF had driven all the way to Beirut and had bottled up the PLO and the 85th Syrian Brigade, the Israelis faced the task of how to get Yasser Arafat and his associates out of Lebanon. Since the capture of West Beirut (the Moslem section of the city) would involve far more Israeli casualties than the Begin government was prepared to accept, Israel's air, land, and sea forces bombarded West Beirut for a full nine weeks—with thousands of bombs and at least sixty thousand shells.[51]

In consequence, the total number of Lebanese civilian deaths, largely in this later phase of the war, probably came nearer to 12,000 persons than the 930 originally conceded by the Israelis.[52] In addition, one should not overlook Israel's deliberate destruction of Palestinian homes in its zeal to help the Phalange drive the Palestinians out of Lebanon.

On August 1, 1982, the UN Security Council unanimously "demanded" an immediate cease-fire, and dispatched military observers to assure that it was maintained. In response, Israel declared that the United Nations "could in no feasible technical way, monitor the activities of the terrorist organizations in Beirut and its environs." A UN presence, the Israelis alleged, would "signal to the terrorist organizations that they are not obliged to leave Beirut."

The U.S. government resorted to its ritual dance routine of taking one step forward, then tripping over its own feet: it approved a resolution couched in abstractions, then blocked any Security Council action to enforce it. Instead, the Reagan administration sent Philip Habib back to Lebanon, this time to serve the Israeli objective of arranging the departure of the PLO; and, through his intervention, a cease-fire was finally established on August 3. But when the PLO leaders obstinately refused to comply with General Sharon's demand that they leave promptly, Sharon canceled the cease-fire, unleashed a heavy bombardment, and sent his troops into West Beirut.

Because Sharon's assault threatened to wreck Habib's negotiations, the President, the next day, called the Israeli bombardment "a disproportionate" move. He told Prime Minister Begin that Israel's behavior raised a profound question about whether it was using American weapons for "legitimate self-defense." Israel should, he urged, return to the cease-fire line of August 2 and stop "unnecessary bloodshed."

Prime Minister Begin responded by assembling in Jerusalem a group of 190 American Jewish leaders, to whom he delivered a bitter harangue. Begin angrily shouted at his audience, "No one should preach to us. Nobody, nobody is going to bring Israel to her knees. You must have forgotten that the Jews kneel but to God."

Israel's cabinet brusquely rejected the President's request to pull back its forces. Israel would, they informed him, keep its troops there as long as the PLO leaders remained in West Beirut. In a further display of intransigence, a "senior Israeli official" warned on August 6 that any U.S. pressure "will have a contrary effect and America will lose all of its leverage. Then what Israel will do is unpredictable, but it could make Beirut look like peanuts."[53]

The United States dutifully yielded, and when, on August 4, the day of Reagan's protest, the United Nations Security Council adopted a new resolution "censuring" Israel for the invasion of West Beirut, America abstained. The President's modest request was simply that Begin defer his destruction of West Beirut long enough for Habib to complete his withdrawal negotiations. The Israeli government replied with condescension coupled with a threat: it might hold back the IDF briefly, but Habib would have to hurry, for Israel was "losing patience." If results were not promptly forthcoming, Israel would intensify its bombardment.

Although on Wednesday, August 11, Israel reluctantly accepted Habib's evacuation plan "in principle," subject to "suggestions for a number of amendments," that did not deter Sharon from mounting the next day the most ferocious attack thus far. It combined continuous saturation bombing with a massive artillery barrage and lasted eleven hours. As two Israeli correspondents described it, "Black Thursday" was a "nightmare"; unofficial tallies reported at least three hundred people dead in West Beirut that day.[54]

This episode overstepped even President Reagan's tolerance. He telephoned Prime Minister Begin to express his "outrage" (so the White House reported) at the continued Israeli attacks. Reagan's indignation was not focused so much on the bloodshed as on the possible crippling effect on Habib's negotiating effort. The only threat made to the Israelis was a message delivered to Begin by the U.S. ambassador that if the August 12 bombardment was not abandoned, Habib would stop trying to negotiate the removal of the PLO leaders.[55]

Despite Reagan's complaints, he took no disciplinary action against Israel's wilfully improper use of its theoretically "strictly defensive" weapons. Far from being a defensive effort, Begin himself, before the Israeli War College, had called the Lebanese campaign, like the 1967 War, not a "war of survival" but rather "a war of choice." Moreover, Reagan acquiesced in Israel's use of cluster bombs. One might have thought that after Carter had protested the Israeli use of cluster bombs in 1978, America would have rigorously blocked their further shipment to Israel. Instead, the U.S. government relied on the agreements of April 10 and 11, 1978, under which Israel had stipulated that it would not use cluster bombs unless "attacked" by the "regular forces of a sovereign nation" that Israel had fought in 1967 and 1973. It had also agreed that it would not use cluster bombs against civilians—a commitment demanded after the CIA had reported that Israel had carpet-bombed South Lebanon's civilian refugee camps with them.[56]

The Israeli government knew, however, that with President Reagan in power, it could disregard these irksome restrictions—which Sharon did with a vengeance. According to a classified CIA report, Israel used nine types of American cluster bombs. There were, another study disclosed, nineteen locations in West Beirut, as well as fifty-one other locations throughout Lebanon, where Israel had used them. A multinational cleanup force in Beirut found more than three thousand unexploded cluster bomblets. Doctors in twenty hospitals and clinics operating in West Beirut signed affidavits that they had all treated cluster-bomb patients.[57]

Confronted by this compelling evidence of misuse and American public indignation, the Pentagon, on July 9, 1982, announced the cancelation of shipments to Israel. The disingenuous character of this order was exposed by the Kisco Corporation of St. Louis, maker of these weapons, who told CBS-TV on September 29 that what was banned for shipment was the bomb casing, which, as the company spokesman pointed out, happened to be the only part of the weapon that Israel manufactured.[58] Even this meaningless suspension was scrapped as part of the second "Strategic Cooperation Arrangement" signed during Prime Minister Shamir's visit to Washington on November 28–29, 1983.[59]

## The Need for a Peacekeeping Force in Lebanon

Once Philip Habib had induced the PLO and Israel to agree to a cease-fire and the evacuation of the PLO forces from West Beirut, he faced the problem of a peacekeeping force. Habib first favored a UN force—which had already been suggested on July 20 by the Soviet Union; the USSR opposed the injection of United States forces into the area.[60]

In spite of Chairman Brezhnev's clear statement on the subject, President Reagan in February 1984 claimed that he would have preferred a UN force had Moscow not blocked his "preference." The record clearly shows, however, that it was Israel, backed by the Americans, who blocked that force.

Since a UN force could have been quickly constituted by redeploying UNIFIL troops already in southern Lebanon, what then did Israel want? In July, Israeli officials leaked a story that President Reagan would deploy American forces in a peacekeeping role. Israel's purpose, some suspected, was to provoke the PLO into rejecting Habib's offers so that the IDF could continue its bombardment.

Yet that leak produced unexpected repercussions in Washington. The thought of committing the Marines to Lebanon was unpalatable to key members of Congress. The Senate majority leader, Howard Baker, remarked that it was "not wise to introduce American fighting men into the Lebanese conflict," and the same sentiment was expressed by Senator Charles Mathias of Maryland and the chairman of the House Foreign Affairs Committee, Congressman Clement Zablocki. Nor, with Vietnam fresh in its memory, did the Defense Department favor the idea. Secretary Weinberger warned against sending troops into such a "volatile area."

Similar advice was tendered by others, including the senior author, by then a private citizen, who told the Senate Foreign Relations Committee in testimony: "We would imprudently hazard the lives of our marines to commit them to an area where anti-Americanism is a dominating sentiment. . . . " The author then added that, although America might facilitate the removal of the PLO leaders,

> there will be plenty of frustrated Palestinians left behind and they may be driven to desperate acts of terrorism by the atmosphere of death and violence that has enveloped the city.
>
> If there must be some third party intervention then, let the troops of other nations undertake it—young men who are not Americans and hence not the natural targets for assassins.[61]

All this advice was disregarded, first because Israel detested the United Nations, and second, because it wanted to have an American presence to support its position. Israel's influence in blocking a United Nations force is well documented. According to a report of the House committee that investigated the nonexistent security precautions of the Marine contingent blown up in the Beirut Airport disaster, "Ambassador Philip Habib . . . testified that a United Nations force to supervise the withdrawal was not acceptable to Israel. Robert Dunn, the U.S. Ambassador to Lebanon . . . testified that the Israelis would not trust any international force unless the United States participated."[62]

Because Israel had programmed the United States to defer to its wishes, the Reagan administration felt constrained to commit an American unit as part of a multinational force. Israel accepted that decision on August 15, 1982, and Lebanon assented on August 29. A contingent of American Marines, along with troops from Britain, France, and Italy, arrived off the Lebanese coast on August 25, and from August 26 to September 11 they covered the evacuation. Then, on September 11, once the PLO leaders had been evacuated, the international force was abruptly withdrawn.[63]

Meanwhile, two other significant events were taking place. The first was President Reagan's September 1, 1982, peace plan; the second was the election of Bashir Gemayel as president of Lebanon.

## Ronald Reagan's Peace Plan

Israel's American propagandists claimed that by invading Lebanon and expelling the PLO, the Israelis had done America a favor. A "liberated" Lebanon would pave the way for "new realities," which would offer "new opportunities" for a fresh start toward resolution of the Middle East conflict. With the PLO expelled, it could no longer interfere with the remodeling of Lebanon. That thesis overlooked the fact that Israel had undertaken its Lebanon invasion with the major objective of evading negotiations with the Palestinians or anyone else.

In a speech at the time, President Reagan pointed out two realities and two issues. The two realities were that the losses of the PLO had not diminished the need to find a just solution for the Palestinian peoples, and that Israeli military prowess had not brought that country peace. The two issues were the strategic threat posed by the Soviet Union and the achievement of peace between Israel and its Arab neighbors. The plan was acceptably orthodox. It called for

—autonomy for the Palestinians in the West Bank and Gaza under some form of Jordanian supervision;
—a freeze on Israeli settlements; and
—the maintenance of an undivided Jerusalem (presumably to remain under Israeli control).

In addition, the plan specifically ruled out an independent Palestinian state and any negotiating role for the PLO.

To some, Reagan's peace plan seemed well timed because it followed the July 1982 dismissal of Secretary Haig. His successor, George Shultz, was thought to carry "little ideological baggage and was seemingly prepared to take a fresh look at Middle East policy. . . . "[64]

The Arabs greeted the Reagan Plan with cautious but generally positive language. It was the first time that the Reagan administration had mentioned any Palestinian element in the Arab-Israeli conflict, and it implied an American recognition that the issue would thereafter be regarded as central to any resolution. Nonetheless, the more cautious Arabs noted the ambiguity in such phrases as "legitimate rights," "full autonomy," "disposition of Jerusalem," "Palestinian-Jordanian entity," and "Israel's final boundaries," as well as the summary rejection of a Palestinian state. The plan, as William Quandt put it, was noteworthy as much for what it left out as for what it said; for example, "Lebanon was briefly mentioned. Syria was not."[65]

*The Israeli Response*

The Begin government's reaction was emphatically negative. Determined to avoid any negotiations on the Palestinian issue, Prime Minister Begin peremptorily declared that the Reagan Plan was a danger to the very existence of the State of Israel and should be rejected as "a lifeless stillborn," and he procured a 50–36 vote in the Knesset against it. During the debate, Begin shouted that Israel would keep unending control over the West Bank and Gaza. "We have no reason to get on our knees. No one will determine for us the borders of the land of Israel."[66]

Begin had long shown a genius for the provocative gesture. To emphasize his disapproval, he flouted Reagan's opposition to new settlements by allocating $18.5 million on September 5 to construct three new ones in the occupied West Bank and announcing his approval for seven others. In addition, the cabinet directed the Ministry of Defense to turn four West Bank military outposts into permanent civilian settlements. Forty-two new West Bank settlements were planned over the next four years, and within five years another 100,000 Israelis were expected to settled in the West Bank, 20,000 in the Golan Heights, and 10,000 in Gaza.

Individual Israeli ministers joined Begin in denouncing Reagan's proposal. Defense Minister Sharon compared the Palestinians to the White Russians in post-1917 Paris and implied that the invasion of Lebanon had forever disposed of Palestinian autonomy of any kind. Foreign Minister Shamir said that, had Israel known about the American peace plan, it would never have returned the Sinai to Egypt.[67]

To cap these angry comments, Prime Minister Begin indignantly protested to Reagan that a semi-autonomous Palestinian entity in the West Bank "would endanger our very existence." Such an enclave, he wrote with characteristic hyperbole, would inevitably lead to a "Soviet base in the heart of the Middle East." Although he had not consulted the United States before annexing the Golan Heights, he was outraged that Reagan had not consulted him before forwarding his proposals to Jordan and Saudi Arabia. Nor was he mollified when the State Department pointed out that the United States was under no obligation to treat his objections as definitive.

In response, the Reagan administration complained that Israel's plans for projected settlements were "most unwelcome," with the White House explicitly stating: "We cannot understand why at a time when broader participation in the peace process is most critical and possible, Israel has elected to extend a pattern of activity which erodes the confidence of all, and most particularly, the inhabitants of the West Bank and Gaza." Secretary of State Shultz added that the Israeli action was "not consistent with the objective of peace."[68]

But in Jerusalem no one with political clout was listening. To underline Israel's determination never to give the Palestinians autonomy of any sort, Shamir informed Egypt that it was not interested in resuming talks on Palestinian self-rule because the situation had become "complicated and more difficult." The talks, he said, could resume only after the situation in Lebanon had been settled.

## The Obligatory Peace Offering

Israel's resistance to all peacemaking efforts of the Reagan administration drew from Shultz only the mildest of rebukes. The administration failed to penalize Israeli obstructionism; on the contrary, it seemed to apologize for its temerity in ever having made its proposals.

Then, true to form, Reagan sought to make amends to the Israeli leaders for having chided them at all. So he asked Congress to augment the annual aid given to Israel, despite the fact that a part of that aid would help fund Israel's Lebanese invasion and expanding settlements program. And, as usual, Congress increased the appropriation over the original request.

CHAPTER SEVEN

# Reagan Continues Until Bush Takes Over

WITH THE ELECTION of Bashir Gemayel in Beirut, Israel had accomplished the first stage of its grand design for Lebanon. The fact that Gemayel had killed the relatives of several prominent Lebanese leaders and had massacred thousands of Palestinians in a refugee camp in 1976 did not deter President Reagan from sending Gemayel a congratulatory message, promising that the United States would "work closely with the new government in the complex and difficult task ahead." American officials confidently asserted that the election would lead to a speedy withdrawal from Lebanon of both Israeli and Syrian troops.

But rather than wait for Bashir Gemayel to be installed as president, his Lebanese enemies arranged for his assassination by bombing the Phalange Party's East Beirut headquarters on September 14, 1982. The next day, in open violation of the August cease-fire agreements, the Israeli Army invaded and occupied West Beirut.

Ignoring Moslem protests, the White House at first refrained from taking any stand on the Israeli move. Then, presumably shamed when Lebanese Prime Minister Shafik al-Wazzan reminded the United States that it had pledged to uphold the cease-fire arrangement, the State Department declared the entry of the Israeli troops a "clear violation of the Beirut cease-fire agreement." The Israeli takeover of West Beirut, the White House added, had been "contrary to assurances" given by Israel on September 15 that the military moves would be "limited and precautionary." In identical statements, the White House and State Department concluded America's protest with the words: "There is no justification in our view for Israel's continued military presence in West Beirut and we call for an immediate pullback."

In response, the Israeli Cabinet bluntly rebuffed the U.S. requests. Israeli leaders contended that the PLO had left behind in West Beirut "about 2,000 terrorists, equipped with modern and heavy weapons." Israel's troops, they asserted, had entered the city only to prevent "violence, bloodshed and anarchy," and "this danger was indeed averted." No one had the temerity to point out that it was the Israeli's original entry into the city that had unleashed that "violence, bloodshed and anarchy."

Israel also announced that it would not pull out of the city until the Lebanese army was able to take control. But, as everyone knew, there was no effective Lebanese army nor any prospect of one, so the Israelis were merely signaling their intention to stay on indefinitely. That did not deter Defense Minister Ariel Sharon from boasting to the U.S. chargé d'affaires, Morris Draper, that "we have saved Lebanon again for you."[1]

## The Sabra and Shatilla Massacres

While the Israelis were proclaiming their devotion to law and order in West Beirut, the Israeli command was arranging action of a different sort with the Phalangists, who wanted to revenge themselves on the murderers of Bashir, their commander. As the list of suspects was lengthy, the Israelis suggested that the Phalange work off its anger by combing through two Palestinian camps, Sabra and Shatilla, to ferret out Palestinian guerrillas. Between September 16 and 18, goaded by their hatred of the Palestinians, the Phalange massacred perhaps as many as 2,000 men, women and children (death certificates were issued for over 1,200).

That obscene affair left Israel in disgrace, and the Jewish American community appalled. Emerging evidence showed that the Israeli commanders, before, during, and after the fact, knew what was going on and did nothing to stop it or punish those responsible. On September 18, President Reagan expressed his horror at the Beirut killings and repeated his demand for an immediate Israeli pullback. In addition, on September 19, the United States voted for a UN Security Council resolution condemning the "criminal massacre of Palestinian civilians in Beirut." The resolution also authorized the Secretary General to investigate the deployment of UN forces to assist the government of Lebanon "in assuring full protection for the civilian population."

The reason it suggested no punishment of the malefactors was that in negotiating this resolution the United States representatives acted as the guardians of Israeli sensitivities. They threatened a veto if the resolution even mentioned Israel or United Nations sanctions. They also attempted to add a proviso that the PLO and Syria should promptly withdraw their forces. In all likelihood, the United States only supported the final watered-down resolution because of the widespread indignation and its embarrassment at being caught in a bald violation of its commitments.[2]

American authorities had induced the PLO fighters to leave Beirut by guaranteeing, on the basis of explicit, unequivocal Israeli assurances, that the families they were leaving behind would be safe. Thus, the United States had put its honor on the line and the refugee massacre had violated it. Prime Minister Sari Nusseibeh of Jordan declared that "Israel has chosen to lay bare the ability, or the credibility" of the United States as "guarantor" of the Beirut Truce Agreement.

Although world opinion was horrified by the massacre, the Israeli government's initial reaction was to ignore the whole matter. Proposals for an independent investigation were vetoed by Begin, who solemnly denounced the claim that Israel had any responsibility as a "blood libel." The clamor in the U.S. Congress, in Jewish American groups, and within Israel itself was so tumultuous, however, that grudgingly Begin had to give way.

Among those most troubled by the massacre was the Beirut correspondent for *The New York Times,* Thomas L. Friedman, who by his own proud admission had, in his youth, been an ardent Zionist. After spending three years covering the developing chaos of Beirut, he was about to be transferred to Israel when the massacre occurred. He went to inspect the site and wrote a masterful report—an almost hour-by-hour reconstruction of the massacre—that was published across four full pages of the *Times* on September 26, 1982. His conclusion was that "The Israelis knew just what they were doing when they let the Phalangists into those camps."[3]

A week later the Israelis granted Friedman a stormy but exclusive interview with Major General Amir Drori, the senior Israeli commander in Lebanon. Drori, Friedman wrote, "had no answers. I knew it. He knew it." So "the next morning I buried Amir Drori on the front page of *The New York Times,* and along with him every illusion I ever held about the Jewish state."[4]

Finally, but reluctantly, the Israeli government set up the so-called "Kahan Commission" to investigate the affair. That Commission found that the Israeli authorities either knew what was going on during the massacre or should have known and, in any event, should have taken effective measures to prevent its occurrence. The Commission also found that the Israeli authorities were lax in supervising the Phalange, particularly given the Phalange's notorious history.

Friedman wrote:

> But for all their inquiring, what was the final outcome? Sharon, who was found by the Kahan Commission to bear "personal responsibility" for what happened in the camps, was forced to step down as Defense Minister and become a minister-without-portfolio instead, until the next Israeli government was formed, when he became Minister of Industry and Trade. Israel's Chief of Staff, Rafael Eitan, who was also assigned blame

> for what took place in the camps, who had lied to dozens of world newsmen when asked if Israel had sent the Phalangists in, was allowed to finish his tour of duty with dignity and was then elected to the Israeli parliament. Brigadier General Yaron was told he could never get another field command, but was then promoted to major general and put in charge of the manpower division of the Israeli army, which handles all personnel matters. After fulfilling that job, in August 1986 he was handed one of the most coveted assignments—military attaché in Washington.
> An investigation which results in such "punishments" is not an investigation that can be taken seriously.[5]

## The Israeli-American Attempt to Reorganize Lebanon

After Bashir's death, his brother, Amin Gemayel, who had handled family business with Syria, was elected president. Israel's agenda remained as follows:

(1) achieving a peace treaty with Lebanon, calling for trade, tourism, and diplomatic recognition;
(2) maintaining the Israeli armed forces in Lebanon until the Syrians removed theirs; and
(3) organizing a strong centralized government to impose Israeli-dictated policies on the whole of Lebanon.

On its face, this plan defied the logic of number. It contemplated that a minority Maronite Christian government representing less than 20 percent of the population and controlling only 10 percent of Lebanon's total area would be able to establish its rule over the whole of the country in the face of resistance from other powerful factions. It was clear that such a tour de force—if possible at all—would require the massive, bloody use of armed intervention over a protracted period.

The United States assumed the role of an indirect supporter of Israel's policies. The Reagan administration seemed quite unperturbed that this involved interfering arrogantly in Lebanon's affairs, helping to impose despotic minority rule on the Lebanese, and subjecting America's military and diplomatic personnel to probable injury or death.

As part of this American effort, American Marines were again deployed to Lebanon on September 29 to serve in a second multinational peacekeeping force that would replace Israeli forces scheduled to leave West Beirut. However, in sending this new Marine detachment, the White House, echoing Israel's views, announced that American forces "would remain until all foreign forces were withdrawn." As neither the Israelis nor the Syrians showed any intention of evacuating Lebanon, the Marines did not have a clearly defined mission with a specific *terminus ad quem.*

In testifying on September 29, 1982, before the House Foreign Affairs Committee, Nicholas A. Veliotes, Assistant Secretary of State for Near Eastern and South Asian Affairs, stated that the prospect of an Israeli-Syrian withdrawal was not "a criterion," but only an "expectation" that the foreign troops would be out of the country by the end of 1982 at the "outer limit."[6]

Having installed a pro forma government in Beirut, the Israelis proceeded with the balance of their agenda. There was talk in Israel about the possible annexation of southern Lebanon, the expansion of Major Haddad's "security zone" in the south, and other projects designed to reduce Lebanon to an Israeli protectorate.

Meanwhile, the Israeli public had grown disenchanted with the war: Israel had failed to achieve a quick and total victory, and had no prospect of doing so. That impasse led Begin to persuade Secretary of State George Shultz to try his hand at dislodging the Syrian troops, whose departure would then permit a parallel Israeli withdrawal. Up to then, Shultz had had little opportunity to display his diplomatic talents; Middle East negotiations appeared to offer him a chance to emulate Kissinger's shuttle diplomacy.

But Shultz was, in the words of Thomas Friedman, too "decent, dignified, and well-meaning" to be effective. He was not prepared to be tough even in private with Shamir, and, like a naive tourist in a *souk,* he declined to bargain but paid whatever he was asked without question. It was not a formula for success.[7]

Before undertaking his Lebanese negotiations, Shultz had met in Cairo with all the American ambassadors in the Middle East, including Robert Pagnelli, America's ambassador in Damascus, who

> bluntly told Shultz that [America's] blatant disregard of Syria's interests made Assad's opposition inevitable. Affronted by Pagnelli's plain speaking, Shultz dismissed the warning. He had no real grasp of Assad's reasons for dreading an Israeli overlordship in Lebanon, nor did he appreciate the depth of Assad's resentment at what the Syrians saw as Washington's "betrayal" over the 11 June ceasefire.[8]

In ignoring Pagnelli's advice, Shultz made a major negotiating blunder. Pagnelli "knew the Syrian mind." Yet wishful thinking carried the day. For reasons best known to himself, Shultz approached Israel, confident that the Syrians must agree to whatever terms he worked out with Begin.

After frenetic shuttling between Beirut and Jerusalem, during which he saw Begin no fewer than six times, Shultz did achieve a draft of sorts. But the agreement of May 17, 1983, was a disappointment to everyone except George Shultz. The Israelis were unhappy because Lebanon had not signed a treaty of peace, and they were annoyed that American intervention had thwarted their hopes for concessions in southern Lebanon, which they had expected to extract from the weak Lebanese government. So the Israeli government let it be known that Prime Minister Begin had signed the agreement only to gain favor with the Americans. They neglected to mention that Israel gained greatly from its secret protocols. Among them was a side letter from Shultz assuring Israel that the IDF need not withdraw from Lebanon unless the Syrians agreed to withdraw at the same time. Since Begin was certain that the Syrians would never withdraw (in which view he was notably correct), he was confident that Israel could legitimately maintain its puppet army in Lebanon as long as it wished.[9]

By the time Shultz visited Damascus on May 7, he had a draft treaty fully negotiated with the Israelis. When he offered that draft for signature to Assad, the Syrians were outraged. Shultz had simply outlined the terms agreed to by the Israelis and presented them as a fait accompli. He showed no willingness to consider Syrian interests. Assad thereupon treated him to "a five-hour history lesson."

> He recited the Arab struggle to contain Israel and their resentment at America's indifference to their aspirations and in supplying support for their enemy. Now the United States proposed rewarding Israel for its aggression. It was to be allowed to change Lebanon's Arab character, to threaten the security of Arab states such as Syria, and to impose its hegemony on the region.

Assad rejected Shultz's entire proposition. The proper course, he advised, was to pursue "the strict implementation of Security Council Resolutions 508 and 509, for which the United States itself had voted."[10]

The rejection of his plan left a permanent mark on Shultz. He returned to Beirut angry and affronted and in an anti-Arab, and particularly anti-Syrian, mood for the residue of his tenure. Six days later, on May 13, Secretary of Defense Weinberger completed the insult to Syrian sensibilities by threatening to attack Syria with "retaliatory force" if it did not accept the Shultz arrangement.[11] No one should have been surprised that when Ambassador Habib went to Damascus with the final terms on May 18, Syria's officials refused even to receive him.

The person most damaged by this agreement was Lebanon's President Amin Gemayel. Because of Secretary Shultz's highly visible role in these negotiations, Gemayel was inevitably accused of having caved in to the United States. Subjected to pressures from every side, the hard-pressed Gemayel tried to temporize, evading formal ratification in the hope of placating the Syrians and Lebanese Moslems while still implying an intention to ratify to please the Americans, Israel, and the Maronite Christians.

President Assad claimed that Syrian troops were in the country under the authority granted them by the Arab League in 1976 with tacit American approval, and he resented comparing his troops (who in his view had legal standing) with those of Israel, which had aggressively invaded the country with no legal justification, and then defied UN orders to leave. Moreover, the Syrians were adamant that the territorial integrity of Lebanon be maintained in the face of Israel's dismemberment plans.

Secretary Shultz and President Reagan seemed oblivious to all this. The White House ignored the storm signals and the President observed benignly at his press conference on May 17 that he was confident Syria would withdraw its troops "because of pressure from other Arab countries."

If there had been any Arab support for the agreement, it quickly vanished when the secret protocols were aired during the Israeli Knesset debate; it was then realized that, contrary to American assurances to the Arabs, the agreement gave Israel special rights in southern Lebanon. By backing Israel's fantasies, the United States had reneged on its own vote in the United Nations calling for total Israeli withdrawal. For President Reagan to charge President Assad with having "reneged" was, therefore, pure effrontery; on the contrary, Assad was the only party in this sordid affair who had displayed a consistent position or who insisted upon thwarting Israel's annexationist schemes.

## The End of the American-Israeli Grand Design for Lebanon

The firmness of the Syrians, and the formidable potential casualties involved in trying to drive them out of northern Lebanon, compelled the Israelis to recognize that their imperial dream had aborted. Israel had suffered badly from its invasion. When an Israeli troop convoy drove through a Shia religious procession killing and injuring several worshipers, it bitterly alienated the Shiite population in the south, on whose support any long-lived Israeli presence in the area would have to depend. So, with Shiite resistance growing, the new Israeli defense minister, Moshe Arens, decided to withdraw to a more defensible position, thus deserting the United States, which was still trying, futilely, to strengthen the Lebanese Maronite government.[12]

It was far from the first example of Israeli disregard of American interests. Israeli troops had frequently clashed around Beirut Airport with American Marines, and the Marine commander had repeatedly complained that his men were being harassed. There were shoving incidents, insults, obstruction of U.S. patrols, and other abrasive encounters. The Israelis responded by blaming the Marines for being drunk, incompetent on patrol, and generally uncooperative.[13]

By now Shiite, Druse, and other pro-Syrian militias were increasing their pressure on the Marines and the American-sponsored Lebanese Army. Thus, if the IDF vacated the high ground above the airport, the void would almost certainly be filled by hostile Druse militiamen, who could make the American Marines' position at the airport untenable. Accordingly, Robert McFarlane, head of the National Security Council, was sent to induce the Israelis to change their minds. The only concession he could extract from them was an agreement to defer their departure until August 31, 1983.

No one has ever explained why the U.S. government did not find some plausible excuse for withdrawing the Marines after Israel removed its troops from the Chouf Mountains. Unhappily, the President's exuberant rhetoric had painted America into a corner. The President had proclaimed that American intervention was indispensable to oppose the Soviet (translation: Syrian) forces.

So, contrary to all reason, the President did not withdraw the Marines but radically transformed their mission in Lebanon from peacekeeping to that of imposing a minority Maronite government on the highly factionalized Lebanese people. He not only authorized the Marines to fire on the Druse, but sent in an impressive armada to shower 5- and 16-inch shells on the Lebanese coast.[14]

Confusion was so widespread that the U.S. government could not get its story straight. On some days, the State Department or the White House told the Congress and the American people that the shelling was intended to protect the Marines from harassing fire from the hills (a pretext hard to argue against). On other days, the objective was described as supporting the Lebanese government in its civil war. The muddling reached a zenith on February 14, 1984, when Navy Secretary John Lehman announced in the morning that U.S. forces were shelling Druse positions to support Gemayel, only to contradict himself, at the White House's insistence, that afternoon by stating that America's shelling was intended to protect the Marines.[15]

Confusion was further compounded by a careless comment of the President. On September 20, 1982, he had announced that the second Marine peacekeeping force would have "the mission of enabling the Lebanese government to resume full sovereignty over its capital—the essential precondition for extending its control over the entire country." That role, of course, had nothing to do with peacekeeping. It put the United States in the position of being a co-belligerent in Lebanon's civil war.

On October 24, 1983, immediately after the bombing of the Marine barracks, the President was echoing the rhetoric of Vietnam days by telling reporters that the United States had "vital interests" in Lebanon because "If Lebanon ends up under the tyranny of forces hostile to the West, not only will our strategic position in the Eastern Mediterranean be threatened, but also the stability of the entire Middle East." Yet, despite this ominous vision, no one even proposed to reinforce the 1,500-man U.S. force.[16]

To justify its position during October 1983, the administration, in effect, declared the Druse to be America's enemies. To reconcile fantasy with doctrine, its spokesmen, television commentators, and many members of the press now began referring to the Druse and others opposed to the Gemayel regime (in other words, 80 percent of the Lebanese) as "leftist forces." There were even those who called Gemayel an American "ally"!

At first, U.S. warships were authorized to fire at Druse and Shiite artillery positions to protect the Marines. Then the Navy used artillery and air strikes to support the Lebanese Army. After that, U.S. aircraft were dispatched on provocative overflights of Syrian-controlled territory. When Syrian anti-aircraft fire caused the capture of the unfortunate Lieutenant Robert Goodman (subsequently rescued through the good offices of Jesse Jackson and President Assad), the United States reverted to random broadside naval shelling that inevitably produced civilian casualties. Finally, the Navy began to bombard Druse positions near the town of Suq al-Gharb. Marine officers were also sent to Suq al-Gharb to help U.S. warships coordinate targets.

By now most Lebanese had formed a resentful view of America. With their own bitter factions proficient at killing one another, they felt no need to import foreign talent. Accordingly, on October 23, 1983, a truck bomb, driven by a Lebanese member of the Hizbullah ("Party of God"), a pro-Iranian group, destroyed the Marine headquarters at Beirut Airport and killed 241 Americans. Simultaneously, another truck bomb hit the French unit and killed fifty-nine. A few days later, on November 4, a similar operation killed sixty persons at Israeli headquarters.[17]

President Reagan, in response, announced that he was "more determined than ever" that the perpetrators "cannot take over that vital and strategic area of the earth."[18] Since the Iranian-backed Shiites could hardly be called Soviet surrogates, the administration insinuated that the attack was the product of Syrian complicity. In doing so, the President was asserting his dogmatic faith in the universal culpability of the Communist conspiracy—or even of all foreigners.

Secretary Shultz did not connect the Marine barracks disaster with America's support for Israel, but considered it merely a further example of Syrian perfidy. To show his disapproval of Syria's continued occupation (and presumably his approval of Israel's behavior during its invasion), Shultz, on November 28 and 29, undertook new negotiations with Israel, which led to a second cooperation agreement.

This agreement went much further toward meeting Israel's demands, even providing for the prepositioning of military supplies. It was astonishingly one-sided. The United States got nothing from Israel, and there is no evidence that it even asked for anything. The agreement's objective was, the administration stated, to "give priority attention to the threat to our mutual interest posed by increased Soviet involvement in the Middle East."

The announced highlights of the agreement were:

1. An increase in U.S. military grants to Israel by $425 million annually.
2. Permission to Israel to use some of this aid to build the Lavi jet fighter in competition with American aircraft producers.[19]
3. The establishment of a U.S.-Israeli Committee to conduct joint military planning and exercises and to arrange for the use of Israeli ports by the U.S. Sixth Fleet.
4. Arrangements for the prepositioning of military medical supplies in Israel for the use by the U.S. Rapid Deployment Force (RDF).
5. Immediate negotiations for a free trade agreement between the United States and Israel, allowing imports and exports on a duty-free and tax-free basis.

These arrangements involved America even more deeply in the Middle East quagmire, and made the United States a co-belligerent with Israel in its war with the Arabs. America provided Israel with on-site supplies that Israel could co-opt at will with no reduction in its regular U.S. military aid.

As might be expected, the first Arab reaction to this agreement was incredulity, followed by anger and perplexity. There was no apparent need for such a treaty since there was no evidence of any "increased Soviet involvement in the Middle East," other than their resupply of Syria, provoked by Israel's gratuitous attack.

Despite administration statements that it had "no plans for joint military planning of military actions against Syria or any other Arab country," the Arabs did not believe a word of it. Israel saw the strategic agreement as the first step toward a formal America-Israeli military alliance.

Why the Reagan administration chose this particular moment to sign an executive agreement with Israel remains a continuing mystery. The most plausible conjecture is that Secretary Shultz saw it as a way to get back at the Syrians for embarrassing him six months earlier over his aborted Lebanese peace treaty.[20]

## Peace Negotiations

Any hope for salvaging some value from Shultz's diplomatic adventure completely faded when President Amin Gemayel formally repudiated the May 17, 1983, accord on March 5, 1984. Though America ought to have foreseen the inevitable demise of this misconceived instrument (which, of course, had no effect without a Syrian signature), the U.S. government declared that

> the proposed agreement still represents the only, agreed formula for insuring both Israel's withdrawal from Lebanon and Israel's legitimate security interests, in a manner consistent with Israeli sovereignty. . . . Those who are responsible for the rejection of the agreement must now bear the responsibility for finding an alternative negotiating formula to bring about Israeli withdrawal.[21]

Meanwhile, suffering from incessant harassment by a local Shiite population, which the IDF had stirred to action by its "iron fist" policy during its occupation, Israeli forces made an undignified departure from Lebanon with, as one Israeli remarked, "their shirttails on fire." They thus left the protection of Israel's northern border in the hands of their mercenaries, the (Maronite) Christian Southern Lebanese Army.[22]

Those developments did not, however, discourage George Shultz from making at least pro forma efforts in the Middle East. He sent Assistant Secretary of State Richard Murphy on exploratory visits. These halfhearted probings disclosed only that the Israelis intended to postpone any definitive peace discussions by a filibuster over the composition of delegations to a peace conference. They constantly reiterated the caveat (to which Henry Kissinger had acquiesced in 1975) that America would not talk with the PLO, and they negated any fruitful negotiation by repeatedly announcing in advance that Israel would not concede one inch of territory to comply with Resolution 242.

The Israelis restricted America's freedom to talk even further by adding as a precondition that the PLO must not only have first accepted Resolutions 242 and 338 of the Security Council but must have formally recognized Israel's right to exist.[23]

Even though Begin had retired in 1983, the Israeli government from 1983 to 1989 still stuck rigidly to his fierce dogmatic views. Begin's effective successor—a man who dominated the coalition by his indomitable obstinacy—was a fellow terrorist of Begin's. At the outset, Yitzhak Shamir had belonged to the Irgun with Begin; then he and a colleague named Nathan Yellin-Mor joined Avraham Stern in 1940 to form Lehi (better known as the Stern Gang). This group was soon busy robbing banks and setting off bombs in marketplaces. It assassinated Lord Moyne and Count Folke Bernadotte, the UN peace negotiator. So rabidly anti-British was the group that (with Shamir's approval) emissaries were sent in 1940–41 to Damascus and then to Athens in an effort to secure German aid by allying with Hitler against the British. The only reason that *démarche* failed was because the Nazis, while tempted by a low-cost chance to harass Britain, deemed it *infra dig* to align themselves with Jews.[24]

After Israel's independence, Shamir had served in the Mossad. In the early 1980s, he and other right-wing agents made arrangements with Rabbi Kahane's Jewish Defense League to assassinate Soviet personnel in the United States with a view to embarrassing Soviet-American relations. Kahane later had to flee to Israel to avoid arrest.[25]

Having embraced Shamir as a friend and ally, the United States submitted docilely to his claimed right of veto over the negotiating process. The only negotiator on whom the Americans and Israelis could agree was King Hussein. But since Hussein, with good reason, insisted that other Arab leaders share the responsibility for any agreement reached with Israel involving territory, he proposed an international conference. His delegation would include Palestinians, whose assent was necessary to make any agreement valid.

Israel rejected the idea and the United States supinely followed suit. Predictably, the other Arabs raised objections as well, demanding an independent PLO delegation—exactly what Israel did not want. Faced by such opposition and PLO waffling on America's conditions, King Hussein withdrew his offer.

Then, in December 1987, the cumulative effect of years of Israeli repression gave birth to the *Intifada* (the uprising of the Palestinians). This conflict came alive for the American people because for weeks the television networks showed pictures of several Israeli soldiers beating some cowering Palestinian youth, usually for throwing stones at them. And, from time to time, there were scenes of Israeli security officials firing Uzi submachine guns at young Palestinians. To demonstrate America's concern, Secretary Shultz in 1988 announced the so-called "Shultz Plan," which was, simply, an update of the 1979 Camp David autonomy proposals.

Although the new plan was evidently tailored to meet the strong prejudices of Prime Minister Shamir, Assistant Secretary of State Murphy found on arriving in Jerusalem on February 9 that the Israeli government was sharply divided. Shamir was opposed to accelerated autonomy, and even Foreign Minister Shimon Peres's lukewarm comment that "anything is welcome" drew down on his head a snappish Shamir accusation that he was willing to "sell everything we have" to the Americans.

Meanwhile, on February 16 an Arab coalition including Egypt, Jordan, Morocco, Saudi Arabia, and Syria formally demanded an international conference, to be co-chaired by the United States and the Soviet Union, at which a so-called "complete solution" could be negotiated.

But the United States had already succumbed to Israel's wishes by vetoing on February 1 a Security Council resolution calling for an overall peace settlement under United Nations auspices. This reinforced what many had long suspected: the United States was determined to monopolize the peacemaking process, but would not permit peace to be made except on Israel's terms.

The shuttle that began February 25 was a purely symbolic affair. The Arabs went along with the Secretary *pour politesse,* confident that Israeli intransigence would spare them the necessity of outright rejection.[26] Meanwhile, the Americans operated in a dream world. With his affinity for conspiracy theories, President Reagan swallowed the Israeli line that the disorders were the work of outside agitators. Thus, if the PLO would only go away, peace would once more reign among the supposedly contented Gazans and West Bankers. Shultz, better informed, at least acknowledged that the riots were "essentially indigenous," although "there has also been interaction with outside forces."[27]

As the Arabs had anticipated, Shultz met nothing but opposition from the Israeli prime minister and his Likud colleagues. Shamir told him flatly that Israel would never give up its authority over the West Bank and Gaza. Moreover, the Palestinians would have to cease their revolt before Israel would even talk to them; otherwise it might appear that Israel was making concessions.

Meanwhile, Shultz had tentatively conceded the possible utility of an international conference, which, advocated by Foreign Minister Peres, was anathema to Shamir. Despite Peres's stipulation that the conference would meet only in opening and closing sessions and that those chairing the meeting would have no veto over private negotiations, Shamir would have none of it. He knew perfectly well that a stalemate would swiftly ensue and the United

States would then come under excruciating pressure to wring concessions from Israel. He also feared that an aborted conference would reveal, beyond a doubt, Israel's obstructionist tactics to a hostile world.

## A New Gift Offering

Having been brusquely rebuffed, Shultz rewarded Israel by giving it more F-15 and F-16 aircraft. That largesse may have been intended to cajole Shamir into cooperation, but its effect was to reward him for intransigence. Thus, when Shultz resumed his fruitless shuttle between Middle Eastern capitals on April 3–8, he seemed more masochist than statesman.

Shultz's new effort was directed at bilateral discussions between the Israelis and King Hussein of Jordan. Hussein, who had talked with Israel's leaders for years, was dubious, and Shamir proved him right. Shamir quickly dismissed Shultz's land-for-peace proposal by claiming that Israel had already complied with Resolution 242 by returning the Sinai to Egypt at Camp David; no further territorial concessions were necessary. Then, piqued by the Secretary's amiable persistence, Shamir said through one his aides, "He is wearing us down, how can we get him to go home?"[28]

The Secretary's disillusionment was complete when neither Israel nor AIPAC applauded his efforts, but instead savagely attacked him for meeting on March 26 with two Palestinian-born American citizens who were members of the Palestine National Council, though not of the PLO. Israel declared that Shultz had violated American law as well as the Kissinger memorandum. Any member of the Palestine National Council, they sweepingly declared, was ipso facto a member of the PLO.[29]

To make doubly sure that the PLO remained intransigent, Israel dispatched a small group of assassins to Tunis on April 16 to gun down the PLO military chief, Khalil al-Wazir (also known as Abu Jihad), who was coordinating the *Intifada* in the Occupied Areas. Abu Jihad's death was immediately attributed to the Israeli government, which, of course, denied it. That prevarication was exposed when an Israeli paper reported that Israel's ten-member inner cabinet had twice discussed this assassination and only Ezer Weizman had consistently opposed it.[30]

## Israeli Recalcitrance Is Again Rewarded

By now the Israeli government had discovered that Shultz's depleted self-respect permitted Israel to do what it pleased. America fully validated this assumption on April 21, 1988, when it signed another memorandum of understanding that officially made Israel a "major non-NATO ally" of the United States.

The memorandum codified the two preceding agreements with various informal working arrangements that had evolved during the Reagan administration. Most significantly, the pact had a term of five years and was renewable, thereby extending the fixed pattern of Israeli-American relations well beyond the Reagan administration. The purpose of the entire exercise, as Secretary Shultz declared, was to bind the United States and Israel so closely together that no future administration could loosen the relationship.[31]

Prime Minister Yitzhak Shamir was understandably ecstatic and declared the new arrangement his "legacy" to Israel. He signed it on April 21 with great fanfare in Jerusalem. By contrast, the Reagan administration signed it in Washington at a quiet White House ceremony, fearing that it might enhance Shamir's election prospects.[32] Even Reagan's advisers realized that this was not the time to dispense favors ostentatiously to Israel.

## Hussein's Royal Shock Treatment

On July 31, the administration was brought face to face with reality when the King of Jordan finally punctured the trial balloon that the press blithely referred to as the "Jordanian Option." The King conceded the primacy of the PLO in the West Bank and withdrew Jordan from any further responsibility for that territory. That gesture caught everyone by surprise, the PLO included.

Israel's American supporters developed differing hypotheses for his move, each one predicting the King's ultimate reentry in the negotiations on behalf of the Palestinians.[33] America's Middle East diplomacy ever since the Lausanne Conference had basically assumed that the Palestinians did not constitute a distinct people and that the King still represented them. Now that view became obsolete.

From Israel's viewpoint, the months following the King's announcement produced a series of ominous events.

First, the Iran-Iraq War came to a sudden end when an exhausted Iran agreed to a United Nations-sponsored truce.[34] The event freed President Saddam Hussein of Iraq to use his army for other purposes (which he did on August 2, 1990, when he invaded Kuwait).

Second, the November 1, 1989, election in Israel resulted in a six-seat gain by ultra-Orthodox religious parties that conditioned their support for a new government on the enactment of certain sabbatarian laws as well as a resolution defining "who is a Jew." This definition, which in effect stigmatized non-Orthodox Jews, had major implications for Israel's continued support by American Jewish organizations.[35]

Third, and most important, the Palestine National Council, meeting in Algiers on November 12–15, 1988, adopted a series of significant decisions. It formally recognized Israel's right to exist and accepted Resolutions 242 and 338. By implication, it thus accepted a two-state solution. Then, on November 15, the Council declared the formation of an independent Palestinian state.

In contrast to the rest of the world, neither the U.S. government nor Israel professed to detect any crucial significance in these statements. America's isolation was further emphasized when Yasser Arafat applied for a visa to appear as an invited guest before the United Nations General Assembly in New York. In refusing to grant the necessary waiver and visa, Secretary Shultz, on November 26, branded the PLO a terrorist organization.

Under the commitment given at the time the United Nations was established in New York, America could not legally refuse a visa unless it could prove Arafat a "security threat," which he was not. The General Assembly voted 153 to 2 (only Israel and the United States dissenting) for a resolution calling on America to rescind its decision. On December 1, Washington rejected that resolution and the Assembly voted 154 to 2 to remove the session temporarily to Geneva, outside the jurisdiction of the United States.

In his Assembly speech at Geneva on December 12 and his press conference the next day, Yasser Arafat restated the PLO position in accordance with the Kissinger memorandum and the 1985 U.S. law so explicitly that the absurdity of the United States' negative position became embarrassingly obvious. If America refused to take Arafat's yes for an answer, it would isolate itself from the rest of the world. If, on the other hand, it declared that the PLO had met the requirements, it risked the wrath of Israel and AIPAC at home. Ultimately, Shultz, at President Reagan's behest and with President-elect George Bush's concurrence, reluctantly declared the PLO in compliance and ordered the opening of talks at a limited level and on circumscribed topics.[36]

As soon as they could organize a government with a Likud premier and foreign minister, the Israelis started a campaign to force the United States to reconsider its decision. They claimed that the ongoing *Intifada* amounted to terrorism; therefore, the United States must break off the talks. They then contended that Arafat had breached his own declaration when splinter Palestinian groups, hostile to him, raided the Israelis in Lebanon. These specious arguments fell flat. Under international pressure, the United States refused to be lured into this trap. It was in that atmosphere that the Reagan administration came to a close.

## Enter the Bush Administration

During its first year, the Bush administration adopted a largely passive role. In time, however, public pressure coupled with Bush's friendship for King Hussein led the administration to urge Prime Minister Shamir to address the Palestinian issue. Responding to that pressure, Shamir came to Washington in early April 1989 with a proposed "plan." The White House imperiously asserted that the Shamir Plan was the sole basis for negotiations.

Shamir proposed that elections should be held in the West Bank and Gaza to choose local leaders to conduct the affairs of the area and negotiate regarding its future. This opened a Pandora's box of questions. Who would run in these elections? How much freedom of speech could the candidates enjoy? Would the Israelis be free to purge the lists of those whom they found objectionable? Would the 100,000 Arabs of East Jerusalem, including most of the West Bank's leadership, be qualified to participate? And if there were to be negotiations on these points, who was to represent the Palestinians?

Despite the Israeli claim that everything was open to negotiation, it soon developed that little could even be discussed. The Shamir government stipulated that the PLO not be represented at the talks; that only residents of the Occupied Areas would be permitted to negotiate or be elected to office; and that inhabitants of East Jerusalem would be excluded because their participation might cast questions over Israel's annexation of that area. Furthermore, Israel insisted on selecting the negotiators for the Palestinian side. It also specified that nothing but the modalities of the elections be on the table; that an independent Palestinian state and other such unpalatable topics could not be discussed; and, finally, that the United States should provide an ironclad written promise that it would support any Israeli position taken then or thereafter, and would walk out of the conference if Israel chose to do so.

By March 1990, much to Shamir's and Foreign Minister Arens's annoyance, the United States had lined up the Egyptians and a Palestinian delegation for a conference at Cairo based on Shamir's terms. But by now the Likud had lost interest. It constantly requested preconditions (labeled "clarifications") that would thwart a successful negotiation before the delegates ever arrived.

Faced with willful procrastination, the Labor alignment in the National Unity Government set a deadline for a definitive answer. Confronted by an ultimatum, Shamir fired Shimon Peres as finance minister; the other Labor ministers resigned; and the government fell on the first vote of no confidence in Israel's history. That event had two effects: It sank Shamir's initiative. It also led to the formation of an extreme right-wing Israeli government ultimately backed by sixty-six members of the Knesset, most of whom were opposed to even the paltry concessions Shamir had offered earlier.

## Other American-Israeli Arguments

At the end of July 1989, Israeli commandos crossed into Lebanon, where they kidnapped and brought to Israel a Shiite leader, Sheikh Obeid, and two companions, hoping to use them as bargaining chips for the release of three Israeli prisoners. In retaliation, the Shiite captors of Lieutenant Colonel William R. Higgins, a kidnapped United States officer attached to the UN peacekeeping force, reported that they had hanged their captive.

That news was greeted with a deluge of recriminations in the United States. Senator Robert Dole, the Republican minority leader, complained that Israel had been obligated to consult with the United States before seizing Obeid and thereby jeopardizing American lives. Israel's supporters then changed their original story and claimed that by seizing Sheikh Obeid the Israeli government was trying to secure the release of all American hostages held in Lebanon. But the Sheik still remains in Israel's hands even though all American captives have been released.

In early 1990, Senator Dole asserted that in order for the United States to find funds for Panama and Eastern Europe, it needed to reduce the aid distributed to the present foreign aid recipients, including Israel. That again triggered a storm of opposition.

## The Problem Caused by the Emigration of Soviet Jews

Jewish Americans had long urged the United States government to apply pressure on the Soviets to grant permission to Soviet Jews to emigrate.[37]

With the Gorbachev revolution, an increasing number of Soviet Jews were applying for visas to America under the American Refugee legislation. As a result, Shamir asked Shultz to close the borders to further Soviet Jewish migrants in order to deflect them to Israel. In refusing Shamir's request, Shultz had been supported by a leading Jewish American refugee organization which was not about to deny the right of choice to its Soviet charges. However, in 1989, AIPAC and other Jewish American organizations pressured Washington to impose a general quota under the Refugee Statute of forty thousand Soviet Jews a year, with an additional ten thousand a year for special cases. American spokesmen tried to explain this action away on the grounds that America could not afford the costs of resettlement and that many Jewish immigrants were not bona fide refugees, merely persons seeking increased economic opportunity.

Given the passionate attachment, the quota did not save the United States any money, for Israel immediately requested an American loan guarantee of $400 million to build housing for the immigrants. Since a number of the Soviet refugees were being settled in the West Bank and East Jerusalem, Bush required a letter from Prime Minister Shamir assuring him that Israel had no plan to build housing for Soviet Jews in the Occupied Territories. Nevertheless, the Israeli government's Housing Ministry, headed by General Sharon, has since issued a report recommending 2,100 new housing units for that purpose and plans for 10,000 more settlers in the Golan.

Israel made its objectives clear when Prime Minister Shamir in January 1991 declared that the Occupied Territories were needed for a "greater Israel" capable of holding all these people, and he reiterated this view later in early September while ordering speeded-up settlements. President Bush heated up the debate when he noted that the Occupied Territories included East Jerusalem.

Following the Iraq conquest of Kuwait in August 1990, President Bush organized a coalition backed by nine Arab states. To keep that coalition intact, it was essential that Israel not participate and that it maintain the lowest possible profile; otherwise support from the Arabs might evaporate. While taking that position, the United States was also proving decisively that it could move its armed forces into the Gulf without Israeli assistance.

This demonstration and the events that followed turned American-Israeli relations on their head. The traditional practice of nations is to reward allies for fighting on their side, but the United States now found itself under pressure to pay Israel for *refraining* from joining the fray. That undermined the whole concept behind the military cooperation agreements and destroyed one of Israel's major points of leverage—its claimed role as a strategic asset. America, it seemed, could protect its interests in the Middle East single-handed, whereas Israel had become, at best, an expensive nuisance.

By making a highly advertised gesture of accommodation to America—i.e., by agreeing not to overfly Jordan, send its bombers through the already overcrowded Iraqi air space, or drop troops in Iraq—Israel was paving the way for a claim against the United States for a total of $3 billion in damages from losses arising out of the war. Ultimately, it reduced that claim to $1 billion, then settled for $650 million with the U.S. proviso that no further funds would be requested until after September 30, 1991.

Earlier in the year, the United States had offered Patriot anti-missile missiles to Israel, which were scornfully rejected. Israel had insisted on waiting for a more highly developed model. Threatened by Iraq with SCUD missiles, Israel suddenly asked for the previously rejected missile defenses. Under these circumstances, the United States felt obligated to send batteries of Patriot missiles, and as Israel had no personnel trained to use them, it also sent American operators. That was an embarrassment to Israel, which had long proclaimed that it would never need American military personnel. The Patriot missiles proved only partly effective, and a few SCUD fragments did cause some minor damage.

## The Baker Shuttle—Part II

Once the cease-fire was in place, President Bush again turned his attention to the Arab-Israeli conflict. He had already told the General Assembly in October 1990 that an Iraqi pullout from Kuwait might provide the opportunity "to settle the conflicts that divide the Arabs from Israel." And on March 6, 1991, in a speech to Congress, he asserted that since peace between Israel and the Arabs would bring "real benefits to everyone," he would, at the conclusion of the Gulf War, "go forward with new vigor and determination" to try to "close the gap between Israel and the Arab states—and between Israelis and Palestinians." Peace between them, he asserted, must be

> grounded in United Nations Security Council Resolutions 242 and 338 and the principle of territory for peace. This principle must be elaborated

> to provide for Israel's security and recognition, and at the same time for legitimate Palestinian political rights. Anything else would fail the twin tests of fairness and security. The time has come to put an end to the Arab-Israeli conflict.

As with the Reagan 1982 declaration, the Bush administration's perception that a window of opportunity for an Arab-Israeli peace had been opened by Iraq's defeat turned out to be overly optimistic. Neither Syria nor Jordan had been defeated and neither was under any compulsion to change its policy. Indeed, Syria's plans to reduce Lebanon (outside that part occupied by Israel) to a quasi protectorate had been measurably improved by the ouster of General Michel Aoun as acting president, while its economic crisis had been relieved by $3 billion of Saudi subsidies. Syria could therefore wait.

The only Arabs urgently in need of peace were the Palestinians, particularly those in the Occupied Areas. But they, disarmed and weak, had no leverage with anyone, and nothing they could offer was likely to induce Israel to lift its heavy hand.

Learning nothing from Secretary Shultz's failures, the Bush administration made the double mistake of allowing itself to be enmeshed in procedural trivia and of basing its peace efforts on a plan devised by Israel before America consulted any Arab state other than Egypt. After Secretary James Baker III's three visits to the Middle East in March through April of 1991, it became apparent that the peace initiative was gradually being whittled down to nothing.

The Israelis insisted that the peace discussions not be under UN auspices, that the United Nations, the European Community, and other outsiders be granted observer status only, and that in order to gain even that small privilege, they would have to agree with Israel's interpretation of 242 as not requiring the return of any more land. Moreover, Israel required that the conference should disband immediately after an opening plenary session into a series of bilateral negotiations between Israel and each of its neighbors and that the conference might not be reconvened.

As could have been predicted, the Syrians announced that they had no intention of turning up at any conference except under UN auspices, and unless Resolution 242 was, in fact, the basis of the settlement. They wanted the United States to guarantee the return of their territory as stated by the resolution and not Israel's unauthorized alteration of it.[38]

Saudi Arabia and the Gulf states, foreseeing the inevitable failure of the whole operation, wished to be left out of the preliminary negotiations until something had been achieved with the states immediately bordering on Israel. That would have meant confining the initial discussion to Lebanon, Syria, Jordan, and a Palestinian delegation.

Israel rejected the President's June 1991 letter asking that it waive some of its requirements, and instead insisted on America granting it the power to veto any member of the Palestinian delegation, which effectively reduced the prospect of participation by representative Palestinians. To add to the confusion, the Syrians, after seeking clarifications, belatedly accepted President Bush's invitation to a conference. They did so with the unconcealed intention of forcing the United States to maintain the principles enunciated at the time of the Kuwait invasion or else lose its position in the Arab world.

Finally, the administration, on the one hand, and Israel and its American supporters on the other, added another source of friction between the two countries. Israel asked for $10 billion of loan guarantees over a five-year period (fiscal years 1992–96) to build housing for Soviet Jews in Israel. In a reprise of the earlier battle over the $400 million loan guarantee, the Bush administration wanted positive assurances that none of this money would be spent on settlements in the Occupied Territories. Israel, for its part, insisted that the question of the loan guarantees must be completely divorced from the settlements problem and Israel's cooperation in the matter of peace negotiations.

Meanwhile, congressmen, even those strongly supportive of Israel, worried about the size of the loan guarantee because it highlighted the high levels of aid to Israel in an era of budgetary stringency. Many middle-class Americans could not afford to buy their own homes. If, as was suspected, Israel came back with demands for up to $40 billion in guarantees to build housing for Soviet Jews, public opposition could be fierce and relentless.

To finesse this question, the Bush administration, after consultation with the congressional leaders (whose assent it sought), announced that the loan guarantee question was to be put off until after January 1, 1992. Since that date fell after the scheduled start of peace negotiations in October 1991, it became clear that the Bush administration, without saying so, was positioning itself to hold up this request should Israel prove uncooperative regarding its attendance at peace talks.

We shall bring this story down to date in Chapter 15.

# PART II

CHAPTER EIGHT

# Homefront Israel—Fragmented and Paralyzed

A PERSISTENT ARGUMENT in support of the passionate attachment is that Israel is the only authentic democracy in the Middle East, and thus warrants massive American encouragement. By regional standards, the contention has merit. Compared with the Arabs' despotic republics or absolute monarchies (with the evolving exception of Jordan), Israel's government generally offers far more freedom.

Democracy has no precise definition; it merely means "rule by the people." Israel largely satisfies the original, limited definition in that its government is established by free elections. But the pertinent question is whether Israel's political system resembles that of a modern Western democracy—a concept that has been broadened to include ideas of social, economic, and political equality or justice.

Most Americans think of Israel's government as vaguely resembling their own. Yet Israel has no written constitution because the founders held fiercely conflicting views on religious matters, personal rights, and the status of the Arabs; thus they could not agree on any common set of principles with rights enforceable in the courts.[1] Having no written constitution, Israel also has no Bill of Rights but only readily amendable fundamental laws, augmented by regulations, some of which were promulgated by the British during a time of social and military crisis (1933–48). As there is no presidential veto and only a limited provision for judicial review, its parliament, the Knesset, functions practically unchecked.

The lack of a written constitution does not, of course, preclude a democracy, as the United Kingdom demonstrates. But the unwritten British constitution (consisting of precedents accumulated over a millennium) is reinforced by a homogenous society, conditioned by common values.

Israel, on the other hand, was founded by peoples of diverse national origins, many of whom had never experienced the blessings of democracy, and during the whole of its existence as a nation it has had to function as a beleaguered garrison state. The inevitable effect has been to aggrandize the power and prestige of its military.

The sharp divisions in Israel's politics largely reflect deeper cleavages in its society: rivalry between its Ashkenazi (European) and Sephardic (African and Oriental) components; between theocratic and secular elements; between Israeli Jews and Israeli Arabs; and between the military and civilian authorities. These differences have so fragmented the political life of Israel as to render it almost ungovernable.

## The Rhythm of Immigration

The population of today's Israel reflects successive waves in the ingathering of Jews.

Before 1882, most of the Palestinian Jews were Sephardic people from the Middle East and the Iberian Peninsula. The early 1880s saw the arrival of principally European Ashkenazi Jews. Over the next fifty years, refugees, primarily from the Russian Empire, increased to the point where the Jewish population of Palestine had become overwhelmingly European.

By 1933, the old Sephardic-Oriental core had been reduced to only one fifth of the total Jewish population. After World War II (1939–45), the Nazi atrocities against European Jews further altered the population profile in favor of the Ashkenazis.

This imbalance equation lasted only briefly. With the creation of the State of Israel in 1948, several Arab states of the Middle East and North Africa expelled their local Jewish populations. The resulting migrations of Jews from Iraq, Syria, North Yemen, and Egypt not only augmented Israel's population but by the 1970s had created a majority of Oriental Jews.

## A Dust of Peoples

The problem of building a nation of Jews with such disparate backgrounds was vividly described by Ben-Gurion as follows:

> There are 55 nations of origin . . . and you have no concept of how great the distances are and how considerable the differences between these national groups. The great majority of our nation is not yet Jewish, but

> human dust, bereft of a single language, without tradition, without roots, without a bond to national life, without the customs of independent society.[2]

And he described the challenge facing the new state: "We must mend the rifts of the Diaspora and form a united nation [and] crystallize this dust of man collected together from all ends of the earth into one national entity."[3]

Although Ben-Gurion succeeded in forming that entity, he could not prevent the ethnic and religious divisions that today render Israel a badly splintered society. Without question, the problem of creating a true melting pot in Israel was far more difficult than in the United States.[4] Mass immigration to America did not occur until the 1880s, nearly a century after independence, by which time the United States had developed its own distinct brand of British-based culture. Massive migration to Israel began immediately after its founding, which meant that the disparate peoples thus brought together shared little but a common religion.

They were not even of the same race.[5] The origins of most Ashkenazi Jews trace back to the Byzantine ruler Leo III, who banished some Jewish rabbis to southern Russia. They providentially arrived just when the Turkic Khan of the Khazars was under pressure to choose between Orthodox Christianity and Islam. To evade a painful choice, he compelled his predominantly Slavonic subjects to convert to Judaism, and it is their descendants, thus converted, who now represent a large part of the world's Jewish population.

Contrary to Nazi myth and even to early Zionist assumptions, the current Polish and Russian Jewish communities have little genetic connection with the ancient Hebrews. Since 1948 the Israeli mix has become ever more complex and diversified, the Falashas of Ethiopia being the latest of many new Jewish immigrants.[6]

## Division Between Ashkenazis and Sephardim

The Ashkenazi and the Oriental Jews (Sephardim) soon appeared as the major elements of division. The Ashkenazis came equipped with Western educations and sophistication. The Oriental Jews from the Middle East and the Maghreb brought to Israel little but their families, their Arab customs, and an abiding hatred for the Arabs who had treated them shabbily.[7]

Conditioned by widely different cultures, the new migrants did not fit easily into an Israel dominated by Ashkenazis, who received preferential treatment in housing, jobs, and education. The Ashkenazi establishment treated the Oriental Jews as a lesser breed, which led the Orientals in turn to disdain everything the Labor Party stood for; Menachem Begin's Likud seemed to them more sympathetic and responsive to their views.

Because Ashkenazi immigration dried up after 1948, Israel's post-independence influx soon consisted predominately of Oriental Jews. Large numbers of Europe's Ashkenazi Jews had been exterminated in the Holocaust; those who had escaped the gas chambers were either Western Europeans who, like the American Jews, saw no need to leave their home countries, or Jews resident in the Soviet Union, who could not leave. These factors resulted in Israel again becoming disproportionately Sephardic. Thus, from 1952 to 1954, the Sephardim, who then constituted only 14 percent of world Jewry,[8] amounted to over 60 percent of Israel's immigrants. This ratio held through the mid-1980s. Because the Oriental Jews possessed fewer marketable skills, they had less temptation or opportunity to emigrate to Western capitals.[9]

In Israel's early years, despite an urgent need for workers, a quota was placed on the immigration of Moroccan Jews. Ostensibly justified by public health concerns, the quota in fact conformed to a popular racist stereotype of Moroccan Jews as exhibiting "chronic laziness and hatred of work."[10]

David Ben-Gurion observed that they "had no education. Their customs are those of Arabs . . . The Moroccan Jews took a lot from the Moroccan Arabs. The culture of Morocco I would not like to have here. And I don't see what contribution Persians [Iranian Jews] have to make." He did not want to see Diaspora Jewish values corrupted by the spirit of the Levant.[11]

Most recently, Israel has received a massive influx of nearly 500,000 Soviet Jews; the total may reach over 1.25 million by 1996. One might think that the balance would swing back once more in favor of the Ashkenazis and the Labor alignment. But the newcomers share the Russian prejudice against Moslem peoples and thus, instead of being potential recruits for the Israeli Labor alignment, they may well be more likely to support the doctrines of Likud and the parties of the right.

Since the Oriental Jews generally have larger families than the Ashkenazis,[12] the effect of their migration has been to orientalize the population. Moreover, exposure to Israel's freer ways has made the Oriental Jews increasingly assertive. Now that the original immigrants' numerous children have grown to voting age, they have not only altered the quality of Israeli politics but have begun, ironically, to undermine the viability of the Israeli democratic system.

The country is now uncomfortably split between two factions: the old Ashkenazi Labor alignment and a new Oriental-Sephardic group that instinctively rallies around the Likud banner. Today, the split is so even that the country is politically deadlocked.

From 1984 to 1990, neither Labor nor Likud was able to command even a precarious majority or form a government without the other. Then Likud, by taking in heretofore ostracized right-wing parties, assembled a 66-vote majority (out of a total number of 120) whose long-range goal was to annex the Occupied Areas and expel their Arab inhabitants.

For years, the Ashkenazis remained in almost complete control of Israeli politics. Because the Sephardim tended to be less well educated, the Ashkenazi treated them as second-class citizens. And since the proportion of Ashkenazis receiving more than twelve years of education is nearly three times that of the Sephardim (roughly 35 percent to 13 percent),[13] Ashkenazis have consistently filled the universities. Not only were Oriental Jews largely confined to blue-collar, nonmanagerial posts, but their family income was only 80 percent of the Ashkenazim. Of Israel's poorest residents, 90 percent were Orientals.[14] In 1984 some 42 percent of employed Ashkenazim were managers, academics, scientists, or professionals, compared with only 18 percent of Sephardim.[15] That disparity was intensified by the fact that Ashkenazis migrated to the cities, leaving Sephardim in less economically developed rural areas.[16]

The 1967 War significantly altered the occupational stratification of Israel by bringing thousands of Arabs in the newly occupied areas into the Israeli work force to perform the menial tasks of Israel's economy. That shift, for example, enabled young Sephardic women to move up to be bank tellers, leaving the char tasks to *Gastarbeiters* (Palestinians from the Occupied Areas). When the 1984 economic crisis increased Israeli unemployment, thousands of Jews refused manual work, claiming "those are jobs for Arabs."[17]

One can easily understand, therefore, why the Sephardim passionately oppose Israel's relinquishing control of the West Bank. Palestinian cheap labor is necessary for their own upward mobility. They can also enjoy the psychological satisfaction of looking down on the Arabs in compensation for their own treatment at the hands of the Ashkenazis. The prominent Israeli novelist Amos Oz records an Oriental Jew discussing the exchange of the Occupied Territories for peace:

> What did they bring my parents to Israel for? . . . You didn't have Arabs then, so you needed our parents to do your cleaning and be your servants and your laborers. . . . If they give back the territories, the Arabs will stop coming to work, and then and there you'll put us back into the dead-end jobs like before.[18]

The class warfare between the Ashkenazis and Sephardim has led not only to violence in the streets[19] but to disagreement over the Occupied Territories. Most Ashkenazis fear that the Jewish character of the state will be undermined by too many Arabs. The solution favored by most in that group is to return just enough territory to get rid of most of the Arabs while populating the residue with more and more Jews. This position reinforces the racist attitudes toward the Arabs held by some Israeli Jews.

The Sephardim have fallen under the influence of Likud and the extreme right. Those parties claim all the Occupied Areas as Israel's divinely ordained heritage; the Arabs not needed for menial labor should be deported. Because of the growing Oriental character of the Israeli electorate, this view is finding increasing support in the Knesset.

Taken together, these factors are turning Israel toward religious conservatism, enhanced right-wing political influence, extremist support for Israel's territorial expansion, and a marked retreat from the traditional social-democratic ideology of Zionism. No wonder the Oriental Jews have become the major power base of the Likud Party (over 60 percent vote for Likud).[20] They had grown up in traditionally authoritarian countries and had had no experience whatever with democracy or democratic forms. The leaders of the Likud—Begin, Shamir, and Sharon—met the standards to which their followers had been conditioned; they were fanatical, ruthless, and xenophobic. Hence the chant of their followers, hailing first Begin and then Sharon as "King of Israel."

## Implications of the Likud Electoral Victory in 1977

After its near defeat in 1973, the Labor Party, which commands about 60 percent of the Ashkenazi vote, began to exhibit both fatigue and corruption—the familiar affliction of a party too long in power. Inevitably, Begin's Likud Party took over.

The profound, though not immediately visible, impact of shifting from Labor to Likud was an explosion of latent racist hatred for the Arabs. Except for the Moroccan Jews, who cherished fond memories of Mohammed V and Hassan II,[21] the Oriental Jews cordially detest the Arabs. As an Israeli sociologist explains: "By expressing hostility to Arabs, an Oriental attempts to rid himself of the 'inferior' Arab elements in his own identity and to adopt the position congenial to the European group which he desires to emulate."[22] Over the next few years ethnic conflict is likely to intensify.[23]

## The Second Source of Dissension—The Trend Toward Theocracy

As often happens, political groups like the Likud that represent the economically disadvantaged tend to be attracted by religious fundamentalism. That affinity has intensified the ingrained rivalry between observant and nonobservant Jews. Most of the Zionists who founded the State of Israel were religiously lukewarm, and today all but a diminishing minority of Israelis still maintain a largely secular attitude toward society and government.

That secular attitude has led to clashes with the stricter sects of Israel's religious community, who differ widely over the propriety of participation in Israel's political affairs. The most idiosyncratic, ultra-conservative sects totally deny the legitimacy of the Israeli state and shun the political process entirely. They believe that before founding a Jewish state Jews have to await the coming of the Messiah, because only under his aegis can a Jewish community be lawfully reestablished in Israel.[24]

By contrast, the nationalist National Religious Party (Mafdal) sees the reestablishment of a Jewish Israel as a precondition to the anticipated Messianic appearance.

Between these conflicting positions are Agudat Israel, Poalei Aguda, and the Sephardic Shas parties. Although they also question the legitimacy of a Jewish state established before the Messiah's arrival, they do participate in politics, but almost exclusively to promote religiously oriented policies. Because these parties represent the swing elements in forming any but grand coalition governments, their members are given cabinet posts and key Knesset committee chairmanships.[25] The 1988 elections greatly augmented their political clout.

## Religious Meddling in Private and Public Affairs

Since the early days of statehood, the Orthodox Jews have forced the government to walk a fine line so as, in the words of Ben-Gurion, to "avoid the division of the House of Israel into two parts."[26] In the predominantly secular communities, local authorities ignore Orthodox strictures, acknowledging the widespread preference for laxer practices; but where strictly Orthodox populations are concentrated, the local authorities not infrequently take militant measures to impose strict doctrines and practices on all.

Israel's ultra-Orthodox Jews strictly follow the *Halakah,* the extensive body of traditional Jewish law. The ultra-Orthodox abuse those whom they regard as immodestly dressed, stone intruding cars and block streets on the Sabbath, harass pathologists for conducting autopsies, violently deny the right of Christian missionaries to seek converts among the Jewish population, harass and persecute non-Orthodox rabbis, shield girls from military service, and burn shops selling sex aids. They also ban movies and sporting events on the Sabbath; they demand military service exemptions for religious school students and deny equal religious or social status to women. Violent physical attacks against deviants from Orthodox Judaism are quite common in Israel.[27]

Rabbinical meddling in the private affairs of Israeli citizens is accepted as a norm. Marriage matters are a rabbinical prerogative, and Orthodox rabbis seek to reduce the role and rights of women in a manner that Western societies would find intolerable.

Consider the following cases:

—If a man indulges in a liaison with another woman, his children by that woman are considered legitimate. But, if the man's separated wife takes a lover and has a family, her children are not only illegitimate but are ineligible to marry any Jew except one similarly situated.[28]

—If rabbinical courts refuse to force a wayward husband to give his wife a divorce, she cannot bring her spouse before the civil courts because

> the Israeli Supreme Court has ruled that only the rabbinical courts have jurisdiction over marriages.[29]

The enforced inferiority of women manifests itself even in funeral observances. In a 1987 incident, female mourners (including relatives of the deceased) were blocked from the grave site by a wall of ultra-Orthodox men; later, Ashkenazi Chief Rabbi Yitzhak David Grossman declared that the *Zohar* (a medieval book of Jewish mysticism) decreed that women mingling with men at funerals can bring disaster on the Jewish people. In proof he cited a series of recent village misfortunes, including a bus accident on a Saturday which the Orthodox attributed to God's displeasure over the desecration of the Sabbath. Ultra-Orthodox Jews also claimed that Israeli casualties in Lebanon were a divine retribution for the alleged "licentiousness" of the Israeli female soldiers.[30]

The ultra-Orthodox invariably object to advertisements showing young women modeling skimpy bathing suits. When bikini ads appeared on bus stop billboards in 1985, fanatics set fire to them. In the end, the advertisements were withdrawn.[31]

Not only do the ultra-Orthodox observe the Sabbath strictly, they demand that others do likewise. Since Orthodox doctrine prohibits riding in vehicles on the Sabbath, the Orthodox insist that chains be strung across the roads in their district to prevent access to vehicles. When their strictures are transgressed, they riot and stone the municipal buses and those riding in them. Sabbatarianism has reached a point where the national airline, El Al, no longer flies on the Sabbath.[32]

More recently, Orthodox Jews in Israel have prohibited Reform or Conservative Jewish groups from conducting services in regular synagogues. The official government position is that Orthodox Judaism is the sole authentic form of that faith. Moreover, Sephardim Chief Rabbi Itzak Nissim has declared that only non-Jewish minorities are entitled to religious freedom; all Jews must adhere to the official line, dictated by the chief rabbis.[33]

Intolerance for proselytizing was shown when, in 1987, the Mormon Church, long a staunch supporter of Israel, proposed to open a study center of Brigham Young University on Mount Scopus. When ninety-six professors published an advertisement containing a letter supporting legislation to block the Mormon project, Abba Eban, former Israeli foreign minister, responded with ridicule in *The Jerusalem Post:*

> If there were a prize for the most ludicrous document ever published since the invention of writing, this one would be a hopeful candidate for the award . . . the defeat of self-confidence by undisciplined panic reechoes in every word and letter of this meanminded text. . . .
>
> How will Moses, Isaiah, the Psalmist and the Rambam compete in Jewish pride and emotion with Israel's good friend, former US Secretary of Agriculture Ezra Taft Benson, whose shrine in Salt Lake City, Utah will now

> become the home of prophecy for the masses of Jewish converted? The learned will give out their cry, *"Benson ad portas!,"* and the sheer silliness of it all invites parody and justifies a tear for the departing glory of Israeli scholarship. . . .[34]

After pointing out two fallacies in the advertisement—first, the authors' love of ghettolike isolation, and second, their belief that the average Jew so lacks attachment to Judaism that he cannot resist missionary arguments—Eban concluded:

> The issue is not Mormon theology, but the principle of free exercise of conscience in a democratic society. . . .
> If Mormonism is to be feared because of its alleged strong capacity for successful conversion(!), should we not equally suppress the institutions of orthodox Christianity and Islam which, with all respect for the Latter Day Saints, have shown a far greater power in this field? . . .[35]

In other religious developments, *The Jerusalem Post* on February 28, 1987, complained that the Yeshiva students (47,000, of whom 17,000 claim military exemption) increase the military burden of the nonreligious. As Ya'acov Morris put it:

> What contribution have all these Yeshavot made to the advancement of creative Judaism? . . . With their mechanical memorizing of hallowed texts, their dialectical acrobatics around the meaning of meanings, their worship of the letter of the Law, they contribute nothing to the building or defense of Israel; they contribute less to its spiritual, ethical or moral present or future.[36]

The religious parties have raised embarrassing questions among the American Diaspora, on whose support Israel depends. Conflict became clear in 1988 when religious party leaders insisted on amending the Law of Return before joining any new coalition. The religious parties wanted to limit the Jews entitled to benefit from that law solely to individuals who had a Jewish mother or had been converted by an Orthodox rabbi.[37] Since 80 percent of American Jews belong to either Conservative or Reformed congregations, that proposal insulted and outraged the American Diaspora.[38]

The most fiercely committed religious element in Israeli politics is the Gush Emunim (Bloc of the Faithful), which represents a powerful and growing form of Jewish fundamentalism. It seeks to impose its own vision of the Jewish state and, according to Professor Ian S. Lustick, "*Kulturkampf* is not too strong a word for the struggle that is now underway. Its outcome will have profound implications for Israel's future and for the evolving relationship between Israel and its superpower partner, the United States."[39]

Gush Emunim, which has indoctrinated the Likud with its "own vision of authentic Zionism," is an umbrella organization. It includes more than ten thousand devoted activists, and it demonstrated its political potency when it helped unseat the Labor government in 1977.

It demands that Jewish sovereignty be reimposed on all those territories once ruled by King David; that authentic Jewish "theocratic despotism" replace nonscriptural Western democracy; and that a third Temple be built to implement the Messianic redemption. The fact that this would involve seizing most of Lebanon, Syria, and Jordan, not to mention demolishing the Moslem holy places, does not concern them. They expect and wish war with their Arab neighbors.

Although Gush Emunim is busy recruiting new members for Israel's largest religious youth movement, Bnei Akiva, from among recent immigrants and middle-class Israelis, its membership is largely concentrated in West Bank, Gaza Strip, and Golan Heights settlements. Officially nonpartisan, it enjoyed until March 1990 the active support of half a dozen cabinet ministers and 35 percent of the Knesset, representing Jews scattered among five political parties.

What differentiates Gush Emunim from the secular Zionism of Theodor Herzl is the repudiation of Herzl's view that "the Jewish nation is a normal nation and ought to be treated as such by the so-called international community."[40] The Gush Emunim view of authentic Zionism, as explained by Lustick, holds, on the contrary, that "Jews are not, and cannot be a normal people. The eternal uniqueness of the Jews is the result of the Covenant made between God and the Jewish people at Mount Sinai. . . . "[41]

Lustick explains the movement's view as follows:

> . . . The implication is that the transcendent imperatives for Jews effectively nullify moral laws that bind the behavior of normal nations. Rabbi Shlomo Aviner, one of Gush Emunim's most prolific ideologues, argues that the divine commandments to the Jewish people "transcend the human notions of national rights." He explains that while God requires other nations to abide by abstract codes of justice and righteousness, such laws do not apply to Jews.[42]

Rabbi Aviner's position, of course, is a modern version of antinomianism, the belief that the truly sanctified are above either human or divinely ordained law.[43]

Fundamentalists, Lustick continues, cannot acknowledge "any real tie between the Palestinians, or any group other than Jews, and the Land of Israel." In Lustick's assessment, Jewish fundamentalism

> remains ideologically the single most coherent and vigorous political force in Israel. Its influence is reflected . . . in Israeli opinion polls. In the late 1960s the vast majority of Israeli Jews regarded Fundamentalists' ultranationalist and religious beliefs and political programs as bizarre extremism. Now, however, some 20 percent of Israeli Jews embrace them.

> Another 10 to 15 percent consider these policies and opinions acceptable, even if they do not fully agree with them. Another 10 to 15 percent firmly back the key Gush demand that no territorial concessions be made in the West Bank and Gaza Strip.[44]

Today, there are 100,000 Gush supporters in the Occupied Areas, and a million backers in Israel as a whole. Because they are both armed and fanatical, this group provides a formidable impediment to the exchange of territory for peace.

## Division Between Arabs and Jews

As late as 1917, over 90 percent of the population of Palestine was still Arab; today, Israeli Arabs are a mere one seventh of the population of Israel proper.[45]

There are Arab majorities in parts of the Negev, "the Triangle" (the area around Umm el-Fahm), and in Galilee where Israel's Arab citizens are heavily concentrated. To overcome an adverse three-to-one Arab/Jew ratio in Galilee, the Israeli government mounted a prodigious effort to seize lands and settle Jews there, until in 1985 Jews finally became a majority.[46] But that did not last, for by 1989 the Arabs had again outnumbered the Jews. The Likud mayor of Nahariya on the coast bans Arabs from taking up residence; he fears an Arab majority in his city.[47]

This racial and nationality rift touches every aspect of both Arab and Jewish life. In a 1980 poll, Israeli Arabs were asked whether they could be equal citizens in, and identify themselves with, the Jewish state; 70 percent replied, "No" or "Doubtful."[48] Asked what produced a sense of identity, 42 percent cited nationality, and only 30 percent religion.[49] In the same 1980 poll, 76 percent of Israeli Jews said they would refuse to work for an Arab superior; only 20 percent would accept an Arab as a neighbor.[50] Racist attitudes toward the Arabs on the part of many Jewish Israelis have compelled the government and private groups to sponsor educational programs designed to promote communal harmony and eradicate Arab stereotyping. Unfortunately, these efforts are hindered by a variety of government policies.

## Discrimination Against Israeli Arabs

Arab unhappiness with their treatment finds its causes in the official and unofficial conduct meted out to them by the Jewish majority.

Land tenure in Israel discriminates heavily against non-Jews. In 1990, only 7 percent of the land was owned by the Arabs, whereas they represent over 15 percent of the population.

The 93 percent of the land not owned by the Arabs is held by the state or the Jewish Land Trust. The Trust, while nominally an independent body, is, under the fundamental laws enacted in 1948, closely connected with the government. Trust land is to be used solely for the benefit of the Jews. Only recently, when the last Arab Bedouins were settled in the Negev, a small amount of Trust land was made available to them, but on very restrictive terms. The Arabs are thus deprived of any independent existence as farmers and must depend on Jewish employers.[51]

## Violations of Due Process of Law

To Americans, conditioned to the adversarial practices of Anglo-American law, it seems remarkable that defendants in Israel have no right to confront their accusers in open court, or to be advised of the exact nature of any charges against them. When a Palestinian named Akram Haniyeh, who was the editor of the East Jerusalem *A Sha'ab* newspaper, was deported from Israel, he accepted deportation in lieu of lengthy imprisonment because the judges refused to give his attorney an opportunity to view the allegedly secret material offered in evidence against him. The justification for this practice is that furnishing such evidence would expose the agents of the Shin Bet (Israel's equivalent of the FBI) and so damage "state security."

The Israeli intelligence agency, Shin Bet, often violates due process. In 1980, it charged Lieutenant Izet Nafsu, a member of Israel's tiny (3,000) Circasian minority, with passing information to a pro-Syrian Palestinian guerrilla and transferring weapons from southern Lebanon to the West Bank. Nafsu protested his innocence. He claimed that he had been deprived of sleep for days, forced to stand for hours out in the cold, subjected to freezing showers, stripped, spat upon, thrown to the floor, and pulled around by his hair, while Shin Bet agents threatened to arrest his mother and his wife, and strip them naked in public if he did not confess. He was charged with and convicted of treason, demoted as an officer, and sentenced to eighteen years imprisonment.

In 1986, a change in the law allowed Nafsu to appeal to the Israeli Supreme Court. That tribunal heard military Judge Advocate General Brigadier Amnon Nevo admit that the Shin Bet had employed illegal interrogation methods, had systematically lied during earlier court proceedings, and had destroyed most of the transcript of Nafsu's interrogation to conceal their wrongdoing. The court ordered the prisoner released and instructed the Attorney General to take "decisive measures to uproot such phenomena."[52]

Instead of profiting from the court's decision in the Nafsu case, the government presented draft legislation to legalize the Shin Bet interrogation techniques. The proposed law was dropped after the second reading only after the Attorney General had announced that he was promulgating new rules permitting the Shin Bet to use techniques generally classified as torture, and declared that the evidence secured by these means would be legally admissible in court. Thus, on the bicentennial of the abolition of torture in judicial proceedings in Spain (the last Western nation to take this step), Israel was placed in the anomalous position of reinstating torture as a respectable part of the judicial process. Not even the 1930s regimes in the Soviet Union, Germany, or Italy were so brazen as formally to legalize such practices, however much they might use them.

Since the Shin Bet has claimed that it has never adhered to the so-called "Judges Rules," which regulate permissible interrogation methods, and admitted that its operatives had consistently committed perjury in court proceedings aimed at establishing the admissibility of evidence, the new regulations will doubtless be exceeded. After all, they were primarily designed to avert criminal proceedings against Nafsu's Shin Bet interrogators.[53]

These revelations are not a surprise. Although between 1948 and 1970 Shin Bet has been accused of murdering seventeen Arabs, only two of the deaths resulted in disciplinary actions against Shin Bet personnel. One man survived an interrogation that included a severe beating and two broken ribs; his testimony led to the dismissal of the Shin Bet chief.

If a prisoner dies in custody, relatives cannot discover whether the officially listed cause of death is correct; it is routinely declared a matter of "state security." Relatives are not allowed to attend the court of inquiry. Nor, to preclude a private autopsy, is the body returned to the family. Such practices prompt the suspicion that reported deaths from "disease" and "suicide" are false, and that it is the Shin Bet agents, not state security, that are protected against public exposure.[54]

## Limitations Placed on Freedom of the Press

While Israel's press is the freest in the Middle East, it must tread warily; the Israeli authorities can and do take arbitrary action against the fourth estate when it suits them.

Such a state of affairs arose after three Palestinians hijacked Bus 300 on April 13, 1984. While Israel professes not to have a death penalty, Shin Bet executed two guerrillas without trial after taking them prisoner on the bus. When the Attorney General proposed a formal investigation of the affair, he was dismissed from office, and, prodded by the coalition government, the president of Israel hurriedly granted pardons to thirteen unnamed persons.[55]

The press fared comparatively better than the guerrillas. On the night that the Israelis aboard Bus 300 were rescued, a newspaper photographer and reporter from *Hadashot* (a sister publication of *Ha'aretz,* the prominent Israeli newspaper) were present at the scene. They photographed Defense Minister Moshe Arens with the bus in the background and also Shin Bet agents leading away the guerrillas, both of whom were obviously unhurt. They also eluded attempts by Israeli soldiers to seize their tapes and film.

The next day, the Defense Ministry announced that all the guerrillas had been killed when the bus was stormed. In answering complaints that Defense Minister Arens had mishandled the whole episode, a Ministry spokesman declared categorically that Arens had not been present.

Responding to this disinformation, *Hadashot* published its photographs the following day along with the text of an on-the-scene interview tape with Arens. Annoyed and embarrassed, Arens closed the paper on charges of violating state security (which meant exposing him as a liar) and shoved the two newspapermen into jail. Following a hue and cry from the press, and much to the minister's unfeigned regret, the reporters were grudgingly released. But the newspaper remained closed for six weeks.[56]

## Arab-Jewish Relations in Israel

The record of communal conflict between Arab and Jewish Israeli citizens makes Arab wariness understandable. As a weak minority, the Arabs have been subjected to highly discriminatory legislation and hostile administrative actions. They feel unwelcome in the country. Charges of disloyalty by the Jewish majority do nothing to reconcile them, even when, like the Druse, their devotion to the state is unquestioned.

Both Arabs and Israelis feel themselves to be embattled minorities—both are right: Israeli Arabs feel persecuted by Israel's Jews; the Jews feel threatened by the Arab's Middle East majority.[57] Each group automatically adopts paranoiac, defensive, confrontational attitudes that fuel the other's instinctive mistrust. No one seems able or willing to break out of this destructive cycle.

Until the influx of Soviet Jews in 1989, demography increased this tension. Before the Soviet influx, Israel's Bureau of Statistics predicted that the percentage of non-Jewish Israeli citizens would continue to rise, slowly, to nearly 25 percent by the year 2005;[58] the statistics would be even more dramatic were Israel to incorporate the 1.75 million Palestinians in the West Bank and Gaza Strip—a possibility that causes consternation in Israel, particularly in government circles.[59] Now the Soviet immigrants have largely—though perhaps only momentarily—relieved the anxiety of an Arab majority.

## The Political Future of Israeli Arabs

Historically, three quarters of Israel's non-Jews have voted in national elections.[60] Although that is an impressive record by American standards, Israeli Jews regard it with misgiving. In the 1984 elections, Arabs cast fully 10 percent of the vote. Of this, 60 percent went to far-left parties outside the political mainstream.[61] Some Arabs voted for Labor, though in 1988 that figure had dropped to 30 percent, largely because of Rabin's *Intifada* policies.[62] In the 1989 local elections, Arab participation exceeded 85 percent;

their vote went primarily to Moslem fundamentalist tickets.[63] Jewish hostility and neglect is steadily radicalizing the Israeli Arabs.

If the Arabs were convinced that the Israeli government would not intervene (as in the past), they could form a party of their own, which might well command twelve to fifteen seats in the Knesset—thus giving them the balance of power. Yet thoughtful Arabs fear that, confronted by such an unwanted political threat, the Jews might, by a simple Knesset majority, strip them of their political rights. The growing Jewish support for schemes to disenfranchise the Arabs, coupled with the growth of a Sephardic majority friendly to authoritarian methods, will further erode Israel's democratic system.[64]

Obviously the recent influx of Soviet Jews has injected a new wild card into all voting projections. If, as now suspected, many of them side with the Likud, it could materially accentuate the anti-democratic trends.

## The Prognosis of Political Paralysis

In recent years there has been a growing sense of decline and decay within Israel. This was summed up by the former chief of Israel Army Intelligence, General Yehoshafat Harkabi, when he noted:

> In recent years Israel has experienced massive decline: a worsening of the public mood, the vulgarization of political thought and language, a degeneration of norms of public conduct, permissiveness in state affairs, demagoguery—the good of the country shunted aside in pursuit of short-term party gains—the domination of mediocrity, the proliferation of falsehoods and rampant deception of the people by their rulers, a magnification of domestic tensions. The responsibility for this decline belongs to a great extent to the Likud government.[65]

Israel appears to have lost its national sense of purpose. The social democrats of Zionist Israel disseminated abroad the image of a country that never existed. They pictured a democracy working toward a Utopian goal: the establishment of a secular community of justice and social order.[66] They sought to cast off the stereotype of the Diaspora Jew—a sickly, urban, non-land-owning, downtrodden exile—and to establish in its place a new, proud, land-owning Hebrew Israeli, clear-eyed, open-minded, and self-assured.[67]

According to Knesset member Amnon Rubenstein, the original Zionist goal was to create "a home and not a temple, a secular nation and not a sacred tribe, a good neighbor waiting for feuds to subside, and not a recluse willing and destined to reside alone."[68]

The Zionist dream of establishing a secular "city on a hill" could not be permanently sustained; people found it impossible to maintain their original self-sacrificing zeal. The ardent socialism that animated Jewish politicians fifty years ago has been substantially superseded by a pervasive desire for self-aggrandizement.

Likud governments have encouraged the thirst for material gain and the "good life" to compensate Israeli citizens for the heavy demands of military service, and the crushing taxation necessary to support a state continuously at war. As a result, Israeli citizens today maintain a living standard far higher than is warranted by Israel's real income. No wonder the State of Israel has been able to afford a long series of trade deficits, regularly funded by the U.S. Treasury and by Jewish communities around the world.

The tone of Israeli society has changed in other regards. For the first thirty years of its existence, financial scandals or official wrongdoing involving bribery were practically unheard of. This can be readily shown by the Rabin affair in 1977, when the prime minister had to resign from office after his wife was found to have a small but illegal bank account in Washington, D.C. Since then, during the mid-1980s, the great bank-share price-fixing scandal cost the Israeli Treasury approximately $7 billion. Only in the summer of 1991, eight years after the alleged crimes, were the responsible bankers put on trial.

Moreover, in her recent reports, the Israeli State Comptroller, a former Supreme Court Justice named Miriam Ben-Porat, suggests that government-related financial improprieties are on the rise. But instead of promptly taking steps to correct the problems she has discovered, Israel's politicians now clamor for her removal. What they object to is not the criminality or mismanagement thus revealed; instead, they clearly dislike her inconvenient exposure of matters the Knesset members and government would prefer to have concealed.

Two recent cases are particularly disturbing for older Israelis. The first one came to a head on March 27, 1991, when Brigadier General Rami Dotan, former chief purchasing officer for the Israeli Air Force, pleaded guilty to bribery, taking kickbacks, and other offenses for which he was sentenced to thirteen years imprisonment. Taking advantage of a law requiring General Electric to give an offshore co-production contract to an Israeli firm for the F-16 engines it was selling to Israel, the general set up a dummy company that siphoned off over $10 million for himself and several other officers and Israeli officials.

Equally alarming was a case that broke a few months later in the United States, when Melvyn R. Paisley, a former Assistant Secretary of the Navy, pleaded guilty on June 27, 1991, to taking a $268,000 bribe. It appears that Mazlat, a subsidiary of Israel Aircraft Industries, Ltd. (IAI) and Tadiran (a computer firm), had a NATO ally procurement contract to furnish the American Navy with drone aircraft. Leaving aside the fact that the technical plans for the planes had apparently been pirated from American firms by Mossad, it soon transpired that the Israelis were unable to master the technology involved. Falling behind schedule, Mazlat gave Paisley the bribe, only to have the contract abrogated when the drones proved seriously defective.

These affairs raise disturbing questions for many Israelis. Are they simply isolated incidents, or part of a growing pattern of improper relationships between American officials and businessmen on the one hand and their Israeli counterparts on the other?[69]

Nor is that the only change. In economic policy, Likud's supporters differ profoundly from the early leaders. They clamor for private initiative, not socialism. Yet they share, and carry further, the expansionist and exclusionist attitudes of the Labor alignment.

No doubt part of the problem, as Amnon Rubenstein suggests, is that "alignment Zionism sought to transform the status of Jews among the nations from a persecuted minority awaiting the coming of the Messiah to equal partners in a secular world . . . [a change in attitude that] required a major mental readjustment."[70] That "mental readjustment" proved impossible for all too many Israelis who continue to cling to their notion of Israel's manifest destiny as a "nation for God's Chosen People." They yearn to revive not only ancient religious traditions, but David's kingdom in all its glory. Consequently, "There is a new revival of Zionism in the land, wearing the mantle of fundamentalism, driven by a single-minded belief in Eretz Israel, thriving in an emotional and intellectual vacuum left by the intellectual bankruptcy of the secularist Labor Party and the Revisionist nationalists [Likud]."[71]

Thus the universalism of the Israeli Zionist founding fathers (and the ancient prophets) is being replaced by the tribalism of the ultra-nationalists and religious fundamentalists, which has historically been the root cause of past disasters for the Jewish nation.

Though the Knesset clearly runs the country, compromise has become an obscene word and political purity a virtue. Factions and one-man political parties proliferate, due to a flawed electoral law that illustrates the evils of proportional representation run amok. No member of the Knesset has a geographical constituency. Indeed, the law allows each party to produce lists for which a citizen must vote *in toto*. Thus, a Knesset member represents no one but those who put him on the party slate. In addition, the law grants a Knesset seat to any "list" that captures at least 1 percent of the vote. Not until March 1992 was it provided that in 1996 the Israeli premier would be elected directly.

Proposed electoral reforms have failed because the two major parties, knowing that they must depend on minor parties for their majorities, refuse to enact political reforms that would offend them. In 1984, twenty-nine parties fielded tickets, seventeen of which elected one or more members to the Knesset. Out of a total of 120 Knesset seats, those held by the main parties fell from 95 to 85. In 1988, twenty-seven parties took the field, of which seventeen won seats. The two major parties together acquired only seventy-nine seats.[72]

Since no single party has ever won a majority in an Israeli parliamentary election,[73] the prime minister forming a cabinet is hostage to small factions. Shimon Peres has observed: "I see the present system as the source of all our political troubles. But I don't see a chance of changing this now."[74] Ben-Gurion could pursue farsighted projects because he was assured of reelection.

His successors, not similarly blessed, are concerned solely for each day's needs. Thus responsible statesmanship becomes impossible.

## Superiority of the Military over the Civil Authorities

The British mandatory emergency legislation, promulgated in the 1930s and 1940s to deal with pervasive terrorism and violence, constitutes today a grave abuse of Israel's legal system. Although terrorism now exists only as the occasional raid or incident, the terrorism laws are selectively enforced. Whenever the government finds it convenient, it may prohibit Israeli citizens from traveling abroad; the authorities also allow Israeli officials to arrest anyone on security grounds and to detain them for six months with an unlimited right of renewal. Such detentions are not subject to any writ of *Habeas corpus.*

Thousands of people have endured such arbitrary imprisonment. For example, the Jewish head of the Alternative Information Center in Jerusalem, Michael Warshewski, was jailed for thirty days, his office files seized, and his publication closed. He was finally released on bail, but trial was recessed for four months to allow the prosecution to seek more damaging evidence. Mordechai Vanunu, who told the world about Israel's nuclear arsenal, was gagged and denied permission to talk privately with his own attorney, thus denying him the change to prepare an effective defense against treason charges.

Another constitutional deficiency is the total lack of any provision for full and prompt payment to any person whose property is seized under eminent domain. Nor is this system of confiscation directed solely against Arabs. During the 1948 War, Jews fled from the Jewish Quarter in Jerusalem. When Israel regained that area in 1967, several persons whose parents had owned property there and who had the requisite title deeds asked for their property back or requested compensation. The Israeli government in one case offered only £15 Israeli (worth $3.80) for property worth £1500 Palestinian ($6,000) in 1947.

Since military actions in "state security" matters (as defined by the military) are not subject to review by the Israeli Supreme Court, the decrees of the Defense Ministry supersede civil law whenever it exercises jurisdiction. This is scarcely surprising considering that Israeli politics has a plethora of retired generals; Rabin, Sharon, Eitan, Peres, Herzog, and Weizman.

Although America protested the deportation of Soviet citizens by the Brezhnev regime, only muffled grumblings have been directed at Israel. Using British mandatory law (under which the British had once deported both Begin and Shamir), the Israelis have summarily deported their own citizens as well as foreigners, and particularly Palestinians in the Occupied Territories.

Citizens of a recognized democracy are entitled to organize parties, write platforms, and present candidates for election. In Israel, these accepted rights are subject to government abrogation. An electoral commission may ban lists by claiming that the party opposes the existence of the state. In 1984, the bans of Rabbi Kahane's Kach Party and an Arab-based *Peace and Freedom* list were overturned by the courts. But in 1988 the grounds were extended to include racism or racist incitation and Kach was again banned under that new category.[75]

The threat of bans inhibits Arab efforts to protect their interests by democratic means. When Israeli Arabs went on strike in the spring of 1988 and rallied to protest their second-class citizenship status, Prime Minister Shamir threatened to abrogate their citizenship if they persisted. Given the Knesset's powers, that was no idle threat. Moreover, according to the polls, 15 percent of Israelis favored deporting all Arab Israelis and another 43 percent favored stripping them of the franchise.[76]

Israel's perpetual warfare with its neighbors, the military tinge of its society, and the growth of right-wing ideologies, bolstered by religious fundamentalism, all threaten Israel's vulnerable democracy.

## Implications of Israeli Disunity

The cleavages in Israel's social fabric have hampered Israel's domestic and foreign policy, and, indirectly, U.S. policy toward Israel.

Political discontent exists over national policies and also over the way in which they are formulated. The extreme elements of the Israeli political spectrum are gaining inordinate influence, while the center is represented by two major political parties that are not responsive to the public's views. Thus, when a 1981 sampling was asked, "To what extent can you . . . influence policy?", 61 percent replied, "Little" or "Not at all."[77]

Given the sharpness of the differences that divide the Israeli body politic, the process of thrashing out policies tends to be unusually vituperative and polemical. As Nadav Safran wrote in *Israel: The Embattled Ally,* "Hyperbole, passion, cataclysmic oratory, and occasional outbreaks of fanatical zeal are the stuff of everyday politics in the tradition inherited by Israel. . . . [Politics] everywhere, and especially in Israel . . . arouse to a high pitch the spirit of partisanship and belligerence."[78]

## Israel, the Military Giant and Economic Mendicant

If political disputes create more heat than light in Israel, the state of that nation's economy is cause not only for debate but serious concern.

There is a small but respectable body of theoretical literature that analyzes the historical experience of a declining hegemonic power. Among its classical examples is Spain (1552–1659). Spain found itself seriously overextended when, flooded with riches from the mines of the Andes, it failed to recognize the transient nature of its good fortune. Instead of using its newfound resources to build up a weak domestic economy, it spent extravagantly at home, pursued imperialistic policies abroad, and obstinately wasted wealth in vain wars to retain vulnerable territories that offered little but prestige and massive expense.

Like Spain in the sixteenth century, Israel is militarily overextended and dependent for both its military machine and its economy (as it now operates) on a perpetual injection of outside resources, this time not from the mines of the Andes but from an annual gift of resources inspired by America's passionate attachment.

Although Israel's population is comprised of about 4.4 million Jewish citizens and 800,000 of Arab descent, the number of Jews is being rapidly augmented by a fresh ingathering of what may ultimately amount to an additional 1 million Soviet Jews. In the long run, this new wave of immigration will no doubt increase Israel's manpower resources; meanwhile, it will impose economic costs for language teaching, job retraining, housing, and finding employment. It is already creating major dislocations in the Israeli economy, displacing Israeli Arabs and Palestinians in the Occupied Territories from menial jobs and exacerbating unemployment for the Oriental Jews.

Many of the new migrants are doctors and other professionals forced to take unskilled jobs in order to earn any kind of living at all. Unemployment and underemployment have reached 12 percent, with 20 percent expected by the end of 1992 if job-producing capital investments are not forthcoming. Understandably, many former Soviet Jews are writing home telling friends and relatives to stay put until things get better in Israel.

Israel's political leaders take it for granted that most, if not all, of these economic costs will be paid by the United States. But that brash assumption ignores recent changes in the long-existing strategic calculus. The end of the Cold War has definitely invalidated Israel's claim to be an essential military barrier against a possible Soviet invasion of the Middle East. The recent fracas with Iraq has made irrelevant Israel's self-asserted role of America's watchdog surrogate guarding the Gulf. America can and will do the job itself, without the political complications that arise every time Israel intrudes itself into a Middle East situation.

For these reasons, the insistent demand of Israel for perpetual and evergrowing American largesse is losing its resonance. Attrition of American support is clearly predictable, with more and more Americans demanding that the President and Congress reevaluate the cost-effectiveness of America's huge annual tribute to Israel.

Thus it seems likely that, sooner or later, the Israelis will have to adjust their plans to take account of the winding down of America's bounty. Insistence on that winding down may well be the only means by which America can provide Israel with sufficient incentives to put its disheveled economic house in order and regain its national self-respect as a self-supporting nation.[79]

At the outset, Jewish business pursuits concentrated on farming the land or using their limited resources for industrial pursuits. The countryside was covered by cooperative farms or by rural villages with attached industrial facilities (Kibbutzim). Agricultural pursuits required water in a land with only the modest levels of rainfall provided by a Mediterranean climate in winter. The use of summer water for farms and the rapid increase in the population of cities clearly mandated the careful exploitation of the available and renewable water resources. Water was always a constricting factor on Israel's economic growth, simply because it rendered largely unusable that part of the country lying within the Negev Desert. Thus growth in the agricultural sector was limited to those areas where there was no water shortage.

Because of the shortage of funds and the initially low level of worker training, industrial investments were at first restricted to basic, labor-intensive industries. After independence, investments were made as well in industries involving larger amounts of capital, more advanced technologies, and higher worker skill levels. The Israeli diamond business, the swimwear business, the defense firms and computer industry exemplify these developments. There remained a need for basic entry jobs for the unskilled Oriental Jewish work force; otherwise, they would have been left unemployed.

By the 1970s, however, changes in the economy foretold future difficulties even when migration to Israel was at a minimal level. These difficulties fall under a number of headings.

First of all, the generation of sacrificing pioneers began to pass from the political scene. Their children understandably wished to reap where their parents had sown and to enjoy lives of a more pleasant and less laborious character. Moreover, the tone of relaxation was set by the Labor government and even more by the Likud bloc regime which succeeded it.

Second, the growth of low-priced industry worldwide, particularly in eastern Asia, destroyed the competitiveness of several basic Israeli industries, textiles above all. But, because of political considerations, the government was reluctant to close down firms that could no longer compete. Since Israeli workers were not prepared to accept Asian wage levels to make their firms competitive, their continued existence was justified by a need to keep Israel self-sufficient in such goods. The result was a system of monopolies supported by state subsidies. These increased the national budgetary deficit and wasted funds needed for more productive investments.

Third, the 1967 War and the occupation of substantial Arab-inhabited territory provided the excuse for a larger active-duty army and a bigger defense budget to deal with the endemic threat of warfare that had replaced the hitherto episodic danger of conflict with its neighbors.

Fourth, the socialistic basis of society, which carried with it the presumption of the government as the employer of final resort, put pressure on the politicians to create jobs within the government for otherwise unemployed persons, which contributed to overburdening the budget.

## The Costs of Excessive Regulation

Aside from the Arab boycott, the plethora of government regulations explains why Israel finds it difficult to attract foreign investment. Money goes where it is welcomed, and Israel is uninviting. Too many Israelis prefer that the members of the Diaspora merely make passive investments in local money market funds or preexisting corporations. They do not favor direct investments because this would bring the foreign entrepreneur into contact with Israeli officialdom, with all the friction and bad will that might thereby be engendered. New foreign investment might even, if enough appeared on the scene, lead to demands for changes in the present methods of doing business, which are the result of cozy deals between various groups in Israeli society who prefer things as they are.

Excessive regulations march hand in hand with high tariffs, government subsidies, and other manifestations of protectionism, while the government grants official monopolies and cartels to friendly firms that turn out low-quality products at high prices.

When Israel's high tariff rates prove less than fully effective to protect the monopoly firms from the cold winds of foreign competition, preposterous regulations are quickly prepared to deal with the case. Israel protects its local industry by such rules as one mandating the use of odd numbers of items so that anyone wanting to sell in Israel has to create a production line exclusively for that limited market. Since Israel is a small market, most firms are unable or unwilling to adhere to such rules in order to trade with it.

## Other Israeli Economic Problems

To enable some exports to compete profitably on the world market, Israel provides substantial government subsidies. For example, Israeli tomatoes are sold at far cheaper prices in the European Common Market than at home. The Israeli government prohibits the sale of West Bank agricultural products throughout Israel or East Jerusalem, since many Israeli farmers could not compete with West Bank producers and thus might not be able to repay the government loans made to their Kibbutzim or other agricultural establishments.[80]

Of course, Israeli protectionism could spoil the dream of opening up a great trading area with the Arab states once peace is concluded. No Arab state will allow Israel to dump its produce in its territory when it has balance-of-payments crises to deal with. Nor is Israel likely to offer the Arab states anything by way of real reciprocity in the sale of goods where the terms of trade favor the Arabs.

Affluence, supported by tax evasion and other questionable practices, is quite evident in Israel. Anyone who visits will note a large number of Mercedes-Benz cars. Israel, it is reported, has one of the highest ratios of cars per mile of paved roads of any country in the world. Traffic jams abound; accident rates are murderously high because of reckless and discourteous driving; bad maintenance, scrimping on road lighting, and other safety measures.[81]

Some housing also verges on the luxurious. The building boom at Elat, Israel's Red Sea port and resort, includes private houses worth $300,000–$400,000. The penury evident in the public finances is definitely not reflected in the conspicuous consumption of Israel's entrepreneurial class.[82]

The Israeli economy today provides evidence of serious difficulties in four key indicators. These include savings and economic growth rates; military expenditures; a domestic budgetary deficit; and the size of the state's expenses vis-à-vis the economy and the foreign trade deficit.

With well over half the government budget eaten up by defense and debt service charges, economies had to be effected in other areas. While there are, per capita, nearly twice as many doctors in Israel as there are in the United States, doctors, nurses, and other health-care personnel are seriously underpaid and the hospital system is starved for funds. In July 1991, the governor of the Bank of Israel responded to the demand of the finance minister, Yitzhak Modai, for further economies in the civil budget by declaring that no further economies could be effected in public health without a disastrous decline in the quantity and quality of service provided.[83]

Public education is also being stinted to a point that threatens the long-term welfare of the nation. In an era when educated persons are increasingly needed to deal with high-technology service industries and with the increasingly complex weapons systems now in use, Israel has had to cut back considerably on the share allotted to education.

As Ami Doran and Eli Teicher were already writing in 1977,

> The Israeli economy hovers on the brink of the abyss. Teachers are being dismissed, schools closed and the school day shortened; and a generation of illiterates is thus being raised. Israel's system of public medicine is in a state of collapse; soon proper medical treatment will be a luxury reserved exclusively for the rich and well-connected. Israel's agriculture is likewise falling apart: the kibbutzim are drowning in a sea of debt while the moshavim [collective farms] fall into the hands of receivers. Israel's elderly live in penury; the threat to reduce old-age pensions persists, and the ranks of the poor continue to grow. Crime is on the upswing, because of both increasing poverty and cutbacks in the police force. People are becoming fed up with life in Israel, as one can see from the growing emigration and declining immigration rates. [Israel] is marching undaunted toward utter bankruptcy in its efforts to turn the entire country into one giant armory.[84]

If Israel has a deficit in its domestic budget, it has an even more serious problem in its balance of international accounts. Before 1977, Israel had run a substantial trade deficit. For a time its current account problem was largely offset by German reparations and even more by the liberality of the international Jewish community, which lent money to Israel at preferential rates. The accumulated debts of the Israeli state in 1977 were approximately $15 billion.

In order to assure its reelection, the new government of Prime Minister Begin, which took office in 1977, adopted the objective of providing greater satisfaction for the people, who had long lived under an austerity program of the Labor Party that had restricted their propensity to consume.

Such a program could not have been adopted at a less propitious time. The oil price shock had led to rapid price increases in the cost of oil, practically all of which Israel had to import. In the early 1980s, interest rates even on short-term loans rose to 22 percent, so that Israel had to pay more and more debt charges in foreign exchange in the middle of hyperinflation. Today, in spite of America's forgiveness, in effect, of all its debt by promising sufficient aid to meet the payments falling due, Israel now owed $20.9 billion for a per capita foreign debt of approximately $5,900.[85] In 1985, debt service on the foreign debt alone had risen to 25 percent of GNP. In 1989, 43 percent of Israel's gross national product was employed for both internal and foreign debt service. Any private person so overextended would usually seek relief in the bankruptcy courts.

Israel's decline in economic stability was partially arrested by an improved world economic climate. Israel saved at least $1.5 billion each year by lower oil prices and lower international interest rates. But the 1987 *Intifada* forced increased defense expenditures, reduced tax revenues, impeded Palestinian purchases of Israeli goods, and dried up tourism. Whereas before the *Intifada*, economic exploitation of the Occupied Territories had been a major source of public and private revenue amounting to at least $2 billion a year, during 1988 the uprising probably cost Israel a net $1.2 billion.

Political and social disunity tend to be self-perpetuating, and a country that depends for its living standard on subsidies from a friendly nation must necessarily be regarded as a declining society. As Professor Robert Gilpin of Princeton University has written:

> A declining society experiences a vicious cycle of decay and immobility . . . on the one hand, decline is accompanied by a lack of social cooperation, by emphasis on rights rather than emphasis on duty, and by decreasing productivity. . . . The failure to innovate accentuates the decline and its psychologically debilitating consequences. Once caught up in this cycle, it is difficult for the society to break out.[86]

Israel represents almost a textbook illustration of these phenomena. The increasing Israeli domestic dissension reflects the country's relative decline in internal strength and external initiative, while the highly contentious foreign policy issues that continually confront Israeli leaders tend to feed domestic political discord.

The rapid changes in Israeli society create a fertile environment for growing complacency and insensitivity. Gilpin notes that a state in decline characteristically undergoes a "psychological shift," with the result that "social values, attitudes, and behavior change in ways that undercut the efficiency of the economy and the dedication of individuals and groups to the commonwealth. Private and public interests that formerly had converged now diverge to the detriment of the power and welfare of the society."[87]

Unwilling to confront all the groups whose special interests would be affected by a change in the status quo, Israel's main political parties drift along. They count on brilliant extempore maneuvers to extricate themselves from conflicts abroad, and they hope to use similar expedients at home. Instead of looking for long-term solutions, they turn, inevitably, to America.

Israel's politicians lavish money on armaments, acquired not for bona fide defense, but for the appearance of power and prestige, with the hope of overawing their opponents into letting Israel keep its 1967 conquests. To date, efforts in this regard have notably failed either to make the Arabs surrender or to secure peace. In pursuing these contradictory policies, Israel's politicians have disregarded Israel's founding fathers' view that Israel must stand on its own and look to others for no more than occasional support.

An Israeli financial manager recently noted that certain Israeli consumption habits have become sacred cows. But, in resource allocation, Israel's national security policy has retained its high priority as the largest untouchable bovine.

Yet, a single-minded emphasis on security-related expenditure could prove self-defeating. As military leaders have repeatedly noted, excessive military spending can lead to the undermining of a society and hence to military defeat. This has particular relevance to Israel, in view of the inherent limitations of its economy.

CHAPTER NINE

# Israel's Colonialist Adventure—Ruling and Absorbing the Occupied Territories

UNLIKE THE PALESTINIANS who had fled in terror in 1947–49, most Palestinians in the West Bank, Gaza Strip, and East Jerusalem stayed put during the 1967 War. Thus, instead of presenting Israeli with a convenient "emptied land," they provided a captive labor supply and a colony to rule at a time when colonialism had ceased to be in fashion.

According to a sociologist, Meron Benvenisti (a former deputy mayor of Jerusalem), who directed a detailed study of the problem, some Israeli leaders in 1967 briefly contemplated withdrawing from the newly occupied territories in exchange for peace, thereby implementing Resolution 242.[1] However, the Arabs decreed at Khartoum in September 1967 that there should be "no peace with Israel, no recognition of Israel, and no negotiations with it." This gave a green light to the Israeli factions that opposed any peaceful outcome. As Benvenisti wrote in 1984: "a new conception took over, which interpreted the Six-Day War as a direct extension of the war of liberation, taking care of 'unfinished business.' The Israeli national consensus, explicitly or implicitly, views the nineteen years during which Palestine was divided as a stage in the realization of national aspirations. . . . "[2] In other words, the 1967 War gave Israel the opportunity to take full possession of even more land than had once been part of the British Mandate. Their means for turning a temporary situation into a permanent advantage lay in planting Israeli settlements in the Occupied Territories.

Although Israel's Labor government initially justified such settlements as a security measure, its Likud successor candidly stated that the settlements were expressly designed to establish squatters' rights, or, as they put it euphemistically, "to create new facts."[3]

Since then, the army has established and protects more than 140 Jewish settlements in the West Bank (including East Jerusalem) and Gaza. They are peopled by over 250,000 Israeli Jewish citizens. The army has taken nearly 70 percent of the land on the West Bank and controls 96 percent of the water supply. In Gaza, it has preempted 33 percent of the land and 80 percent of the water for the exclusive benefit of 3,000 Israeli settlers at the expense of 700,000 resident Palestinians. Very little, if any, compensation has been paid for nearly 1,700 square miles of confiscated real estate, together with its related buildings.

Meanwhile, for a quarter century, the Israeli Army has dominated and ruled the Occupied Territories in apparent violation of almost every principle of the UN Charter and the Geneva and Hague conventions. A whole generation of Palestinians is being wantonly destroyed in mind, if not in body. The Israeli military has already killed more than 1,000 young Palestinians, mostly for throwing rocks at Israeli military vehicles and security personnel; it has closed universities for three years, and primary and secondary schools for at least two, presumably on the colonialist principle that to keep the natives tractable, one must keep them ignorant.

Israel has refused to repatriate thousands of Palestinians displaced during the 1967 fighting, and has illegally deported about 1,400 Palestinian community leaders from many strata, including lawyers who tried to safeguard Palestinian rights through legal channels, on the ground that they were all terrorists. The real ground for these continuing deportations has been to eliminate any prospective local leaders, while Israel substitutes appointed collaborationists as the Palestinian representatives.

Israel's illegal and inhumane conduct is amply documented by the findings of Amnesty International and the annual Human Rights report of the State Department. Israel subjects Palestinians in the Occupied Territories to arbitrary arrests and thereafter denies them procedural rights; it imposes collective punishments; it mistreats and often tortures detainees, of whom there are now reported to be more than five thousand imprisoned illegally in Israel. At one time or another, it has arrested or imprisoned one in four inhabitants under occupation. It destroys or seals Arab suspects' houses, or those of their relatives, and detains individuals without charge or trial for renewable six-month terms. Israel prevents the reunification of families; it confiscates lands and destroys crops, including olive or citrus groves. Finally, and most insensitively, it diverts scarce water resources to fill the swimming pools and water the lawns of Israeli settlers, leaving the Palestinians to trudge sun-wracked miles toting cans of water from the nearest well.

The revolt against Israeli repression has been going on for five years, and still no one abroad does anything to check Israel's practices or seek redress of legitimate Palestinian grievances. Not surprisingly, the Palestinians' growing frustration has led to internal fighting, chiefly the liquidation of alleged collaborators. But despite Israeli press pictures about the horrors of Palestinian death squads, one should keep in mind that the Israeli Army TV station has reported the use of Israeli soldiers dressed in Palestinian garb, which suggests that not all the deaths squads are of Palestinian origin.[4] The presumed Israeli intention in showing such a telecast was to strike terror in other Palestinians and create the impression that the *Intifada* (like earlier revolutions) has begun to devour its children.

Israeli authorities, who encouraged radicalization by persecuting the PLO, have still left untouched Hamas, a Sunni fundamentalist body related to the Moslem Brotherhood and dedicated to Israel's violent destruction. Only after Hamas murdered a number of Israelis in Gaza did the government in Jerusalem belatedly realize its mistake and change its policies.

Israel's settlements program has now reached the stage where only the exertion of external pressure can achieve a reversal. As Benvenisti put it in 1984, ". . . the processes set in motion in 1967 and accelerated in recent years have created social, economic, and political interactions between Israel and the territories that have assumed quasi permanence."[5]

With the help of massive construction financed by the government (and with covert but major U.S. assistance), Israeli settlers have flocked into the Occupied Territories. They have established special enclaves and have quickly displayed the attributes of arrogance and racism of a colonialist age. Faithful to that tradition, Israel has granted the settlers a multitude of preferences, including the extraterritorial protection of its own domestic laws, rather like the Western residents in China or the Ottoman Empire before 1914.

According to Benvenisti, preemption and new settlements had, by 1986, transformed the Occupied Territories from an international problem to a purely internal one. By this he presumably meant that, because Israel was militarily superior to the Arabs and the United States would furnish the support necessary to maintain that superiority, what happened to the Occupied Territories and their inhabitants would now be decided by Israel alone. Although Benvenisti would himself prefer a liberal solution, the outcome will most likely be dictated by Israel's racist and anti-Arab attitudes.

The long-term objective of the right wing is to diffuse Jewish citizens so widely throughout the Occupied Territories that any demarcation of Jewish and Arab areas in the West Bank would resemble the map of Thuringia in the pre-1914 era. This was conveyed to the senior author in 1978 when Ariel Sharon, then minister of agriculture, told him that Israel planned to move 100,000 Jewish Israelis into the Occupied Areas. A short time later, Sharon amplified his intentions by his response to a question from a friend of the authors as to whether the Israelis intended to leave any Palestinians in the Occupied Territories. Sharon replied with a grin, "We'll keep enough for labor."

Sharon was not arbitrarily inventing the figure of 100,000; he was heralding the "World Zionists Organization Master Plan," whose goal was to achieve

> maximal distribution of a large Jewish population in areas of high settlement importance. . . . The plan . . . "diverts . . . settlement activity away from the subsidized, rural, communal villages to the demand forces [pushing] for semi-urban settlements of high quality of life in demand zones." Based on that strategy, more than 80 percent of total investment has been directed to the West Bank metropolitan areas of Jerusalem and Tel Aviv.[6]

Raja Shehadeh, a West Bank lawyer and a member of the British Bar, concluded in a study made for the International Commission of Jurists that

> the policy which Israel has been pursuing in the West Bank is intended to drive out the Palestinians, to take over their land, and eventually to annex the occupied territories. In a lecture given in the Spring of 1980 at Jerusalem's Hebrew University, Aharon Yaniv (former chief of Israeli military intelligence) said: "Some people talk of expelling 700,000 to 800,000 Arabs in the event of a new war, and instruments [operations plans and military orders] have been prepared (for the contingency)."

One may ask why, if Israel intends to absorb these territories, it has not formally annexed them. Quite possibly the Israelis feared that formal annexation prior to filling up these lands with Jews and pushing out the Arabs might provoke the United States, or other nations, into taking effective action to block this plan. When annexation does come, Israel wishes to present the world with a fait accompli.[7]

In addition, if Israel did formally annex the Occupied Territories on the ground that they had always been Israeli territory unlawfully seized by Jordan and Egypt in 1948, then it would follow that all the inhabitants would automatically become Israeli citizens. But this would mean that they could elect over a third of the Knesset—which would immobilize the current government or force it to revert to an unworkable grand coalition.

Actually, the Arabs in East Jerusalem and the Druse in the Golan Heights were offered Israeli citizenship, but declined it on grounds of principle. Probably, the West Bankers and Gazans would act the same way, though that is a chance Israel dares not take. Annexation without offering citizenship would seriously undermine Israel's claim to be a bona fide democracy and weaken its standing in America.

## The Illegality of Israel's Conduct in the Occupied Areas

Although disputed by the Israelis and their American protagonists, there is little doubt that Israel's settlements program and other aspects of its conduct in the Occupied Territories violate international law.

Israel behaves as though it had acquired sovereignty over the territories, but in fact, under established international law, all that Israel achieved by military conquest (which in turn has accounted for more than half the territory it now governs) was the status of "belligerent occupant." A belligerent occupant possesses only a temporary and de facto authority to protect its security interests, and it is subject to various substantive limitations designed to protect the inhabitants.

We make this point to emphasize Israel's dubious status in the Occupied Territories and the conditions which treaties and statutory law have now imposed on it. The fact that under such law Israel is merely a "belligerent occupant" and therefore subject to severe limitations is wholly rejected in action if not in theory by the Israeli government. In fact, at the time of the passage of Resolution 242, the Israeli negotiator Abba Eban dismissed with scorn that provision of the preamble to the resolution which reaffirms the proposition that "the acquisition of territory by force is inadmissible, in accordance with the United Nations Charter, the principles of international law, and relevant Security Council resolutions."

The relevant treaties and conventions are the Hague Convention IV adopted in 1907, which the Israeli Supreme Court held binding on the State of Israel in the so-called "Elon Moreh" decision in 1979, and Geneva Convention IV, one of four Conventions adopted in 1949 to ensure that abuses practiced by the Axis powers could not be legally repeated. The Fourth Geneva Convention, "Relative to the Protection of Civilian Persons in Time of War," puts responsibility for its enforcement on all of the signatories (including the United States) by the following language:

> The High Contracting Parties undertake to respect and to ensure respect for the present Convention in all circumstances.

The provision "to respect" means to abide by a Convention; the provision "to ensure respect," added in 1949, means that if one state is in violation, others are also in violation unless they take energetic measures to compel the erring state to comply. Consequently, if Israel violates the Convention, other signatory states are accessories after the fact, unless they stop such practices. Although the United States has declared many Israeli practices unlawful or a violation of Palestinian human rights, it has utterly neglected its duty to stop these criminal acts or to allow the Security Council to do so.

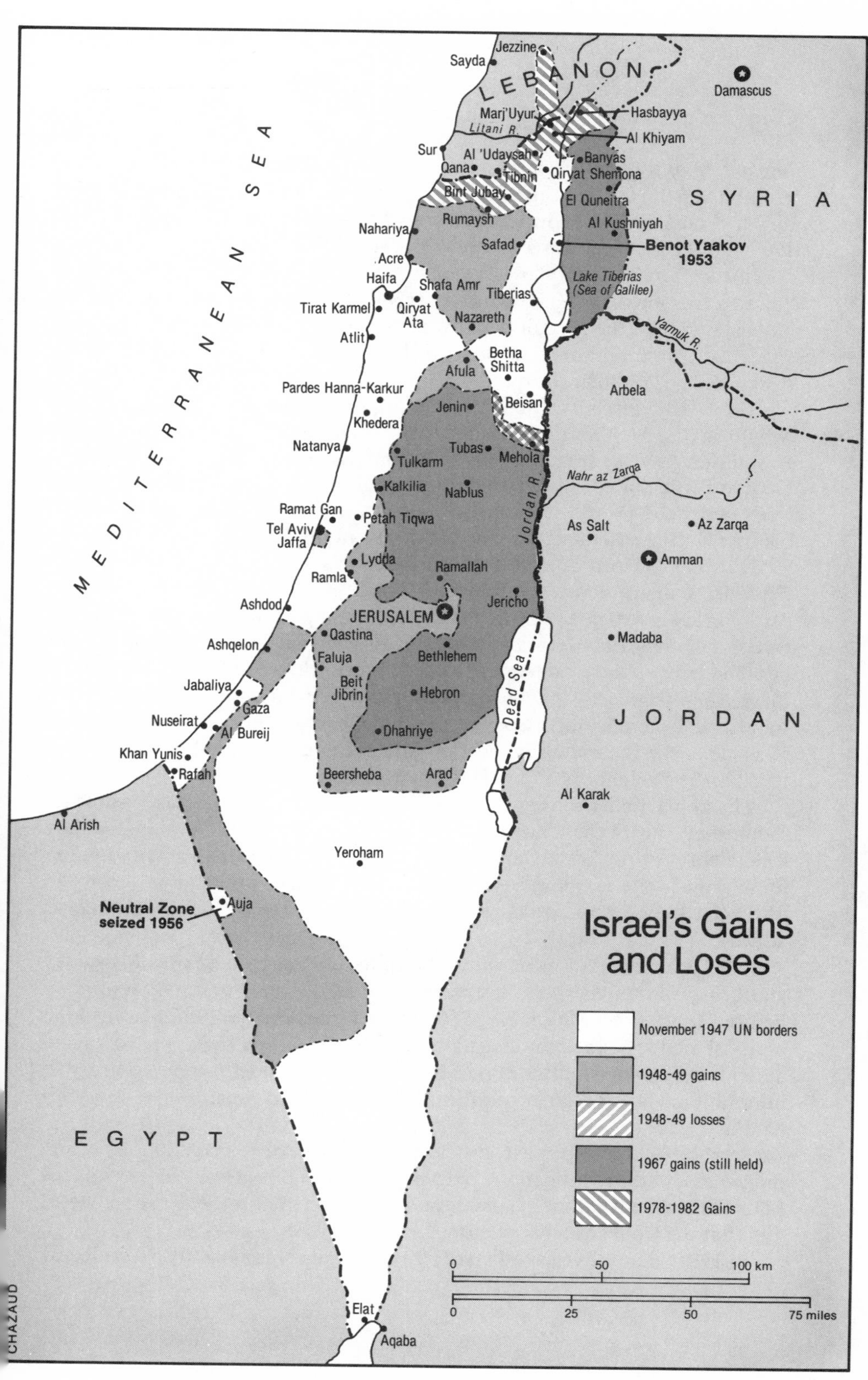

Israel's Gains and Loses
November 1947 UN borders
1948-49 gains
1948-49 losses
1967 gains (still held)
1978-1982 Gains
0 50 100 km
0 25 50 75 miles
MEDITERRANEAN SEA
LEBANON
SYRIA
JORDAN
EGYPT
Damascus
Amman
JERUSALEM
Sayda
Jezzine
Hasbayya
Marj'Uyur
Litani R.
Al Khiyam
Sur
Al 'Udaysah
Banyas
Qana
Tibnin
Qiryat Shemona
Bint Jubay
El Quneitra
Rumaysh
Al Kushniyah
Nahariya
Safad
Benot Yaakov 1953
Acre
Haifa
Shafa Amr
Tiberias
Lake Tiberias (Sea of Galilee)
Tirat Karmel
Qiryat Ata
Nazareth
Yarmuk R.
Atlit
Afula
Betha Shitta
Arbela
Pardes Hanna-Karkur
Jenin
Beisan
Khedera
Natanya
Tubas
Mehola
Tulkarm
Nahr az Zarqa
Kalkilia
Nablus
Jordan R.
Ramat Gan
Petah Tiqwa
Tel Aviv Jaffa
As Salt
Az Zarqa
Lydda
Ramla
Ramallah
Ashdod
Jericho
Qastina
Madaba
Ashqelon
Bethlehem
Faluja
Beit Jibrin
Hebron
Jabaliya
Gaza
Dead Sea
Nuseirat
Al Bureij
Dhahriye
Khan Yunis
Rafah
Beersheba
Arad
Al Karak
Al Arish
Yeroham
Neutral Zone seized 1956
Auja
Elat
Aqaba
CHAZAUD

The most directly pertinent violations by Israel of the Fourth Geneva Convention fall into the following categories.

*Implanting of settlements in the occupied areas:* While an occupying power is prohibited from transferring part of its own civilian population into the territory it occupies, Israel routinely violates both the Hague Convention IV of 1907 and the Geneva Convention IV of 1949 in that regard.[8]

Just before he left office, President Lyndon B. Johnson declared that "Arab governments must convince Israel and the world community that they have abandoned the idea of destroying Israel. But equally, Israel must persuade its Arab neighbors and the world community that Israel has no expansionist designs on their territory."

The Nixon administration first referred to the settlements programs in a debate in the UN Security Council in September 1971 which resulted in Resolution 298. At that time the U.S. ambassador to the United Nations, George Bush, stated: "We regret Israel's failure to acknowledge its obligations under the Fourth Geneva Convention, as well as its actions which are contrary to the letter and spirit of this Convention."

During the Ford administration, America's ambassador to the United Nations, William Scranton, told the Security Council in March 1976 that "substantial resettlement of the Israeli civilian population in Occupied Territories, including East Jerusalem, is illegal under the Convention and cannot be considered to have prejudged the outcome of future negotiations between the parties on the locations of the borders of states in the Middle East. Indeed, the presence of these settlements is seen by my government as an obstacle to the success of the negotiations for a just and final peace between Israel and its neighbors."[9]

The applicability of these conventions to the Occupied Areas became an established part of the United States policy on April 21, 1979, when the then legal adviser of the State Department, Herbert J. Hansell, issued an opinion finding that "the *establishment of the civilian settlements in those territories* [the West Bank and Gaza] *is inconsistent with international law*" (emphasis added).[10]

U.S. characterization of the settlements as "illegal" was reaffirmed by another respected lawyer, Secretary of State Cyrus Vance, in testimony before Congress on March 21, 1980, where he said: "U.S. policy toward the establishment of Israeli settlement in the Occupied Territories is unequivocal and has long been a matter of public record. We consider it to be contrary to international law and an impediment to the successful conclusion of the Middle East peace process. . . .

"Article 49, paragraph 6 of the Fourth Geneva Convention is, in my judgement, and has been in the judgement of each of the legal advisers of the State Department for many, many years, to be . . . that settlements are illegal and that the Convention applies to the territories."

In 1981, Hansell's carefully researched opinion was abruptly overruled by a nonlawyer, Ronald Reagan, who announced with the total confidence of ignorance that the settlements were legal. In Reagan's view, they were simply an "obstacle to peace." Subsequently, the Bush administration has waffled on whether the settlements are illegal or not. Given its demands for an end to settlements based only on diplomatic grounds, the underlying basis of American policy in this area has become hopelessly muddled.

*Destruction of private property and humiliation of residents:* The IDF routinely breaks into Palestinian homes, often during the night, humiliating the residents, stealing and wilfully destroying their property. Such acts are illegal under Hague Regulations, Articles 46(1) and 47, and Article 33(2) of the Geneva IV Convention.

*Interference with religious rights:* Disrupting religious services of the occupied population is a direct violation of Hague Regulations 46(1) and of Article 33(2) of the Geneva IV Convention. The Government of Israel routinely interferes with religious observances and has, from time to time, threatened to ban or banned Moslem worshipers from the Temple Mount mosques.

*Attacks on hospitals and hospital personnel:* During disorders, Israeli occupying forces invade hospital and medical facilities, arresting and removing seriously wounded people, harassing medical personnel, and destroying hospital equipment. Such acts are forbidden under Articles 18(1) and 20 of the Geneva IV Convention.[11]

*Physical violence against protected persons:* "Murder, torture, corporal punishments" of any civilian population are prohibited by Article 31 of the Geneva IV Convention. Such activities on the part of the Israeli authorities, both before and during the *Intifada,* have been repeatedly reported.

*Collective and guilt-by-association punishments:* "Collective penalties, including curfews, and likewise all measures of intimidation" are prohibited under Article 33(1). Because no protected person may be punished for an offense he or she has not personally committed, this provision clearly rules out the punishment of persons related to the accused. Similarly, reprisals against the inhabitants of Occupied Areas (who under the terms of the Convention are protected persons) are expressly forbidden under Article 33(3). Yet the Israelis routinely impose curfews and destroy or seal the houses of suspects or their relatives even before the arrested person has been found guilty of any crime, or indeed without any criminal finding whatsoever.

*Unjustifiable destruction of private property:* An occupying power is specifically prohibited by the Geneva IV Convention, Article 6, from destroying real or personal property owned by private persons or others. Israeli forces have destroyed hundreds of homes and farmers' crops without any bona fide justification, falsely asserting military necessity. The Israeli authorities systematically laid waste to the entire Syrian city of Quneitra in 1974 in a time of truce, when no hostilities were in progress.

*Seizure and plunder of private property:* The seizure of private property is also prohibited to the occupying power by Geneva Convention IV, Article 56. Plundering is expressly forbidden by the Hague Convention IV, Article 47. Yet, Israel has seized over half the land in the West Bank from private persons and plundered the homes of Quneitra's inhabitants.

*Unlawful tax collections:* Articles 49 and 50 of the Geneva Convention IV of 1949 relating to civilians prohibit the levying of taxes in an occupied territory and the diversion of such funds to the treasury of the occupying power. From 1967 to 1987, Israel routinely extracted each year $80 to $100 million more from the Occupied Territories than it expended in them.

*Unlawful deportations:* Deportations of protected persons, or the imprisonment of such persons in the territory of the occupying power, are explicitly forbidden under Geneva IV, Articles 49(1) and 76. The only exception permitted is the temporary removal of civilians to ensure their safety during combat operations. Nevertheless, with a perversity worthy of Dickens's Seth Pecksniff, Israel's High Court of Justice has refused to issue a judgment based on this protocol because it has not "entered the canon of Israeli law via legislation by the Knesset."[12] Israel's ratification of the Geneva Conventions makes this provision binding on Israel whether the Knesset says so or not.

*Closing of schools in the occupied areas:* Israel's action in closing schools in the Occupied Areas violates Article 50(1), which requires the military occupant to "facilitate the proper working" of such institutions.

*Deprivation of procedural and substantive due process of law:* Under Article 66, civilians under occupation are entitled to trial by "properly constituted, non-political military courts," and under Article 72(8) they are entitled to the assistance of a "qualified advocate or counsel." They are also entitled to a specific bill of particulars regarding the charges against them (Article 71[3]). But the Israeli military authorities have routinely denied trial or proper legal assistance to civilians in the Occupied Areas. The defense cannot ascertain and answer specific charges because the Israeli authorities declare the evidence to be a matter of "state security."

*Commission of aggressive annexations:* When the Axis powers used their domestic laws to annex portions of the territories they occupied, the Nuremberg Tribunal held such annexations illegal. The same principle and the pertinent Security Council resolutions apply to Israel's purported annexation of East Jerusalem in 1967 and 1980 and of the Golan Heights in 1981.

*Specification of grave breaches:* Article 51 of the First Geneva Convention (which applies to all four conventions) states:

> Grave breaches to which the preceding Article relates shall be those involving any of the following acts, if committed against persons or property protected by the Convention: wilful killing, torture or inhuman treatment, including biological experiments, wilfully causing great suffering or serious injury to body or health, and extensive destruction and appropriation of property, not justified by military necessity and carried out unlawfully and wantonly.[13]

The horrible suffering imposed by the Nazis particularly on the Jewish people, their deportation from their homes, the seizure of their property without compensation, their enslavement, maltreatment, and slaughter, ought to have inspired the Israelis to make a particularly careful effort to observe these rules. Unhappily, current Israeli authorities now appear to be repeating most of the abuses the Geneva Conventions were intended to prevent.

## The Means by Which Israel Carries Out Its Violations

The turbulent political history of the Occupied Territories bequeathed to the occupiers a whole basketful of laws—Turkish, British, and Jordanian. The Israelis have taken full advantage of this unique storehouse. In each individual case they have selectively applied those laws that best serve their purposes; and, to cover any lacunae, they have empowered their military authorities to promulgate whatever new regulations they might find convenient. New regulations have normally been represented as amendments to old laws; in fact, most have been new legislation or a repeal of earlier statutes that interfere with Israeli objectives.

The Israelis found the Jordanian laws most useful for their purposes. Thus, in 1970, according to Raja Shehadeh:

> Moshe Dayan proposed that a governmental committee be set up to study Jordanian laws with a view to replacing them with Israeli laws. A month later, Dayan withdrew his suggestion. After evaluating the situation he realized that applying Israeli law over the West Bank would be tantamount to annexation, which was not a step that Israel was politically ready to take. . . . The same advantages for Israel could be gained if Jordanian law were preserved and the Area Commander made substantial amendments to it. The Area Commander then began to exercise more freedom in amending Jordanian law to meet Israel's needs. . . . In effect the Area Commander assumed full legislative power.[14]

After he assumed that "full legislative power," the area commander of Judea and Samaria (Central Command) had by 1991 ordered over 1,400 new amendment orders. Many of these amendment orders were not published and were, therefore, unavailable to lawyers trying to advise clients on their rights. In one case, the military authorities pretended to follow a land-usage law pertaining to a large East-West highway in the central West Bank region, by printing the required official public notices in Hebrew, then posting them in a locked Israeli military office inaccessible to the Palestinians. When an Israeli secretly gave some Arabs copies of the documents and the Arabs' lawyers filed the requisite objection papers within the prescribed deadlines, they were jailed on the ground that the public notice was a state secret, which it was unlawful for them to possess![15]

*Destruction of houses and restrictive land and water-usage regulations:* Long before the *Intifada,* Israeli military authorities arbitrarily destroyed houses built by Palestinians on lands that their families had owned for generations. The Israelis justified these demolitions by claiming that there was no proof the houses had been built with official license. In fact, in a classic Catch-22 maneuver, the Israeli military masters seldom granted such licenses.

In another case, the Israeli military administration reversed a Jordanian law granting a certain category of land (15 percent of the West Bank's area) to its peasant cultivators. The land was then declared (despite land registration forms and tax receipts) once more state property, after which the Israeli military expelled the owners, destroyed their homes, and refused all compensation.

Retroactive laws of this sort have long been standard procedure for the occupying Israeli authorities. Nor are the courts in the Occupied Areas, or Israel, entitled to review such practices. The law is whatever the commander says it is.

The Israeli authorities presumably have two reasons for these practices: One is to keep the properties undeveloped or without dwellings on them, so that the Israelis can more easily expropriate them. The second is to force the Palestinians to leave, or at least to move into urban areas where they become economically dependent on the occupiers.[16]

A typical example of this process was that of a Palestinian family which had tried to obtain a permit to build on family-owned land, but "after years, they gave up and built without a permit."[17] They lived in their new house for only two years, then unexpectedly received an order to demolish it. They appealed, but before the appeal was heard, the bulldozers had razed the building after giving the Palestinian mother only five minutes' notice to vacate her house before it was destroyed. "What can I move outside in five minutes? I could take my children or my furniture. I took my children and left everything." She watched the bulldozers destroy her home, her possessions, the fabric of her life. She and her children then squeezed into the already crowded house of a neighbor.[18]

Similar incidents occur regularly. In June 1989, Israeli authorities reported that they had bulldozed more than 550 allegedly illegally constructed houses in the Occupied Territories. When asked about this unconscionable record, an Israeli official indignantly dismissed the query. The homes, he maintained, "were destroyed because they violated government plans for roads, nature preserves, or other land use." In fact, the principal substantive use for any of this land so far has been to provide building sites for Jewish settlers.

Furthermore, the Israeli Army, before and since the *Intifada,* using the 1945 British emergency regulations as pretext, has illegally dynamited 220 homes of Palestinians, or their relatives, accused but never convicted of offenses against the Israeli occupation.[19] According to Ms. Katz, before the *Intifada* only an Arab suspected of murder or an equally severe crime saw his or her family's home blown up. "Now authorities destroy as punishment homes of those suspected of throwing stones."[20]

The simple fact is that the Israeli government and most Israelis view all the land in the former British Mandate as theirs by right. In their unflattering view, all this land has to be "redeemed" for exclusive Jewish use from its Arab owner-occupiers. The ownership of land by any non-Jewish person is illegitimate, and therefore, land acquired at Arab expense is justifiable, regardless of the means employed to that end.

*Abuse of the land laws:* The Palestinian population has suffered most from abuses of the land laws. With their deep sense of family, Palestinians revere properties that have been in a family for generations.[21]

In the Occupied Territories, the military authorities have manipulated the potpourri of laws and regulations with complete disregard for the Palestinians, who are not viewed as inhabitants, whereas the Jewish settlers are considered legal residents. A complex of intricate technicalities has developed over twenty-four years of occupation.

Raja Shehadeh's 1985 study concludes that Israel is pursuing its West Bank policy by the following means:

—giving inalienable ownership and possession of the land to Jewish settlers and Zionist agencies for the exclusive use of Jews. The most recent figure for West Bank land already so acquired is 2,150,000 dunums (a dunum is 1,000 sq. meters), or 40 percent of the total area of the West Bank;

—using regional . . . and road planning schemes . . . to prevent the Palestinians from developing and using the remaining land;

—conferring on Palestinians . . . a legal status . . . with none of the rights, privileges and guarantees normally enjoyed by nationals or permanent residents. . . .

—pursuing policies of harassment and intimidation . . . and denial of . . . basic human rights, including the right to self-determination.[22]

*Preemption of the water supply:* In an arid land where water is almost more precious than oil, Israeli settlers may drill as many new wells as they wish. By contrast, the Palestinians may never drill any new wells, or even replace or upgrade their wells or pumps—and such regulations are sternly enforced.

Because agriculture in the West Bank largely involves the efficient use of water, any drought or the inability to drill wells could prove disastrous, especially since the number of operant Arab wells is diminishing year by year. Land lying fallow because of a water shortage might lead to claims that it had been abandoned, thereby permitting the Israeli Army to confiscate it as "waste state land."

Israel maintains strict limits on Arab water consumption, not only to encourage the Palestinians to leave but also because Israel itself has a threatening water shortage. It uses 100 percent of its own renewable water resources and has already commandeered 80 percent of the groundwater of the West Bank. Another 16 percent of the aquifer water is reportedly used by the Jewish settlers, who make up about 10 percent of the population, leaving the residual 4 percent for the Palestinians who constitute 90 percent.[23]

Moreover, Israel is now exploiting the waters of the Litani River in Lebanon, which is probably why it has surreptitiously extended its "security zone" to the town of Jezzin, twenty-five kilometers to the north of the original zone. In Gaza, Israeli settlements have been built on seized land over three large aquifers, which are now exclusively used by Israelis. These are rapidly being depleted and are filling with salt water. When Israel exhausts these resources, it must either reduce its water consumption or take over additional contiguous Arab territory to maintain its water-use levels.[24]

Palestinian agriculture is slowly being strangled as the Israelis use their road policy and edicts of the local Jewish planning councils to destroy vast numbers of fruit trees, which the Palestinians are forbidden to replant—even on their own land—without permission. Most painful is the destruction of olive trees, which take almost a generation to bear fruit. Here again, Israel's unavowed but obvious goal is to stifle the Palestinian economy, and force the Palestinians into economic dependence on Israel both for goods and employment—in flagrant violation of the Fourth Geneva Convention, Article 52.

In addition, the Israeli government scants the public services in the Occupied Areas for which it has taken exclusive responsibility—public health, education, agriculture, justice, and road building, among others. The Israelis levy taxes on the Palestinians for these services, but they provide them with fewer benefits than the settlers receive, while the Palestinian tax revenues are diverted for the Israeli benefit of new settlers.

Before the *Intifada,* Israel could not blame its discriminatory skimping on budgetary stringency. The Israeli economy was benefiting from cheap Palestinian labor as the government garnered a $80 million annual tax surplus from the West Bank; it was also profiting from the $150 million a year transferred from the Arab world to West Bank inhabitants and the $435 million provided by the PLO-Jordanian Committee between 1979 and 1984.[25] Now it is paying heavily for its inhumanity. The annual direct costs of the *Intifada* amount to roughly $150 million, and the indirect losses in tourism and other costs are aggregating roughly $1 billion; and, because of the expulsion of Palestinians from the Gulf states, the remittances to their families in Arab countries have been greatly reduced.

By the early 1980s, the injustices in the Occupied Areas had become so blatant that on April 29, 1981, a commission headed by Deputy Attorney General Yehudit Karp was appointed to sift the slag heap of complaints. Based on a case before the Supreme Court, the Commission was ordered to investigate Arab allegations of illegal treatment. A year later, on May 21, 1982, the Karp Report was filed and a censored version was belatedly released on February 7, 1984. The Commission found that:

—Of seventy cases randomly sampled, fifty-three had been closed without police action. Furthermore, the Attorney General's office could not give the Supreme Court any assurances of a better performance in the future.

—Brigade 202 of the Israeli Army stood by and watched settlers from Kiryat Arba (an illegal Israeli settlement) enter Hebron (a major Palestinian West Bank city) after a curfew and vandalize a substantial amount of property. The brigade made no arrests and recorded not a single name, even though the soldiers knew many of the settlers.

—Arabs rarely file complaints, because those who do have been threatened by the settlers with physical violence; not surprisingly, the army regularly refused to provide protection, though the Geneva Convention requires that it do so.

—Since the police rarely acted upon a complaint, the Arabs had long since given up hope of justice from the Israeli authorities.[26]

*The Jerusalem Post* summarized its views on February 8, 1984:

> The Karp Report bears out the initial suspicion that a systematic miscarriage of justice is being perpetrated in the West Bank. Jewish settlers, wishing to assert their rights to the area, take the law into their own hands and refuse . . . to cooperate in police investigations. . . . The police, deferring to the army, fail to stand on their own rights, and the army tends to look benignly on those it views as its soldiers. The result . . . is that files are closed without anyone being booked. [pp. 1–2]

## THE INTIFADA ("SHAKING OFF")

The December 1987 outbreak had long been building up, for demonstrators in the territory had become increasingly bold. Israeli troops found that firing into the air was a fruitless exercise, since the demonstrators merely jeered at the soldiers, while panicked Israeli civil employees abandoned their cars on the streets of Gaza, later to find them burned. The local operations log of the civil administration showed, according to Ze'ev Schiff and Ehud Ya'ari, that during 1987, as compared with 1986, there were 133 percent more demonstrations in Gaza and 178 percent more burned cars, 100 percent more stones thrown, and 68 percent more roads blocked.[27]

The fact that the IDF found itself unable to tamp down the situation increased its appearance of weakness, which in turn escalated the boldness of the attacks. Nevertheless, when the outbreak finally occurred, the Israelis were taken by surprise.

What differentiated this outburst from earlier incidents was that it involved the entire Palestinian population—young and old, male and female, town and country, religious and secular.[28]

It is now clear that the *Intifada* had been developing for many months. The only real question was: when would it begin? When the authors talked to Palestinian residents in the West Bank in 1985, they wondered why the Palestinian population had tolerated the IDF's inhumane treatment for so many years. In 1987, accumulated passions exploded.

Many wars have insignificant causes, and the proximate cause of the *Intifada* was an otherwise routine road accident. On December 8, 1987, an Israeli truck hit a car carrying residents of the Jebalya refugee camp, the largest in the Gaza Strip, killing four of the passengers and badly injuring the others. The incident was broadcast on the radio and provoked rumors that it had been a cold-blooded act of vengeance by a relative of an Israeli stabbed to death in Gaza's main market a few days earlier. The Palestinian press immediately described the accident as "maliciously perpetrated," and some Israeli Army units braced themselves for demonstrations during the funerals.

Early in the evening, as thousands of mourners returned from the rites, their procession turned into an assault on an Israeli outpost; young and old flung stones into the compound. Soon rioting spread throughout the camp, and this time, in contrast to past incidents, the Palestinians did not return to their homes by nightfall. They continued rioting well past 11:00 P.M.

Meanwhile, the local Israeli commander shrugged off the incident. "You don't know these people. They'll go to sleep now and leave for work first thing in the morning as usual. You'll see." Due to this false confidence, the area was not reinforced or placed under curfew. Before dawn, most of the roads and alleyways leading from the Jebalya camp had been barricaded, and that morning the rioting began again in earnest.

Although the American public followed the events on the evening news, Israeli commanders tended to treat it as simply another disturbance like those they had often dealt with before.[29] But Israeli military forces on the spot soon discovered that the atmosphere had wholly changed. Indeed, Israeli soldiers were disgusted that they had received such meager briefing on the Palestinian mood and, on the last day of their tour, fifty-nine of one company's officers and enlisted men signed a petition to the Chief of Staff protesting the "lack of guidance, backing and appropriate equipment given to the soldiers of the Israeli Defense Forces holding the territories."

The result was a chain reaction of anger. The battalion commander wrote a letter calling the petition "insolent"; the company's commander and his deputy were dismissed for having signed the petition. When the local commander, Itzik Mordechai, asked Defense Minister Rabin for additional troops, his request was denied.

After the *Intifada* started, Rabin quickly moved to arrest demonstrators; 750 were reportedly arrested in one night raid at the Burayj refugee camp.[30] By the end of the month, more than 1,200 Palestinians, mostly between the ages of seventeen and twenty-seven, were in custody.[31]

## Management of the Intifada

Who actually manages the *Intifada*? Geoffrey Aronson speaks of the "Unified National Command of the Uprising" which, for the first time in a generation, "represented a vibrant, popularly supported clandestine network capable of organizing an evolving strategy of persistent, large-scale civil disobedience and demonstrations."[32] There are, he says, six organizations represented in the Unified National Command. Each organization in the Command presents its own draft of a leaflet. The leadership then redrafts a version to be faxed to the PLO for approval, then faxed back to the West Bank, where the final version is printed and disseminated.[33]

On the Israeli side, containment of the uprising has been entrusted to a succession of ministers beginning with Yitzhak Rabin, who established the initial pattern of colonial repression. The right wing pressured Rabin to crush the rebellion speedily, in order to subvert U.S. Secretary Shultz's tentative plans for an international conference based on Resolution 242. A right-wing political party, Tehiya, demanded that the soldiers be permitted to shoot demonstrators without waiting until their lives were threatened, and demanded that the government deport, without appeal, the "hundreds of leaders and inciters whose names the Shin Bet has, including the Muezzins who incite from the mosques."

Sharon, then minister of trade and industry, savagely denounced Rabin's policies and joined Tehiya in advocating the deportation of "every rioter who lifts a hand against an IDF soldier." Rabin announced: "We will not be able to solve the problem in the territories by the method of detentions and the use of force which are allowed by law. It is probable we will have to use grave economic measures in order to convince [the Palestinians] that it is impossible to continue with violence any more."[34]

On February 24, a Palestinian stool pigeon for Israel, Muhammad Ayid Zaharana, was lynched in the village of Qabatiyeh, which the Shin Bet saw as a threat to the network of Palestinians whom it had recruited as collaborators. Rabin therefore decided to make that village an example, placing it under a complete blockade for over a month. Running water, electricity, and cooking gas were shut off, and outside medical assistance was forbidden entry. No export licenses were granted, which created special economic hardship, since the community's largest source of income was the export of stone.[35]

Similar measures were applied throughout the West Bank, until the uprising seemed to have settled into a war of attrition; but by May 12, 1988, the Palestinians recognized that they would never achieve their objective of an independent state without some major demonstration like a labor boycott.[36]

The *Intifada* has made it impossible for any American to brush aside the pictures of Israeli bullying that nightly appeared on American television. (Of course, the conditioned reflex of Israeli spokesmen has been to denounce the coverage as unfair.)

Israel's widespread abuse of the Palestinians has produced a copious literature. For example, an excerpt from the Amnesty International 1989 *Annual Report* described human rights violations during the first two years of the *Intifada:*

> More than 25,000 Palestinians were arrested in connection with the *Intifada* (uprising) which began . . . in December 1987. More than 5,000 of those arrested were held in administrative detention without charge or trial; some were prisoners of conscience. Hundreds of other Palestinians were summarily tried and imprisoned. At least 40 Israelis were imprisoned as conscientious objectors for refusing military service in the Occupied Territories and others, possible prisoners of conscience, were brought to trial on political charges. Thousands of Palestinians were victims of beatings while in the hands of Israeli forces; at least nine were reported to have died as a result. There were also many incidents in which Palestinians were shot in circumstances suggesting that Israeli forces had deliberately used excessive force. In a number of cases Palestinians were reported to have died as a result of deliberate misuse of tear-gas. Several political detainees died in custody in suspicious circumstances. One death sentence was imposed but there were no executions.[37]

To reinforce the findings of Amnesty International, two other reports should be noted. First is the official report to Congress on the status of individual human rights, issued on February 21, 1990, and second, a report by Save the Children.

The Israeli brutality displayed during the *Intifada* cannot be attributed solely to undisciplined local actions. Israeli soldiers in the West Bank and Gaza were indisputably carrying out Defense Minister Yitzhak Rabin's official orders. His instructions to his troops on January 21, 1988, were crystal clear: "The first priority is to use force, might, beatings." Then, contrary to history and fact, he added: "No demonstrators have died from being thwacked on the head."[38]

Geoffrey Aronson, the editor of the report on Israeli settlements, says that the policy had in fact "been in effect since the first week of January [1988], when the IDF, stung by international reaction to the high Palestinian death toll in December, turned to methods short of gun fire to reimpose fear on the Palestinian streets."[39]

The daily newspaper *Hadashot* commented that Rabin's announcement had "merely converted a *de facto* situation that prevailed since the beginning of the riots into one of a *de jure* nature. As of tomorrow morning, beating is a free for all."[40]

How the occupation forces interpreted Rabin's instructions was illustrated by a report in *Ha'aretz*.[41] In late January 1988, during the second month of the *Intifada,* the report states, Captain A. was ordered to arrest certain Palestinians in the small village of Hawara outside of Nablus and to inflict mayhem on them. When the captain objected to the immorality of his instructions, he was told that the orders came "from on high."

So, in compliance with explicit instructions, the captain rounded up twelve persons, shackled and bused them to a remote orchard, where flannel was stuffed in their mouths, while the bus driver revved up the motor to drown out the Arabs' cries.

> And then the soldiers obediently carried out the orders they had been given:
> —to break both their arms and both their legs by clubbing them;
> —to avoid clubbing anyone on their heads;[42]
> —to remove their bonds after breaking their arms and legs, and to leave them at the site;
> —to leave one local [Palestinian] with broken arms but without broken legs so he could make it back to the village on his own and get help.

The *Ha'aretz* story continues:

> The mission was carried out to the full. In the course of [carrying it out], most of the wooden clubs used by the clubbers broke. . . .

Only at the beginning of May, four and a half months later, did the Red Cross learn the story and lodge a severe complaint—which resulted in a pro forma investigation. The *Ha'aretz* report then states that "since the incident in Hawara some of the officers involved have been promoted in assignment rank. No one has been brought to trial."[43]

The Israeli government continues to vaunt its "purity of arms" (i.e., that its armed forces religiously adhere to the laws of war); yet well-documented instances of misconduct occur and are swept under the rug. For example, two Israeli soldiers attempted to bury three Palestinians alive. The victims were rescued from the final ministrations of the bulldozer before suffocation; yet for this act of attempted murder the Israeli soldiers received sentences of only three months each. What this proved was that, in embarrassing cases that cannot be concealed, a mild punishment might be administered;[44] but, more often, the perpetrators are rewarded for their diligence.

Such sordid conduct profoundly disgusts many Israelis as much as it does American observers. The Israelis, however, should take no satisfaction from the fact that an increasing number of West Bank killings are apparently committed by Palestinians. The disclosure that Palestinians are killing alleged collaborators in no way justifies the unfairness and severity of Israel's occupation policy; it suggests, on the contrary, that the Occupied Areas have been forced into a state of moral collapse where neighbor preys upon neighbor. Hamas and the PLO now strive to destroy each other's followers.[45]

Since April 1990, Moshe Arens, once more the defense minister, has attempted to give the *Intifada* a lower profile. In lieu of Rabin's policy of going out of the way to seek confrontations with Palestinian youths, Israeli forces confine themselves to keeping main roads open and avoiding areas whose control is not vital to the occupation. As a result, clashes and casualties are less frequent, and the control of many areas, despite complaints from General Sharon, has passed by default to the local Palestinians.

## Keeping the Natives Ignorant

Israel's pretext for closing the primary and secondary schools[46] was that they served as a staging area for organized stoning attacks against Israelis and a place where youths plotted mischief. Yet Israel's action ignored a universal phenomenon: adolescents left at loose ends are far more likely to get into trouble than those occupied with their studies or regular jobs.

For almost two years after the *Intifada* started, Israeli authorities not only closed the schools for 320,000 elementary and high school students and 18,000 college students, but treated any attempt to arrange informal education as a criminal act. Whenever the Israeli Army discovered clandestine classes improvised by the universities or secondary teachers in the West Bank and Gaza Strip, it promptly closed them and arrested their organizers.[47] But that policy was not uniform; well-educated Palestinians discovered that they could tutor their own children at home, but that if a neighbor's child were invited to sit in, the house would be raided by Israeli soldiers.

In the fall of 1989 the primary and secondary schools were reluctantly reopened; yet, despite the absence of disorder, they were closed again during November and December 1989 because the Israeli authorities feared possible riots on the anniversary of the PNC declaration of independence on November 15 and the second anniversary of the *Intifada* on December 8. To conceal their intentions, they declared these closures to be simply a normal interlude between terms.

In late 1989, the Parliament of the European Economic Community voted to suspend official scientific cooperation with Israel until all colleges and universities were reopened. In response, the Israeli authorities grudgingly permitted the reopening of sixteen community and vocational colleges on February 26, 1990.[48]

Israel's belated actions did not fully satisfy the European Parliament because the six major universities in the Occupied Areas, which had been shut down in October 1987, had not been reopened. Early in 1991, the Israeli authorities announced that the universities would be reopened one by one; the last, Bir Zeit, resumed classes in 1992.

## The Israeli Predicament

The *Intifada* has so far been restricted to the Occupied Territories, which few Israelis visit, and the Israeli press frequently observes that the country must learn to live with it indefinitely. As Hirsch Goodman, an Israeli newspaper commentator, stated on American television when asked how the Israelis viewed the *Intifada:*

> I believe it has become routinized. It is something we have learned to manage even though we can't like it. I think the army has learned to adapt to it. The economic cost is marginal, four percent of the defense budget. It has not impacted on our relationships with Egypt and has not impacted on our international relations. Tourism is back in the country. Our relationship with the American Jewish Community is good.[49]

What is most striking about Goodman's statement is the narrow self-absorption that now seems to characterize a great deal of Israeli thinking. Even though Israeli forces were regularly killing each day at least one and often several Palestinian youths—the total now exceeds 1,000—the *Intifada* seemed to strike many Israelis as no more than a nuisance. Yet the *Intifada* should not be dismissed as a built-in aspect of Israeli life. It will not remain indefinitely merely a contest between stone-throwing students and well-armed Israeli forces. The dark chronicle of revolutions teaches that initially mild uprisings will, if prolonged, almost inevitably escalate into bloodier clashes. Even a brief revolution can quickly get out of hand—as Romania demonstrated in December 1989.

Yet the present Likud government obstinately refuses to deal with the PLO (or any Palestinians). As Prime Minister Shamir declared: "For the PLO, a Palestinian state is a minimum. Therefore, anyone who engages in negotiations with it in effect accepts this principle. What else can one talk about with the PLO, if not about a Palestinian state?" This analysis helps explain the obduracy of Shamir and the hard-line Israelis, since they equate dialogue with the PLO as an *"a priori* acceptance of a Palestinian state."[50]

## The Settlements Policy of the Bush Administration

The Bush administration has refused to say that Israel's settlements policy is not consistent with law. It muddied its position further when our UN representative abstained on a resolution offered by the Human Rights Commission, which called on Israel not to settle new Soviet immigrants in the "Palestinian and Arab" territories that Israel captured in the Six-Day War.

On February 25, 1990, Secretary of State James Baker, testifying before a congressional committee on the proposed $400 million loan guarantee for housing in Israel, stated that funding should be made contingent on the cessation of further Israeli settlements in the Occupied Territories. Later the same day, Bush implied that his opposition to Israeli settlements in the Occupied Territories included East Jerusalem.

The President's statement not only provoked the usual rage from pro-Israeli circles but the Senate majority leader, Senator George Mitchell, referred to it as a "gross blunder." In the face of loud outcries from Jewish organizations on this highly sensitive problem, and after an expression of concern by Mayor Teddy Kollek of Jerusalem, the subject was dropped. Still nobody, including the President, made the effort to point out that President Bush was simply repeating the official U.S. government position that UN Ambassador George Bush had stated to the United Nations on September 25, 1971. At that time, he had first endorsed a 1969 statement before the Security Council by his predecessor, Ambassador Charles Yost. Then Bush had added (relying on the Fourth Geneva Convention) that the U.S. government considered East Jerusalem to be "occupied territory and thereby subject to the provision of international law governing the rights and obligations of an occupying power."

Recent statements and reports clearly indicate that the United States is well aware of Israel's violations of human rights in the Occupied Territories. The U.S. government has declared several aspects of Israeli rule, including its territorial annexations and settlement schemes, to be a hindrance to American attempts to end the Arab-Israeli conflict, but administration actions fall far short of the effective countermeasures needed to stop these excesses.

CHAPTER TEN

# How Jewish Americans Became a Power Force in American Politics

IN THE EARLY DAYS of Jewish immigration, the first priority of the newly arrived Jew was to become integrated into American society as quickly as possible. Many of the early arrivals regarded Zionism as a hindrance to assimilation; they feared that it might convey a sense of divided loyalties. Indeed, many joined explicitly anti-Zionist organizations such as the Council on Judaism.

While keeping their Jewish cultural identity, most Jewish Americans preferred to pursue what sociologists call "the politics of group integration."[1] Thus, a large number avoided involvement in Zionism until the Holocaust and the actual creation of Israel. They adopted reformist liberalism—which largely explains why so many Jews today prefer the Democratic Party.

But, as the British Mandate drew to an end, more and more Jewish Americans began to empathize with the European Jews struggling to establish themselves in Palestine. Some even developed a savage resentment at the immigration constraints imposed by the mandate authorities.

Supporters of Israel made effective use of public relations. For Jewish Americans, the novel *Exodus,* an idealized story of the Zionist experience, acquired a degree of authority comparable to holy writ.

Yet *Exodus* was not the product of a virgin birth; its origin has been described by a public relations practitioner named Art Stevens in a book called *The Persuasion Explosion.* He writes that

> skillful public relations can speed up the acceptance of a concept whose time has come. A striking example of this involved eminent public relations consultant Edward Gottlieb. In the early 1950s, when the newly formed State of Israel was struggling for recognition in the court of world opinion, America was largely apathetic. Gottlieb, who at that time headed his own public relations firm, suddenly had a hunch about how to create a more sympathetic attitude toward Israel. He chose a writer and sent him to Israel with instructions to soak up the atmosphere of the country and create a novel about it. The book turned out to be *Exodus* by Leon Uris. His novel did more to popularize Israel with the American public than any other single presentation through the media.[2]

With overblown verbiage, the struggle of Europe's Jews against British bureaucracy was celebrated in an advertisement written by the playwright Ben Hecht. It appeared in 1948 shortly after the Irgun and the Stern Gang had blasted holes in the thick walls of Acre Prison and freed twenty-nine of their colleagues,[3] attracting nationwide comment. It read:

> The Jews of America are for you. You are their champions. . . . Every time you blow up a British arsenal, or wreck a British jail, or send a British railroad train sky high, or rob a British bank, or let go with your guns and bombs at British betrayers and invaders of your homeland, the Jews of America make a little holiday in their hearts.[4]

The shrillness and insensitivity of Hecht's words, however, repelled all but the most extreme sector of Jewish American opinion. Several Jewish American leaders conveyed that sentiment in December 1948, when Menachem Begin announced that he intended to visit the United States.[5] Alarmed by the refusal of "the top leadership of American Zionism" to "campaign against Begin's efforts" or "even to expose to its own constituents the dangers to Israel from support to Begin," a group of America's most distinguished Jewish leaders published an open letter in *The New York Times* on December 4, 1948, signed by, among others, Albert Einstein, Sidney Hook, Seymour Melman, and Hannah Arendt. The letter sharply warned the American Jewish community not to support "this latest manifestation of fascism," asserting that Begin's party has "within the Jewish community" preached "an admixture of ultra-nationalism, religious mysticism and racial superiority." It then noted that

> During the last years of sporadic anti-British violence, the IZL [Irgun] and Stern groups inaugurated a reign of terror in the Palestine Jewish community. Teachers were beaten up for speaking against them, adults were shot for not letting their children join them. By gangster methods, beatings, window-smashing, and widespread robberies, the terrorists intimidated the population and exacted a heavy tribute.

And the letter continued:

> The discrepancies between the bold claims now being made by Begin and his party, and their record of past performance in Palestine bear the imprint of no ordinary political party. This is the unmistakable stamp of a Fascist party for whom terrorism (against Jews, Arabs, and British alike), and misrepresentation are means, and a "Leader State" is the goal.

Most of the Jewish community had been horrified at the Deir Yassin incident, to the extent that the Jewish Agency sent a telegram of apology to King Abdullah, and although Begin and his party had little appeal for Americans, the Israeli cause made quantum gains after the Allied armies discovered the full extent of the Nazis' genocidal program.[6]

## Israel's Quest for a Sponsor

From Herzl to Ben-Gurion, Zionist leaders have envisaged Israel's need for a major patron and, inevitably, America has found itself in that role—largely because of its sizable and talented Jewish community. Israel's American friends have well understood that they could help most effectively by focusing their political clout on Congress, keeper of the purse strings. To achieve that rapport, they needed a persuasive theme and an effective lobbying organization to coordinate and channel their support.

At the outset, Jewish Americans sought to justify requests for congressional aid to Israel on humanitarian and idealistic grounds. Israeli leaders and their American friends soon recognized, however, that this angle might lose its appeal. Israel's heady victory in the 1967 War brought a change of approach. For both Israelis and Jewish Americans, that war spawned a new mythology. It cast the powerful Israeli Defense Forces in the role of a latter-day David.

With its impressive record of military victories, a prosperous and well-armed Israel could, they contended, serve America as a staunch ally, blocking the spread of Soviet and radical Arab influences, safeguarding the Gulf and the oil fields on the Gulf's littoral, and providing irrefutable intelligence on the whole Middle East.

Their argument was tactically inspired. A former AIPAC director, Morris J. Amitay, pointed out at a 1983 conference that congressmen would be more inclined to vote money for Israel based on its demonstrated strategic value than on its "moral authority."[7]

That theme was made even more explicit by the U.S. correspondent for *The Jerusalem Post,* Wolf Blitzer, who commented in a book published in 1985:

> It was not all that long ago when most Americans tended to cite primarily moral and emotional reasons for their support of Israel . . . but . . . the case for stressing the strategic side of this story has intensified in recent

> years. Israeli officials themselves have encouraged this trend, fearing that the massive sums of U.S. military and economic assistance to Israel might cease to be acceptable to the American public and Congress unless explained in such a hard-nosed way. If Israel were shown to provide a useful military and strategic service to the United States on the other hand, the aid becomes justified on the basis of self-interest, as well as national morality.[8]

Through constant repetition and the absence of skeptical challenge, Israel's claim of "strategic value" to America became the principal justification for America's aid to Israel. It soon evolved into what some anthropologists call a "fact of the mind"; and it found particular resonance with a succession of American presidents from Johnson to Reagan who viewed American policy in the Middle East (as well as elsewhere) in a Cold War context.[9] As a result, Israeli self-esteem and ambitions ballooned. Israel, its leaders claimed, was capable of taking on any power on earth, including the Soviet Union.

The distinguished *New York Times* correspondent Thomas L. Friedman has pointed out in his book *From Beirut to Jerusalem* that Israel plays two roles for American Jews: "one as a visible symbol which places the Jew in the world and integrates him with dignity, and the other as a haven that could protect the Jew from a world turned hostile." Before the 1967 War, the "balance between these two roles was very much weighted in favor of Israel as a safe haven and not as a symbol of Jewish identity."[10] Friedman illustrates the change of attitude by the comments of a senior American Jewish official who confided to him:

> "Before 1967, Israel in the eyes of many American Jews was a nation of nebachs. In my family, Israel was where we sent our used clothing. . . . That is how I thought of the place—a place you send used clothes to."
> After the 1967 war, the perception of Israel in the mind of many American Jews shifted radically, from Israel as a safe haven for other Jews to Israel as the symbol and carrier of Jewish communal identity.[11]

The reason for this, Friedman comments, is that after American Jews had comprehended the magnitude of Israel's 1967 victory, they said to themselves:

> My God, look who we are! We have power! We do not fit the Shylock image, we are ace pilots; we are not the cowering timid Jews who get sand kicked in their faces, we are tank commanders; we are not pale-faced wimps hiding in yeshivas, we are Hathaway Men, handsome charismatic generals with eye patches.[12]

This shift of image inspired the American Jewish community to revise its political strategy. Its lobbyists now portrayed an exciting vision of Israel as a major military nation that could, if "given the tools," not merely defend itself but also become America's bastion against Communist ambitions in the Middle East.

Friedman has described the relationship with America that developed:

> Although Israelis and American Jews began dating and fell in love after 1967, they never got married; they never made that total commitment to each other. . . .
> As with any love affair, it was only skin deep; the two parties didn't really know that much about each other. In many ways, American Jews liked Israel for her body and Israelis liked American Jews for their money.

But, he adds:

> The relationship worked as long as the two parties dealt with each other in a facile, superficial manner—as long as not too many Israelis moved to America and saw how attractive life there really was compared to life in Israel, and as long as those American Jews who went to Israel never got off the tour bus or, if they did, met only heroes and dead people and got right back on again.[13]

Thereafter, writes Friedman, there came "a process of mutual discovery." It began, he suggests, in 1973, when Egyptian forces crossed the Suez Canal, "and American Jews realized that their Israeli heroes were not supermen after all. This was reinforced by the banking scandals and exposure of corruption under the Labor governments. . . ."[14] And finally the old order was replaced in 1977 by the tough right-wing Likud Party of Menachem Begin.

## The American Fundamentalist Constituency

Besides the 5 million American Jews, Israel's American constituency has always included a significant percentage of the 40 million Evangelicals who view Israel as a partial fulfillment of biblical prophecy. Fringe elements among them believe that Christ will come again once the Jews have established a state, gathered all the Jews in Israel, and built a third Temple. The world would then end and practically all the Jews would be killed at Armageddon. The few Jewish survivors would convert to Christianity.

Today, the Fundamentalists support conservative policies that most liberal Jewish Americans oppose, such as school prayer. Their belief in biblical prophecy is compatible with Likud Party tenets. In fact, when Begin was warned that Fundamentalist aid was forthcoming only because American religious hard-liners believed that a new Jewish state was necessary for the second coming of Christ and the conversion of Jews to Christianity, he is reported to have responded: "I tell you, if the Christian Fundamentalists support us in Congress today, I will support them when the Messiah comes tomorrow."[15]

Israel, therefore, possesses a substantial asset in the remarkable spread of fundamentalism in the United States. Until recently, five Fundamentalist organizations were spending $50 million a year broadcasting their views, and there were three Christian television networks. But lately, the Fundamentalist movement has suffered setbacks. The Moral Majority has faded; sexual and financial scandals have weakened the so-called "televangelists." The Fundamentalists still have considerable political clout, however, and they are well represented in Congress by spokesmen such as Senator Jesse Helms and others from the South and West.[16]

## Israeli Espionage and the Pollard Affair

As a new nation surrounded by Arab adversaries, Israel has concentrated great effort on perfecting its abilities to gather and interpret intelligence data. At the same time, it has shared some of that data with the American services, although perhaps not so much as Israel publicly maintains. Carrying out Israel's intelligence depends on a network of agencies that cover a variety of intelligence tasks, ranging from industrial intelligence that support Israel's burgeoning industries, to political spying even on Israel's best friend.

The practice of industrial espionage has produced a number of disturbing incidents. In the 1950s there was substantial evidence that Israel had procured a shipment of uranium for its nuclear program from the Apollo Corporation in Pennsylvania. Though the Jewish owner of that firm was subsequently the target of an extensive FBI investigation, the case was left without indictment because of a lack of admissible evidence tying that disappearance directly to the owner.

In 1986, an Israeli commercial attaché in New York, not covered by diplomatic immunity, was arrested on the premises of a Long Island firm, then charged with breaking and entering and attempted burglary. When apprehended, he and a companion were busy rifling the company files. The attaché had apparently sought to buy a patent held by the corporation, but had been rebuffed.

On May 16, 1985, one Richard Kelly Smith of California was indicted on sixteen counts by a grand jury for violating the Arms Export Control Act by supposedly selling krytons—devices to trigger nuclear weapons—to the Heli Trading Company of Israel.

On December 12, 1985, American intelligence agencies discovered that the Israelis had procured the specifications for the new chrome process used to plate the gun barrels of the MI (Abrams) tank; and in December 1990, they found that Israel had pirated American technology to make cluster bombs and had sold the process to other nations.

In a report prepared in 1979, but updated and released in 1986, the CIA asserted that so far as spying and industrial espionage were concerned, Israel was a close second to the Soviet Union, an avowed enemy.

But all these incidents seemed insignificant when compared with the military espionage activities of Jonathan J. Pollard, a Jewish American employed as a civilian analyst for the U.S. Navy. For over a year, he secretly had procured information of a kind useful only to Israeli intelligence. It also included a wide range of material not directly or indirectly concerned with the Arabs or Israel's defense concerns. Defense Secretary Weinberger testified before the court in secret session that Pollard had done great damage to the United States and had carried off a truckload of the highest classified documents.

Israel's disingenuous explanation was that this was a rogue operation, carried on by Israeli intelligence operatives without government authority. Israel also promised its full cooperation with the American investigation.

However, when the Americans sought that cooperation, including interviews with the operatives who had handled Pollard, Israel refused to allow its personnel to leave Israel and pointedly refused to return all but a small fraction of the stolen documents.

Any doubt of Israel's official complicity in this affair was dispelled by its treatment of the so-called "rogues." As in the case of those involved in the Sabra and Shatilla massacres, the operatives were showered with rewards. The chief of the office in Israel that compiled the "want lists" for Pollard was given a lucrative position in a government-owned chemical works. Air Force Colonel Aviem Sella, who was Pollard's handler, was posted to a key air base in Israel, made a brigadier general, and thus put on the ladder heading toward the position of Chief of Staff of the Israeli Air Force. Only a cutoff of U.S. intelligence sharing forced Sella's premature retirement.

In spite of this, Israel, Pollard, and Pollard's American defenders (who are busy trying to get him released) sought to justify Pollard's conduct in a number of ways.

First, they claimed that his conduct was not really espionage because he had been working for a friendly country. Thus, no damage had been done to U.S. interests, Secretary Weinberger's testimony to the contrary notwithstanding.

Second, Israel was entitled to engage in such activities because other countries were spying in America.

Third, Israel was entitled to the information it took and which the U.S. government had improperly withheld from it, Israel's judgment in these matters being the determining one.

Fourth, Pollard was acting from a patriotic devotion to that country, despite the fact that he was then and is now an American citizen. It was little wonder that this last argument, as will be seen, struck a raw nerve in the American Jewish community.

The plain fact was that Pollard's motivations, whatever he might represent them to be, were clearly based not on moral principle but on the more tangible principal one deposits in a bank. The evidence proves conclusively that he accepted $30,000 in cash, a fur coat and a diamond ring for his wife, a free trip to Europe and Israel. He also accepted the promise of $300,000 to be deposited in his name in an Israeli bank.

Some Israelis, more sensitive than others, questioned the wisdom and propriety of spying on a country they constantly refer to as Israel's "ally." Among these was Isser Harel, the former head of Mossad, who labeled Pollard's suborning "sheer idiocy": "Should we create a situation in which people in the U.S. may even consider Jews a security risk? It was irresponsible, stupid of us." He also said: "Using a Jew as a spy was a . . . major blunder. Israel's intelligence community has purposely refrained from using Jews in their home countries so as not to risk putting entire communities in compromising positions. . . . As far as possible, we would rather rely on others, not Jews. . . ."[17]

The American Jewish community reacted to these disclosures with mixed emotions. Though its members were naturally sympathetic to Israel, they were deeply concerned about how the disclosures might compromise Jewish Americans with their Gentile fellow citizens. They shared the view stated by a former head of Mossad that it was madness for Israel to use American Jewish agents because it would simply cast a shadow over the patriotism of the entire Jewish community and open the way to charges of dual loyalties or even of disloyalty to the nation whose citizenship they held.

Many members of the Jewish community had long contended that their activities in support of Israel were unobjectionable because Israel and the United States had congruent interests. The Pollard affair clearly suggested otherwise. Prominent Jewish leaders and organizations heaped denunciation on Pollard and on the government that had used him, and tacitly supported his life sentence, even though that risked violating a well-enforced taboo—that no Jew not living in Israel should ever criticize the Israeli government.

## The Background for the American Jews' Political Effectiveness

Certain basic facts distinguish Jewish Americans from any other ethnic group:

*First:* About a fifth of the Jews in America (1 million) are actively involved in promoting Zionist causes.[18] These activist Jews are, as Rabbi Arthur Herzberg has observed, motivated by a universal kinship. "The sense of belonging to a worldwide Jewish people, of which Israel is the center, is a religious sentiment, but it seems to persist even among Jews who regard themselves as secularists or atheists."[19]

These sentiments are strengthened by years of what the sociologists call "marginality." Writes the political scientist Charles Liebman: "support for Israel becomes not only support for a state . . . or for its inhabitants—rather, support for Israel is the symbol of one's Jewish identity."[20]

*Second:* More than any other group in America, Jewish Americans have a strong tradition of both charity and political activism. They contribute with great generosity to major philanthropies, feel at home in an active political environment, and have a flair for efficient organization. Although they constitute only about 2.5 percent of the population, approximately 90 percent of them vote in presidential elections as compared to a general average that varies between 40 to 55 percent.[21]

Moreover, Lee O'Brien, who has written a standard book on Jewish American organizations, notes that "This high level of voter participation goes hand in hand with financial donations to candidates. . . . American Jews are estimated to donate more than half the large gifts to national Democratic campaigns, and an increasing amount to Republicans as well."[22]

The clout that Jewish Americans exercise in American politics is far incommensurate with their population. Their power derives primarily from an active interest in public affairs and a willingness to work hard for causes in which they believe. It derives also from their flair for understanding the electoral process, their gift for efficient organization, and, most of all, from their dedication to philanthropy, reinforced by supersensitive peer pressure among members of a group forced together by a discrimination still apparent in far too many sectors of American society.

## The Assigned Role of Jewish Americans

Israeli leaders have taken full advantage of these characteristics of American Jewry. They have made crystal clear that they expect Jewish Americans to lobby for Israeli interests with members of both the executive and legislative branches, and to present and defend Israel's case to major American opinion makers. Jewish Americans are orchestrated to persuade powerful congressional leaders that Israel's government is both righteous and wise, and that Congress should accede to its requests without asking questions. Moreover, they should, as individuals, lavish philanthropic benefactions on Israel.[23]

Until recently, only a handful of Jewish Americans openly challenged that assignment, keeping their views to themselves. But today, some who are paying the bills no longer propose to stand mute. In their view, one does not have to leap off a high bridge before pointing out the folly of it.[24]

For a long while, Jewish Americans were able to convince themselves—and others—that Israeli and U.S. interests were invariably congruent. But after the Pollard case, the rise of the *Intifada,* and other incidents, many more American Jews began asking questions. They were further upset when Israeli right-wingers like Shlomo Aviner claimed that the Jewish people should be expelled from America and sent to Israel. Those who failed to come to Israel, he tastelessly asserted, were faithless assimilators.[25]

The American Jewish attitude toward Israel and vice versa was explored in Philip Roth's novel, *The Counterlife.* As Shuki, his young Israeli protagonist, says to Nathan Zuckerman, the American Jew visiting Israel:

> You think in the *Diaspora* it's abnormal? Come live here. This is the *homeland* of Jewish abnormality. Worse: now *we* are the dependent Jews, on your money, your lobby, on our big allowance from Uncle Sam, while *you* are the Jews living interesting lives, comfortable lives, without apology, without shame, and perfectly *independent*. . . . The fact remains that in the Diaspora a Jew like you lives securely, without real fear of persecution or violence, while we are living just the kind of imperiled Jewish existence that we came here to replace. . . . We are the excitable, ghettoized, jittery little Jews of the Diaspora, and you are the Jews with all the confidence and cultivation that comes of feeling at home where you are.[26]

Roth belongs to that growing group of American Jews who explicitly assert that the United States is their promised land.[27]

That attitude disturbs and angers Israelis. They deeply resent that fewer and fewer Diaspora Jews look to Israel for leadership. If American Jews are unwilling to migrate to Israel and assume the country's burdens directly, they should at least refrain from offering advice. Lucius Aemilius Paulus, the Roman general, delivered a famous admonition to armchair strategists. On assuming command of Rome's legions fighting against Macedonia in 168 B.C., the doughty warrior suggested that if his critics thought they could do better, "Let them not refuse their aid to the state, but let them come with me into Macedonia." The army, he said, was like the crew of a ship embarked on a dangerous voyage. Those who stayed in Rome should not, he averred, "from the safety of the shore, assume the office of a pilot."

Various developments have, however, challenged the assigned roles of the American Diaspora and the Jews in Israel. During the negotiation of a coalition government after the 1988 elections, both Likud and the Labor alignment, disenchanted with the grand coalition that had existed from 1984 to 1988, sought to form a government with the aid of the indispensable religious parties. These minority parties demanded not only an appropriate allotment of cabinet seats and committee assignments but enactment of a law declaring that only conversion to Judaism by Orthodox rabbis was valid when applying for Israeli citizenship.

The possibility of a government formed on this basis aroused Jewish Americans (80 percent of whom belong to Conservative or Reform congregations) to virtual mutiny. Committees met and a strong delegation was dispatched to Jerusalem to convey the American Diaspora's disapprobation in no uncertain terms.

In the end, the Americans won. The grand coalition was reluctantly revived, even though Likud had already lined up a two-vote majority in the Knesset for a narrowly based right-wing and religious-party coalition.[28] The experience confirmed Eisenhower's 1957 view that America can indeed compel policy changes in Jerusalem when it chooses to take a firm stand.

Confronted by the growing theocratic trend in Israeli life and the embarrassing need to explain away Israeli civil rights violations, the American Jewish community is being pushed toward a decision. The older generation—

the present leadership—proposes to support Israel regardless of whether it has to abandon its own principles in the process. The younger generation, while not openly opposing Israel, has quietly withdrawn its active support. The refusal of some Jewish Americans to go to Israel during the *Intifada* was resentfully noted in Israel. No less to the point, in a revolt against AIPAC's views, announcements were made that independent lobbies will hereafter speak out on their own.[29]

## The Organizational Structure That Multiplies the Political Muscle of American Jews

Today, the center of the complex system of Israeli organizations in the United States is AIPAC.[30] According to I. L. Kenen, its founder and longtime director,

> In 1950, Israel appealed for American financial assistance to help absorb the huge influx of Jewish refugees and immigrants between 1948 and 1950. Always worried about the Arab reaction, our State Department was then adamantly opposed to any economic aid for Israel, which, it insisted, would deepen Arab bitterness. Accordingly, Israel's American friends concluded that they must appeal directly to Congress for enabling legislation. That was the beginning of the pro-Israel lobby, now called the American Israel Public Affairs Committee (AIPAC).[31]

As AIPAC is specifically a lobbying organization, it is precluded by statute from making direct campaign contributions and thus it need not register as a political action committee (PAC). With an experienced staff of sixty presided over by a strong executive, Thomas Dine, who was once an administrative assistant to Senator Kennedy, AIPAC pursues its goal of protecting the interests of a foreign government.

AIPAC finesses its inability to make direct campaign contributions by maintaining close communications with the eighty-plus PACs around the country that favor the Israeli cause. Its interlocking connections and directors with these PACs provide readily available funds when necessary.[32]

### *Nationwide Organization Alerted to Respond*

AIPAC issues "Action Alerts" to more than a thousand Jewish leaders countrywide. An "Alert" will usually prod the sympathetic recipient into dropping in on his congressman, or sending him a letter or a telegram.[33] As if on command, legions of other supporters will buttonhole owners or editors of their local newspapers and bombard their representatives in Washington. Nor does any critical newspaper article, column, or advertisement ever lack a prompt answer by some prominent individual of some pro-Israeli organization.

AIPAC maintains a computer list of key contacts for every member of

Congress—people who personally know or at least contribute heavily to the legislator and who can be counted on to reach him or her on issues of concern to Israel.[34] The contact's wealth is less important than his ease of access to the lawmaker, including the President of the United States.

Most of the AIPAC staff devote their time to mobilizing AIPAC members and writing propaganda pamphlets. The frontliners, a corps of skilled lobbyists, tirelessly roam the halls of Congress to press the point at hand.[35] Publicity is AIPAC's most effective weapon. AIPAC issues many propaganda tracts and publishes the *Near East Report,* a weekly newsletter mailed to about sixty thousand people and sent free to all congressmen, high government officials, and many media VIPs. A supplement called *Myths and Facts* is distributed to campuses. It attempts, for example, to dispel such "myths" as the accusation that the Palestinian refugees were deliberately frightened into flight during 1948–49.[36]

Paul Weyrich, a political analyst and former Senate aide, explains how AIPAC uses these publishing assets:

> It's a remarkable system they have. If you vote with them, or make a public statement they like, they get the word out fast through their own publications and through editors around the country who are sympathetic to their cause. Of course it works in reverse as well. If you say something they don't like, you can be denounced or censured through the same network. That kind of pressure is bound to affect Senators' thinking, especially if they are wavering or need support.[37]

### *Regular Indoctrination Meetings*

Annual morale boosters are held in Washington, where AIPAC's members listen to speeches by major politicians and the Israeli ambassador.[38] At one AIPAC meeting, then Vice President George Bush attacked the Democrats for being "soft on anti-Semitism" and reassured the membership about the administration's continuing battle against it. Nearly two thousand AIPAC members, including a small group of Christians, attend these affairs.

One conference highlight is the invariably upbeat annual report of Thomas Dine. He recites, by rote, that U.S.-Israeli relations have never been better. With sincere conviction, he asserts that "a whole new constituency of support for Israel is being built" in precisely the areas where "we are weakest—among government officials in the state, defense and treasury departments, in the CIA, in science, trade, agriculture and other agencies." Israel, Dine reiterates, is now treated by the United States as an "ally, not just a friend, an asset, rather than a liability, a mature and capable partner, not some vassal state."[39]

Thus bolstered, the AIPAC members return to their homes rededicated to promoting the well-being of a foreign country in which they assiduously refrain from living. To keep them "up to speed," AIPAC conducts tightly scheduled annual workshops in its five regions.

AIPAC provides ongoing intelligence about congressional activities. It keeps track of how every congressmen and senator votes, and it concentrates on the chairmen and other leading members of key committees that pass on legislation which affects Israel.

As a result:

—it can and does target available resources through political action committees;
—it provides speech materials and background guidance for sympathetic legislators during relevant committee hearings; and
—it systematically provides election-year help to marginal members and discourages backsliding by threatening to support rival candidates against congressmen who do not toe AIPAC's line.

Exhibit I (below) is a fair sample of the political money spent by Jewish organizations and the care with which it is distributed. Dine explained how much progress AIPAC has made: "We are not a PAC, we're a movement, a political factor, neither liberal nor conservative, neither Democratic nor Republican. We're the top of the iceberg of the pro-Israel community. We figure to expand support for Israel through the rest of the century."[40]

AIPAC does not try to influence Israel's policies vis-à-vis America's interests; it simply seeks to accommodate whatever Israeli government is in power. That point was well made by Kenneth Bialkin, a principal spokesman for the Jewish American community. Before the 1984 Israeli elections, Bialkin was quoted in *The Jerusalem Post* as stating, "If the Alignment wins and changes Israel's policies, we will support them; if the Likud wins and pursues a strong line in the West Bank we will get behind them."[41]

Although Bialkin was paraphrasing, perhaps unconsciously, Stephen Decatur's theme of "our country, right or wrong!", there was a significant difference. Stephen Decatur was speaking of his *own* country, America. Bialkin apparently neither knew nor cared that Israel's pursuit of "a strong line in the West Bank" contravened an expressed objective of American policy.

The Israeli lobby's hold over Congress was described by Robert G. Kaiser, then an editor of *The Washington Post.* On May 27, 1984, in an article entitled "The U.S. Risks Suffocating Israel with Kindness," he wrote that the House and Senate were competing over which "would give more to Israel this year." The Reagan administration had requested $850 million in economic aid (in addition to military aid), and he notes:

> The Senate Foreign Relations Committee—whose chairman and ranking Democrat are both up for reelection this November . . . quickly upped the ante to $1.2 billion, an increase of nearly 50 percent. This worried members of the House Foreign Affairs Committee. . . . "We can't let them be more generous to Israel than we are," some said. In the end, the House committee proposed $1.1 billion, "but it will come out of conference at $1.2 billion," a knowledgeable member predicted.

EXHIBIT I

Contributions by Pro-Israeli PACs
to Key Members of Congress and the Senate, 1984–90

| State | Name and Party | Senate House | Committees[1] | 1984 | 1986 | 1988 | 1990 | 1980–90 Total |
|---|---|---|---|---|---|---|---|---|
| AZ | De Concini (D) | S | A(D,FO), I | 0 | 1,000 | 30,000 | 3,000 | $ 63,000 |
| CA | Lantos (D) | H11 | FA(E&ME) | 24,450 | 1,750 | 3,250 | 7,250 | 36,700 |
| CA | Levine (D) | H27 | FA(E&ME) | 24,300 | 20,000 | 4,800 | 20,680 | 69,980 |
| CT | Gejdenson (D) | H2 | FA | 67,350 | 31,829 | 29,450 | 27,000 | 155,629 |
| FL | Mack (R) | S | FR | 3,750 | 1,550 | 36,622 | 2,500 | 44,422 |
| FL | Smith (D) | H16 | FA(E&ME) | 48,230 | 55,800 | 32,950 | 15,100 | 152,080 |
| FL | Fascell (D) | H19 | FA | 76,500 | 18,500 | 18,250 | 10,000 | 123,250 |
| IL | Simon (D) | S | FR | 49,539 | 4,500 | 23,013 | 262,655 | 339,707 |
| IL | Michel (R) | H18 | I | 27,750 | 5,250 | 3,750 | 5,000 | 41,750 |
| IL | Durbin (D) | H20 | A | 82,149 | 5,350 | 13,075 | 9,066 | 109,640 |
| ME | Mitchell (D) | S | I | 0 | 7,500 | 15,000 | — | 22,500 |
| MD | Sarbanes (D) | S | FR(NE&SA) | 3,000 | 0 | 25,000 | — | 28,000 |
| MA | Kennedy (D) | S | AS | 2,000 | 6,750 | 16,000 | 1,000 | 25,750 |
| MI | Levin (D) | S | AS | 31,725 | 1,000 | 10,575 | 243,000 | 286,300 |
| MI | Wolpe (D) | H3 | FA | 48,900 | 27,750 | 19,100 | 51,200 | 146,950 |
| MN | Durenberger[2] (R) | S | — | 2,250 | 8,250 | 143,000 | 2,000 | 155,500 |
| NE | Kerry (D) | S | — | — | — | 89,000 | 2,000 | 91,000 |
| NV | Bryan[3] (D) | S | — | — | 49,750 | 74,250 | 3,000 | 127,000 |
| NJ | Lautenberg (D) | S | A(D,FO) | 5,250 | 12,000 | 200,050 | 12,000 | 229,300 |
| NJ | Torricelli (D) | H9 | FA(E&ME) | 93,000 | 13,700 | 7,500 | 9,300 | 123,500 |
| NM | Bingaman (D) | S | AS | 22,500 | 9,000 | 95,850 | 500 | 127,850 |
| NY | Downey (D) | H2 | — | 44,964 | 7,500 | 9,390 | 7,250 | 69,104 |
| NY | Mrazek (D) | H3 | A(FO) | 107,934 | 16,419 | 14,670 | 6,700 | 145,723 |
| NY | McHugh (D) | H28 | A(FO),I | 76,500 | 12,000 | 5,500 | 6,050 | 100,050 |
| ND | Burdick (D) | S | A | 0 | 5,000 | 55,750 | — | 60,750 |
| OH | Metzenbaum (D) | S | I | 0 | 6,000 | 173,285 | 3,000 | 182,285 |
| OH | Feighan (D) | H19 | FA(E&ME) | 77,700 | 52,750 | 4,000 | 5,500 | 139,950 |
| IE | AuCoin (D) | H1 | A(D) | 74,850 | 17,500 | 9,100 | 1,450 | 102,900 |
| PA | Kostmayer (D) | H8 | FA | 74,100 | 28,500 | 32,250 | 15,750 | 150,600 |
| TN | Sasser (D) | S | A(D) | 1,500 | 1,000 | 38,000 | — | 40,500 |
| TX | Wilson (D) | H2 | A(D,FO),I | 24,600 | 6,750 | 500 | 6,000 | 37,850 |
| TX | Bustamante (D) | H23 | AS | 46,950 | 5,750 | 5,800 | 750 | 59,250 |
| UT | Owens (D) | H2 | FA(E&ME) | 0 | 15,600 | 30,300 | 48,900 | 94,800 |
| WA | Miller (R) | H1 | FA | 13,000 | 12,250 | 51,698 | 29,600 | 106,548 |
| WV | Byrd (D) | S | A(D),AS | 0 | 0 | 5,500 | — | 5,500 |
| WI | Obey (D) | H7 | A(FO) | 15,300 | 26,750 | 23,600 | 42,950 | 108,600 |

1. COMMITEES

Senate: FR: Foreign Relations (NE&SA: Subcommittee on the Near East and South Asia);
AS: Armed Services; A: Appropriations (D: Defense; FO: Foreign Operations);
I: Select Intelligence.

House: FA: Foreign Affairs (E&ME: Subcommittee on Europe and the Middle East;
AS: Armed Services; A: Appropriations (D: Defense; FO: Foreign Operations);
I: Permanent Select Intelligence.

2. His 1988 funding was clearly a reward for services rendered in the Iran-Contra hearings.

3. Given to purge Senator Hecht, a Jewish American, who had supported administration arms deals with the Middle East.

1990 SOURCE: *Washington Report* (April 1981), vol. IX, no. 11, pp.17–23.

Kaiser points out that such episodes are rarely covered by the media, since "in Washington, reporters and politicians share a cynical understanding that Israel and its American friends constitute probably the single most effective lobby in the country; they take its victories for granted." He then adds:

> Ask a senator or congressman on one of the committees involved if anyone this year seriously questioned whether the huge amount of American aid to Israel was a good idea, and you are more likely to get a laugh than an answer.[42]

It is not surprising, therefore, that Dine has been singled out as one of the most influential men in the capital, and that AIPAC has been described by *The New York Times* as "the most powerful, best-run and effective foreign policy interest group in Washington."[43]

### *A Network of Pro-Israeli Organizations*

Beyond AIPAC, there are thirty-eight major Jewish organizations[44] and scores of smaller ones nationwide. Although each has its own specific program, they are all more than willing to assist AIPAC. Leaders of the major groups sit on AIPAC's board, which enables it to exert grass-roots pressure far beyond its own membership. The major groups also belong to the Conference of Presidents of Major American Jewish Organizations. Heretofore, the Presidents' Conference has focused primarily on the executive branch while AIPAC concentrates on the Congress, a division of labor that, with AIPAC's increasing strength, now seems redundant.[45]

## The AWACs Incident—A Turning Point

The most significant demonstration of the lobby's power came in 1981, when President Reagan, at the beginning of his administration, encountered opposition to the sale of AWACs to Saudi Arabia (see Chapter 6). By any measure, the deal was good for the United States. It would, as the President saw it, help the Saudis defend their oil fields on which Europe and Japan depend, guard against attacks from Iran, and it would enrich the American economy by $8.5 billion from the sale of planes and spare parts. Thus the sale had everything going for it—except AIPAC.

AIPAC was dead set against the deal, ostensibly because it endangered Israel's security, but more likely because the AIPAC leaders wished to teach the new administration a lesson. It was not that the AWACS posed a threat to Israel. Indeed, former Israeli Defense Minister Ezer Weizman denied any dangers, because the planes were slow and could be easily shot down.[46] Nonetheless, pitted against the sale, the lobby deployed its formidable forces.

As Roberta Feuerlicht, a Jewish American writer, recounts, AIPAC's campaign even intruded into her synagogue. On Yom Kippur, the rabbi's sermon before the prayer is usually devoted to a text in the Talmud. But in 1981, the pre-prayer sermon in her synagogue was devoted to a denunciation of AWACs. The rabbi told the congregation that "Jews must fight the 'outrageous' charge that there is a Jewish lobby. . . . At the same time, he inconsistently urged his congregants to fight against the sale of AWACs."[47]

Congressmen were bombarded by petitions and by anti-AWACs tracts written by AIPAC staffers. They were lectured endlessly by AIPAC representatives. AIPAC sent every member of the relevant committee a free copy of the novel *Holocaust.*[48] Full-page ads appeared in major newspapers denouncing the sale to "an oil arrogant, oil greedy nation."[49]

The confrontation ran from April to October and became so nasty that the exasperated President on October 1, 1981, complained at a press conference that "it is not the business of other countries to make American foreign policy."[50] Because of AIPAC's campaign and in spite of White House pressure, on October 14 the House overwhelmingly voted 301 to 111 to turn down the sale. One naysayer was the influential Daniel Rostenkowski, chairman of the Ways and Means Committee, who later admitted that, while he favored the sale as a matter of policy, he had voted against it to avoid tangling with the Jewish lobby.[51]

Since it requires both houses to reject a weapons sale, the President had to invest considerable time and prestige over the next two weeks pressuring the Republican-controlled Senate. Although AIPAC had managed to induce fifty-four senators—more than a majority—to sign a letter publicly opposing the sale, the President personally lobbied those senators, warning them against succumbing to AIPAC. In the end, the sale was approved on October 28 by a narrow 52 to 48 vote.

The approval came with restrictions that seemed to question the Saudis' honor as well as infringing on their sovereignty. The restrictions (in the form of a presidential letter to the Senate) promised that the AWACs would be deployed only within the boundaries of Saudi Arabia; that the security of American technology would be protected; that the Saudis would share any AWACs information only with America; and that the sale would assure "substantial assistance" from Saudi Arabia to the Middle East peace process.[52]

Congress was thoroughly brainwashed by the AWACs incident.[53] Some legislators who had yielded to Reagan's importunings and voted for the sale suddenly found themselves labeled "anti-Semites," a favorite lobby tactic. Thus, a New York Jewish newspaper wrote of Maryland's Senator Charles Mathias, a highly principled man who regarded the sale as in America's interest, "Mr. Mathias values the importance of oil over the well-being of Jews and the State of Israel. The Jewish people cannot be fooled by such a person, no matter what he said, because his act proved who he was."[54]

AIPAC treated its near defeat of the bill as a victory, and as soon as it was passed established a new publication, *Saudi (AWACs) Watch,* ostensibly to monitor Saudi compliance, but in reality to undercut Saudi Arabia. Saudi oil policy was called anti-American; Saudi aid to the Palestinians was labeled support for "PLO terrorism"; the Saudis were chided for not bullying other Arab states to surrender on Israel's terms.

AIPAC later bragged about its AWAC fight in letters soliciting new members. In a 1982 mailing, it noted that "we almost won!" and went on to declare:

> To look at this figure [$6 billion in aid] in terms of what *your own membership in AIPAC means in aid to Israel, consider this: On a budget of just $1.8 million, AIPAC successfully lobbied Congress in 1981 for $2.2 BILLION in foreign aid. This means that every membership gift of $35 to AIPAC resulted indirectly in $42,777 of US AID TO ISRAEL!* (Emphasis in original)

## AIPAC's Current Status

In mid-1986, a former AIPAC staff member, Richard B. Straus, wrote in *The Washington Post* that "American Middle East policy has shifted so dramatically in favor of Israel" that it could only be described as "a revolution." He quoted AIPAC's Tom Dine as saying that Secretary of State Shultz is the "architect of the special relationship," which, Dine added, "is a deep, broad-based partnership progressing day-by-day toward a full-fledged diplomatic and military alliance." Straus commented: "State Department Arabists acknowledge that Arab interests hardly get a hearing today in Washington." One former State Department official observed: "We used to have a two-track policy. Now only Israel's interests are considered."[55]

Another AIPAC secret weapon is its network of ardent Israeli supporters in the federal departments and agencies that affect the fate of Israel. During Lyndon Johnson's presidency, some influential pro-Israelis functioned in the top echelons of government. Below these powerful men was a coterie of Israeli supporters in lesser jobs but no less important in their cumulative influence. A comparable number of Israeli sympathizers has persisted throughout succeeding administrations, including Bush's.[56]

Their presence has greatly enhanced the effectiveness of AIPAC, because a corps of pro-Israeli supporters in Congress and the executive branch assures an institutional bias. During Reagan's administration, these bureaucratic supporters were dubbed the "Israeli Mafia."

Equally intrusive are the eager pro-Israeli congressional staffers on Capitol Hill. Large congressional staffs are organized like the executive branch in miniature; specific individuals are assigned to keep track of particular topics. To an extraordinary degree, the staff assigned to watch the Middle East is composed of dedicated pro-Israelis. Referring to senatorial staffs, former

AIPAC director Morris Amitay observed that "There are now a lot of guys at the working level up here who happen to be Jewish, who are willing to make a little bit extra effort and to look at certain issues in terms of their Jewishness. . . . These are all guys who are in a position to make the decision in their areas for these Senators." Adds an unidentified aide: "It's long been known that several staff people support Israel. But we don't do it for money the way some paid lobbyists do. We do it out of a very, very passionate commitment."[57]

Another example: In 1983, an Israeli government official gave a special briefing to the senior aides of about fifty prominent Senate and House members on why Israel had to remain in Lebanon and why Reagan's peace plan could not work. AIPAC followed up that meeting with memoranda to members of Congress and persuaded *The Washington Post* to publish an Op-Ed piece by Dine entitled "Pressuring Israel Is Dumb."[58] This whole effort was a direct attempt to influence Congress to back Israel's opposition to Reagan's September 1982 peace plan.

To further encourage the support of key aides, AIPAC works with Israeli universities to provide congressional staff members with expense-paid tours of Israel. The ten-day trips concentrate on burnishing Israel's image. As Israel's backers have reformulated their appeal, the pitch has shifted so that visitors see Israeli military maneuvers more than its cultural institutions.

AIPAC has been equally active in trying to prevent legislators from visiting Arab countries. In 1983, the National Association of Arab Americans, working with the World Affairs Council of Amman, invited all congressmen and their spouses on an expense-paid trip to Jordan with a side visit to the occupied West Bank. AIPAC's *Near East Report* scoffed at the idea and assured its readers that Israel would prevent the congressmen from inspecting West Bank conditions firsthand. In the climate of fear generated by AIPAC, only three congressmen were prepared to make the trip. The project was dropped for lack of interest.[59]

## Assuring Representation in the Congress

Although the number of Jewish senators and representatives seems excessive relative to the Jewish presence in the population at large, not all Jewish members of Congress are strongly pro-Israel. In fact, the prime targets of AIPAC are non-Jewish members. AIPAC follows the electoral fortunes of both its enemies and its friends; whether they are Democrats or Republicans does not matter, AIPAC's sole interest is whether they toe the AIPAC line.

As AIPAC reported a year after the 1981 Saudi-AWACs imbroglio, all fourteen of Israel's Senate supporters were reelected; so too were two new Jewish senators, while the number of Jewish House members increased from twenty-four to thirty, despite the loss of a freshman member. In many cases, only pro-Israeli candidates were running on both sides.[60]

Among AIPAC's closest non-Jewish supporters in the Senate have been

Joseph Biden, Alan Cranston, Dennis DeConcini, Christopher J. Dodd, Daniel K. Inouye, Robert W. Kasten, Jr., Edward M. Kennedy, George J. Mitchell, Daniel P. Moynihan, Bob Packwood, Donald W. Riegle, Jr., Paul Simon, and John W. Warner.[61] In the House, AIPAC's major supporters have formed what *The Jewish Post* has described as a "pro-Israel caucus" under the leadership of Barney Frank, Benjamin Gilman, Stephen Solarz, Tom Lantos, Mel Levine, Larry Smith, Henry Waxman, Charles Wilson, and Sidney Yates.[62]

AIPAC obviously pays particular attention to the members and staffs of those Senate committees that control relevant policies and purse strings. The House Foreign Affairs Committee and the Senate Relations Affairs Committee receive especially close scrutiny. An AIPAC representative attends every open meeting of those two committees and assiduously contacts members and staffers alike to voice AIPAC's views. Closed meetings are attended by pro-Israel senators or congressmen or by aides who quickly report back to AIPAC.

## Efforts to Suppress Independent Opinion

Among AIPAC's publications is a 1983 pamphlet, *The Campaign to Discredit Israel.* In 154 pages it lists 21 organizations and 39 individuals as anti-Israel. AIPAC also published a roster of unfriendly administrators and teachers at colleges across the country.[63] A similar "enemies list" has been circulated by the Anti-Defamation League of B'nai B'rith. It mentions thirty-one organizations and thirty-four ex-congressmen. As Paul Findley has remarked, "These . . . blacklists [are] reminiscent of the worst tactics of the McCarthy era."[64]

Edward Tivnan, a writer and television producer who is the author of *The Lobby: Jewish Political Power and American Foreign Policy,* describes the way in which AIPAC uses one of its blacklisting pamphlets:

> Since 1977, AIPAC had been sending out annually a Xeroxed "Who's Who" list of "anti-Israel" organizations and personalities . . . *The Campaign to Discredit Israel* was nothing more than a campaign to discredit critics of US-Israeli policy—a hit list for local Jewish leaders to refer to whenever anyone came to town to discuss the Middle East.[65]

Congressman Paul McCloskey of California replied to a questioner during the 1980 elections that Israel's policies were hampering peace in the Middle East. "The next day," McCloskey recalled, "the Anti-Defamation League charged that my [McCloskey's] remarks were patently anti-Semitic."[66] AIPAC and other groups have assiduously claimed that opposition to Israeli policy equals anti-Zionism, and anti-Zionism is anti-Semitism.

Viewed objectively, it seems astonishing that Jewish organizations and

Israeli spokesmen should employ the charge of "anti-Semitism" so carelessly as to trivialize it. "Anti-Semitism" is a term freighted with a long and ugly history. It conjures up images of vicious civic discrimination, the religious persecutions of the Inquisition, the Russian pogroms, and the ultimate horror of the Holocaust. Any Jewish American who equates that term with critical comments on transient Israeli policy implicitly acknowledges that he cannot defend Israel's practices by rational argument.

Is it anti-Semitic, for example, to point out repeated Israeli violations of the 1949 Geneva Conventions? Or to suggest, as the State Department did from 1979 to 1981, that the implanting of settlements in the Occupied Areas was illegal? The overuse of the term "anti-Semitism" gives the practitioners of real anti-Semitism a quasi-respectability, just as Joseph McCarthy devalued the term "Communist" by recklessly applying it to anyone whose views deviated from his own.[67]

In addition, the haphazard use of this odious term is clearly intended to stifle criticism of American policies in the Middle East. When it is pointed out that Jewish Israelis constantly criticize their government's policies, the rejoinder is that only Jews may disagree with other Jews. Yet Israel's defenders constantly attack the Pope and the Roman Catholic Church for not recognizing Israel.

Charges of anti-Semitism can occasionally backfire. In 1990, Jewish Senator Rudy Boschwitz of Minnesota, the only defeated incumbent senator, found himself in a tightening race against Paul Wellstone, a college professor and also a Jew who predicts the creation of a Palestinian state. Not content with $144,150 of pro-Israel PAC money, Boschwitz sent out a circular letter to his state's small Jewish community attacking Wellstone, not because of his PLO stand, but because he had married a Gentile and was not bringing his children up in the Jewish faith. Word of this hatchet job reached the non-Jewish electorate, whose members, angry at such religious bigotry, came down decisively on Wellstone's side. Boschwitz now works for the Jewish Institute for National Security Affairs (JINSA), a body devoted to arranging the release of sensitive technology and high-tech weaponry to Israel.

## Jewish Fundraising

Unquestionably, a large amount of campaign money raised—perhaps 90 percent—particularly for Democratic candidates, comes from Jewish sources. Eighty percent of the Democratic 1952 presidential campaign funds (the senior author was then closely acquainted with these matters) came from that source. The Republicans, while less dependent, are thought to receive nearly 60 percent of their funds from Jewish contributions.

A lot of contributions, as Stephen Isaacs, the author of *Jews and American Politics,* explains, are not made to secure preferment or favors, but for status.

> People like to get invited to the White House, to the governor's mansion. They like to be on the dais when the political person is speaking. They like to be on the inside. . . . And for Jews, who . . . traditionally have felt excluded . . . to be accepted at the very highest levels by political figures . . . is important, and gives them a sense of belonging and acceptance that they might not otherwise get or they aren't satisfied with merely in the business world.[68]

AIPAC's method of operation has been explained by Richard Curtiss, executive director of *The Washington Report on Middle East Affairs.* In 1984, PACs proliferated. Jewish PACs assumed disguises by adopting nondescript names like Badger PAC, Desert Caucus, Five Towns PAC, Goldcoast PAC, and so on. The only PAC bearing a name mentioning Israel, Zionism, Judaism, or even the Middle East, quickly camouflaged itself as "Texas PAC." By June 30, 1984, such PACs had spent more than $4 million on congressional races. These funds were particularly effective since much of the support went to sparsely inhabited western states, where campaign costs for television and print ads cost much less, so every dollar goes farther.[69]

As the February 26, 1985, *Wall Street Journal* observed on its front page:

> a *Wall Street Journal* review of Federal Election Commission records shows that the network of Jewish political-action committees has greatly multiplied its clout since the 1982 elections. Measured in their dollar-generating power, the Jewish PACs are emerging as one of the most potent single-issue lobbies in the US. . . . Taken together, the Jewish PACs gave $1 million more during the 1984 elections than the nation's largest PAC, the 110,000-member Realtors PAC, which gave $2.5 million.

By the 1986 congressional elections, there were over ninety pro-Israel PACs. They spent $2 million by June 30, and $4,302,765 by December 31.[70]

Federal law prevents a PAC from donating more than $5,000 to a candidate. But since the Jewish PACs are all legally unrelated, they can, collectively, give very much more. And though they are not supposed to collaborate in support of particular candidates, there is no doubt that they systematically do. (In fact, very few PACs confine their contributions to candidates running in their own districts.) For example, as of June 30, 1988, one pro-Israeli PAC had donated over $86,000 to twenty-six Democrats and six Republicans in states where dollars buy far more television time than in its home district. Although that PAC was headquartered in Pennsylvania, it had contributed to no candidate in either Pennsylvania or Delaware.

As another example, Jewish PACs in 1984 pumped more than $100,000 into each of seven congressional races; in four cases, their choices won.[71] Through personal contacts and AIPAC's avalanche of publications, no PACs have trouble discerning the official line as to which candidates are to be supported and which opposed.

To illustrate how carefully Israeli PAC money is targeted, Exhibit I (see page 212) lists the total contributions of Israeli PACs in four elections—1984, 1986, 1988, and 1990—to key congressional members or chairmen of those committees having a particular role in authorizing aid to Israel.

## AIPAC's Role in Presidential Elections

The standard tools of pro-Israeli groups seeking to influence presidential elections are massive financial contributions and strong attacks on opposition candidates. Such practices began in the early 1950s with Abraham Feinberg, president of the American Bank & Trust Company of New York, who is credited with being the first major Jewish fundraiser in America. According to Stephen D. Isaacs,

> Feinberg's activities started a process of systematic fund raising for politics that has made Jews the most conspicuous fund raisers and contributors to the Democratic Party. As one non-Jewish strategist told this writer, "You can't hope to go anywhere in national politics, if you're a Democrat, without Jewish money."[72]

The large Jewish contributors commit their money only after they have carefully interrogated candidates on their views about Israel. That lesson has been painfully learned by a number of putative presidents, including George McGovern in 1972, who failed a test to which he was subjected at a dinner given by rich Jewish American businessmen whose collective worth amounted to billions of dollars.

During the question period, McGovern was asked by the financier Meshulam Riklis: "Senator, just what is your position on Israel?" McGovern replied that the only hope for a settlement was a negotiated peace worked out in a world forum like the United Nations.

McGovern's mistake was twofold. First, he assumed that a reasonable position could win over reasonable men. On the contrary, his interlocutors believed that a candidate was properly prepared only if he told them what they wanted to hear.[73] Second, he failed to appreciate the bitter hatred of the Jewish community toward the United Nations and all its works.

Former Senator James Abourezk met the same fate when, in a small gathering, he refused to endorse arms aid for Israel. As a result, he said later, "They never contributed a dime to my campaign."[74]

Other presidential candidates, such as Senator John Glenn in 1984, have felt the wrath of Israel's supporters when they dared to express an independent judgment on the Middle East. Although Glenn had consistently supported aid for Israel, he committed three unforgivable offenses in the eyes of the Jews. These transgressions were enumerated by William Safire in *The New York Times* (February 2, 1983) shortly before Glenn announced his candidacy.

> On the sale of our most sophisticated fighter-bombers to Saudi Arabia, Senator Glenn has come down on both sides. In 1978, he voted for the Carter Administration's sale of F-15s that caused the Israelis to doubt America's commitment to its safety; two years later, he voted against the Reagan Administration's enhancement of those F-15s and the sale of AWACs.
>
> On the raid that destroyed the Iraqi reactor's prospective "Islam bomb," Senator Glenn denounced Israel's "vigilante tactics" and condemned "one of the most destructive events in recent history."
>
> On recognition of the PLO, Senator Glenn . . . said in 1981 . . . "It wouldn't hurt to sit down with the PLO and see if we can find any commonality."

This hardly seems like the record of an anti-Israel zealot; but Safire went on to relate Glenn's "worst night" where, of four speakers, Glenn was the only critic of Menachem Begin's illegal use of U.S. weapons outside of Israel's borders. Consequently, Glenn received few Jewish donations, so that in 1986 his campaign ended up a record $2,838,733 in debt.[75]

Such venomous tactics obviously make presidential contenders go to extreme lengths to curry AIPAC's favor. Witness the degrading spectacle of both Gary Hart's and Walter Mondale's promise to move the U.S. Embassy to Jerusalem in 1984. Such a move, as even Ronald Reagan admitted, would destroy America's standing not merely among the Arabs but throughout the entire Moslem world.[76]

Mondale's fear of AIPAC reprisals became so hysterical that he ordered his finance director, Thomas Rosenberg, to return five $1,000 checks donated by Americans of Arab ancestry. Gary Hart, not to be outdone, paid off a $700,000 campaign loan and severed all further ties with an Arab-owned Washington bank.[77]

## The Stick Rather Than the Carrot

AIPAC's influence in Congress does not derive solely from using Jewish PAC money to support candidates; it is also a powerful deterrent to candidates who do not meet rigid pro-Israeli tests. Because AIPAC has managed to defeat or harass candidates so successfully, it operates a virtual reign of terror among congressional members. AIPAC not only helps steer the spending of PAC money, it also influences the very substantial contributions of rich Jewish Americans who, under the First Amendment, are free to spend their own money to back an opposing candidate without restriction, so long as they do not coordinate their efforts with the candidate.

The most notorious example of its vengeance was the 1984 defeat of Senator Charles Percy of Illinois—which demonstrated that even the most powerful and well-entrenched senators can be dislodged if they affront the AIPAC.

Senator Percy, chairman of the Senate Foreign Relations Committee, voted in support of Israel 87 percent of the time, yet he had, in AIPAC's eyes, committed three unforgivable sins. In 1975, he returned from a tour of the Middle East saying that "Israel and its leadership, for whom I have a high regard, cannot count on the United States in the future just to write a blank check." Second, he urged Israel to deal with the PLO, adding that in his view, Yasser Arafat was "more moderate, relatively speaking, than other extremists such as George Habash." Finally, he had voted to support the AWACs sale to Saudi Arabia.

When Percy came up for reelection in 1984, he met a massive anti-Percy campaign in the Jewish community. His primary opponent called Percy "Israel's worst adversary in Congress." And a full-page newspaper advertisement featured a photograph of Arafat with the caption: "Chuck Percy says this man is a moderate."

Although he survived the primary, vast amounts of Jewish money began pouring in to the campaign of his Democratic opponent. Fifty-nine Jewish PACs contributed $321,825 out of an estimated $3.1 million contributed by Jews for his defeat, in a campaign where spending exceeded $10 million. Tom Dine, the head of AIPAC, bragged: "All the Jews in America, from coast to coast, gathered to oust Percy. And American politicians—those who hold public positions now, and those who aspire—got the message."[78]

But Percy's defeat can even more be attributed to a Californian named Michael R. Goland, who spent $1.1 million on television and billboard space and direct mailings to support Percy's opponent, Paul Simon.

Goland's personal spending in the Percy-Simon campaign earned him instant notoriety among politicians, who quite properly fear such zealotry. Their fears were justified when, in the middle of 1986, Goland personally appeared in Washington to oppose a Saudi arms package. Minnesota Senator Rudy Boschwitz set up a number of appointments for Goland with senators known to support the sale. As columnist Mark Shields observed,

> With all the subtlety of a knee to the groin, Boschwitz, according to White House and Senate Republican sources, told the Senators that this was the same guy who had spent all that money to beat Percy because he disliked Percy's lukewarm support of Israel. Consistent with Boschwitz's delicate touch, Goland reportedly told the GOP senators to consider the possibility of one of those Saudi missiles falling into the hands of a terrorist who would use it to shoot down a civilian airliner, killing Americans abroad. Then, reports indicate, Goland asked them to imagine the political repercussions of a TV commercial of that airplane wreckage—yes, the one with the dead Americans—reminding home state voters that the Senator had voted for such arms sales. This was no idle threat.[79]

The Israeli lobby was also effective in mobilizing Jewish support from outside the state to oppose Republican Jim Abdnor, when he ran for reelection as senator from South Dakota in 1986. His opponent received nearly $400,000 from Jewish groups, while Abdnor received nothing. Since he lost the election by 4 percent of the vote, the outcome was presumably influenced by the extra funds his opponent commanded.[80]

In addition to defeating Percy and Abnor, pro-Israeli forces also defeated two incumbent congressmen, Paul Findley of Illinois and Paul "Pete" McCloskey of California. Findley had routinely supported Israel and had been reelected to Congress nine times. But in 1980, he had had the temerity to meet publicly with Chairman Yasser Arafat and to support recognition of the PLO. Israel's supporters promptly labeled him a "practicing anti-Semite" and called him "one of the worse enemies that Jews and Israel have ever faced in the history of the U.S. Congress." Pickets dogged him with the chant: "Paul, Paul, he must go. He supports the PLO."[81] Although Findley sailed through that year with a comfortable 56 percent of the vote, nationwide Jewish opponents of Findley poured money into the 1982 campaign of his opponent, Richard Durbin, who won by 1,407 votes. That led Thomas Dine of AIPAC to boast: "This is a case where the Jewish lobby made a difference. We beat the odds and defeated Findley." He estimated that of the $750,000 in contributions that Durbin had received, $685,000 came from Jews.[82]

McCloskey suffered very much the same fate. A highly decorated Marine veteran and a sixteen-year member of Congress, he undertook to run for the Senate in 1982. Although he had consistently voted for aid to Israel, he had increasingly questioned the growth of that aid and was critical of Israel for squandering its American-supplied resources on building illegal settlements in the Occupied Territories. He had also made the grievous error of attacking AIPAC directly. In a *Los Angeles Times* article, McCloskey had stood up for AIPAC's right to lobby, but he had also observed that if the United States were to work effectively for peace in the Middle East, the power of that lobby must be recognized and countered in open and fair debate. And he stated: "I had hoped that the American Jewish community had matured to the point where its lobbying efforts could be described and debated without raising the red flag of anti-Semitism."[83]

The obvious response of the angered pro-Israeli forces was to smear McCloskey as an anti-Semite. The Heritage Southwest Jewish Press employed hyperbole to describe him as "number one sonovabitch," "crummy," "sleazy," and it damned his "obscene position against the Jews of America." Columnist Paul Greenberg charged that McCloskey had accused the Jewish lobby of "busily subverting the national interest." The *B'nai B'rith Messenger* published a totally false story that McCloskey had proposed that all rabbis be made to register as foreign agents.

Another victim of a smear campaign was Faye Williams, a 1986 candidate to become Louisiana's first female black member of the House. Jewish groups viciously attacked her in the November election because her campaign manager, Sam Burgan, was an American of Jordanian extraction. Although she supported Israel and opposed the PLO, Sheldon Beychok, head of a pro-Israel PAC disguised as "Louisianans for American Security," sent mailgrams urging her friends to withdraw their support because "she is a PLO sympathizer."

Of course, not all of AIPAC's efforts to purge candidates are successful. As early as July 1, 1986, they had poured $128,000 into John V. Evans's campaign and gave Senator Steven Symms (R-ID) nothing. Symms's crimes were that in 1977 (when he was still a congressman) he had dared to visit Libya, promoting the sale of Idaho wheat, and had supported the AWACs sale in 1983. Symms barely edged out Evans and was the only survivor of the Jewish PACs that year.[84] John Chafee (R-RI) was equally lucky in 1988 to turn back an attempt by Jewish groups seeking to remove him from the Senate in favor of Lieutenant Governor Richard A. Licht (who happened to be Jewish).

Most Jewish Americans angrily reject any suggestion that support for Israel derives largely from the activities of AIPAC or the other Jewish American organizations. They prefer to think that it expresses the unprompted sentiments of Americans—sympathy for the Jewish people and admiration for Israel as a strategic asset.

Although individual Jewish Americans disparage the importance of AIPAC and the other organizations, AIPAC's leadership invariably takes a very different view. Thus, AIPAC's chairman, Thomas Dine, has shown no inhibitions in boasting of AIPAC's role in electing or defeating senators and congressmen, or of its success in blocking legislation that would, in AIPAC's judgment, harm Israel.

Dine has obvious reasons to inflate his lobby's reputation. Not only does its effectiveness bolster his Capitol Hill clout, but AIPAC can operate only if there is a constantly augmented flow of funds from the American community to PACs and other pro-Israeli organizations.

Of course, the contradiction between the assessment preferred by individual Jewish Americans and that preferred by the lobby's leaders complicates the problem of determining causation. So, in sorting out the answer, the authors conclude that AIPAC and the other Jewish American organizations provide unsurpassed machinery for exploiting the basic materials of a successful appeal: the sympathy of America for the tragic past of the Jewish people; its admiration for Israel's achievements; and the erroneous contention that Israel provides America with a surrogate bastion against Soviet intrusion into the Middle East. No one can precisely assess the contributions of any of these factors, but in combination they have demonstrated remarkable success.

However, these successes cover one fact that the friends of Israel would do well to keep in mind. Support for Israel as a matter of conviction as opposed to mere political expediency is very shallow—not more than 15 percent or so of each House of Congress. It is easy to get one hundred senators to sign a letter supporting some pro-Israel position when there is not, at present, any serious or focused countervailing pressure to oppose

AIPAC-sponsored policies. But, should the Jewish community become divided and flag in its pro-Israel zeal, or should significant groups begin to express opposition, such congressional support could melt away with lighting speed. American opinion has a tendency to veer suddenly from one extreme to another and many congressmen today tend to resemble weathervanes rather than lawmakers with strong convictions.

# PART III

CHAPTER ELEVEN

# American-Arab Relations: The Neglected Leg of the Triangle

AMERICA'S RELATIONS WITH the second leg of the Middle Eastern Triangle, the Arabs, have been muddied by incomprehension, biased by a lack of sympathy, and marred by two-way mismanagement. This has resulted from Arab suspicion and disunity and from America's ignorance of the Arab people, their culture, recent Arab history, and evolving political trends in the Arab world.

## REASONS FOR AMERICA'S FAILURE TO UNDERSTAND THE ARABS

Most Americans feel comfortable with Israelis, whom they view as products of Western culture, but all too many tend to regard the less familiar Arabs with what George Washington called "habitual animosity."

The ordinary American knows of very few Arabs as Arabs. For example, how many know that Doug Flutie, the football star, or F. Murray Abraham, the actor who played Antonio Salieri in the film *Amadeus,* are Arabs? Most American Arabs do not think of themselves as Arabs, but as Lebanese or Iraqis or Syrians or Saudis.

Americans generally err in viewing all Moslems as Arabs, often confusing Iranians with Arabs and look on the Islamic religion as exotic and mysterious. They know little of its doctrines and consider all Moslem practitioners—whether Sunni or Shiite—as backward, unfriendly Third World peoples.

Unlike Britain, the United States, with its proportionally smaller foreign trade and latent isolationist tendencies, has produced few major scholars or writers to describe and romanticize the Arab world—no Charles Doughty or Richard Burton or T. E. Lawrence—and few Americans visit the Arab capitals of the Middle East except as bankers and businessmen narrowly intent on making deals, or as tourists haggling over bargains in *souks.* Neither group absorbs any substantive knowledge of the culture or develops any respect or affection for Arabs except as rich potential business partners.

The ethnocentric bias of American education denies young Americans even the scantiest acquaintance with the debt the West owes to the Arab peoples in science, mathematics, art, and other aspects of civilization.[1]

As stated by an historian, Professor William E. Leuchtenburg:

> From the perspective of the American historian . . . the Arabs are a people who have lived outside of history . . . one may read any standard account of the history of America, until the most recent times, and derive from it the impression either that the Arabs have had no history or that it was only of the most inconsequential sort.[2]

According to Michael Suleiman of Kansas State University, if the Arabs register at all on most Americans, "they are viewed as a Middle East people who have changed little since the time of Christ and who, in the twentieth century, have opposed Western penetration of the area and are locked in mortal combat with Israel. . . . "[3] Arabs have often been portrayed on the screen as wily types swathed in caftans or burnooses, murderously pursuing each other on horses or camels across the desert.

Recent television portrayals of the male Arab are scarcely more flattering. He is quite often satirized as a person of vast unearned wealth, squandering his riches on conspicuous consumption and the lustful pursuit of women. Another view depicts him as a sinister terrorist or as a sleekly dressed con man of dubious morals, perfidiously using his Harvard Business School education to extort more money for Arab oil from the hard-pressed American consumer.

Part of that misconception arose because America came late on the Middle East scene; not until after World War II did our countrymen have much in the way of official dealings with Arab nations. Prior to that time, early in the nineteenth century the United States had done little more than send a series of punitive naval expeditions against the petty potentates of the Barbary Coast whose piratical depredations finally exceeded even Thomas Jefferson's high threshold of patience. In a skirmish with Tripoli (later enshrined in the Marine Corps song), the United States tried a ploy that later became a shoddy pattern; it enlisted the aid of a deposed former Pasha of Tripoli, promising that it would restore him to the rule of his province—although it promptly abandoned him when his brother decided to come to terms.[4]

The right of the Jewish people to a homeland of their own has been widely accepted and applauded by the American people, but only recently have an increasing number of Americans begun to recognize that the Palestinian Arabs also have a claim worth serious examination. Because the Arabs have—foolishly and ethnocentrically—regarded the virtues of their cause to be self-evident, they have neglected until recently to try even to elucidate their position to Americans. Most important, their efforts have been hampered by internal dissensions. Finally, they face the formidable competition of the highly effective propaganda of America's dedicated Jewish community. The Arabs lack a wealthy domestic lobby to promote their story.

Even more important, while there are over 7 million Arabs versus 5.6 million Jews resident in America, it was not until 1988 that they made their presence felt politically in Michigan in the Jesse Jackson campaign, and at the Democratic National Convention. This has alarmed the Jewish community, and it was announced in July 1991 that a group had been formed to fight Arab political power at the grass roots. Finally, there is still residual animosity toward the Arabs because of the 1973 oil embargo.

## The Rise of Palestinian Nationalism

Before the British Mandate, Palestine was a political wasteland, a mosaic of competing families and fiefdoms.[5] Each family and its attendant clique sporadically changed sides on issues in order to block some rival clique.[6]

Such factionalism and the absence of pragmatism may explain why the Palestinians turned down a British proposal that they form a government to administer the territories allocated to them when the partition proposal (Resolution 181[II]) was adopted by the UN General Assembly. Instead, many fell back on what now appears a fatuous excuse—that forming a government would constitute recognition of what they regarded as the illegal partition of the country.[7] It was a lamentable error, for so long as the Palestinians lacked any framework of national identity and a unifying political structure, they could not build support through a feeling of common nationality, much less draw strength from a state of their own. They thus fell piecemeal victims to the better organized Israelis.[8]

## Why Have the Arabs Consistently Lost to Israel?

The initial assumption of the Palestinians who had fled in 1947–48 was that the neighboring Arab states would regain their land and restore them to their homes. Why were the Arabs unable to accomplish this? Why were they so inadequate on the battlefield?

The most obvious explanation was that the founders of Israel were of European stock and the initial settlers were cultured European Jews, well versed in the most up-to-date industrial and agricultural technology then available in the world. Israeli's founders also possessed practical combat experience. Service in World War II advanced their knowledge of modern military planning, and the use of modern equipment. As time went on, they benefited from the unparalleled bounty of America, which was fast becoming the world's military leader. Because they were viewed as disloyal during World War II, the Palestinians were, in contrast, excluded from military service and thus had no experience with the organization of modern military forces or the tactics and strategy of modern warfare.

Besides, most of the new Arab states were concentrating on the development of their own countries. If they paid attention to Palestinian affairs, it was only to try to grab portions of the territory for themselves, or to use the Palestinian issue to promote collateral agendas.

When Israel was born, most of today's Arab states did not yet exist as nations or had only recently become nations. Only Saudi Arabia and the North Yemen had been independent before World War II, and by 1948 only six Arab states had achieved membership in the United Nations. Egypt, Syria, Iraq, Lebanon, and Saudi Arabia had joined in 1945; the Imanate of the Yemen did not become a member until September 1947. In North Africa, France yielded its protectorates in 1955, and its other territories in the early 1960s. The British and Italian Arabic colonies were all independent by 1960. The residue of the Asian Arab states, chiefly on the Arabian peninsula, did not become independent until 1967 or 1971.

Many of these newly independent states started out as monarchies, but one by one the monarchies were overthrown and replaced by radical anti-Western military officers determined to purge Western influences. Corruption, incompetence, and despotism, however, did not disappear with the monarchies.

As new nations, they faced baffling problems organizing their own governments. With the exception of the oil states, they were all short of money. They had little time to devote to a war which was at best tangential to their interests. Only their sense that the Palestinians had been unjustly treated, combined with the belief that their former colonial masters, the Western powers, were responsible, served to keep this issue alive.

The United States thus faced a growing tide of anti-Western radicalism. The fact that its government initially blamed Soviet machinations reflected the prevailing Cold War atmosphere; in most cases, the Soviet Union simply attached itself to the new regimes, which welcomed its support in the face of American opposition. So the United States, in fact, furthered the spread of Soviet influences. Instead of disassociating itself from unsatisfactory governments and identifying itself with modern, reformist elements in the Arab world, the United States generally opposed change of any sort. Too often, the actions it did take were unhelpful.

First, hoping to check the radicals, the United States promoted rivalries between the conservative and the radical states. This fed Arab suspicions that the moderate regimes had sold out to Israel and the Americans, and that the United States wished to thwart the Pan-Arab dream of a federated nation by dividing and controlling the Arabs in a neocolonialistic manner.

Second, the United States grew ever closer to Israel, thereby offending Arab opinion from the Atlantic to the Indian Oceans. Israel's claims to have saved Lebanon for the United States in 1982 served to fuel Arab fears that America was using Israel as a bullying enforcer of its unpopular Middle Eastern policies.

Third, the United States constantly sought not only to oppose but to depose unfriendly "radical" governments, as was the case with John Foster Dulles's campaign against Nasser. Dulles seemed blind to the obvious fact that no former colonial people would willingly align themselves with their erstwhile masters, especially while Britain and France still ruled fellow Arabs in colonies or protectorates. But it was an article of faith with Dulles that any nation not irretrievably committed to basic American positions was an enemy; neutralism was immoral.

Moreover, after 1980, the United States vented its spleen against the Khomeini regime by "tilting" toward the Iraqis who had started the Iran-Iraq War (not without, one must note, considerable Iranian provocation).[9] And the United States is now quarreling with Jordan, whose growing representative institutions evolving through their opposition to American policies may result in more, not less friction.

## The Rich Versus the Poor

The divisions among the Arab states derive, partially, from wide disparities between those with oil and those without it. Per capita income in the Arab League member states runs from a pathetic $200 a year in Djibouti to $29,000 in Qatar.

The aid provided by wealthy states to their poor Arab cousins has consisted primarily of military outlays. Thus the Gulf states alone provided about $100 billion to bolster Iraq in its war with Iran (1980–88). Economic development aid, however, has totaled less than half that much ($43 billion), After the Iraqi invasion of Kuwait, it was revealed that profit-minded Kuwait and Saudi Arabia had each invested more than $100 billion in the United States, Western Europe, and Japan, rather than in poor Arab nations urgently in need of capital.[10]

## The Additional Factor of Intrastate Rivalry

Not only have there been a multitude of interstate rivalries between Arab governments but also intrastate quarrels within Arab regimes that are often minority governments. The government of Iraq, for example, primarily represents the 15 percent minority that are Arab Sunni Moslems. The government of Syria is dominated by a 15 percent minority of Alawites, an extreme Shia Moslem sect. Until its recent movement toward more representative government by the election of a parliament in November 1989, the Hashemite Kingdom of Jordan was largely dependent on a minority of Bedouin tribesmen heavily represented in the army.

In most Arab countries the army is the only educated and effective force for cohesion. The officers, however, have too often been selected for their loyalty rather than their competence. For example, the Syrian Air Force in 1982 primarily used Alawite personnel as combat pilots when well-educated Christians and Sunni Moslems might have done better.[11]

Unsupported by basic public opinion, most regimes have for years resorted to one-party systems kept in power by the police and the army. Fears of internal rebellion have made them understandably reluctant to commit their military forces to battle except in defense of their own territory. Such fears are well founded in history. Military coups have overthrown governments in Egypt, Syria, North Yemen, Libya, Tunisia, Algeria, the Sudan, and Iraq. Coups have been attempted in Jordan, Morocco, and South Yemen. Assassinations have cut down chiefs of state in Iraq, Egypt, Syria, and Jordan. Under these circumstances, many rulers prudently keep their armed forces near at hand so as to be readily available to defend their personal security and keep their regimes in the power.

## The Inadequate Military Response

After the breakdown of the Lausanne Conference in 1948, Arab leaders shrilly reiterated the need to eliminate the so-called "Zionist entity." But the fiery hyperbole of Arab rhetoric has continued to exceed Arab action. As can be seen in Table 1 (page 241), the building of Arab armies proceeded only lethargically. The Arabs thus ended by having the worst of two worlds. They were unwilling to take effective measures to redress the just grievances of the Palestinians, while vociferously promising to do so. But they refused to work toward an accommodation with Israel that, with great power assistance, would have resulted in peace and some restitution for the Palestinians.

After their defeat in 1967, the Arab states again called loudly for war but did little or nothing to prepare for it. Syria tried halfheartedly to beef up its army between 1967 to 1973, but only managed to double its strength from

60,000 to 125,000. Although greatly improved in quality by 1973, the Egyptian Army was not materially increased in size. Jordan, as a confrontation state, accepted a subsidy from the Saudis, but spent most of it on nonmilitary projects. Between 1973 and 1980 Iraq, the only active noncontiguous Arab state, doubled its army, from 101,800 to 220,000 men. This increase was spurred by a Kurdish revolt and troubles with Iran, not by any plan to confront Israel.[12]

After the Camp David Accords had led to the neutralization of Egypt in 1978, Syria was left to face Israel alone. Deeply disturbed by their lonely status, the Syrians once more exerted themselves, pushing their strength up to 200,000 men in 1982. Only after the Lebanese War in 1982, when Syrian forces were gratuitously attacked by General Sharon, did President Assad of Syria resolve to achieve "military parity" with Israel.[13]

Nonetheless, because of its support for Iran, Syria failed to persuade any of its neighbors to join it. Consequently, Syria is now mired in a $15–20 billion debt to the Soviet Union.[14]

## Arab Military Mismanagement

The histories of the 1948, 1956, 1967, 1973, and, most recently, the 1991 Gulf War over Kuwait all display an incredible series of Arab military errors. These wars demonstrated that the Arabs were unable to translate their analyses of the balance of forces into sensible and effective policies. In each conflict, Arab leaders pursued provocative actions that provided Israel or the United States with made-to-order opportunities for attacking them. Palestinian communal fighting with the Jews in 1947–48, the invasion of the former mandate by the Arab states in 1948, the guerrilla raids from the Gaza Strip in 1955 and the Suez Canal seizure in 1956, the mobilization in the Sinai and the blockade of the Straits of Tiran in 1967, and the invasion of Kuwait in 1990, all fall into this category. In each case, the Arab regimes failed to anticipate the formidable reaction of their enemies.

When confronted by vigorous opposition and knowing that military defeat was all but certain, the Arab governments acted as if they expected the United States, the United Nations, the Soviet Union, or some other outside power to rescue them from the predicament of their own making. Even in those cases where the United Nations and the Soviet Union tried to build a bridge to permit their retreat, they obstinately refused to budge. The saving of face and prestige within the Arab bloc were, in retrospect, more important to many of them than the protection of their countries and the lives of their citizens.

The Arab governments' disregard for the safety and welfare of their troops was scandalous and unforgivable. Arab states more than once went to war knowing not only that defeat was inevitable but that the conflict could have been avoided.

The Charge of the Light Brigade, the result of a blunder, was, as the French commander put it, "Magnificent, but it is not war." There is nothing magnificent about the Arab governments that sent their overmatched troops to be massacred by the enemy.

Although Arab commanders are at last learning to apply Western military technology, and presumably will in time master the present weapons systems, they do not appear to be making comparable progress on the strategic, political, and tactical aspects of warfare, especially airpower. Antiquated arms and adoption of the Soviets' overcentralized command system, with a resulting dearth of local commander initiative, may have made things worse.

Except for the 1973 War, when the Arabs were on the strategic and tactical offensive, and adequately prepared in advance, their military planning has been abysmal. Despite the creation of a combined staff prior to 1967, no serious coordination or planning occurred before hostilities. Iraq's defeat in the Gulf War acutely illustrated this deficiency. Despite lengthy hearings before the House Armed Services Committee in which America's tactical alternatives were spelled out and a sweep around the western end of Kuwait recommended, Iraq refused to take precautionary measures. As a result, the value of the individual Iraqi soldier was grossly maligned.

## The Relations of Arab Nations with the Soviet Union

The Arabs first turned to the Soviet Union for weapons and diplomatic support in 1955, when they decided that the Tripartite Declaration by the United States, Britain, and France limiting arms imports to the Middle East was serving only to maintain Israel's arms advantage. Sensing possible benefits from cultivating the Arabs, the Soviet Union stepped in as a supplier first of Egypt, and then of Iraq, Syria, Kuwait, the Yemens, Libya, and Algeria.

After their defeat in 1967, the Arabs turned again to the Soviet Union, but found that although Moscow was quite prepared to deliver more and better armaments, it would not risk war with America in order to force Israel to withdraw its settlers and soldiers from the West Bank, Gaza, and the Golan Heights. So, after the 1973 campaign, Egypt turned to the United States.

## The Illusion of Pan-Arabism

By far the greatest Arab defect was the lack of unity. Nasser utilized the myth of the Arab nation to glorify Pan-Arabism by persuading the Arab multitudes that they were the inheritors of the vast Arabian Empire that ran from the Atlantic Ocean to the Persian Gulf in the seventh through the ninth centuries. They had a common language and a common religion. There was, so Nasser contended, no reason why the Arab peoples should not multiply their strength and importance in world affairs by combining their resources into a large, unified, efficient military entity. This approach enabled Nasser to talk to the Arab peoples over the heads of their governments.

The apparent charm of the idea was, however, not confirmed by experience. Unions between Arab states, with the possible exception of the two Yemens, proved to be short-lived. Nasser's Egypt did manage to unite with two other countries (Syria and the North Yemen) in the early 1960s, but that experiment failed because Nasser exploited the resources and insulted the feelings of his merger partners to the point where they broke away.

The Gulf War, where Iraq fought a number of Arab countries, presumably put an end to the Pan-Arab concept, though it did demonstrate its possibilities. Arab nations have found it difficult to criticize one another, but they tend to stand together against outside criticism of Arab conduct; thus, Western denunciations in early 1990 of Saddam Hussein's use of poison gas against the Kurds aroused the Arabs to rally around him in a show of unity. Only when the Iraqi strongmen broke the unity convention by overrunning Kuwait in August 1990 and threatening adjacent Arab states were a majority able, after much soul searching, to stand up against him. That in turn broke a long-standing taboo against any but unanimous intra-Arab decisions.

If Pan-Arabism failed as an instrument to mobilize Arab fighting strength, it also failed bitterly as a mechanism for shaping and negotiating a durable peace. The number of occasions where Arab selfishness and disunity torpedoed opportunities to achieve a peaceful settlement is appalling.

## Palestinian Efforts at Self-Reliance

Experience over time had evidently convinced the Palestinian people that no group of Arab nations could ever unite sufficiently to halt Israel's expansion and regain their seized lands. They therefore reluctantly concluded that they must rely on their own efforts.

The Zionists, after all, had begun with no state of their own. But by dedicated work, vast help from Jewish groups around the world, and brilliant improvisation, they had built a compact armed force so potentially powerful that once they had announced the existence of their new state, they could effectively defend it against the disorganized national armies of neighboring Arab states. Why should not the Palestinians, in effect, repeat the Zionist performance?

By 1964, Egypt and Syria were trying to outbid each other to establish their bona fide Pan-Arab credentials.[15] Their rivalry dominated a January 1964 summit meeting called in Cairo.

Nasser had compromised his authority by his loose talk about launching a war against Israel to frustrate various Israeli water diversion projects, even though he was by no means ready to fight. In his eagerness to maintain his position as the number-one Arab leader, Nasser sought to induce other Arab regimes to approve his position.[16]

The Arab nations used the summit primarily to conceal their own lassitude while still giving a verbal impression of vigor. To that end, they designed a new organization, the Palestine Liberation Organization (or PLO). As its head, they installed an ex-diplomat, Ahmed Shuqayri, but his incompetence soon became glaringly apparent, even to Arab leaders. Shortly thereafter, a Palestinian group called Al-Fatah won fame through guerrilla attacks on Israel culminating in a skirmish at Karameh on the East Bank in 1968. In February 1969, the Palestine National Congress installed Al-Fatah's leader, Yasser Arafat, as chairman of the executive committee of the PLO, thus effectively making him its leader.

Soon, Arafat's PLO found itself caught up in an inter-Arab struggle as various Arab leaders tried to dominate the new organization. Nasser viewed it as his creation and expected deference. The Syrians, whom Nasser hated, viewed the PLO as a sign that "the Ba'ath had been neatly outmaneuvered by its main competitor for the favor of the Arab masses—Nasser—and had lost to him the initiative in pro-Palestine action: a complete reversal of the situation before the summit meeting."[17]

Even with new leadership, what could the PLO do? All the Arab states except Syria and Algeria opposed guerrilla activity, which they saw as reckless adventurism.[18] King Hussein of Jordan banned any guerrilla operations from his country. He feared that the PLO would challenge the legitimacy of the "Jordanian entity," which would invite devastating Israeli punitive raids.

After the 1967 War, the oil-rich Gulf states began to fund both the PLO and Al-Fatah.[19] Emboldened by that backing, the PLO sought recognition by the world powers in the hope of gaining the respect that would enable it to negotiate as an equal with Israel and thus clear the way for an independent Palestinian state. After a disastrous clash with Jordanian forces in September 1970, the PLO decided to work with the Arab regimes rather than antagonize them. Arafat recognized that Israel was too powerful to be tackled in open combat and the Arab nations too weak to serve as jumping-off points for guerrilla forays against it. Only from Lebanon, which no longer had a functioning government, could the PLO harass Israel without local interference.

By 1974, the PLO's pivotal role in resisting Israel and its subsequent popularity persuaded the Arab governments to accord it the status of "sole, legitimate representative of the Palestinian people"—a decision that greatly complicated the peacemaking process for the future.

## Israel's Lebanese Adventure, 1982–85

When the PLO moved its "base camp" into the Shia and Christian areas of South Lebanon in 1969–70, it violated its own ground rule, which was to operate only in areas where the Palestinian population formed a majority. The Palestinians totally alienated the local Christian and Shia residents, who, besides enduring retaliatory raids by Israelis, had also been preyed upon by

Palestinian robbers masquerading as "tax collectors," and suffered other brutal excesses. The Lebanese happily welcomed the expulsion of the Palestinians in 1982 and its weak government continues to oppose a resumption of Palestinian operations against Israel from Lebanese soil.

## Box Score of PLO Achievements

The record of the PLO is a mixture of limited success and substantial failure. To its credit, it has created a new Palestinian identity and put the Palestinians on the world map; to its discredit, the association of some of its member groups with terrorist activities has inspired an active distaste for the Palestinian cause.

In 1979, Yasser Arafat boasted: "In the 1950s John Foster Dulles used to say that the new generation of Palestinians would not even know Palestine. But they did! The group that made the [March 1978] operation against Israel were nearly all of them born outside Palestine, but they were prepared to die for it."[20] Were it not for the PLO it seems most improbable that the concept of "a Palestinian people" would even exist today.

Al-Fatah, by far the largest component of the PLO, has become more conciliatory since the mid-1960s, compelling most of its auxiliary groups to accept various concessions to moderate opinion. In 1969, it engineered the change of a phrase (and objective) in the PLO Charter from "the liberation of Palestine" (which was widely interpreted to mean the destruction of Israel) to the establishment of "a secular, democratic state in Palestine" in which Jews, Christians, and Moslems would live as equals. Since the Jews are committed to a state dominated by themselves, and since they construed the PLO offer as insinuating (correctly) that non-Jews were being discriminated against in Israel, this olive branch was furiously rejected. The Fatah-PLO leadership also signed, in 1981, an unprecedented cease-fire with Israel in southern Lebanon, and further agreed to impose it on any would-be dissidents.[21]

Many Arabs argue that the PLO has finally achieved the first items on its agenda: it has jelled Palestinian nationalist sentiment and has aired the Palestinian cause so dramatically that it can no longer be ignored. U.S. polls indicate that 53 percent of Americans favor self-determination for the Palestinians and an independent Palestinian state.[22] Yet Congress, under Israeli influence, continues to dismiss the PLO and the Palestinians as a gang of bomb-throwers ineligible for serious diplomacy or of having a country of their own.

Still, this seemingly important list of achievements cannot conceal the fact that the Palestinians have been unable, either by negotiation or by force, to recapture a single acre of the territory allotted to them in the 1947 UN Partition Resolution.

## The Fatal Flaw in the PLO Structure—The Inclusion of Member Groups with Disparate Objectives

As events evolved, it became increasingly clear that the PLO had limited its effectiveness by undertaking to represent Palestinians with conflicting interests and aspirations, and that Israel's conquests had created different groups of Palestinians whose historic grievances could not be solved by a single simple solution. They are as follows.

*First:* The Palestinians who departed from the mandate territory before, during, or after the 1948–49 War, or in 1967, can achieve the restoration of their homeland only through the destruction of Israel. Having been unable to rebuild their lives in other Arab countries, they have been packed into refugee camps for at least two generations, where they brood on their grievances and fall back on hashish dreams of Israel's ultimate demise.

*Second:* The West Bank and Gaza inhabitants *are* at home, and can regain control of their lives without the destruction of Israel; they merely require the withdrawal of the Israelis from the Occupied Territories. The Arab residents of the Golan Heights similarly want their land to be returned to Syria.

*Third:* The Palestinians who remained in Israel and acquired Israeli citizenship find themselves in an awkward situation. As Arabs, they resent Jewish discrimination and reject Israel's efforts to dominate every aspect of their lives. Yet, fearful for their own modest rights, they, though sympathetic, are reluctant to identify too closely with their fellow Palestinians in the Occupied Territories.

*Fourth:* The Palestinians who have made a new life for themselves, chiefly in Jordan but also elsewhere, still have strong ties with both their fellow Palestinians under occupation and those in the camps. Unlike the refugees, they have much to lose in another war and therefore would greatly prefer a peaceful solution.

## The Clarification of Jordan's Position

In a press interview in March 1985, King Hussein of Jordan conveyed his obvious displeasure at the paltry results of his pro-United States policy. Any residual doubts he may have had about planning a new strategy were conclusively settled in 1986 when, bowing once more to Israeli pressure, America abandoned its agreement to sell modern military equipment to Jordan.

The King's July 31, 1988, speech renouncing Jordan's connection with the West Bank was sparked by the belated realization that Washington's 1967 promises of Israel's evacuation of the West Bank were hollow. His comments imply that America's refusal to state forthrightly where it stands, is undermining its position in the Middle East.[23]

The tendency of U.S. administrations to make friendly sounds and yet to fail to move forward has finally persuaded the Arabs that American words should not be taken at face value; they are merely a ploy to string the Arabs along. Furthermore, the Arabs regard Israel's violations of American laws and attacks on Arab interests as attributable to American government backing. Increasingly, the U.S. government is finding that America's vaunted claim to preferential influence with Israel is losing its effectiveness because of a repeated refusal to use that influence.

America's waffling on the meaning of Resolution 242; its blocking of punitive actions to coerce Israel to reverse its annexations of East Jerusalem and the Golan Heights (compared with its vigorous response to Iraq's would-be annexation of Kuwait); its refusal to enforce the Geneva Conventions; its inability to sell arms to Arab states have blunted any Arab incentive to cultivate America's friendship.

TABLE 1

**Arab-Israeli War Strengths**

| | Arab Armies | | Israel | |
|---|---|---|---|---|
| | Participating | Nominal | Total Mobilized Forces | |
| 1948[1] | 50,000 | (70,000) | 80,000 | |
| 1956[2] | 100,000 | (125,000) | 150,000 | |
| 1967 | 225,000 | (330,000) | 275,000 | |
| 1973[3] | 371,000 | (481,500) | 400,000 | |
| 1982 | 50,000 | (242,500) | 75,000 | (500,000) |
| 1990[4] | (1,600,000) | | (645,000) | |

1. Participating Palestinians, 24,000; Arab state armies: Lebanon, 2,000; Syria, 2,000; Jordan, 10,000; Egypt, 12,000.
2. Does not include the French and British forces.
3. Participating: Egypt and Syria, with brigades from Jordan, Saudi Arabia, Morocco, and Kuwait, and a division from Iraq.
4. Syria, Jordan, Iraq, and Saudi Arabia.

SOURCES: *Encyclopaedia Britannica* year books; Institute for Strategic Studies, *The Military Balance 1970–1971, 1990–1991.*

The fact that some Arab governments chose to go along with the Bush-Baker diplomatic moves following the Gulf War arose from several calculations, none of which indicates any trust or affection for America. One element was the collapse of Soviet power, meaning that the Arab states must avoid burning their bridges in Washington. Another calculation lay in the hope that Washington could be shamed into a position where it must either deliver on its peace promises and uphold established levels of international morality, or else completely destroy its position among the Arabs, and generally damage its authority in the world.

Finally, the Arab world is now coming to fear that time is running out for a peaceful settlement of the Arab-Israeli struggle and the protection of the Palestinians living under occupation. If the settlements program is allowed to continue much longer, the Arabs will soon be confronted by unacceptable alternatives. They can either let Israel get away with the seizure of their territory and the mass expulsion of the Palestinians still resident in the Occupied Territories, or they must at last prepare seriously for war, which alone, if successful, could force out the settlers.

For these reasons, the Arab governments have wisely sought a peaceful solution. Peace can be achieved on equitable terms if the U.S. government is prepared to make the effort. Nor is the decision solely for America to make. The American economy is still dependent on Middle East oil, and this dependence will grow. Arab Gulf state investments in America can also be used to apply economic pressure by withdrawing capital from American markets, thereby seriously reducing employment. There are also dangers from which America has heretofore been spared, but to which frustrations and a continuation of the present war might ultimately lead, that the struggle might be transferred to American soil.

CHAPTER TWELVE

# Terror and Reprisal

IN THEIR INTENSE desire to secure a Palestinian state, the PLO and Fatah have recently aspired to international recognition and respectability. The Palestinian radicals, on the other hand, have a different agenda: they favor enlarging their armed attacks on Israel or its sympathizers around the globe as a means of chivvying the major nations into compelling the formation of a Palestinian state.[1] Terror is the last resort of those who cannot solve their grievances by conventional political means.

Lacking a state of their own, the Palestinians resorted to terror when they discovered that they were getting nowhere either with negotiations or with conventional war. It was clear that the Arab nations were not about to regain their territory for them, and few non-Arab nations were prepared actively to alleviate, their plight; terror seemed the quickest way of attracting world attention.

To be sure, the Palestinian terrorist groups have not proved very efficient. Though the Israelis complain that they are in great danger from the PLO's allegedly systematic terrorist campaign,[2] an analysis shows that Palestinian terror has rarely been systematic, and it is not the PLO itself but radical fringe groups that have usually been its perpetrator. Most of the Palestinian-sparked terrorism has been uncoordinated, ineffectual, and directed against innocent parties whose deaths can neither benefit the Palestinian cause nor damage Israel in any way.

In retrospect, one can assign much of the PLO's past and present malfeasance to Arafat's failure to follow Ahmed Shuqayri's advice when he transferred the leadership of the PLO to Fatah. Arafat was strongly urged to exclude all other existing Palestinian organizations from the PNC (Palestine National Council). At the same time, the PLO's main financiers—Saudi Arabia, Kuwait, and Qatar—asked Fatah to assume total control.

But in the face of this advice, Arafat invited into the PLO's fold two other groups. One was the Popular Front for the Liberation of Palestine (PFLP), headed by Dr. George Habash, a lapsed Christian Marxist dentist, who emphasized organization and planning prior to taking violent action. His party held that only a complete housecleaning of Arab governments, by violent revolution, would foster the preparations needed to destroy Israel. The second was the Popular Democratic Front for the Liberation of Palestine (PDFLP), headed by Naif Hawatmeh; it also regards the current Arab regimes as reactionary and ripe for revolution. As a result of a self-imposed rule of unanimity, the extremist leaders until 1989 held a veto over Arafat's activities.[3]

Although self-defeating, Arafat's acceptance of these groups had a grain of logic. Confronted with a community that was scattered around the Middle East, and with competing groups under the influence of various Arab states, he evidently thought his best bet was to include all groups and work through consensus. While understandable at the time, this decision subjected the PLO to hobbling political constraints and made it responsible—in the public eye—for the terrorism of its radical fringe components.

Why, then, did Arafat decide to share power? In a 1983 interview, Salah Khalaf, one of Fatah's four founders, explained that since the PLO had been originated by Egypt, Fatah leaders were afraid of Cairo's interference. Therefore, they wanted some other groups to come in with them. He also pointed out that as it was not a government in being, the PLO, unlike Algeria, could not always control its guerrilla groups.

Even though the PLO received ample financing from oil-rich Arab states, attracted a large roster of trained personnel, and had abundant targets available, it inflicted surprisingly few casualties.[4] In retrospect, it seems clear that all its terrorist activities have gained is unfavorable worldwide attention, while critically retarding any progress toward peace. Palestinian apologists say that violence would have been worse if the Fatah leadership had not still clung wistfully to the hope of an ultimate diplomatic solution. Yet to reach that goal, the PLO needed a modicum of respectability, which terrorism by its very nature denied.

The comparatively limited character of PLO actions can be seen in the fact that Israel's semi-official statistics credit Arafat's organization with only 36 out of 435 terrorist raids from 1968 to 1984.

It is interesting to note that although Israel's state terrorism occasionally results in the attempted kidnapping or death of a PLO leader, there have been to date no reports of murder attempts against Israeli leaders—Israel's president, prime minister, or any cabinet members—whether at home or abroad.[5]

There has emerged no PLO counterpart of General Sharon, who has repeatedly clamored for the assassination of Yasser Arafat.[6]

## The Program of the Radicals

Dissatisfied with the passivity of PLO moderation, the radical fringe groups have pursued their own aggressive agenda. But they have apparently launched too few effective attacks to compel Israel to change its policies, and too many indiscriminate operations for the good of their own reputations.

In spite of the impression conveyed by the American media, only a relatively small group of radicals has undertaken the bloodiest terrorist attacks. Most of the radicals not only do not take orders from Arafat, they would kill him if they could. Many of the radical leaders—George Habash, Naif Hawatmeh, Ahmed Jebril, or Abu Nidal—actually relish violence. Hence it was one or the other of them who masterminded the attacks in Rome and Vienna in late 1985; the massacre at the Istanbul synagogue in 1986; and the earlier infamous Lod Airport affair in 1972, when Japanese Red Army radicals, recruited by George Habash, spread death, injuries, and terror among Christian pilgrims. They were also involved in the Munich Olympic Games attack, the *Achille Lauro* affair, and a wide range of other incidents. The more recent 1988 Pan-American plane crash at Lockerbie, Scotland, has now been attributed to Libyans.

Far from helping the Palestinian cause, these episodes have dealt it a critical blow. They confirm the widespread American impression that Arabs are bloodthirsty fanatics, thereby providing Israeli supporters with heavy ammunition to discredit the very idea of a Palestinian state. In sum, these attacks have proved futile as well as barbaric; they have outraged world opinion, yet done Israel comparatively little harm. After all, more people were killed on Israeli highways in 1990 alone than have been killed in the totality of bona fide terrorist attacks since 1949.[7]

The Israeli authorities are far more concerned about the potential damage that could be done by a coordinated terrorist campaign than they are by the current level of violence, which puts them in a strong moral position against their opponents at comparatively modest cost to themselves. They constantly worry that the vital tourist trade might be diminished by systematic attacks on the airlines that service Israel. Israel's important fruit and vegetable trades were seriously disrupted by a poisoning incident in the 1970s, which was fortunately not repeated. Persons giving Israel large gifts and businesses making investments have been targeted by nothing worse than the Arab boycott.

## Israel's Response—Reprisals as Counterterrorism

Israel has reacted to the Palestinian use of terror by a campaign of counterterror which it labels a "reprisal policy."

General Mattityahu Peled is a retired Israeli military leader who works for peace and reconciliation with the Arabs. To deal effectively with the terrorist phenomenon, he contends, one must first subject it to clinical probing like an illness. He has noted, for example, that "the term terrorism is often conveniently used to avoid the need to get to the roots of the phenomenon." To isolate its fundamental causes, he has written,

> it is necessary to consider the grievances and final goals of the different actors. One must assume, for example, that among the young men and women who lived through the horrors and the massacres in Sabra and Chatila, there will always be enough recruits for terrorist missions, regardless of proposed measures to counter them.[8]

Peled then asks the central question: "what exactly is meant by the term 'an act of terror'?" He notes that when the American government protested to Pretoria about its reprisal raids against neighboring countries which sheltered members of the African National Congress (ANC), South Africa retorted by inquiring what the difference was between its actions and the U.S. attack on Libya. The obvious answer: the U.S. raids and Israel's raids meet with State Department approval, whereas South Africa's and the Palestinians' do not.

General Peled commented that the Israeli position, when analyzed, leads to the absurd conclusion that, "in a confrontation between the armed forces of a state and forces that are as yet unable to establish a state of their own, such as a national liberation movement, the former would be conducting a legitimate war and the latter would be committing acts of terrorism."[9]

Years ago, Shamir himself had even more vividly pointed out the similarities between terrorism and reprisals. At that time he was defending terrorism as practiced by his Stern Gang:

> There are those who say that to kill [an individual] is terrorism, but to attack an army camp is guerrilla warfare and *to bomb civilians is professional warfare. But I think it is the same from the moral point of view. . . .* It was more efficient and more moral to go for selected targets. In any case, it was the only way we could operate, because we were so small. For us it was not a question of the professional honor of a soldier, it was the question of an idea, an aim that had to be achieved. We were aiming at a political goal.[10]

But are not the Palestinian terrorists also "aiming at a political goal"—the right to create an independent state of their own? Was not that exactly what motivated Shamir and Begin four decades ago? Now that Shamir's role has shifted from poacher to gamekeeper, his pious denunciation of terrorism reeks of hypocrisy.[11]

Professor Noam Chomsky recounts an anecdote, which he attributes to Saint Augustine, about a pirate captured by Alexander the Great. Alexander asked the pirate, "How dare you molest the sea?" To which the pirate replied, "How dare you molest the whole world? Because I do it with a little ship only, I am called a thief; you, doing it with a great navy, are called an Emperor."[12]

That story has symbolic relevance to Israel's actions taken under the rubric of "reprisals." Is there—or should there be—a clear distinction between the morality of a small group's actions and the counteractions of what Israelis have styled the world's fourth or fifth strongest armed forces?

Mainstream Israeli attitudes toward reprisals have steadily blurred from the moral view originally expressed in 1936 by David Ben-Gurion:

> What good can Jewish terrorism do for us? It will not intimidate the Arab gangs or their captains. . . . Those who protest against the policy of "self-restraint" are really not asking for self-defense or an organized campaign against the gang, but for retaliation on any chance Arab, which is no earthly good for us, let alone being morally wrong.[13]

### *The Effectiveness of Reprisals*

An unpublished doctoral dissertation by Barry M. Blechman, written in 1971 at Georgetown University, investigates the effectiveness of Israeli reprisals.

Blechman explains that until 1954 the Israelis either did not mention their own reprisals or, when pressed, claimed that they were the work of purely private groups. Ever since that rationalization was exposed by Force 101's activities at Qibya in 1954, reprisals have been openly carried out by Israeli government personnel.

Up to 1970, Blechman found little evidence that Israel's reprisals policy had deterred Palestinian guerrilla actions. Before 1967, guerrilla actions showed some reduction for a few weeks after an Israeli retaliatory strike. But generally speaking, attempts at chastising the guerrillas with reprisals only increased the tempo of their attacks.[14]

Nonetheless, Israel's reprisals had one useful effect: they persuaded the contiguous Arab states to prohibit the Palestinians from operating guerrilla bases on their territory, as they often have in the past. That goal achieved, some Israelis hoped they could induce their Arab neighbors to make peace, or at least be more cooperative. Yet, except for Egypt, that did not happen.

### *The Legality of Reprisals*

When the Israelis first undertook reprisals in the communal fighting preceding World War II, they followed with reasonable fidelity the rules later laid down by the Naulilaa Incident Arbitration as well as other established precedents of international law. Those rules require, among other things, that when a country conducts a retaliatory attack, it must make as certain as possible that the reprisal is carefully directed at the individual or individuals who actually planned, or participated in, the outrage that triggered the reprisal.

The rules also require that before launching any reprisal a nation must first exhaust all other legal alternatives, including presenting its claims to the United Nations for indemnification. In addition, the response must be reasonably proportionate to the provocation. But when, in order to avoid casualties to their own military personnel, the Israeli's resorted to air attacks, they inevitably killed or wounded innocent men, women, and children living near PLO installations; they also destroyed schools, hospitals, and mosques.[15]

The Israeli rationalization for killing so many civilians was that for propaganda purposes, the Palestinians have deliberately located their headquarters in or near civilian concentrations. That is a specious excuse. Obviously, the Palestinian leadership does locate itself in refugee camps to be near their supporters. If the Israelis insist on bombing such headquarters, then they must accept the responsibility for the civilian losses involved instead of trying to blame the guerrillas or the host government.

When at the outset of the Arab-Jewish communal warfare, Jewish officers tried to aim their attacks exclusively at the perpetrators, Menachem Begin expressed exasperation at the Haganah's obsession with the "historical, philosophical justification" of reprisals, and he derided their concern with what he called "mathematical relationships."[16] He thereby put himself on record as favoring indiscriminate and unlimited retaliation, a policy both he and Yitzhak Shamir pursued while they were prime ministers.

### *The Security Rationale for Reprisals*

The root of Israel's reprisal policy, as Barry Blechman notes, is the biblical injunction "an eye for an eye," and he quotes a passage from Abram Sachar, to the effect that "The law of retaliation, the grim response of the desert to actual or fancied injury, was part of the Hebrew tradition until late in the prophetic age. Kinsmen avenged each other's wrongs with relentlessness. *Lex Talionis* was the only justice conceivable."[17]

Tradition, while no doubt a contributing element, is only part of the explanation. Israel's reprisals are also rationalized on the racist contention that the Arabs understand nothing but force. Therefore, any failure to respond to an act of terrorism is interpreted by the Arabs as a sign of weakness.

### *Reprisals as a Response to Internal Politics*

Blechman found extremely limited results from Israel's reprisal practices, appraising them as follows:

> At a minimum, the reprisal policy has failed as a means of alleviating border conflict and bringing about a general settlement. . . . At a maximum, through their apparent effect on Arab political systems and on individual Arabs' mental frameworks of incentives and disincentives . . . they have contributed to an intensification . . . and a consequent escalation of military activity. . . .[18]

Why, in view of their limited effectiveness, have reprisals become such an automatic element of Israeli policy? Blechman believes that retaliation helps Israeli governments to satisfy public anxiety by providing "a counterfeit form of redress." Popular rage and frustration is released through attacks on the neighboring Arabs. Reprisals thus operate as a "compensating mechanism." Because the Arab perpetrators cannot be brought to justice, "the shocked and enraged populace is soothed" by an equally savage attack on Arab civilians. Although Israeli leaders presumably have "a more sophisticated understanding of the consequences" of revenge, they have conned themselves into believing that the frustration of their beleaguered populace compels them to "respond with reprisals."[19] But all too often, reprisals are the equivalent of collective punishment, which both treaties and established international law have explicitly outlawed. Thus, as the Israelis put it, " . . . if a saboteur cannot be captured, the village which has harbored him, inadvertently or not, will be attacked."[20]

### *Israel's Most Effective Rationale for Reprisals*

In one of Israel's rare glosses on its reprisal policy, General Moshe Dayan, in a lecture to Israeli staff officers, revealed that the main objective was to dissuade neighboring Arab states from providing the terrorists with bases from which they could mount attacks:

> It is not easy for Arab governments and armies to combat infiltration . . . the motive which could lead to a campaign against infiltrators must be the advantage of the Arab country and not of Israel . . . the motive that could . . . make the people understand why—must be something hard and real and certain; reprisal actions by the Israeli army and the fear of such actions. . . .

Dayan continues:

> We cannot guard every water pipeline from explosion and every tree from uprooting. We cannot prevent every murder of a worker in an orchard or a family in their beds.

> But it is in our power to set a high price on our blood, a price too high for the Arab community, the Arab army, or the Arab government to think it worth paying.
> We can see to it that the Arab villages oppose the raiding bands that pass through them, rather than give them assistance. It is in our power to see that Arab military commanders prefer a strict performance of their obligation to police the frontiers rather than suffer defeat in clashes with our units.[21]

The Israeli position, therefore, could be summarized as follows: Any raids made on it constitute an aggression on the part of the state from whose territory such raids were mounted. Israeli spokesmen have further argued that if the state is responsible, then all individuals living in that state are collectively responsible for its wrongdoing. Therefore, retaliation against *any* members of that community constitutes a fair and proportionate retaliation. Such logic, which justifies collective punishment, was specifically disavowed at the Nuremberg Trials and is categorically proscribed by the Geneva Conventions.[22]

The policy has succeeded to this extent: a weak Jordan must crush the PLO to avoid Israeli raids; Syria dares not provoke Israel until it is ready for open war. Only Lebanon, until lately, has offered a haven from which the guerrillas may launch attacks, and soon this may end, except for Lebanese groups attacking Israelis and their henchmen in the "security zone" in the south.

Blechman concludes that Israel has accepted the long-range consequences of its reprisal policy "in exchange for benefits of a psychological nature within the Israeli political system and tactical, short-run benefits in the frequency of Arab initiated hostilities."[23]

## Proportionality After 1954

In order to determine total casualties and Israel's degree of adherence to the rules of proportionality, we examined the records of terrorist incidents in the years 1971–88, based on *The New York Times* and other public records.

Admittedly, our numbers are not perfectly accurate since newspaper reports are incomplete and not all incidents were deemed newsworthy by each publication. Nonetheless, from 1949 to 1969, we have found records of 1,310 Arab attacks and 325 Israeli reprisals, resulting in 1,980 Israeli casualties versus 3,298 Arab deaths and injuries, for a ratio of 1 Israeli loss for every 2.25 Arabs killed.

In 1970, after Israel went over more heavily to the use of aircraft, we found that there were 282 Israeli dead to 2,512 Arabs killed, for a ratio of nearly 9 Arabs killed for every Israeli. However, from 1979 to 1985, we could find records of only 65 Israelis killed, whereas 1,741 Arabs were reported dead. This gives a kill ratio of about 27 Arabs for every Israeli. Such a level of slaughter suggests that the Israeli response to Arab attacks has been seriously disproportionate and may well help explain the intensity of Arab animosity toward Israel.[24]

Secretary of State George Shultz advised America to take Israel as its role model in dealing with terrorism. His recommendation might be taken with a grain of salt. In copying Israeli practice, the United States has, for example, announced that it will not negotiate with terrorists, or pay ransom to them. This high-toned policy fell somewhat flat when it presently transpired that the United States was selling Iran weapons to secure the release of hostages held by Iranian operatives in Lebanon. Some thought the approval Shultz gave to a Hebrew text advocating the murder of those whom one suspected of an intention to murder oneself in poor taste, since preemptive murder does not accord with American laws defining legitimate self-defense.

More substantively, Brian Urquhart's excellent biography of Dag Hammarskjold contains sharply contrasting views. When in 1956 Ben-Gurion complained to Hammarskjold that his condemnation of Israel's retaliatory actions against the Palestinians had "encouraged Egypt and Jordan to commit outrages," the UN Secretary General replied:

> You are convinced that the threat of retaliation has a deterrent effect. I am convinced that it is more of an incitement to individual members of the Arab forces than even what has been said by their own governments. You are convinced that acts of retaliation will stop further incidents. I am convinced that they will lead to further incidents. . . . You believe that this way of creating respect for Israel will pave the way for sound coexistence with the Arab peoples. I believe that the policy may postpone indefinitely the time for such coexistence. . . . I think the discussion of this question can be considered closed since you, in spite of previous discouraging experiences, have taken the responsibility for large-scale tests of the correctness of your belief.[25]

## America and Terrorism

There are other aspects of Israel's counterterrorism campaign which should not pass unnoticed. One of these is Israel's instigation of murders and assassinations abroad committed by Mossad or its armed forces. Israel has tried on several occasions to kill Yasser Arafat. Despite its pro forma denials, its role in the death of Abu Jihad is a matter of public record. Israeli agents, seeking to kill those connected with the Black September attack on Israel's athletes at Munich in 1972, murdered, in a case of mistaken identity, an innocent Arab waiter in Oslo.

Other similar activities have also come to light. In 1980 an Egyptian, Yahia Meshad, was murdered in his Paris hotel room. He had been working with Iraq on its nuclear program, and his death, as Israeli radio pointedly observed, would set back the Iraqi program at least two years. On March 22, 1989, Gerald Bull, a Canadian ballistics expert who was working on an Iraqi long-range cannon project, was shot to death outside his Brussels apartment. He had, so his son reported, been warned that Mossad, Israel's Secret Service, wanted him killed.

The United States has failed to take cognizance of any of these activities. Had the PLO perpetrated these crimes, the State Department would have promptly issued a statement on the subject. The fact that Israel is the suspected party and the U.S. government spokesmen remain silent clearly implies at a minimum American assent to such practices. Certainly, it is on the same moral plane as the CIA pamphlet encouraging Contra supporters to assassinate Sandinista leaders in Nicaragua.

David Lamb, who covered the Middle East for the *Los Angeles Times,* has commented that "the White House appears unaware of the relationship between peace and terrorism and seems unable to explain why Americans or American property are the targets of about one-third of all terrorist attacks." But he suggests that

> if one plotted the increasing number of terrorist incidents and the increased degree of official U.S. support for Israel, as measured by UN votes, arms shipments, American policy statements and unchallenged Israeli actions, the two lines would run in tandem right up the graph.
>
> And as long as the peace process lies dormant . . . and . . . as long as weapons continue to pour into the Middle East like Christmas-gift toys from the superpowers and as long as the United States and the Soviet Union keep regional tensions high by competing for domination, terrorism will have an atmosphere in which it can flourish.

Finally, Lamb concludes, the choice Washington must make is between a policy of automatic support for "the minority, often to the detriment of the majority, and one that recognized the need to play by the same rules when dealing with decent people, be they Arab or Israeli."[26]

Though Americans can consider themselves fortunate that for the present this sordid tale of slaughter has been largely confined to foreign nations, there is no assurance that this country will be permanently immune. If the peace process breaks down, what assurance do we have that America's porous borders will not be infiltrated and terrorist operations carried out against our people? If or when that does occur—and let us pray that it does not—the American government, if it continues to back Israeli state terrorism, will not be able to claim legitimately that this country is a totally innocent victim.[27]

# PART IV

CHAPTER THIRTEEN

# The Financial Costs of the Passionate Attachment

America's foreign aid programs have, at different times, been justified on different grounds.

In the immediate postwar period, the United States Marshall Plan provided economic assistance that enabled the shattered nations of Western Europe to rebuild.

In a second phase, which began under President Truman and reached its high point during the Kennedy years, America concentrated on helping nations in the so-called Third and Fourth Worlds to attain an economic development that would enable them to achieve self-generating growth. Aid was also furnished to countries that suffered Cold War subversion and communist external pressure.

## Israel's Special Aid Status

Then the politicians and lobbyists superseded the academics and restructured the foreign aid machinery to advance their own political and military objectives. One result of this pragmatic *coup d'état* was that Israel replaced India as the prime recipient of America's largesse.

Although the initial justification for America's aid to Israel was compassion for the tragedy of the Holocaust, leaders of the pro-Israeli lobby veered away from relying solely on emotion. They based their appeal instead on the hardheaded calculus of security. By blocking potential Soviet penetration in the Middle East, Israel could, they contended, serve a vital American interest. That rationale has, however, now lost relevance with the end of the Cold War, the disintegration of the Soviet empire, and the Gulf War.

Taken in combination, these new developments have put the Israeli leaders in an awkward position. Israel's claim to be a vital American strategic asset is now obsolete, and its brutalities to the Palestinian people have marred America's earlier compassion.

Today, U.S. foreign aid policy is no longer guided by a coherent strategy; it reflects, instead, the aberrations of America's domestic politics. The program is so distorted that the more than $3 billion of aid annually given to Israel, plus the $2.1 billion assigned annually to Egypt, comprise more than one third of the amounts appropriated for America's entire foreign aid program.

Of the total amount of foreign aid America earmarks for specific countries ($10.3 billion), Israel takes 28 percent and Egypt 20 percent, while the remaining 52 percent is divided 18 percent to other countries of the Near East and Asia, 15 percent to Latin America and the Caribbean, 10 percent to Europe, and 8 percent to Africa.

Thus, the United States concentrates a large part of its limited aid on a relatively wealthy country while, on a per capita basis, giving little more than pennies to the Third World. Moreover, Israel's GNP in 1990 was $40 billion, or $10,000 per capita; any country with a GNP per capita of $6,000 or more in 1988 is classified by the World Bank as a "high income economy."[1]

By the standards of a World Bank Report, ninety-nine countries have a per capita GNP less than Israel's. In relation to other Middle East countries outside the Gulf oil producers, Israel is extremely rich; even by European standards, it is moderately rich. Still America continues to provide it with aid that on a per capita basis is seven hundred times what we give to Africa, where hunger and hardship are a continuing rebuke to the conscience of civilized humanity.

In inflation-adjusted terms, the cumulative total of America's aid to Israel exceeds the aggregate assistance the United States gave Western Europe under the Marshall Plan. Yet Israel's population of 5.2 million (of which 4.4 million are Jewish Israelis) is barely 2 percent of the population that shared in the Marshall Plan.

In furtherance of its colonizing efforts in the territories, the government is enticing the settlers by offering them a subsidized and lavish life style.

> The settlers in the West Bank are no exception. Some Jewish settlers there are putting up $200,000 homes with comforts that range from heated towel racks to solariums. If a peace treaty ever requires an Israeli withdrawal, Washington may have to pick up the cost of compensating Jewish settlers, privately estimated at more than $35 billion.[2]

The Senate minority leader, Senator Robert Dole, has placed an even higher valuation on the newly constructed houses in the West Bank settlements. After completing a trip to Israel in the spring of 1990, he reported to the Senate:

> I visited one new settlement near Bethlehem. I saw there, new homes being provided to settlers under Israeli government subsidies. There were probably one hundred or more houses already built, and another 30–40 under construction.
>
> They were not shacks. They looked like they might fit in pretty well somewhere off Embassy Row in the District, or in Fairfax or Montgomery County. An American official resident in Israel estimated that, if identical houses were built in an urban center in Israel, the likely cost would be in the range of $300,000 to $400,000 per unit.[3]

Dole then continued, addressing the $400 million housing guaranty request then before the Senate:

> . . . what kind of housing is likely to be built as a result of these guarantees? The existing program requires that 90 percent of any guarantees be provided for housing for people with below-median income. This bill waives that requirement entirely.
>
> . . . There are no restrictions—and, in fact, no U.S. Government management or oversight, period—in the law, none.
>
> This is, in effect a blank check, in terms of how the loans can be used in supporting a housing program.
>
> . . . If it intends to build modestly priced housing for large numbers of people, why do we need to waive the standard 90 percent requirement I mentioned above?
>
> I think all Americans—especially those struggling with their own mortgages, or totally shut out of the housing market, have a right to answers to those questions.
>
> . . . We also have countless tens of thousands of homeless in this country.
>
> We do not hear their voice much, but they might ask: What about us?
>
> And they might ask it more loudly when they find out we are about to embark on a big program to provide housing to people living in a foreign land—especially if we are leaving open the possibility that we will be subsidizing housing for a privileged few, instead of many needy people.
>
> So I guess it is fair to add this question to my list: "How do we justify this program . . . ?"[4]

Providing funds for this type of housing is, of course, only one further addition to the multiplicity of financial costs for America of its passionate attachment to Israel. Some major cost items benefit Israel; a second category does not, but still results from Israeli pressure.

## Direct Aid That Benefits Israel

Between 1948 and fiscal year 1991, Congress has approved net loans and grants for Israel aggregating $53,531 billion.[5] That aid has contained both economic and military components. It includes outlays through the Economic Support Fund (ESF) and the Foreign Military Sales (FMS) programs.[6]

Through 1961, aggregate U.S. aid to Israel had totaled only $508.1 million, split roughly 50-50 between grants and loans. In addition, Israel has used its political leverage to persuade the American Congress to grant it a long list of exemptions to restrictions that are strictly applied to America's other foreign aid recipients.

In dealing with any matter affecting Israel, Congress responds more obediently to AIPAC than to its own budget-cutting mandate. The discipline of the Gramm-Rudman-Hollings (GRH) Act, designed to reduce America's budget deficit, required severe cuts in almost all government programs. Yet Congress passed a supplemental appropriation to compensate Israel for its mandatory reduction. The Congressional Research Service has published the following table, which shows first aid appropriated, then the GRH reduction, and finally the balance after taking account of a supplemental appropriation:

(in millions of dollars)

| | | | |
|---|---|---|---|
| Economic Support Fund | $1,200 | $51.6 | $1,148.4 |
| Foreign Military Sales | 1,800 | 77.4 | 1,722.6 |
| Fiscal year 1985 | | | |
| *supplemental* ESF | 750 | 0 | 750 |
| Total | $3,750 | $129.0 | $3,621 |

For fiscal year 1991, Congress voted a $400 million loan guaranty, ostensibly to be used to pay for the resettling of Soviet Jews. Under that proposal, member firms of the Israeli construction industry would borrow from American commercial banks at a concessionary interest rate made possible by a U.S. government guarantee of 90 percent of the principal sum.

In addition, Congress gave Israel $650 million in compensation for losses suffered during the Gulf War; ordered the transfer of $700 million of surplus American military goods assigned to NATO for Israeli use; and further ordered the storage of $300 million of military supplies in Israel.

In response, Defense Minister Moshe Arens announced that because of inflation and the geometric rise of the cost of weapons systems, Israel would request an increase in arms aid from $1.8 billion to $2.5 billion a year, starting in fiscal year 1992.[7]

The $3 billion of directly appropriated aid, usually taken as the totality of America's assistance to Israel, therefore severely understates America's contribution. In response to a request from Congressman Lee H. Hamilton, chairman of the Subcommittee on Europe and the Middle East of the House Foreign Affairs Committee, for a statement of "all types of direct assistance provided to Israel by the United States," the State Department (after canvassing the other relevant departments and agencies) produced the figures listed in Table 2 (page 280), which show that the appropriate amount for U.S. direct assistance to Israel is not the $3 billion directly appropriated for that purpose, but, according to official sources, is $3.75 billion. When one includes the saving to Israel that America makes possible by permitting it to refinance its FMS debt, the amount of Israel's effective aid is increased by $150 million a year—raising America's annual contribution for the benefit of Israel to an aggregate of $3.90 billion.

Senator Robert Dole proposed in April 1990 that America should consider a 5 percent cut in the aid provided the present recipients, including Israel and Egypt, to free funds for the pressing needs of Eastern Europe. As might have been expected, Dole's proposal evoked a storm of vitriolic protests from fellow senators and members of the House. He reportedly commented at the time that, although some of his fellow senators were publicly attacking him, they were privately as critical of Israel as he was: ". . . they won't say it out loud, but they grab you in the cloakroom and tell you, 'You're right. I can't say it because I'm running' but 'When I've been here as long as you have, I'll be able to say it.' "[8]

On May 1, 1990, in a speech on the Senate floor, Dole discussed the extraordinary concessions and special privileges granted Israel. Counting all the extraordinary concessions, he said, the United States provides Israel with "nearly $4 billion—not the $3+ billion usually cited—in aid every year. That includes direct aid and side benefits. Some of those side benefits are not widely understood by the American public—perhaps not even by some members of Congress."[9]

Dole's assertion that the aid approached $4 billion derived from a study made (at his request) by the Congressional Research Service (CRS), under the direction of its Middle Eastern specialist, Clyde R. Mark. The study analyzed the value to Israel of the principal special benefits of over thirty items. The most important of these was the decision of Congress to waive completely the repayment of annual FMS aid for fiscal year 1981 and subsequent years, and the decision in 1985 to accord ESF aid the same gratis treatment. That effectively placed all U.S. aid to Israel on a gift basis.[10]

Another concession was to treat Israel's granted funds as, in effect, an increment to its general revenues. As a result, the United States deprived itself of any viable means of ascertaining how Israel was spending its American gifts, even when it was suspected of using them to undercut U.S. interests.[11] The lack of accountability became starkly clear in 1991 when the U.S. government determined that no U.S. aid should be used for settling Soviet immigrants in the West Bank. Yet there was no way of checking how such aid was being used.

As revised in 1979, the program further undermined the concept of accountability. It reduced the obligations of the Israeli government to keep books on our economic aid, supposedly used solely for the purchase of American goods, to simply giving a general assurance that Israel would buy an unspecified amount of civilian imports from the United States. Since there is no check on whether that assurance is being honored, Israel's "buy American" promises can be easily evaded. Indeed, the program's loose oversight may well have stimulated the excessive consumerism that has debilitated the Israeli economy.[12]

Congress also gave Israel a special dispensation in drawing down the aid provided. Originally, FMS recipients of $100 million or more per year had been required to draw down proportionately on their FMS loans and grants.[13] But in the early 1980s Israel was permitted, as a special favor, to draw down the grant portion of its FMS funds before drawing on the loan portion. Israel took full advantage of this dispensation. The CRS "Issue Brief" of December 31, 1987, showed that Israel had "about $156 million in 'unexpended' funds in its FMS account."[14]

Furthermore, according to Senator Dole's CRS Report, the practices applicable to other loan recipients prescribe that "FMS funds are [to be] used for purchase of goods and services in the United States, and are not used to finance research and development (R&D)." But it notes that as an exception, "Israel is allowed to finance R&D in the United States with FMS funds."

That waiver's origin[15] dates to the time when Israel undertook to build the Lavi plane. Although that ill-conceived project was canceled in September 1987, Congress continued to earmark a portion of Israeli aid funds for R&D and procurement of other projects. The CRS Issue Brief notes that for the fiscal years 1987 to 1989, America gave Israel permission to use $150 million of its FMS funds for U.S. and $400 million for Israeli R&D and procurement of "advanced fighter aircraft."[16]

Major defense programs involving the development and procurement of new military instruments required that the purchaser pay in advance the full amount of the multi-year purchase. But, according to the CRS Report, the United States now allows Israel to pay only that portion of the FMS loan funds due in the current year. This provision enables Israel to "buy other equipment with the FMS funds that would have been committed to pay for multi-year purchases. Cash flow financing implies that the U.S. will guarantee future FMS levels to pay for the deferred installments."

Since Israel still has substantial loans outstanding, it has naturally wished to reduce the annual burden of repayment. Congress materially helped it by another exceptional privilege. The CRS Report continues: "In practice, most countries have 12 years in which to repay FMS loans. Israel and a few other countries were granted a 10-year grace period, during which only a reduced interest payment was made, followed by a 20-year repayment period." Such delayed payments enabled Israel to "utilize its funds for other purposes during the grace period, and then repay loans in deflated [*sic*] dollars."[17]

In 1981, Israel requested negotiations with the United States to eliminate trade barriers between the two countries. In 1983, Israel and the United States agreed to establish a "free trade area" to eliminate trade barriers over a ten-year period.[18] The free-trade-area agreement gives Israel preferential access to U.S. markets at the expense of many American interests. Yet there have been no signs of reciprocity; in fact, as noted in Chapter 8, the U.S. government has complained to Israel about alleged administrative and other restrictions it was placing on the free flow of American goods and services to Israel.

## Other Privileges and Concessions

There are a number of additional concessions and privileges granted to Israel, some of which can be briefly summarized.

—In 1988, Israel's congressional supporters attached a provision to the foreign aid bill that sets the cost of U.S. military weapons. Known as "fair pricing," this method prohibits the United States from including in Israeli aid any costs for overhead, research, and development of weapons—which saves Israel an estimated $56 million a year. The U.S. taxpayers pay the costs—through surcharges on arms purchased by the U.S. armed forces.

—Israel has been granted status as a non-NATO ally, which will entitle it to the same treatment as NATO countries in the cooperative development of defense weapons. It also benefits Israel in bidding for U.S. defense contracts, as well as in buying U.S. defense equipment and services.[19]

—Israel was invited to participate in developing and building the Strategic Defense Initiative (SDI). The Reagan administration included Israel in planning the SDI for two reasons: it provided Israel with a substantial contract for its defense industry, and it secured the backing of the Israeli lobby in America to keep the SDI alive.[20]

—The 1990 Department of Defense bill includes almost $25 million for the "Popeye" air-to-ground missile. Israel also receives American help in developing the "Arrow" anti-tactical ballistic missile (ATBM) to counter the ballistic missiles now possessed by several Arab states. The Arrow development will cost $300 million per year for the next three years, of which the United States will pay 80 percent and Israel 20 percent; half of that 20 percent will come from FMS funds. During the SCUD attacks on Israel, the Arrow proved ineffective; and in view of the impending substitution of upgraded Patriot missiles, there is no need for this costly program, except to provide Israeli weapons designers and munitions workers with make-work employment.

In addition, as noted in Chapter 8, a $12 million unmanned surveillance aircraft (Drone) procurement contract had to be canceled for nonperformance even after the Israeli contractor bribed an Assistant Secretary of the Navy in an effort to avoid the cancelation.

—To stretch its aid dollars even further, Israel has sought funding from other U.S. budget accounts. Thus Congress appropriated about $180 million in the fiscal year 1990 Department of Defense budget for the United States either to purchase Israeli-manufactured military hardware or to subsidize Israeli weapons research.

—Israel requires American companies that provide arms under the FMS program to buy an equivalent value of goods from Israel. Offset programs, to be sure, are frequently required by governments that buy arms with their own money. But Israel uses *Alice in Wonderland* logic; it compels American manufacturers to buy Israeli goods to offset the arms the United States government has given Israel as a gift. Israel's offset rebates are reported to cover about 45 percent of its American aid. An aviation industry association study found that on twelve contracts over five years, U.S. firms were compelled to purchase Israeli goods amounting to $262 million. In early 1988, General Dynamics pledged to buy $800 million in Israeli defense equipment partially to offset a $2 billion arms sale paid for by American gift aid.[21]

In connection with that practice, the General Accounting Office has warned:

> If any FMS recipient country is granted approval to purchase its own goods as an integral part of the program, or other recipient countries are allowed to use their FMS credits to purchase goods in that country when U.S. sources are available, it could be used as a precedent for other recipients and cause an adverse impact on the U.S. economy.[22]

That is, of course, a bureaucratic paraphrase of George Washington's more eloquent warning against giving "concessions to the favorite nation of privileges denied to others," which results in a "disposition to retaliate in the parties from which equal privileges are withheld." To avoid the full fury of such ill-will, the United States has, from time to time, felt obliged to pacify other disgruntled countries by according them equal privileges, thereby multiplying American sales losses abroad.

The summary of the CRS Report states also that, in addition to U.S. government assistance, "Israel receives about $1 billion annually through philanthropy, an equal amount from short- and long-term commercial loans, and about $500 million or more in Israeli bond proceeds." Philanthropy, particularly from the United States Diaspora, is thus a major resource for Israel, since for every three dollars that Israel receives from the U.S. government, one additional dollar purportedly comes from private contributions.

## Costs of Subsidizing Israel's Arms Industry

Israel's own military requirements provide too small a market to permit production runs long enough to enable its industry to manufacture at competitive costs. Therefore, Israel's arms producers have achieved the requisite volume by acquiring a substantial position in world markets, which puts them in direct competition with American producers.

That buildup directly contradicts a primary principle that has from the beginning governed America's foreign aid grants—that the resources provided should not be used to compete with American producers in world markets. However, AIPAC and Israel's other friends have inveigled Congress into giving Israel the money and technology to become a potentially effective competitor of America in the sale of sophisticated weapons.

Under the 1970 Defense Development Data Exchange Agreement with Israel, the United States "permits and facilitates the exchange of information important to the development of a full range of military systems, including tanks, surveillance equipment, electronic warfare, air to air and air to surface weapons, and engineering."[23] Consequently, Israel has been given, gratis, access to systems like aircraft electronic countermeasures technology, in which the United States invested $2.5 billion between 1965 and 1970.[24]

Transfers are effected through the release of so-called "technical data packages"—the entire complex of blueprints, plans, and types of materials required to construct the new weapons. More than 120 such packages were given to Israel between 1970 and 1980. As of July 1982, 19 separate data exchange annexes covering individual projects had been included, and a twentieth was under negotiation. In some reported instances, Israel has sold the technology thus acquired to other powers. The Chilean production of cluster bombs and the Chinese Silkworm missile are notable examples of this.

The United States has permitted Israel to co-produce U.S. defense equipment through licensed production at a "higher level of technology" than any other FMS credit recipient.[25] Furthermore, a Memorandum of Agreement (MOA) signed in 1979 enables Israeli industry to compete in the procurement market for Department of Defense purchases. Its Annex A calls for an expanded data exchange program, cooperative research and development, and for the exchange of scientists. Its Annex B contains an open-ended list of over 560 items (since enlarged) used by U.S. forces on which Israel can bid. Using that list, Israel has performed overhauls on F-4 components, sold assault weapons to the U.S. Marine Corps, and obtained contracts to provide American defense agencies with radar, ammunition, and pharmaceutical supplies.[26]

The practice of subsidizing Israel's armaments industry began on July 22, 1977, when President Jimmy Carter agreed to add $107 million in U.S. foreign aid funds so that Israel could build the Merkava (Chariot) tank in Israel. Although a reluctant Carter specified that the Merkava tank "was considered a onetime exception,"[27] that did not deter Israel from later demanding and receiving another $50 million to expand its production capacity from eighty to one hundred tanks per year.[28]

## The Fiasco of the Lavi—A Serio-Comic Saga

When Israel first proposed building a low-cost replacement for its aging U.S.-built A-4 aircraft, the United States agreed to the use of FMS credits for that limited purpose only—it also specified clearly that such planes were solely for Israeli use.

However, the situation changed drastically when the Israeli government and its lobby lured the American authorities into subsidizing an Israeli aircraft to fulfill an American presidential directive issued on January 3, 1980, which established the requirements for an FX international fighter.

Producing the requisite aircraft would normally have been undertaken by an American company, assisted by a government subsidy during the design and development stage. But this time the directive explicitly stated that "the United States government" will "not provide funding for the development of the aircraft, and aircraft companies will assume all financial and market risk." The American manufacturers quickly realized that meeting the government's requirements might well result in their bankruptcy, as had nearly happened several times when producers had accepted high-risk exposure in developing a new generation of aircraft without government help.[29]

Then, incomprehensibly, having denied any subsidy to an American manufacturer, the U.S. government subsidized instead an ill-conceived Israeli effort to build the same kind of plane.

During the initial meetings in 1982, the Israelis had disingenuously assured the American government that Israel did not intend to offer its projected new high-performance plane (the Lavi) on the export market; the plane was intended merely to fill the expected requirements of the Israeli Air Force (IAF) for three hundred such planes by the late 1990s. Yet early the following year the Israel Aircraft Industries, Ltd. (IAI) issued a marketing brochure entitled "Lavi—the affordable fighter." That brochure outlined plans to sell some 407 Lavis to Argentina, Chile, South Africa, and Taiwan. Eventually, the Israelis hoped to capture (primarily from American firms) 17 percent of the developing-country military aircraft market between 1988 and 2000, in direct violation of American regulations and previous Israeli assurances.

Their marketing literature hopefully referred to a possible war between

Argentina and Chile over the Beagle Islands and optimistically estimated that Israel had a 50 percent chance of selling one hundred Lavi fighters to the prospective combatants. But when Pope John Paul II arbitrated the Beagle Islands dispute, he scotched most of Israel's sales plans.

The Pentagon opposed the Lavi from the beginning. When Israel first briefed the State Department in late 1981 on its ambitions for the Lavi, there was "general incredulity." One State Department official remarked that "they were going to build this airplane. All they needed was American technology and American money."[30] The proposal reminded another State Department official of the old tale of a man with a stone, who offered to use the stone to cook soup for a stranger. If the stranger would only find him a pot, water, some carrots, potatoes, onions, meat, and seasoning, he would benevolently share the soup with the stranger. It was an apt analogy; by the time the Lavi project was finally killed, the United States had provided more than 50 percent of the technology and more than 90 percent of the funding.

What ultimately broke the camel's back was that, in spite of lavish American subsidies, Israel proved unable to build a cost-competitive plane. Only after production had fallen three years behind schedule did other branches of the Israeli Defense Force complain that the Lavi project was consuming an inordinate share of American funds urgently needed for other military programs. In his annual report, released in July 1987, the Israeli state comptroller, Yaacov Maltz, commented that the project had been badly administered from the beginning. Furthermore, "a great many of the significant and essential decisions were made with information that was without basis, inadequate, tendentious and lacking proper cost estimates." The president of one American subcontractor told the senior author that "the Israelis simply did not know how to build a modern, large, high-technology plane."

Comptroller Maltz's report was based on the Israeli defense establishment's decision in 1985 that it would build only 210 planes, even though such a large cutback in the proposed production run would obviously increase the "average cost of each plane." In 1987, *The Jerusalem Post* reported that only one hundred Lavis were to be built, which would raise the unit cost from $15 million dollars per plane to more than $30 million.

However, even that critique did not persuade Israel to drop the project. According to the U.S. General Accounting Office, which had been asked to examine the situation, "Israeli officials expressed the hope that by the early 1990s, U.S. budgetary constraints will have run their course and that additional funding will be available for the U.S. government to assure successful completion of the Lavi program."[31]

Even after its demonstrated failure, Israeli leaders insisted that the project must continue because its cancelation would prompt Israel's technical elite to seek jobs abroad, taking their precious skills with them—a constant Israeli anxiety. Thus, before Israel's quarreling cabinet finally agreed to heed U.S. advice (which they did late in 1987 by a one-vote margin because the project was draining too much American aid from the army and navy), Ambassador

Thomas Pickering (later U.S. ambassador to the UN) had to assure them that if the United States would provide a $400 million increase in aid, it could be converted to Israeli currency. The Israelis wished to secure a "promising potential" for research and development of weapon systems that would maintain an adequate level of employment in the Israel Aircraft Industries, Ltd.[32]

## The Sour Result for Northrop and the American Taxpayer

The Carter directive of January 3, 1980, had made it clear that no American producer should assume that meeting the requirements outlined for an FX international fighter would guarantee that the Pentagon would buy the finished product. Even so, one courageous American plane manufacturer, the Northrop Corporation, took the gamble. Northrop spent roughly $1 billion of its own funds to develop the high-quality F-20 Tigershark, which was highly praised in technical circles, but rejected by the U.S. military bureaucracy because of a desire to standardize aircraft.

Forced to seek purchasers abroad, Northrop soon discovered that Western European markets were effectively reserved for European aircraft manufacturers, whose governments were helping to peddle their products. That left only one major national group rich enough to purchase the Tigershark: the Persian Gulf states. Once again, Israel and AIPAC used their political muscle in Congress to prohibit licenses for Northrop to sell its planes to Arab purchasers.

As a result of this whole mess, Northrop was forced to absorb $1 billion in R&D losses (partially offset by some federal tax rebates). The U.S. government added substantially to its foreign account deficit by letting Israel use close to $2 billion of the funds the United States gave it to try to build an aircraft that, had it been successful, would have usurped an important market segment from America's own industry. And when Israel finally demonstrated that it could not produce a competitive plane, America even funded the cancelation charges under Israel's subcontracts with U.S. component manufacturers. No matter what happened, this entire scheme left America a sure loser.

Had America conducted such a transaction with any nation but Israel, there would have been a loud and protracted national outcry, complete with congressional investigations. But, unsurprisingly, the passionate attachment assured a cover-up.

## Analysis of the Lavi Affair

The Lavi saga raises cogent questions. How could a project consistently held infeasible by the Defense Department be allowed to go forward at an ultimate cost to the American taxpayers of roughly $2 billion? If obtaining subsidy money for the Lavi was a conspicuous triumph for AIPAC, it was a disaster for U.S. interests. In 1983, Northrop board chairman Tom Jones sent identical letters to Secretary of State George P. Shultz and Defense Secretary Caspar W. Weinberger. Jones sharply complained that the U.S. government was funding foreign competitors to the detriment of U.S. industry: "The policies and political issues raised by such a precedent are indeed profound. They involve the exporting of U.S. jobs at a time of high unemployment and difficult economic conditions."[33] These indictments were well founded. A subsequent study by the Congressional Research Service concluded that the Lavi project had cost the American economy 6,000–8,000 jobs, beyond those lost by Northrop.

Not even Israel prospered from this harebrained undertaking. Some of the results were manifested in:

—The loss (on cancellation) of 3,000–4,000 jobs in Israel's most important industry;
—Increased friction between the Israeli Air Force and its army and navy, which saw the Lavi as a monster devouring the sustenance of their own projects.

In a larger sense, the episode reflects two basic elements in Israeli life: The first is a belief that Israel is capable of anything, even a project wildly disproportionate to its resources. The second (which reinforces the first) is Israel's heretofore well-founded conviction that it will always have access to Uncle Sam's deep pockets.

The Israeli public was bitterly angry with the leaders who canceled the project, and blamed the United States for urging them to do so. The real lesson went unheeded: Israel is not a superpower, but a tiny nation whose only conspicuous resource is a pool of superbly talented individuals.

When the Reagan administration denied subsidies to American manufacturers for FX fighter production while subsidizing a competing Israeli plane, it not only discriminated against American producers but also between American airframe manufacturers. Northrop had to bear the whole cost of developing the F-20, whereas Grumman, which had subcontracted with IAI to build the wing and tail assemblies for the Lavi, was bailed out by the U.S. government with the FMS funds America had permitted Israel to use to pay cancelation costs.

This whole lamentable history, as was pointed out in *The Washington*

*Post* on August 6, 1986, also illustrates the incestuous relationships between AIPAC and the U.S. Congress. One of Israel's most outspoken advocates in Congress is Representative Charles Wilson (D-TX), a member of the House Appropriations Defense Subcommittee. Wilson first learned about the Lavi during a visit to Israel in April 1983, when he met Minister of Defense Moshe Arens, a former aircraft engineer and principal promoter of the project. On his return, Wilson asked AIPAC to draft a legislative amendment authorizing Israel to use American aid money for the Lavi program.

The AIPAC-drafted amendment designated for the Lavi's development $550 million ($150 million more than IAI requested) of fiscal year 1984's $1.7 billion military aid package—$300 million to be spent in the United States and $250 million in Israel. Because the Israelis had been unable to spend all the previously allocated $500 million, for fiscal year 1985 the request was reduced to $400 million. Of this $400 million, Israel was allowed to spend $250 million at home and $150 million in the United States. The practice in subsequent years was largely the same; the U.S. Congress obligingly approved $400 million in fiscal years 1986 and 1987, and $450 million in fiscal year 1988, despite firm Defense Department convictions that Israel would never be able to develop a marketable plane.

If the project made no sense for the United States, it did have value for Israel as a domestic relief device. In the early 1980s, unemployment was a pressing concern. Its Kfir fighter jet production line was going to close down, which would depress its largest industry: aircraft. Thus, Israel's rationale for this vast U.S. subsidy was its need to prevent unemployment—hardly a justification under U.S. law.

Another pro-Lavi contention was that the high-performance aircraft America was selling to certain Arab states might, in time, erode Israel's qualitative edge. Israel's possession of the Lavi would make it easier for the United States to refuse to sell its most advanced fighters to Arab countries. Since Israel would be making its own high-performance aircraft, the Arabs could no longer argue that the United States should sell high-performance aircraft to them as long as it was selling such planes to Israel.

## The Cost of Aid to Egypt

In computing the indirect costs of the passionate attachment, one must also consider the price of negotiating and maintaining the Camp David Accords with Egypt. Egypt is the second largest recipient of U.S. aid after Israel. In inducing it to sign the Camp David Accords, U.S. negotiators promised Egypt that it would receive the same amount of aid as Israel. However, Congress has, by sleight of hand, managed to fix America's aid to Egypt at an unacknowledged 70 percent of its aid to Israel. Even so, U.S. aid keeps Egypt neutralized and hence is an additional boon to Israel. So, too, is the 1991 $7.5 billion write-off of uncollectible Egyptian military debts, nominally in exchange for Egypt's services in the Gulf War.

Although America's generosity has materially increased the burden on American taxpayers, it has not always pleased Israel. The evolution of special privileges and concessions for Israel has inevitably led Egypt to demand those same favors, whereas the Israelis have jealously resisted the United States granting Egypt any such concessions because, so the congressional report states: "The Israelis . . . desire that the United States maintain its special relationship which means favorable treatment. In Israeli eyes, the linkage is eroding part of the their special relationship."[34]

In simple terms, Israel wants to so arrange matters that it and it alone is America's special friend in the Middle East. It would much prefer that America had sour relations with all the Arab states so that Washington would be compelled to put all its Middle East eggs into Israel's basket. American would then have no choice but to back Israel in anything that it does. Thus, Israel's intense effort to prevent arms sales to Saudi Arabia is not so much motivated by the ostensible fears for Israel's military security as it is a reflection of Israel's irrationally jealous fears that decent American relations with any Arab state will undermine Israel's special position in Washington.

## The Economic Costs of the 1973 Oil Boycott

We have recorded thus far only those costs to America that benefit Israel. But we must also, in reckoning the total cost of our special relations with Israel, include the costs imposed on America that are not to Israel's advantage. For example, a number of Israeli actions may actually have made Israel more rather than less vulnerable to attack from its neighbors.

In the early 1970s King Faisal of Saudi Arabia, an Islamic leader, was infuriated by Israel's continued occupation of the sacred city of Jerusalem, and as a head of state, was also deeply disturbed by President Nixon's lavish increase of U.S. military assistance to Israel.[35] He therefore agreed to finance the war that Egyptian President Anwar el-Sadat was then planning to break the Middle East impasse, and further, to use his oil weapon against the West.

This message was conveyed in April 1973 by Sheikh Ahmad Zaki Yamani, the Saudi oil minister, both to Secretary of State William Rogers and the Treasury Secretary, George Shultz. He told them that if OPEC was to quench the West's insatiable appetite for oil, the West must restore Arab control over Jerusalem. Yamani also met with National Security Adviser Henry Kissinger, who said, "I hope you have not mentioned this to anybody else," and regretted that Yamani had already spoken to Rogers and Shultz.

Yamani's reaction, as reported by Robert Lacey in his history of the Saudi royal family, was as follows:

> Afterwards, the Oil Minister wondered why Dr. Kissinger should be so concerned to keep the threat of the Arab oil weapon a secret. The Security Advisor had talked in terms of Arab image and of the importance of the Arabs not appearing threatening or extreme in American eyes.

> But Yamani, who like many Arabians, feels that Dr. Henry Kissinger's Jewishness hampers his impartiality in Middle Eastern matters, did not accept the Security Advisor's counsel at face value. Dr. Kissinger, in the Oil Minister's opinion, could not care less about the Arab's posture . . . the Security Advisor was concerned to prevent the American public from reflecting too deeply on the price they might have to pay for supporting Israeli military conquest. . . .

In an interview with *The Washington Post* on April 18, Yamani cautioned the United States to adopt a more evenhanded approach to the Arab-Israeli conflict. The following day a *Post* editorial downplayed Yamani's remarks, commenting that "it is to yield to hysteria to take such threats as Saudi Arabia's seriously."

Unhappily, the Nixon administration shared the *Post*'s skepticism, and decided that Yamani was acting without King Faisal's authority. To prove otherwise, the King promptly granted an unprecedented U.S. interview, in which he warned: "America's complete support of Zionism against the Arabs makes it extremely difficult for us to continue to supply U.S. petroleum needs and even to maintain friendly relations with America."[36]

Nevertheless, the Nixon administration evidently adopted the contention of Israeli Foreign Minister Abba Eban, who asserted that "There isn't the slightest possibility of an oil boycott. The Arab states have no alternative but to sell their oil because they have no other resources at all."[37]

Although that comment reflected the opaque logic which then prevailed both in Washington and Jerusalem, King Faisal was determined to register his deadly serious intentions. Consequently, he summoned board chairman Frank Jungers of the Arabian-American Oil Company (ARAMCO) and sternly reiterated his threat of an oil boycott.

Jungers alerted both the White House and State Department, but his advice "was ignored"—even though oil men everywhere knew that Faisal "never acts on a whim. He never breaks his word. When he speaks, he never tells you anything unless he means it."

That same month, Faisal told four other leading oil men that "You may lose everything. Time is running out." The oil men again tried to warn the Nixon administration. Unhappily, neither the White House nor the State Department paid them heed; Kissinger refused even to see them.[38]

Finally, in September, the King told *Newsweek* that "logic requires that our oil production does not exceed the limits that can be absorbed by our economy," and he urged Washington to disavow "Zionist expansionist ambitions." Contemptuously, George Shultz dismissed the King's remarks as Arab "swaggering," while President Nixon observed that "oil without a market . . . does not do a country much good."[39]

When Egyptian and Syrian forces attacked Israel on October 6, 1973, the four chairmen of ARAMCO's controlling companies explicitly informed Nixon on October 12 that increasing military aid to Israel "will have a critical and adverse effect on our relations with the moderate Arab countries."

That the Saudis meant what they said was first made emphatically clear when an extraordinary meeting took place at the Sheraton Hotel in Kuwait shortly after the war began. There the OPEC nations decided unilaterally to raise the price of a barrel of oil from $3.01 to $5.12, a jump of $2.11—the largest increase ever. No longer would the Arab oil states bargain with the producing companies before raising prices.

On Thursday, October 18, King Faisal sent President Nixon another admonitory message: "If the United States continues to stand by the side of Israel, then the [U.S.-Saudi] relationship will risk being diminished."[40] But, trying to rally Jewish support for his Watergate-beleaguered presidency, Nixon moved briskly to flout such advice. The following day, October 19, he submitted a $2.2 billion special request to Congress for emergency aid to Israel—more than half of which was in grant form. The Arabs reacted with fury.[41]

King Faisal was particularly enraged at Nixon. The United States had repeatedly spurned the king's warnings, flaunted its support for Israel, and was now provocatively challenging the whole Arab world. So the next morning (October 20), Saudi Arabia announced the imposition of a total oil boycott against the United States. The kingdom would no longer sell it the average of nearly 600,000 barrels a day. This statement had a domino effect on other Arab producers—including Abu Dhabi, Algeria, Bahrain, Kuwait, and Qatar—all of which, by quickly following suit, caused an economic earthquake that was felt around the world. The boycott remained in force until March 18, 1974; industrial output plummeted, particularly in America. Older Americans will not soon forget their exasperation, or the nerve-wracking pump lines. Endless hours were consumed each week in often fruitless searches for stringently doled out gasoline.

Hard as it is to estimate the precise impact of the 1973 War on the American economy, there is no disagreement that the cost of the oil boycott looms large. In reviewing American aid to Israel, former Secretary of State Cyrus Vance told the Senate Foreign Relations Committee that "If only one tenth or one twentieth of these accelerated [oil] price increases could be directly ascribed to the 1973 War and the embargo, it would reflect another $15–30 billion in war-related costs." General Ira Eaker (World War II commander of Allied Air Forces in the Mediterranean) was more explicit. The 1973 War, he maintained,

> cost this country at least $4 billion. It used up scarce reserves of weapons and supplies. It reduced the purchasing power of American consumers. General Motors, during the embargo, laid off 65,000 workers and put 5,700 more on temporary furlough, and further depressed the entire U.S. economy since this move had repercussions on GM's 13,000 dealers and 45,000 suppliers.[42]

Secretary Henry Kissinger estimated the direct costs to the United States at $3 billion, and the indirect costs, mainly from higher oil prices, at $10 to

$15 billion. He added: "It increased our unemployment and contributed to the deepest recession we have had in the postwar period."[43]

A final reflection of the costs of the U.S. action in 1973 came in 1978 as part of the Camp David deal. There, the U.S. government agreed to guarantee Israel's oil supply for fifteen years—potentially a commitment that could prove extremely costly.[44]

In addition, but completely forgotten, was the cost to the United States and Europe of the closing of the Suez Canal from 1967 to 1975—estimated at well over $10 billion and arising from America's lax approach to securing peace in the Middle East.[45]

## American Losses Through the Denial of Arms Sales to Arab Nations

It is impossible to determine precisely the total cost to America of technology transferred to Israel, and the loss to American industry when Israel diverts aid funds for in-country expenditure. Nevertheless, one can make a solid estimate of the financial and economic costs when AIPAC blocks American arms sales to Arab nations, which it does with great regularity. American industry—and the American economy as a whole—has suffered heavily from AIPAC's manipulation of Congress. It is particularly painful when AIPAC prevents sales to Arab nations, since they pay cash while the United States gives arms free to Israel.

Several of Israel's military leaders have pointed out that U.S. military equipment in Arab hands would pose no menace to Israel. Any U.S. weapons bought by the Arabs would be subject to strict restrictions as to use and deployment—and, unlike its treatment of Israel, America would enforce those restrictions. Thus, AIPAC's virtuosity with Congress actually harms Israel's security, for it forces the Arabs to buy arms from nations such as Russia or Western Europe, countries that place no restrictions on their use.

By blocking sales to nations disliked by Israel, AIPAC has deprived American industry of profitable sales and foreign exchange. It has also successfully diminished America's ability to restrain the Arab nations while enabling America's competitors to gain a strong toehold in the rich Arab market both now and for the future.

America showed premonitory symptoms of that malaise in 1963 and 1964 when, in order to avoid a showdown with Congress and the pro-Israel lobby, the Johnson administration advised the Saudis to buy British Lightning jet fighters. In theory, America's losses were to be offset by the British purchase of U.S. defense equipment, but, due to British budgetary problems, that never occurred.[46]

In the 1970s, the Defense Department and U.S. Air Force made several extensive studies of Saudi air defense needs and recommended that the Saudis buy a highly mobile, sophisticated air fleet as the most effective and cheapest defense system. The sparsely populated land area of Saudi Arabia is as large as the United States east of the Mississippi, and its oil reserves (one fourth of the world supply) and coastal shipping appeared vulnerable to air raids.

Accordingly, the United States proposed selling the Saudis about one hundred F-15s, even though the Saudis had well-trained pilots for only sixty. But, fearing AIPAC's congressional influence, the Ford administration decided to hold off the sale until after the 1976 election. Eventually, despite an all-out Israeli lobby push, the Carter administration induced Congress to approve the proposed sale of the first sixty planes in May 1978.[47] Although the remaining F-15s were to arrive in the early 1980s, the outbreak of the Iran–Iraq War in 1980 led the Chairman of the U.S. Joint Chiefs of Staff, Lieutenant General David Jones, to urge the Saudis to change their priorities and buy AWACs (airborne warning and control aircraft). Until the Saudis could acquire their own, the United States would immediately lend five planes, to be returned later. Though Carter agreed in November–December 1980 to take the heat for that sale on an emergency basis, the incoming Reagan administration postponed the project for further study. In February 1981, it decided to move ahead.

The President secured final congressional approval of the AWACS sale during the honeymoon period of his first year only by putting his popularity on the line, and by paying Israel a "peace offering" or, more accurately, a bribe in the form of a $300 million increase in its annual FMS credits. In November 1984, Secretary Weinberger is reported to have flown to Riyadh with a (still-classified) letter confirming to the Saudis that the administration would press for the remainder of the promised planes soon after the President's second inauguration. By February 1985, however, National Security Adviser Robert McFarlane told the Saudis that AIPAC was threatening to raise a big fuss, so the Reagan administration could not keep its promise.

Still, the Saudis maintained the pressure for two months, while the Reagan administration stalled. Finally, to get the administration off the hook, McFarlane, copying President Johnson, urged the Saudis to buy alternative planes in Western Europe. Fearful of loosening their ties with the U.S. defense industry and anxious to avoid criticism, the Saudis requested a letter from the White House confirming that it had no objection to such alternative procurement. The President complied—even though it was a substantial diversion of lucrative business away from hard-pressed American manufacturers to competing foreign industry.

At this point, the Saudis once again tried to influence America to resist Israeli pressure on a key issue. They had tried it the first time with an oil blockade which exploited their leverage as a supplier; now they tried to utilize their leverage as the best customer of America's aircraft industry.

In June 1985, on instructions from the King, the Saudi ambassador to Washington, Prince Bandar, called on Prime Minister Margaret Thatcher at 10 Downing Street and inquired about buying comparable planes from Britain. An overjoyed Mrs. Thatcher assured Prince Bandar that there would be no problem, and urged the Saudis to purchase other items as well. Worried about high unemployment in Britain and a balance of payments deficit, Thatcher actively involved herself in the sale, even inviting Prince Bandar to meet with her during an August vacation in Austria. The British royal family was also pressed into service to help cement this deal—with good reason. Contracts for the planes alone were worth approximately $9 billion.[48]

That transaction opened the Saudi door for British industry. When Mrs. Thatcher subsequently heard that the Saudis needed two new air bases to handle the planes, she flatly told them that she thought Britain was entitled to sole construction and procurement rights. The Saudis readily agreed. The American contractors were discarded for a further British gain of $5 billion.

Then, since the Saudis would also need spare parts, maintenance services, and related outlays during the planes' lifetime, the British procured contracts for an additional $5 billion. Thus, the first Saudi Tornado purchase amounted to at least a $20 billion revenue loss for the U.S. economy.

On March 11, 1986, with Britain's triumph confirmed by contracts signed on February 4, Senator Alan Cranston (D-CA), a key member of the Senate Foreign Relations Committee, launched a preemptive strike against a plan to sell the Saudis roughly $1 billion worth of Sidewinder air-to-air missiles, Stinger anti-aircraft missiles and launchers, Blackhawk helicopters, Harpoon missiles, and advanced electronics equipment. Saudi Arabia, he declared, was "scorning basic American interests in the area."[49] He was joined by a bipartisan group of eleven pro-Israel congressmen—led by Mel Levine (D-CA)—who sent Reagan a letter stating that further weapons sales to Saudi Arabia could not be justified.

The administration responded dutifully. When the package was finally presented to Congress, it had been reduced to a little more than $350 million and included only missiles already in the Saudi arsenal. Even so, Senator Cranston had little trouble in lining up at least fifty senators to block the proposal. When congressional sanction was finally secured on June 5, all that remained of the original billion-dollar-plus proposal was a $265 million package of air-to-air and air-to-sea missiles. Senator Cranston, who had led the opposition, cheerfully declared that "[the Saudis] got ten percent of what they wanted."[50] In his misplaced joy, the senator took no account of where this AIPAC-inspired victory would lead.[51]

To wit, less than two years after the 1986 sale, the British sold the Saudis additional Tornado aircraft, calculated by U.S. government agencies and the media to be worth a minimum of another $30 billion. An executive memorandum prepared in 1988 by a senior policy analyst of the Heritage Foundation (a conservative, normally pro-Israel think tank) summarized the publicly known facts of the transaction as follows:

> Through this commitment, called by experts the arms deal of the century, Britain, in effect, has supplanted the United States as Saudi Arabia's main

> source of arms. Under the terms of the agreement, the British will provide the Saudis with 48 Tornado fighter bombers, 6 Hawk Jet Trainers, 80 helicopters, 6 minesweepers, millions of dollars of electronic gear, and 2 airbases.
> The Saudis decided to seek British arms because past efforts to obtain American efforts have been denied, delayed or reduced by the U.S. Congress. According to a Saudi official, "we would prefer to buy weapons from the United States. American technology is generally superior. But we are not going to pay billions of dollars to be insulted. We are not masochists.' "

The analyst continues:

> The new Saudi-British deal reveals the United States, not Saudi Arabia, as the masochist. In losing the largest arms sales in Middle East—perhaps world history—the U.S. has lost important benefits. Economically, the United States has been deprived of a major boost to its balance of trade and thousands of jobs. Militarily, the United States has lost an opportunity to increase the ability of American military forces to use Saudi logistical and maintenance support systems, or possibly even Saudi warplanes, in a crisis. Most important, the U.S. stands to lose political influence in Saudi Arabia and leverage over how Saudi military forces are deployed. The loosening of Saudi-American military ties may unravel a broader Saudi-American political relationship and lead other Arab states to question defense cooperation with Washington.[52]

After 1992, Saudi Arabia will need to replace what is left of its American-built aircraft. If the American airframe industry loses out on that order, losses may double yet again. The European airframe manufacturers have already invited Saudi financial participation in the building of the next generation of high-performance aircraft. Moreover, incalculable added costs may arise from America's diminished political leverage in Saudi Arabia, which, since the Gulf War, is at a record high point.

The sales of Tornados in 1986 and again in 1988 resulted in a conservatively estimated $70 billion revenue loss for the U.S. economy, or a total loss to U.S. labor from these two sales alone of 1.7 million man-years of employment, based on the Department of Commerce estimate that $1 billion in sales equals 25,000 jobs. And that does not reflect the Saudi-British civilian contracts that will surely follow this deal. The 1988 financial statement put out by British Aerospace estimates the value of both contracts for their twenty-five-year life as £150 billion ($225 billion).[53]

During 1990, Saudi Arabia bought $7 billion in arms from the United States as the first installment of a $20 billion purchase, on an understanding with Secretary of Defense Richard Cheney that at the conclusion of the Gulf War the administration would go forward with the balance of the package—or $13 billion of additional arms.

But at a meeting of AIPAC on March 19, 1991, which was attended by approximately one half the Senate and nearly one hundred House members, the AIPAC agenda was enthusiastically approved. Its principal emphasis was on blocking arms sales to Arab countries.

As a result, the Bush administration promptly changed its mind about the $13 billion of high-tech weapons for the Saudis. Instead, it put the request on hold, pending a larger agreement on the general issue of arms sales, which of course postponed the transaction for months, if not permanently. The excuse was that since the offensive capability of the Iraqi Army had been greatly reduced, Saudi Arabia no longer needed all of the military hardware it had requested.

This excuse did not fool the Saudis; instead, Prince Sultan, the Saudi defense minister, told reporters that the United States "must understand our needs and our ambition of trying to maintain the stability of the region." And although his government wanted the American defense companies "to be the main supplier," the Saudi government "would look elsewhere" for weapons "if there are things that will inhibit the United States from supplying us." In spite of all this, congressional supporters of Israel indicated they would still oppose the rest of the projected Saudi arms sale because it would damage the credibility of U.S. efforts to control arms proliferation in the region.[54]

That incident gave new pungency to an old grievance. During the Iran-Iraq War, the Saudis first wanted to buy Lance missiles with a range of 75 miles from the United States. To avoid certain conflict with AIPAC, the United States turned them down. The Saudis forthwith sent Prince Bandar to Beijing, where he bought Chinese-made missiles with a conventional warhead range of 1,600 miles. Outraged that the Saudis had acquired by stealth a new weapons system without their knowledge, or permission, Israel's American friends demanded that the United States compel the Chinese to stop the sales. Only then was it revealed that the Chinese missile guidance system had been perfected by a team of Israeli technicians working in Beijing at their own government's behest. Investigators also discovered that some American technology given gratis to Israel had been illegally sold to the Chinese to help improve their product. After this unsavory revelation, Congress and Secretary Shultz quickly dropped the whole matter.[55]

Individual Israel enthusiasts do occasionally deviate from the AIPAC line, when it enriches their constituents. In 1988, one of Israel's most assiduous Senate supporters, Senator Rudy Boschwitz (R-MN), induced Congress to approve a Saudi purchase order for Bradley personnel carriers built in his home state. In this case, the welfare of Israel appeared to take second place to his desire for home-state contracts.[56] Similarly, with congressional—and presumably AIPAC—assent, the United States has sold Stinger missiles to the Afghan rebels, paid for by Saudi Arabia, even though AIPAC has since 1985 persistently blocked the sale of Stingers to the Saudis for their own use. And Saudi Arabia has not been the only Arab nation which AIPAC has prevented from buying American arms.

Qatar, also unable to buy Stingers directly, managed, by means unknown, to buy thirteen on the black market. Sensitive to congressional prejudices, Secretary Shultz sent Assistant Secretary of State for Middle East Affairs Richard Murphy to Doha to demand the return of the missiles or their serial numbers. Qatar's defense minister (the Crown Prince) stood his ground, despite threats to terminate all future American arms deliveries. Murphy left empty-handed.[57]

The Heritage Foundation memorandum mentioned earlier cites a proposed sale of $1.9 billion worth of U.S. weapons to Kuwait, whose reflagged vessels the United States escorted until early 1989, and adds:

> Kuwait . . . poses little threat to Israel. Israeli Defense Minister, Yitzhak Rabin, was unperturbed about a proposed arms deal when he met with U.S. Congressmen during his recent visit. . . . Yet Congress often reflexively opposes arms sales to Arab states because of its simplistic view of Israeli security needs. . . . If Congress stays on this flight path then Israel can find itself surrounded by Arab states armed with Soviet and West European weapons, unconstrained by American strings and Washington's ability to control the flow of spare parts and logistical support.[58]

A June 1985 proposal to sell Jordan forty advanced jet fighters, mobile anti-aircraft missiles, and Stinger missiles was derailed even before it was officially announced, when Senators Edward Kennedy (D-MA) and John Heinz (R-PA) introduced a resolution with at least seventy co-sponsors claiming that arms sales to Arab countries "jeopardize both the security of Israel and progress toward peace in the Middle East." Later that year, Congress overwhelmingly approved postponing the sale until March 1986, unless Jordan and Israel had in the meantime entered into "direct and meaningful talks." Aware that AIPAC could block the deal altogether, the administration eventually shelved the transaction indefinitely.[59]

When its efforts to buy military planes from America were blocked, Jordan retaliated by buying civilian planes from the European Airbus consortium instead of Boeing. Since Jordan's King Hussein was convinced that the United States must be written off as a supplier, his government in 1988 bought from France twenty Mirage-2000 fighter jets worth an estimated $350 million. The deal also reportedly called for the French to refurbish fifteen of the thirty-four Mirage F-1s Jordan had acquired in 1979.[60]

The diversion to Europe of Arab weapons purchases has already produced long-range problems for America. The enormous orders received from Saudi Arabia that were diverted to Europe by AIPAC's manipulation of Congress have enabled European producers to keep production lines running well into the 1990s that they would otherwise have been forced to shut down. Since plans already exist for the next generation of aircraft, financed by current profits, American aerospace firms can anticipate not only diminished revenues for the present but increased competition in the future. Ironically, this situation will probably, on balance, diminish Israel's security.

This point has not impressed either AIPAC or its congressional supporters. Unhappy at being bypassed by Arab purchases abroad, Israel's supporters tried to cut off these sales by diplomatic activities that ignored the State Department. Congressman Mel Levine wrote to Prime Minister Thatcher complaining about her sales of weapons to Saudi Arabia and her apparent lack of interest in Israel's security and welfare. Primarily anxious to promote the welfare of her own country, Thatcher tartly told Levine to mind his own business.

AIPAC also sought to stir up public opinion regarding these developments and its own role in causing losses to American industry. For example, AIPAC denounced foreign governments that entered into Arab arms agreements and Americans who complained about the resulting financial losses as immoral money grubbers.[61] One might find logic—or at least an appearance of logic—in AIPAC's efforts if they involved a principled objection to arms sales per se, or were truly beneficial to Israel, but all too often their exertions have had the opposite effect.

Furthermore, when the 1981 AWACs sale was concluded, the Saudis promised the United States that the planes would not be based at Tabuk, a Saudi airfield less than 100 miles south of Israel. Since the British have never required such guarantees, some of the new Saudi Tornados (one of the world's best ground attack planes) are now based at Tabuk. As one expert commentator wrote: "Based at Tabuk, it would certainly constitute more of a threat to Israel's air force bases than F-15s based elsewhere in the Kingdom."[62]

## The Financial Costs of the Passionate Attachment: A Summary

From the foregoing, it is obvious that the elements entering into any assessment of the total annual costs of the passionate attachment are both complex and subjective. Because we have no incontrovertible way of computing the aggregate costs to the American people and the American economy of the present American/Israeli relationship, we begin with the incontrovertible minimum—the $3 billion in economic and military aid annually legislated by Congress. To this must be added the special privileges Israel has extracted, which contribute, Senator Dole has estimated, at roughly $1 billion additionally. Thus no one can seriously deny that Israel receives from America at least $4 billion of annual aid, plus extras, or that in seeking to support Israeli interests, America also provides Egypt over $2.1 billion per year.

Although those payments represent heavy costs for America, they are only a fraction of the total burden borne by all sectors of American society—taxpayers, industrial workers, bond or shareholders—when American companies have lost markets for political purposes or have been prevented from making lucrative sales by the intervention of AIPAC. These losses occur at a particularly sensitive time when America is scaling down its defense purchases and there are heavy layoffs in the defense industries.

Another key point: Camp David, by inducing Egypt to make peace with Israel, and thus eliminating the most powerful member of the hostile coalition, should have resulted in reduced arms and economic aid to Israel. Yet, what has happened? An examination of Table 2 shows that total aid to Israel from fiscal years 1979 to 1991 had risen to over $40 billion versus the $12.8 billion from 1948 to 1973. If all outstanding requests are granted for fiscal year 1992, the direct cost of Israel to the United States could be close to $5 billion a year—without taking acccount of housing loan guarantees or other possible disbursements.

But these financial items are not the only sources of expense. The political and moral costs of the passionate attachment have also to be considered. And from the both moral and financial aspects, the fundamental question is: Are we getting anything faintly resembling a reasonable return from the costs we are incurring?

TABLE 2
**U.S. Assistance to Israel in Fiscal Year 1989**
*(Dollars in millions)*

| | Amount |
|---|---|
| **Military** | |
| Foreign Military Sales (FMS) grants (of this amount, $550 million is spent in Israel) | 1,800.00 |
| U.S. Air Force exercises | .02 |
| U.S. Navy: | |
| Crew liberty | 27.0 |
| Exercise fees | .1 |
| Port service fees | 2.4 |
| Helicopter maintenance | 1.5 |
| Ship maintenance | 6.2 |
| SDIO: | |
| Arrow | 60.8 |
| Test bed | 5.0 |
| Hypervelocity gun | 1.4 |
| Evaluation of Israel weapons for possible U.S. purchase | 1.5 |
| Construction of U.S. facilities in Israel | 9.56 |
| Congressionally mandated reduction of FMS administrative costs for *Pease Marble III* (F-16) | 20.0 |
| DOD procurement from Israeli companies | 354.2 |
| Multinational force and observers (one half of United States; one-third share of total assessed budget of $73.4 million) | 12.23 |
| **Total Military Expenditure** | 2,301.91 |
| **Grants** | |
| Economic Support Fund (ESF) cash transfer | $1,200.0 |
| Interest earned on lump-sum cash transfer | 76.7 |
| Refugee assistance (RP Bureau to United Israel Appeal) | 28.0 |
| American schools and hospitals abroad | 6.9 |
| Cooperative development program | 5.0 |
| Cooperative development research program | 2.5 |
| Middle East regional cooperation program (one half of $5 million trilateral United States–Egypt–Israel program) | 2.5 |
| Arab-Israeli Peace Scholarship | .75 |
| Bi-national foundations (grants from joint endowments to joint U.S.-Israel projects): | |
| Science | 18.0 |
| Industrial research and development | 14.4 |
| Agricultural research and development | 7.5 |
| VOA/RFE/RL transmitter relay station | 30.04 |
| **Loans/Guarantees** | |
| Export-Import Bank: | |
| Intermediary loans | 16.8 |
| Medium-term guarantees | 2.9 |
| Short-term insurance coverage | 33.2 |
| **Total Nonmilitary Expenditure** | $1,440.19 |
| **Grand Total** | $3,742.1 |

SOURCES: Information compiled from Departments of State, Defense, and Agriculture, AID, and Export-Import Bank.

TABLE 3

**Direct Costs of the American-Israeli Relationship, 1948–91**

*(dollars in millions)*

| | 1948–73 | 1974–78 | 1979–91 |
|---|---|---|---|
| **Direct Financial Costs Benefiting Israel** | | | |
| Direct aid, loans (total $53,531) | 3,189[1] | 9,695 | 40,647[2] |
| **Special Preferences That Benefit Israel** | | | |
| Payment of economic aid funds up front to Israel—not in equal installments throughout the year, at an added interest cost to the U.S. of $50 million per year, 1984–91 | — | — | 400 |
| Refinancing U.S.-Israeli debts of $1.3 billion at 9%, instead of 11%, with U.S. guarantee, 2% per annum to 1993 | — | — | 144 |
| Israeli offset program, whereby U.S. firms are compelled to buy Israeli goods for arms sales to Israel, paid for by the U.S. Treasury | — | — | 3,000 |
| **Indirect Costs Benefiting Israel** | | | |
| Free use of $2.5 billion of U.S. arms patents, amortized | — | — | 250 |
| Concessionary tariff arrangements, lost tariffs, reduced U.S. sales, etc., from 1984 | — | — | 1,000 |
| Loss of sales of U.S. military aircraft and other weapons to markets which the U.S. government forfeited for political reasons, enabling Israel to under its embargo | — | — | 1,000 |
| Israeli domestic weapons purchases since 1977, used for the Merkava tank and Lavi fighter | — | 157 | 2,400 |
| **Total Cost of Special Privileges and Indirect Aid That Have Benefited Israel (1948–91)** | $3,189 | $9,852 | $48,841<br>$61,882 |

1. $1,608 million was paid in the years 1971–73, after the War of Attrition. The quantum jump in aid therefore can be said to date to 1970–71.

2. This figure does include for 1991 the $650 million for Gulf War aid, $700 million of NATO arms ordered transferred, and $300 million of supplies ordered stocked in Israel, but not the $400 million loan guarantee.

TABLE 4
## Indirect Costs of the American-Israeli Relationship, 1948–91
*(dollars in millions)*

| | 1948–73 | 1974–78 | 1979–91 |
|---|---|---|---|
| **Indirect Costs That Do Not Benefit Israel** | | | |
| Losses on non-Saudi Arab arms sales and civilian goods through activities of AIPAC | — | — | 8,450[1] |
| Loss to the U.S. economy from the 1986 Saudi-U.K. arms deal | — | — | 20,000[2] |
| Loss to the U.S. economy from the 1988 U.K. arms deal | — | — | 50,000[2] |
| Loss to the U.S. economy from Arab oil embargo, economic slowdown, and increased oil prices | 1,500[3] | 2,500[3] | — |
| Cost of UNRWA. Expense of fortifying U.S. embassies and other added government expenses attributable to the passionate attachment | 450 | 150 | 2,100[4] |
| **Cost of Camp David Accords** | | | |
| Aid to Egypt 1977–91 (adjusted to reflect the possibility that even without the passionate attachment, the U.S. would have given Egypt at least $500 million of economic aid per year from 1977 on) | — | 851 | 21,244 |
| | $1,950 | $3,501 | $101,905 |
| **Total Costs That Do Not Benefit Israel (1948–91)** | | | $107,356[5] |

1. Excluded from consideration are the tax revenue losses on private gifts, which have been estimated at $20 billion.

2. The British claim the life value of both contracts (see text) at £150 billion or $225 billion. The Saudi vice minister of information put the number at $68 billion for the second contract.

3. Some estimates place the direct and indirect costs as high as $30 billion.

4. Only half of the security modifications are charged to the American-Israeli relationship ($1.2 billion).

5. This does not include any costs for the Gulf force. Total costs if the highest figures were used would come to over $341 billion.

CHAPTER FOURTEEN

# The Political and Moral Costs of the Passionate Attachment

DEEP IN THE CONSCIOUSNESS of most Americans is the conviction of America's exceptionalism. Our country's first settlers, especially New England's Puritans, were determined that the colonies would be firmly guided by divinely ordained moral standards. As the United States emerged and matured as a nation, its citizens accepted the tenet that morality was the quintessential condition for sound government. America should, they thought, so conduct itself as to be—in biblical parlance—"a light unto all nations" or, in today's much drabber argot, a "role model" for other countries.

Almost four centuries have now passed, and in pursuing its passionate attachment to Israel and formulating its policies toward the Middle East, America has all but abandoned its long-standing ideals—to its own moral and political detriment. This failure to live up to earlier—and still avowed—principles has damaged it both politically and morally. When America violates its accepted principles (or condones their violation), it both tarnishes its image and distorts the people's vision of their country. This latter consequence is the more subtle and, ultimately, the more harmful.

In the last few decades, America has progressively redefined its moral objectives; it now puts special emphasis on the elimination of colonialism, racial and ethnic discrimination; on the advancement of human rights; and on the removal of bars to economic opportunity created by inefficient state socialism. These newly prominent values have been given such priority in American policy that their distortion by our passionate attachment to Israel casts mortal doubt on the sincerity and credibility of our leaders.

This doubt has gained particular credence from the fact that our government has permitted Israel to frustrate America's use of arms sales as an instrument of policy. As a matter of principle, the United States has, for some time, denied the right to purchase its armaments to three types of countries:

1. Certain Third World nations—thereby discouraging ruthless and corrupt generals from wasting their nations' limited resources on expensive and unnecessarily sophisticated weapons to satisfy their egregious vanity.
2. South Africa and other despotic violators of human rights.
3. Terrorist states, or those engaged in aggression against their neighbors.

## Economic Reasons Why Israel Undercuts America's Policies

Israel regularly insists that it shapes its own policies consistent with America's. But there are firm limits on its ability to do that. To be free to sell or withhold the sale of weapons in accordance with moral and political standards, Israel needs a sufficiently large and diversified industrial base so that arms sales do not constitute a critical part of its GNP. That, however, Israel does not possess. An in-depth report by Israel's Jaffee Center for Strategic Studies has found that between 1980 and 1984, weapons constituted at least 20 percent of Israel's industrial exports.[1] State-owned arms factories today employ 18 percent of the Israeli labor force, while the state-owned Israel Aircraft Industries, Ltd., was, and is, Israel's largest employer and exporter.

Military production, the study found, amounted to 30 percent of Israel's GNP. It also pointed out that a conversion to consumer-goods production would be a radical and, at best, a long-term operation.[2] Thus, because Israel must sell armaments to survive, it cannot afford to be choosy about its customers.

Not only are arms sales necessary for survival, but a large proportion of the armaments must be sold abroad; the Israeli Defense Force (IDF) cannot offer its munitions industry enough orders to justify the long production runs required to make its products competitive in the world market. Yet, long runs and reduced prices to the IDF are desperately needed to finance Israel's overblown defense budget.

Thus Israel is caught in an insoluable problem. It is largely limited to those markets that more efficient competitors are boycotting, and where, denied its preferred sources, the purchasing country is willing to pay extravagant prices. In practice, therefore, a disproportionate share of Israel's arms export sales have been confined to markets embargoed by the United States and other supporters, thereby putting Israel in very shady company.

To conceal its dependence on this marginal business, Israel deals through private intermediaries whose actions can be disavowed, thus avoiding any overstepping of Congress's tolerance.

Because Israel's arms customers largely comprise countries under embargo, it forms a "Who's Who" of the world's less reputable regimes, principally in Latin America and Africa. An expert on Israel's arms sales, Professor Aaron Klieman of Tel Aviv University, has described Israel's typical customer.

It is, he writes,

> most likely to be a non-western country, with a defense-conscious government, rightist in orientation, in which the military is either the actual or approximate focus of power. It is confronted by a security threat, originating either domestically or from a foreign country . . . like Israel, it too is isolated diplomatically and under international criticism and, therefore, encounters problems in meeting military requirements from other sources of supply.[3]

Most of these customers turn to Israel for the arms denied them by the United States because of their notorious abuse of human rights. Professor Benjamin Beit-Hallahmi quotes a prominent right-wing Guatemalan politician as saying in an interview: "The Israelis do not let this human rights thing stand in the way of business. You pay, they deliver. No questions asked, unlike the gringos."[4] The professor has also written:

> . . . What Israel has been exporting is the logic of the oppressor, the way of seeing the world that is tied to successful domination. What is exported is not just technology, armaments, and experience, not just expertise, but a certain frame of mind, a feeling that the Third World can be controlled and dominated, that radical movements in the Third World can be stopped, that modern Crusaders still have a future.[5]

Israel has developed relationships through arms sales both with Latin American countries and several of the new African nations. Besides selling to pariah governments, Israel also acts as a service center where shoddy governments or disreputable opposition forces can get technical help for their activities.[6]

A sampling of Israel's dubious customers forms the balance of this chapter.

## Central and South America

In Colombia, a former Israeli intelligence officer named Colonel Yair Klein, associated with the "Spearhead Company" (a recruiting outfit for hired guns), was reputed in 1988 to have trained gunmen in the employ of Colombia's Medellín drug lords. Colonel Klein claimed that he worked with "the complete approval and authorization of the Israeli Ministry of Defense."[7] During the same period, a shipment of Israeli arms, ostensibly meant for the Antigua defense forces, was diverted to Colombia, where some of the weapons were used for political assassinations by the drug cartel.

In Panama, General Noriega hired two Israeli citizens to manage his infamous activities. The most notorious, Mike Harari, had headed Mossad in Central America and Mexico until his retirement in 1979. Harari acquired notoriety when Israeli agents under his charge killed a Moroccan waiter in Littlehammer, Norway, mistaking him for the Black September gang member who murdered the Israeli athletes at the 1972 Olympic Games in Munich.[8] The incident of the Moroccan waiter reminds the senior author of a small jingle that was current during the Tong Wars among Chinese merchants in Chicago's Chinatown during the 1920s. "He shot at Wei Wing, but he winged Willie Wong,/A slight but excusable slip of the tong."

Harari subsequently undertook various business operations with General Noriega, and allegedly extracted kickbacks from American businesses wishing to invest in Panama. In the process he acquired the nickname "Mr. 60 Percent."

From 1980 to 1989, Harari served as Noriega's commercial attaché and honorary consul in Tel Aviv,[9] and he helped to keep Noriega in power during 1989, when the United States was seeking to oust him. Although the United States asked Israel to recall Harari and thus stop aiding Noriega, Israel insisted that it was powerless to control its errant citizens abroad.

At the end of 1989, when American troops invaded Panama and overthrew the Noriega regime, they reportedly seized Harari as a prisoner of war, but, on orders, America's military spokesmen denied that event. Since then new evidence shows that Harari was indeed arrested by U.S. forces, then released, reemerging in Israel on January 5, 1990—just after Norway had announced it was seeking his extradition to Oslo to stand trial for the 1973 murder of the Moroccan waiter. Quite likely, the Bush administration wished to avoid the embarrassment of either having an Israeli tried as a terrorist or rejecting Norway's extradition demand.[10]

Israel also cut across American policy in Guatemala, which in 1976 made plans to seize Belize, then still a British colony but about to achieve its independence. To support British policy, the Ford administration cut off arms aid to Guatemala. President Carter renewed the cutoff in 1977 because of Guatemalan human rights violations.

But Israel quickly came to the Guatemalans' rescue; it eagerly sold Galil rifles and other weapons, including counterinsurgency aircraft, armored personnel carriers, and patrol boats.[11]

Israel has trained, assisted, and advised Guatemala's army in its campaign against the country's Indian majority. The army has massacred at least 45,000 Indians, bombed or burned their villages, driven 100,000 into Mexico, and forced another 1 million people to abandon their homes and enter strategic villages under threat of execution. It has also killed those who did not agree to the government's reeducation programs in "strategic villages," nominally modeled on the Israeli Kibbutz. In these villages, Guatemalan Army officers make all the decisions and pocket all the profits: the residents are treated as slave labor.[12]

Given Guatemala's long string of dictatorships, its scant regard for human rights, and its general bloody-mindedness, the United Nations Assembly adopted resolutions in 1982 and 1984 calling on member states not to ship or sell arms to Guatemala. Israel continued its shipments.[13]

Israel has also been active in El Salvador. When the Carter administration cut off military aid to that nation in 1977 because of human rights violations, Israel moved to fill the vacuum with Uzis, ammunition, and even napalm. Israel sold the regime 85 percent of all its arms until late 1980, when U.S. aid was restored. As usual, Israeli advisers followed the arms.[14]

Although the United States expressed shock at the savagery that pervaded El Salvador, Israel induced the Reagan administration to permit it to make $21 million of its American aid funds available to that country in 1981. The next year, as per the agreement, the United States restored the money to Israel.

Israel's relations with Nicaragua began even before the State of Israel existed. General Anastasio Somoza, Sr., had opened a door to the Israelis by supplying arms to the Haganah (at a fat profit), and all during the Somoza regime Nicaragua maintained close relations with Israel, supporting it in UN proceedings even more faithfully than did the United States.[15]

To prop up the Somoza regime during its struggle to survive in 1978–79, Israel began as early as mid-1974 to furnish Nicaragua with warships, aircraft, and Super-Sherman tanks. When the Carter administration imposed a boycott on arms shipments to Managua in 1977, Israeli sales increased. The Somozas used Israeli planes and Israeli-taught methods, like the carpet bombing of rebel-held areas, which greatly increased both the casualties and the animosities of the Somoza/Sandinista war.

The actions of the Sandanistas in taking over in July 1979 afflicted Reagan with an obsession to rid Central America of a regime then tied to Castro. At first he used the CIA to try to achieve that end. But when the American government's connection with the hostilities came to light, Congress passed the Boland amendments, prohibiting U.S. aid to the Contras. That executive-legislative confrontation incited the pro-Contra elements in the American government to use Israel as a surrogate power—a practice that offended many thoughtful Israelis. Both *The Jerusalem Post* and Abba Eban expressed opposition to Israel turning itself into an instrument for thwarting the expressed will of the U.S. Congress. As *The Jerusalem Post* put it in an editorial entitled "Unsavory Trade," on April 26, 1984:

> This would mean that Israel had become a mercenary of the U.S. administration in a course of policy that is highly controversial in the United States itself. . . . To sell arms out of necessity—more justifiable in Israel's

> case than in that of the other countries in this awful trade—is one thing. To act as the agent of the CIA that is being hemmed in by the U.S. Congress is another altogether.

Abba Eban was equally emphatic in an 1984 interview in *Moment:*

> So far as Israel specifically is concerned, I think we ought to want to be more of a regional power and less of a world power spreading our Uzis and Galil guns all over the world. Where you have an Uzi or a Galil, somehow an Israeli flag appears. And we ought to avoid being the instrument of anybody else. What I dislike is the notion that if it's not convenient for the United States to arm a certain country because that country isn't popular or because Congress is parsimonious or because the Americans are sensitive to the human rights issues, Israel can be drafted to act as an American surrogate. That's certainly a role we shouldn't accept and that the United States shouldn't seek to impose upon us.[16]

Nonetheless, Israel continued to help the Contras as much as it could without being so obvious about it as to anger Congress. Here, as in other cases, the Israelis were American surrogates and were also active partners with the executive branch in flouting or circumventing U.S. laws and Congress's control over appropriations.

For example, Israeli specialists in guerrilla warfare flooded into Honduras and Costa Rica, along with captured Soviet bloc arms destined for the Contras.[17]

Israel's connection with Costa Rica began in the 1960s and 1970s, but became close in 1982, when President Monge took office.[18] Aided by the Reagan administration, Israel concentrated on creating a proposed Costa Rican army (the country then had only a minuscule National Guard), on the pretext that the Sandinistas were planning an attack. Meanwhile, Monge courted such an attack by purchasing Israeli small arms, and putting airfields and base camps at the Contras' disposal.

Before long, the Costa Rican people realized the dangers of Monge's policy. The press revealed that Costa Rican officials were taking bribes to facilitate Contra operations. It was rumored that the Israeli ambassador was obligingly equipping the Contras with arms and false passports to make possible drug shipments to North America and arms shipments south.

In the end, Costa Rica paid heavily for Monge's blindly pro-Israeli policy. Arab governments broke off diplomatic relations, and cut Costa Rica's coffee quota to signify their disapprobation. In 1986, President Arias was elected on a platform of repudiating the previous pro-Contra policy and ending the Israeli connection.[19]

Most abhorrent of all Israel's Latin American connections was its major arms dealings and cordial relations with the former president of Paraguay, General Alfredo Stroessner, who was notorious for protecting Nazi war criminals, including Dr. Josef Mengele. Before his overthrow in early 1989, Stroessner had been denied arms by the United States because of his appalling human rights record. Israel filled the breach by selling him the required weapons, mostly small arms for the army.

Next door to Paraguay lies Argentina, then headed by a military junta with which, in 1974, Israel's government had established friendly relations despite the junta's infamous human rights record and its open anti-Semitism.

Even after the Argentine junta invaded the Falkland Islands in 1982, Israel continued to supply it with weapons, ignoring the fact that America officially backed Britain. Business was business. After the war, the Israelis made haste to replace Argentina's losses with Nesher and Mirage planes, Gabriel missiles, spare parts, and ammunition.[20]

Israel was equally active in Chile. After America had embargoed arms sales to Chile in 1977 as a penalty for human rights violations, Israel continued to sell arms to the Pinochet regime. Prominent members of the Israeli government regularly visited Santiago, and passed on to Chile such U.S. secrets as how to make cluster bombs, one of the most strictly embargoed items in the American arsenal. Once they learned to make these bombs themselves, the Chileans exported a large part of their output to Iraq (1980–88).

## Sub-Saharan Africa

Before 1967, Israel had managed to gain a substantial beachhead in sub-Saharan Africa through various economic and technical assistance programs, designed in large part to encourage the support of African nations in the UN General Assembly. After 1967, and more particularly after the early 1980s, the Israelis found themselves with little representation in that part of the world. Thereafter, their relations with African countries south of the Sahara were largely restricted to those blocked by American embargo from access to the competitive world arms market.

From its earliest days, Israel had sought allies among those states adjoining Arab nations. Among those countries targeted by Israel were the Moslem Somalis, then backed by the Soviet Union, and the Eritrean secessionists who, although half-Christian, also had ties with the Arab world.

To check them, Israel allied itself with Ethiopia. But a reversal of alliances occurred in 1973 when Emperor Haile Selassie was overthrown, the monarchy abolished, and a Soviet-backed Communist regime led by Colonel Mengistu took control of Ethiopia. The United States then shifted its support to Somalia, while the oil-rich Arab states increased their aid to the Eritreans. Israel thus found itself without friends in the Horn of Africa.

Eventually, in 1989, with Colonel Mengistu's army disintegrating in the face of a domestic rebellion and with Soviet support fading, Israel decided to reengage itself with Ethiopia. Although the United States was eager for the colonel's overthrow, Israel renewed diplomatic relations with Mengistu in

November, and (according to London's *Sunday Times* of December 1, 1989) signed a secret military pact to provide captured Soviet arms, ammunition, training, and intelligence to the faltering Ethiopian Army. As a reported quid pro quo, Mengistu allowed Ethiopia's Jews to migrate.

It was also reported at that time that Israel had sold cluster bombs to Mengistu for use against the rebels. Since the only cluster bombs available to Israel were provided by the United States or made with American technology, the Bush administration admonished that their resale by Israel was prohibited without U.S. approval. Israel followed its usual ritual; it first denied that it was selling cluster bombs at all. Then it fell back on the equally mendacious contention that the weapons were made in Israel without resort to American technology.[21]

## The South African–Israeli Connection

Israel's close relations with South Africa deserve special scrutiny, because the Israeli and South African regimes have more in common than Israel's American partisans find it convenient to acknowledge. Both Israel and white South Africa base their claims to their respective lands on divine covenants. Each asserts that its people arrived first in the area, and are therefore entitled to rule regardless of the rights and views of other resident peoples. Each pursues a policy of punishing neighboring countries that serve as sanctuaries for would-be guerrilla raiders. Each nation suffers from a trade embargo. Each country maintains a discriminatory attitude toward the nonelite peoples.

Today, South Africa is moving under President De Klerk, with the support of an overwhelming plebiscite, toward an abolition of apartheid and ultimately a more equitable sharing of power with its black majority; but no parallel reforms are visible in Israel's relations with its Palestinian residents.

In order to help South Africa sidestep prohibitions against its trade, Israel assists that country's industry by camouflaging the point of origin of its products. For example, South African diamond merchants annually forward nearly $800 million worth of diamonds from Johannesburg to Tel Aviv for cutting and polishing. The Israelis then sell them abroad, for a total of about $1 billion, bringing a $200 million trade profit. The processed gems are marked "Made in Israel," which permits them to enter the Common Market and the United States.

South African semi-finished goods are often sent to Israel for "finishing processes"—which sometimes involve no additional work whatever. They, too, are labeled "Made in Israel" and shipped to the European Common Market and the United States. The value of this clandestine trade has been estimated at between $2 billion and $4 billion annually.

Israel and South Africa have a long record of selling weapons to each other. Israeli-made Uzi submachine guns were delivered as early as 1955, and ever since 1971 they have been made under license in South Africa. In 1962, Israel sold South Africa thirty-two Centurion tanks; and when, in 1967, de Gaulle embargoed spare parts to Israel following the Six-Day War, South Africa made up that deficiency by supplying key parts for Israel's French-made Mirage jets. Israel has also sold six missile boats and a variety of other military hardware to South Africa.[22]

Four hundred M-113A armored personnel carriers, and 106mm recoilless rifles, both made in the United States, were delivered to South Africa via Israel. The Israeli Galil rifle is produced in South Africa under Israeli license as the R-4, and since 1981 has been the standard weapon of the South African ground forces. South Africa's reconnaissance Drone aircraft are produced by Israeli Aircraft Industries, Ltd., as Mozambique discovered in May 1983, when it shot down a Drone bearing an Israeli identification number.

Although the United Nations Security Council has prohibited all arms shipments to South Africa, Israel is assisting Pretoria to produce both light and heavy conventional weapons, including jets and armored vehicles. The Armaments Corporation of South Africa (ARMSCO) was created with Israeli inspiration and advice. The two governments are mutually supportive, not merely through massive shipments of armaments but also through less visible activities: supplying components, unfinished assemblies, dual-use technologies, and licensing and co-production arrangements.

Much of the technology for South Africa's arms industry has come from the United States via Israel. America disapproves of South Africa and boycotts it. Israel helps South Africa by passing on what America has given it.[23]

In 1986, the Israeli magazine *Tavori* stated with regard to South Africa: "It is a clear and open secret known to everybody that in army camps one can find Israeli officers in not insignificant numbers who are busy teaching white soldiers to fight black terrorists, with methods imported from Israel."[24]

Perhaps the most assiduously concealed of all Israeli/South African enterprises has been their collaboration to develop nuclear weapons. Although the Israelis have been bold and agile in purloining various nuclear materials in Europe or the United States, South Africa is the only source from which Israel can obtain sufficient uranium to develop its own nuclear potential.

Until the archives in both countries are opened, the exact nature of the Israeli/South African nuclear relationship can be only circumstantially established. In August 1977, South Africa proposed a test of its nuclear weapons in the Kalahari Desert. Pointed Soviet inquiries and domestic pressures compelled the United States to insist that South Africa cancel such a test, which it ostensibly did. Nevertheless, on September 22, 1979, and again on December 16, 1980, American satellites detected flash explosions on an island belonging to South Africa. Shortly thereafter, an Israeli delegation, headed by Defense Minister Ezer Weizman, visited South Africa.

Whether this test was conducted separately or jointly by Israel and South Africa is not publicly known. On December 21, 1980, Israeli state television carried, without commentary, a British program which suggested that the

1979 flash came from a test of a naval nuclear shell.

The U.S. government has never taken any official position regarding that September 1979 explosion; it has also deliberately ignored the fact that both South Africa and Israel are among the very few countries that until 1991 had not ratified the Nuclear Non-Proliferation Treaty,[25] and, to our knowledge, it has brought no serious pressure on either country to ratify it. On June 22, 1991, South Africa announced it was adhering to the 1968 Treaty; but no similar announcement has been made by Israel.[26]

The recent South African missile tests reflect the consequences of Israel's infusions of technicians and American technology. On May 3, 1991, *The Washington Times* reported that American spy satellite photography had detected the imminent launch of a Jericho II-type missile on South Africa's Arniston range.

Meanwhile, confronted by leaks from government sources mentioned in two NBC broadcasts starting October 25, 1989, Israel has denied any South African/Israeli missile connection. The CIA simply states that it has no irrefutable evidence, which implies that some evidence may exist. Therefore, in spite of the usual denials, one may reasonably infer that a joint program is, in fact, under way.[27]

## The Israeli-Iranian Connection

Beginning in the days of the Shah, Israel and Iran have had a long-standing commercial, intelligence, and military relationship. The Shah's secret police, Savik, were trained by Israel. The relationship flourished because Israel pursued its so-called "outer ring policy," which involved using Iran as a means of preventing Iraq from launching or joining an Arab war against Israel.

The U.S. government was almost certainly aware of Israel's post-1979 dealings with Khomeini's Iran.[28] On May 26, 1982, General Sharon, then the Israeli Defense Minister, spoke of Israeli arms sales to Iran with American approval, a claim denied at the time by the State Department.[29]

New revelations in an article by Seymour M. Hersh in *The New York Times* of December 8, 1991, contain persuasive evidence that even though the Reagan administration was energetically promoting a public campaign known as "Operation Staunch" to stop worldwide transfers of military goods to Iran, Israel was aggressively pouring arms into that country in order to sustain the Iran-Iraq War and thus keep two potential enemies preoccupied with each other.

Hersh's report, based on extensive *New York Times* investigations, disclosed that Secretary of State Alexander M. Haig, Jr., and Prime Minister Menachem Begin made a deal in 1981 under which the United States would review and approve Iranian requests to Israel for American-made spare parts and other equipment. However, as revealed by that investigation, the Reagan administration rescinded the agreement when, in the spring of 1982, it found that the Israeli defense minister, Ariel Sharon, was selling American-made military equipment without Washington's permission.[30]

According to the comments of Major General Avraham Tamir, an Israeli Defense Ministry official, lists of requests were regularly given to American ambassador Samuel W. Lewis, in accord, General Tamir insists, with "an understanding with Secretary Haig." Hersh's report maintains that the administration made no effort to curb "what became a steadily increasing flow of American-made arms from Israel to Iran."

In spite of America's vigorous advocacy that other nations conform to Operation Staunch, Hersh reports that "The Reagan administration continued to replenish Israel's stockpile of American-made weapons, despite clear evidence that Israel was shipping them to Iran."

Hersh continues:

> At the height of the Israeli program, a former Israeli official said, "The Israeli covertly chartered a large number of cargo ships, registered in Denmark and Liberia. They carried arms between the ports of Eilat in Israel and Bandar Abbas on Iran, making the round trip once a month."
>
> Chartered aircraft from Argentina, Ireland and the United States were also used to fly American-made arms to Israel and in some cases, directly to Teheran.

And further:

> Ari Ben Menashe, a former Israeli intelligence operative, said Israel had also established an undercover office in New York City to direct the covert purchases of American-made military equipment for sale to Iran.
>
> Among those weapons, other officials said, were some of the most advanced arms in the American arsenal, including Hawk anti-aircraft missiles, Lance surface-to-air missiles, TOW anti-tank missiles and armor-piercing shells. Under American law, Israel was not permitted to resell weapons of this sort without approval from Washington.

Menashe, it later appeared, was among the Israeli officials and operatives who brokered the arms deals involved in the current Irangate dispute.

> On behalf of the Israeli Government . . . he helped manage a worldwide network of private arms dealers and shippers responsible for selling American arms worth several billions of dollars.
>
> One former high level Central Intelligence Agency official who saw reports of the Israeli arms sales to Iran in the early 1980s estimated that the total approached $2 billion each year.[31]

The new investigation found quite contradictory statements by the American side. On January 29, 1981, Secretary of State Alexander Haig volunteered at his first news conference: "Let me state categorically today, there will be no military equipment provided to the government of Iran, either under earlier obligations and contractual arrangements or as yet unstated requests." But ten years later, in a PBS television interview, Haig acknowledged that Israel might have shipped some American arms to Iran, and added: "If that happened, it happened through the good offices of somebody on the White House staff, and I don't discount that. That could have happened."

After this story broke in the *Times* on December 8, 1991, the current Secretary of State, James A. Baker III, gave it a tentative confirmation in a television interview.

## The Political Costs of the Passionate Attachment

This review could be extended to include many more instances where Israel has deliberately tried to vitiate America's trade policies. Apart from trade policy, we have also demonstrated that the passionate attachment has led America to follow a pattern of hypocrisy in at least two areas of policy:

1. When America silently watches while the Israeli Army systematically violates the human rights of Palestinians in the Occupied Areas. America's indulgence of Israel in this regard is all the more glaring in contrast to its reaction to Iraq's grab of Kuwait.
2. When it declares opposition to the spread of nuclear, biological, and chemical weapons, and intercontinental ballistic missiles, then turns a blind eye to Israel's activities in all four areas.[32]

In view of Israel's practices, why are the Saudis not justified in acquiring ICBMs from China as they did in the spring of 1988? After all, Israeli technicians, using American technology, worked with the Chinese in developing those missiles. How, therefore, could the United States now complain to China about using its technology when our government had known for years that Israel was selling it recklessly? Neither before nor after this incident did America penalize Israel for so doing.[33]

Why should anyone in the future pay attention to our requests for adherence to embargoes directed against international wrongdoers when we encourage or allow selected favorites to reap rich profits from trafficking with the delinquent?

So long as our country keeps silent while a nation it subsidizes persistently disdains international principles, it makes a mockery of its claim to moral leadership.

# PART V

CHAPTER FIFTEEN

# Recommendations

THE FADING OF the Cold War and the more recent events of the Gulf War have redefined the position of Israel in relation both to the United States and to the Arab-Israeli struggle.

Taken together, these two developments materially transformed the nature and significance of the conflict between Israel and the Arab nations. No longer is it a critical aspect of East-West relations; it is now merely a discrete regional rivalry.

Disabled by the logic of geography from directly participating in any conflict that does not immediately touch its borders, Israel is severely limited in the deployment of its military power. Precluded by politics from joining any Middle East coalition, it can no longer seriously claim to be an indispensable protective shield for America's Middle East interests.[1]

As seen by the U.S. Secretary of State, James A. Baker III, the confluence of these two epic events offered a long-awaited chance for Israel to negotiate directly for peace with its Arab antagonists. But though Israel had long proclaimed that face-to-face negotiations with Arab governments were among its most cherished objectives, Shamir and his colleagues still demanded unprecedented conditions as Israel's fee for reluctant participation. Against his better judgment, Baker conceded that Israel might veto the makeup of the Palestinian delegation. He also accepted Israel's stultifying condition that the negotiators would not mention the creation of an independent Palestinian state or the status of East Jerusalem.

In inaugurating negotiations, Baker proclaimed as a legitimizing assumption that all the players in the drama were eager not only for peace, but a peace that accorded with principle and justice. But, as he soon found, the objectives of the Shamir government were quite different. It did not wish peace but Arab capitulation. It hoped that by joining the negotiations it could perpetuate the status quo long enough for it to fill the Occupied Territories with so many Jewish settlers as to render territorial revision politically impossible. By those means the Shamir government, in its own jargon, planned to "create new facts" that could then be presented as a fait accompli.

Fortunately, Secretary Baker and President Bush quickly recognized the implications of Israel's tactics. They soon found that Shamir's instincts regarding the Occupied Territories were not the lofty objectives Baker had assumed.

At the moment this is written (April 1992), the United States is at long last insisting on a principled solution; it is taking modest steps to influence Israel in that direction. In his search for peace, Baker has benefited from Israel's demand for help as it prepares to absorb thousands of Soviet Jews freed from Soviet domination.

Yet no one has pointed out that Israel's problems in funding the absorption of the new immigrants were basically of its own making. At the first indication that the Soviets might relax their restriction on the right of Jews to emigrate, Prime Minister Shamir requested that the U.S. curtail the right of those Jews to enter America and thus force them to move to Israel. When the U.S. government, on grounds of principle, refused to comply, Israel activated Jewish American organizations to persuade their friends in Washington to close America's Vienna-Rome immigration center and place a visa cap on Jewish refugees from the Soviet Union. Some Jewish American refugee organizations instinctively opposed such a visa cap as arbitrarily restricting the freedom of choice of beleaguered Jews, but under pressure from their peers, they soon capitulated.

As the Israelis had hoped, America's action blocked Soviet Jews from exercising their first choice of coming to America. But few Israelis foresaw the full magnitude of the burden that the costs of relocation would impose on their nation's resources. When they did fully grasp all the implications, the Israelis then approached the United States with a demand that, while continuing its customary subsidy, America should in addition supply Israel with loan guarantees of $10 billion over the next five years.[2]

Aware that the spectacle of America granting these loan guarantees might seriously prejudice the ongoing Arab-Israeli negotiations, the Bush administration first gave Israel a qualified answer. It would provide such guarantees for a limited period of two years, then reexamine the situation. But it would do so only if Israel definitively ceased to settle any Soviet Jews in the Occupied Areas.

Shamir indignantly rejected America's conditional offer. "Who are the Americans to tell any Jew where to live?" In response, Baker expanded his conditions to require that America might provide the loan guarantee but only if Israel would cease to build *any* new settlements in the Occupied Areas, except those that might be already under construction on a fixed date.

Thereafter, there ensued a quiet debate among Israeli economists as to whether the country could or could not get along without the loan guarantees. In an interview with the economic affairs correspondent of a leading Jerusalem newspaper, Finance Minister Yitzhak Modai asserted that "even without the loan guarantees, Israel would undoubtedly be able to supply all the needs of the immigrants." Modai added that "this would not necessarily affect the standard of living enjoyed by long-time Israelis."[3]

## Israel's Economy Could Survive the Elimination of American Aid

Widespread attention to the question of whether Israel needed the loan guarantees soon revived the larger question as to when, if ever, America might prudently discontinue its whole aid package.[4] Although the termination of America's aid might cost Israel money, it would greatly improve the country's international political standing. Israel would cease to be a mendicant nation and would instead become a self-supporting and hence self-respecting member of the international community.

Though some sensible Israelis have long yet quietly cherished the objective of self-sufficiency, government spokesmen continue by rote to contend that the perpetuation of America's subsidy is vital to Israel's very survival.

Is that really true? Some respected economists who have studied the problem have reached the firm conclusion that, by improving its national efficiency, Israel could in a short time position itself to survive the total loss of American aid.

History illuminates that point. During the quarter century from 1949 to 1973, America stringently limited its aid to loans, to a cumulative total of $3.2 billion. Then, beginning in 1974, the United States recklessly turned out its pockets. During the following seventeen years (from 1974 to date), our country provided Israel with aid aggregating over $53 billion. Moreover, after 1984 all America's aid took the form of gifts, while, in addition, the U.S. forgave substantial past loans.

One might have expected that this unprecedented expansion in aid would have materially increased the growth rate of Israel's GNP. But its effect was quite the contrary. In contrast to the 9 percent figure of the earlier period, the growth rate of Israel's GNP since our 1973 aid expansion never exceeded 5 percent a year, and, particularly after the Likud bloc took over in 1977, that rate, except for one year (1986), fluctuated feebly between 1 and 3 percent.

The reasons for this apparently irrational result are a matter of speculation. A most likely explanation is that America's quantum increase in aid—

and the implication that America would continue to play Santa Claus to the same spacious degree indefinitely—deprived Israel of the incentive needed to put its house in order. Abstractly, that operation should not be difficult. Merely by eliminating certain obvious economic drags inherent in its history, structure, and practices, the Israeli economy should be restored to its earlier growth pattern.[5]

These economic drags are easy to identify. The state owns directly or indirectly 93 percent of the land in Israel proper, and the country derives more than 20 percent of its national income from government-controlled enterprises. Even private sector businesses are so overregulated that individual initiative—and efficiency—are smothered.[6]

The greatest restraints on Israeli production derive from its stifling bureaucracy and the relatively low competence of its state-owned unprofitable industries, where the value of a worker's output is less than half that of his counterpart in the United States. Industries managed by bureaucrats prodigally consume vast governmental expenditures and subventions, while their top-heavy bureaucratic structures contribute to exorbitant inflation. These factors, in turn, inhibit capital formation while encouraging barter, corruption, tax evasion, and black market activities.

Added to all this are the painful costs of Israel's recently accelerated colonization program for its Occupied Territories. That program imposes a steady drain on capital resources to build new housing and maintain repressive control of the territories' Palestinian inhabitants.

Thomas G. Donlan, the editorial page editor of *Barron's,* wrote on February 17, 1992:

> Throughout the Israeli economy, restructuring is still mostly a matter of words.
>
> Thanks to borrowing and aid, the government can spend more than $40 billion a year while the economy produces only about $55 billion. Some $5.5 billion of those government outlays go for a hopeless mess of public subsidies to industry, transportation, housing, health, loans and so forth. That's almost equal to the defense budget of the tiny nation surrounded by enemies. The people that "made the desert bloom" subsidize farmers' income with one hand and food prices with the other hand. Individual income taxes average 56%. Tax evasion is correspondingly large. Some analysts guess the untaxed cash economy accounts for 25% of national output.[7]

Overhanging these economic burdens are the formidable costs of Israel's armed forces, which absorb about 25 percent of its annual budget and GNP compared with a diminishing 6 percent for America. Israel's military expenditures drain an excessive volume of resources. They could be significantly reduced were Israel to make peace with its neighbors.[8]

A sensible economic program would require Israel to concentrate on reducing all obstacles to rapid growth while the United States and Israel simultaneously reached agreement on timing the elimination of American aid.

Even though Finance Minister Modai and certain other political leaders have privately whispered that they would welcome a program of substantially reduced aid as an incentive to restructure its economy, Israel's cabinet has given it no support. Almost every member of the cabinet controls a ministry which he regards as his own patronage fiefdom. That fiefdom gives him both power and status, and he will defend it against every assault of economic logic. In the words of one widely read Israeli columnist, "Control over the economy translates into political domination."

Unhappily, the trend toward further government ownership still continues. The government has expanded the public payroll from 18 percent to nearly 29 percent of the total work force, and has nearly doubled its share of the gross national product from 59 percent in 1973 until, during the period 1983–91, it ran between 90 and 110 percent of GNP.

But that does not necessarily call for a pessimistic prognosis. The Israeli government could largely free itself from its humiliating dependence on America's generosity by following a blueprint suggested by Professor Stanley Fischer, who served from 1984 to 1987 as consultant to the American Department of State on the Israeli economy, and Dr. Herbert Stein, who was chairman of the Council of Economic Advisers under Presidents Nixon and Ford. They argued in a jointly written article that:

—Israel should move with increasing speed and determination to privatize banks and other government-owned firms and get enterprises back into non-state ownership and control where they will be subject to the discipline of the market.

—It should correct labor laws and regulations that obstruct adjustment of wage rates to market conditions, abolish measures that impede the employment of new immigrants, impede operation of plants on second and third shifts, and weaken incentives for unemployed workers to seek work;

—It should apply stern fiscal and monetary policies to reduce inflation from the present rate of 20 percent a year to 15 percent, and thereafter to 5 percent or less;

—It should reduce to zero within three years its budget deficit, now running at about 5 percent of gross national product;

—It should abolish all protective measures that shelter Israel's industry and agriculture, and so expose them to "the discipline of foreign competition," and, at the same time, it should drastically shrink the government bureaucracy by downsizing and streamlining regulatory structures;

—It should abolish all remaining controls on foreign-exchange transactions;

—It should substantially reduce government regulation and the bureaucracy that administers it.[9]

To promote this program, they conclude, Israel should establish an independent commission to review the regulations and recommend the elimination of those that impede the operation of the market.

This need to reform Israel's economy is expressed by both concerned Israelis and informed American visitors to the country.[10] As Robert J. Loewenberg, president of the Institute for Advanced Strategic and Political Studies, writes:

> Israel's economy is stagnant because of the perpetuation of an antiquated socialist system, propped up by U.S. aid and Jewish philanthropy. . . . Customs and nontariff barriers to imports protect inefficient companies from having to compete, forcing Israelis to pay twice the world prices for many consumer goods. Businesses rely on Government grants and export subsidies rather than on judgment and skill to make investment decisions.[11]

He then points out that one quarter of all goods and services are under price controls and that wages are set not by the market but by Histadrut strikes.

Joel Bainerman, an Israeli economic columnist, writes in *The Jerusalem Post:*

> It's important for both pro-Israel supporters and anti-Israeli voices to understand that Israel isn't, by definition, dependent on U.S. aid. The moment that faucet is shut, Israeli leaders would be forced to cut the national budget and sell off state-owned assets. . . . But as long as the yearly overdrafts are paid for by foreigners, the politicians will never voluntarily release their control over the economy.[12]

In watching the Soviet empire disintegrate, America has insisted that before it and other Western countries provide substantial aid, the new nations broken off from that empire must show tangible progress toward market economies. Why, then, should America not apply that same standard to Israel by curtailing its assistance until Israel takes visible steps to privatize the residue of its state-owned institutions—and employ the funds derived from their sale (estimated at $15 billion) to restructure and rebuild an efficient, profit-driven society? There is no way our country could benefit Israel more than by pressing its leaders to abandon the residue of a system based on an intellectually bankrupt concept.

## Reforms America Needs—"Physician, Heal Thyself"

If Israel's economy and society are badly warped by its failure to come to grips with modern realities, America faces even greater challenges than Israel. Its economy is stagnant to the point where its resources must be stingily allocated. In addition, its political system has been commercialized, and subtle electoral corruption has become an accepted part of the system.

Although still the richest country in the world, the United States faces a monumental task in rebuilding and modernizing both its physical and human infrastructure.

Americans can easily see the defects of their country's physical infrastructure. The system of roads and highways of which we were once so proud is rendered hazardous by potholes, dangerous tunnels, and faulty bridges, and is thus quite inadequate for present traffic levels. America's physical infrastructure needs at least $2 trillion of deferred maintenance. Its rate of investment in productive plant is far less than that of its competitors. America's federal and local governments are threatened by an ocean of debt, while American industry has been plundered by raiders and starved of capital. Eighty percent of our middle class is unable to purchase affordable housing, which means that America is creating a new wave of "street people" who cannot find shelter.

There are, of course, well-established methods for correcting our physical infrastructure—it is merely a question of money. Far more difficult to correct is the sad state of our complex human infrastructure. On that task we are making no measurable progress—quite the reverse.

In 1900, one out of twelve American adults was functionally illiterate; today, the figure is one out of five. A functional illiterate cannot read a want ad, fill out a job application, or do elementary banking. He or she cannot even read their children's report cards. The number grows every month. The fact that the largest group of adult illiterates is between twenty and thirty-nine years old assures that the next decade will see an acceleration in the educational crisis as the figure rises from one out of five to one out of four. Only a masochist could gain pleasure from the thought that the world may remember twentieth-century America primarily because it witnessed the increase of the percentage of its functional illiterates from 8 to 20 percent.[13]

Professor Lester C. Thurow, dean of the Sloan School of Management at MIT, has confirmed much of this gloomy analysis in an article speculating on which of the major competitors will dominate the twenty-first century—whether America, Japan, or a united Europe. He awards the prize to Europe.

In making that judgment, he describes some of the weaknesses in America's competitive position as follows:

> . . . America has squandered much of its starting advantage by allowing its educational system to atrophy, by running a high-consumption, low-investment society, and by incurring huge international debts. Among the major competitors, none is preparing less for the economic competition that lies ahead.
>
> American investment is simply not world-class: plant and equipment investment per labor force member is far below that of either Germany or Japan, non-defense research and development spending is 40 to 50 percent less than that of Germany and Japan; physical infrastructure investments are running at half the level of the late 1960s. . . .
>
> The second understrength player on the American team is the nation's work force. . . . That part of the U.S. work force that does not go to college is not up to world standards. Those who complete their education with high school are behind their European and Japanese counterparts when they graduate and [they] receive less skill training thereafter. And work force participants who do not graduate from high school (29%) have average skill levels found only in the Third World.[14]

The consequences pervade every aspect of life, with a disastrous effect on America's economy. The nation pays over $200 billion a year for unemployment, underemployment, health, welfare, and incarceration costs. Only 80 percent of our adult population is eligible for our labor pool, while Germany and Japan can count on literate work forces of 95 percent of their populations—employees ready to contribute to their countries' modern economies.

If we fail to educate our citizenry adequately, we also discourage them from self-education by neglecting our libraries. In many communities, libraries have either been permanently closed or are open for only a few hours for a few days each week, and the situation is rapidly deteriorating.

We pay heavily for these delinquencies both in productivity and social costs. Over 70 percent of our nation's prison population are illiterate, over 60 percent are still functionally illiterate when released. In Japan, where a convict cannot be released until he can read and write, the rate is 5 percent. No wonder our inner cities are cesspools of unemployment and drug-related crime.

This shocking state of affairs had made its mark on our political institutions, which can function rationally only with an informed population. Today, not more than half the eligible voters turn out for a presidential election, and fewer still for state and local elections. The crass commercialization of our electoral system has increased the cost of running for office to such an extent as to limit the range of candidates to those who are personally wealthy or prepared to sell out to powerful lobbies. Congress mutters darkly about the nation's electoral problems, but fails to agree on a sensible system of public funding such as exists in other major democracies, because that system is opposed by powerful lobbies.

At the same time, our government has no adequate policy to deal with absorbing and educating the tidal wave of Hispanic and Oriental immigrants projected to reach America's shores within the next few years.

Although not all of America's problems can be resolved solely by increasing available financial resources, lack of funding is still the most insistent complaint of our federal and state governments. Our nationwide obsession with an intractable budget deficit has become so intense that, except for a few sacrosanct exceptions, Congress will fund no new programs without insisting on commensurate reductions in other outlays.

Israel's progress toward becoming self-supporting is relatively straightforward. It needs to privatize its economy, modernize its political institutions, and make the neccessary adjustments that will equip it to live without America's charity. It must abandon its expansionist fantasies and make peace with its neighbors on a basis consistent with international law. The measures required to achieve these objectives have been carefully studied and are widely known; all that is needed is the political will that only outside incentives can provide.

Yet rather than bolstering that political will, America has imposed a major disincentive by conspiring with Israel to perpetuate an unbalanced relationship that rests on the fragile assumption of a big brother's perpetual generosity. Our country should now meet the test of real friendship. It should tell Israel's leaders the stark truth free from diplomatic euphemisms so as to help them confront squarely the uncertain and unworthy future inherent in their present practices and policies.

## The Role of the American Jewish Community

Many Americans naturally assume that our government might best communicate the need for curtailing aid to the government in Jerusalem by channeling that message through the leaders of American Jewish organizations. Those organizations should, in theory, be eager to encourage Israel's economic and social reforms and America's diplomatic efforts to achieve regional peace and disarmament. One might also assume that they would take pride in enabling Israel to stand on its own feet.

Unhappily, Jewish Americans have been conditioned by their peers to abjure offering advice to the leaders of a country in which they themselves have chosen not to live. Thus, an acute sense of inferiority and even of guilt restraints Jewish Americans from risking the disfavor of Jerusalem.

Most American Jews have, after all, been indoctrinated from infancy with sensitivity to Israel's long practice of treating Diaspora Jews with contempt. That phenomenon has been vividly described by Professor Howard Sachar of George Washington University:

> For many decades, it was a principle of Zionist ideology to write off the Diaspora, to regard Jews overseas not only as half-Jews but virtually as half-men. At times, criticism of Diaspora Jewry approached a kind of

> involuted anti-semitism. . . . Again and again, the Zionists described Jewish life in *Galut*—itself a pejorative term for the Diaspora, connoting a state of permanent alienation—as one of poverty, powerlessness, and degradation.[15]

In view of this attitude, it would be difficult, if not impossible, to recruit Jewish American experts of high reputation to develop a formula for the termination of American aid. They would almost certainly be ostracized by their peers for selling out the cause.

If Israel's leaders would prove allergic to any advice from Americans on how they might make their country's economy more efficient, they would be even more outraged were Jewish Americans to suggest revisions in Israel's electoral system. Although, as we have described in Chapter 8, their present electoral rules guarantee political fragmentation and hence paralysis, those rules also offer Israeli politicians an opportunity for highly sophisticated wheeling and dealing which they would not willingly give up.

## Possible Role of the European Community

Leaders of the institutions of the European Community (EC) have made clear more than once that they are dissatisfied with Israel's treatment of the Palestinians in the Occupied Territories. The Community first showed its disapproval in 1989 by insisting that produce from those territories be labeled as such (the Israelis were trying to sell it as their own to take advantage of tariff preferences). When Israel refused to budge, the EC imposed an embargo on its fruit, vegetables, and flowers. Israel angrily but quickly complied with Brussels' wishes.

Later in 1989, the Community cut off technical cooperation with Israel until it reopened the schools and universities in the Occupied Territories. Again, Israel assumed a defiant posture. But, barred from the use of patents and other benefits, Israel reopened the secondary schools, then the trade schools, and is slowly reopening the universities, although the most respected university in the West Bank (Beir Zeit) was not allowed to reopen until April 1992.

In 1991, Israel was notified that although its application for associate membership in the Community had been approved, it could not go into effect until Israel had made peace with its Arab neighbors. That triggered furious denunciations coupled with growing anxiety in Israel as to what would happen if, as many feared, Israel were effectively excluded from its largest market.

Unfortunately, America has not applauded these disciplinary actions. U.S. governments have long maintained that the Middle East is America's private hunting preserve; they resent any poaching by our European allies that would, they assert, only get in the way of our own nation's efforts.

These sporadic instances of intervention suggest, however, that in stimulating Israel to make the hard decisions required for a settlement, the United States might gain useful support from the European Community.

## Involvement of the UN Security Council

The UN Charter provides that five "permanent nations" (the United States, Great Britain, France, China, and the Soviet Union) may exercise a right of veto in the Security Council. Almost as soon as the United Nations was created the Soviet Union began using that special privilege, largely to prevent the admission of anti-Communist members. But the United States rigidly abstained from exercising its own right of veto for twenty-five years. Instead, it took comfort from the thought that the power of logic and the virtue of its positions would enable it to persuade other member nations to vote with it.

President Nixon's decision in 1970 to break precedent and cast our country's first veto was therefore a memorable one.[16] Since then, America has found it far easier to say nyet through a veto than to rely on the arts of persuasion, and has used its veto right seven times as often as the Soviet Union. By the end of 1991 it had cast 69 vetoes, of which 39 were devoted to avoiding even mild censure of Israel. In practically all cases where it has used its veto to protect Israel, America has acted alone. Even such friendly nations as Great Britain and France have refused to join in our Israeli-inspired vetoes, and have either voted for the relevant resolution or abstained.

So far, Israel has rejected any United Nations role in the peace process. Israel's negative attitude is apparently based on the ground that there are numerous Arab member nations; hence, the Arab side could mobilize enough Third World countries to outvote Israel in the General Assembly. Israel long held a particular grievance against a tactless and gratuitous resolution passed by the Assembly on October 17, 1975, that identified Zionism as racism. That complaint, however, is now a part of history; in December 1991, America successfully secured its repeal by a decisive General Assembly vote of 111 to 28.

Today, because the Security Council has a more limited membership than the General Assembly, there is little reason to believe that Israel could not get a fair hearing in that forum. Israel's resistance is presumably based on the fear that the Council would insist on enforcing the Charter's principles and therefore require it to play by rules it persistently flouts.[17]

If, under pressure from the Security Council, the parties should still not resolve their differences, the UN Charter provides for the possible use of coercive measures. To invoke any of the enforcement measures provided in Chapter VII of the Charter, the Council must first find the existence of a "threat to the peace, breach of the peace, or an act of aggression."

Presumably, Israel's continued recalcitrance would justify one or more such findings. Yet, barring an abrupt and drastic change in the domestic political climate, an American administration unwilling to reduce or phase out aid to Israel would be even less willing to invoke the economic sanctions provided by the UN Charter. Such sanctions, after all, would punish the Israeli people and not merely their recalcitrant government. It would thus work directly against America's emotional commitment to Israel's welfare.

The Council is probably not in a position to draft a comprehensive settlement based on established principles and impose it on the parties, since, during the drafting of the Charter, that power was denied it at the insistence of some smaller nations. Yet there are certainly no inhibitions on the Council's authority to pass resolutions on specific violations of the Charter or of established international law. The Security Council has, in fact, passed at least four legally binding resolutions that, if accepted by, or enforced against, Israel, would dispose of major issues in the current dispute. In fact, the United States representatives to the Security Council have voted to approve, or at least abstain on, the following resolutions:

—Resolutions 471 (June 5, 1980) and 476 (June 30, 1980), by which the Security Council declared illegal the building of Israeli settlements in the Occupied Areas.
—Resolutions 465 (March 1, 1980) and 478 (August 20, 1980), by which it invalidated Israel's annexation of East Jerusalem.
—Resolution 497 (December 17, 1981), by which it declared void Israel's annexation of the Golan Heights.
—Resolution 490 (July 21, 1981), by which it invalidated Israel's indirect occupation of southern Lebanon and mandated Israel's withdrawal.[18]

Once adopted by the Council, these resolutions, unhappily, quickly became merely symbolic. America again caved in to Israel's persuasion and threatened to use its veto to prevent the Security Council from any follow-up action.

How greatly this contrasts with the position of President Eisenhower, who had a deep commitment to principle and to the UN as the protector of principle. When Israel refused to comply with the Security Council and withdraw its forces following the Suez Affair, he resorted to national television on February 20, 1956, to tell the American people why America should force Israel to comply with the Security Council resolution.

> If we agreed that armed attack can properly achieve the purposes of the assailant, then I fear we will have turned back the clock of international order.
>
> If the United Nations once admits that international disputes can be settled by using force, then we will have destroyed the very foundation of the organization and our best hope of establishing world order. The United Nations must not fail. I believe that in the interests of peace the

United Nations has no choice but to exert pressure upon Israel to comply with the withdrawal resolutions.[19]

Unfortunately, no president since Eisenhower has reacted so incisively; instead, they have either appeased Israel by offering to use America's veto or have conspired with Israel to prevent any further action.

## Content of an Ideal Clarifying Resolution

Our country blocked these follow-up resolutions in response to the passionate attachment. If we lived in what the humorist Don Marquis used to call "an almost perfect world," America should, even at this late date, introduce a new resolution clarifying the ambiguities still remaining in past resolutions.

That clarifying resolution should cover the following points:

—The Palestinians should be granted the opportunity for self-determination in accordance with Assembly Resolution 3236, with a carefully spelled out limitation on the arms permitted in an independent Palestinian state.[19]

—The city of Jerusalem should be kept united as a municipality, with its government entrusted to a condominium composed of Israel and the new Palestinian state. It should also be understood that Israel and Palestine could each make it their seat of government.

—Palestinians living outside the state should be permitted to opt either for citizenship in the nation in which they now reside or Palestinian nationality. Funds should be provided to the new Palestinian state through international channels to pay the costs of resettling the refugees.

—Israeli settlers should be strictly forbidden to settle in the territories seized by Israel in the 1967 War.

—The resolution should ideally provide that existing settlements in the Occupied Areas be dismantled and the Israeli settlers returned to Israel proper. But if that would threaten to precipitate a major disturbance approaching civil war, the resolution might provide alternatively that the settlers could either resettle in Israel proper or those that insist on remaining in the Occupied Areas must be governed by the same laws as the Palestinian residents.

—Israel should be required to evacuate the Golan Heights together with its Israeli settlers, in exchange for a Syrian treaty of peace with Israel. The Heights should be demilitarized and a strong UN peacekeeping force should be put in place to monitor Syria's compliance.

—Israel should evacuate Lebanon and abandon its mercenary army.

—Jordan would be required to open its borders and demilitarize its part of the Jordan Valley.

—The Arab nations should cease to apply their embargo against Israel, and allow the free movement of people.

## Further Corrective Measures

In view of the general shortage of water in the area, Israel must draw 40 percent of its fresh water from aquifers in the West Bank. That enables those who wish to annex the Occupied Territories to contend that Israel cannot safely entrust vital water supplies to a potential enemy.

What is needed is an Arab-Israeli settlement that will place firm restrictions on water usage, and an agreed plan for sharing water on an equitable basis.

Special attention must also be given to halting the flow of costly arms into the Middle East at the risk of impoverishing all inhabitants of the area outside the oil-producing states. The proposed Security Council resolution should include provisions for a UN-enforced arms agreement, limiting the arms-producing countries from exporting arms to the region and restricting local arms production.

Finally, America should promptly renew the project (periodically mentioned by both Israel and Egypt) to make the area a zone free not only of nuclear weapons but also of biological and chemical weapons. That action should be taken swiftly because Israel's Dimona reactor is nearing the end of its life and will require replacement—at an estimated expense to Israel of $2 billion.

## Areas of Possible Compromise

The provisions we have outlined for inclusion in a clarifying resolution reflect the application of established principles of international law and should, were they fully carried out, end the primary issues of the Arab-Israeli dispute on terms that would leave minimum incentives for renewed conflict. Yet the enforcement of all these terms would be possible only in a situation free from the constraints of domestic politics, and the world is not now approaching that state of perfection nor likely to do so in the foreseeable future.

Hence we are forced to fall back on the shopworn apology that "the perfect is the enemy of the good." Only those individuals detached from reality believe that either side can realize its full desiderata and that peace can be achieved without some compromise by each side. What, then, might be the possible areas in which compromises could be made that do not destroy the objectives needed for a lasting peace?

Earlier in this chapter, we described the views of Professor Herbert Stein on the problems and possibilities of the Israeli economy. In his testimony before a congressional committee, Professor Stein noted that Israel had prepared "a scenario of the course of its economy over the next few years while immigration is expected to be at a high rate." He went on to suggest that "It should extend that scenario for a subsequent period of, say, five years in which U.S. aid should be gradually phased out."[21] That, of course, is on the dubious assumption that the United States will have granted the loan guarantees Israel demands.

Such an extended waiting period would, in our opinion, be a grave mistake. Israel would inevitably regard it as another golden opportunity for procrastination. Rather than speedily reforming and restructuring its economy, it would be more likely to concoct ingenious reasons why America should continue its aid indefinitely; meanwhile, it would accelerate the colonization of the Occupied Territories and thus further its tactics of "creating new facts."

Israel has often demonstrated its mastery of delay. Because it outwaited America during the Lausanne Conference, nothing came of those efforts to prevent decades of slaughter. Israel similarly torpedoed the negotiations following the Camp David meeting, thus limiting their application to bilateral issues. America succeeded in getting Israel to withdraw from the Sinai in 1956 only because Eisenhower made clear by word and action that he would brook none of Israel's filibustering practices.

In the light of this experience, we should discourage any compromises that would delay action on the Palestinians' request for an independent self-governing state of their own. Should the settlement provide some period of preparation and adjustment before the independent state comes into being? If such a period is provided, it should be as brief as possible. Under close UN supervision, the Palestinians should concentrate on

—developing the mechanisms for holding elections, including identifying those Palestinians entitled to vote;
—drafting a constitution;
—limiting the armaments and internal police forces of the new state; and
—legitimizing political parties.

If it should prove impossible to avoid a waiting period, one can be sure that the Israelis would invent a thousand reasons for extending the duration of the period as long as possible.[22] America should vigorously oppose such stalling tactics. An overwhelming amount of study and discussion have been devoted to determining the safeguards essential to establish such a Palestinian state without menace to, or compromise of, Israel's legitimate security interests.

If our suggestions seem to imply that Israel must make more compromises than the Arabs, that is largely because the Israelis have almost always triumphed both in military and diplomatic encounters with the Arabs. Israel's remarkable success in "cleansing the land" (achieved through fear and force at the time of its War of Independence) established de facto boundaries within which Israel might have lived and prospered. But its conquests in the 1967 War fed its expansionistic reflexes to disregard the requirements for a peaceful future. Those reflexes drove it to turn what was, in international law, the status it had earned by war (that of a "belligerent occupant") into that of an imperial state ruling its colonies.[23]

In contrast to Israel, the Arabs have sometimes tried, timidly and usually under pressure, to make some concessions. No longer do they incessantly proclaim that Zionism is responsible for all the Middle East's distresses, nor insist on the destruction of Israel. In Geneva on December 14, 1988, Arafat affirmed "the right of all parties concerned in the Middle East conflict to exist in peace and security, including the state of Palestine, Israel and their neighbors."

The Israelis are a rational people, and if they are faced with a fait accompli (a tactic they constantly utilize in their own diplomacy) one might expect them to adjust rationally. They might greatly benefit from the shock of a "cold douche," leaving them to improvise quickly such adjustments as are necessary.

As presently administered, Israel's program for settling Jews in the Occupied Territories is tailormade to produce bloody and brutal chaos for an indefinite future.[24] Anyone who talks sweetly about peace, then piously contends that expansionism is vital to Israel's security, is dooming Israel to unending conflict.

Meanwhile, America must strictly enforce the halting of further Jewish colonization of the Occupied Territories. Otherwise, any hope of peace will be totally frustrated and new areas of friction and impatience will further erode the Israeli-American relationship.[25]

Our leaders should not overlook the need to establish a united Jerusalem under control of an Arab-Israeli condominium. Nor should they neglect to make that united Jerusalem available to serve as the capital of both Israel and a new Palestinian state.

The Security Council might outline arrangements for joint governance of the Golan Heights, provided that the Heights are first demilitarized and evacuated.

## George Washington's Advice Revisited

Let us return to the wise remarks contained in George Washington's farewell address, summarized in the opening pages of this book.

From the bits and pieces of history we have reviewed, it is clear that America's passionate attachment to Israel has both distorted America's policies and imposed an enormous burden on the nation's economy. Our Western European allies have, as members of the EC, tried several times to convince our government to take a more principled position.

By ignoring their advice, America is violating the sound counsel of

George Washington's colleagues, principally Alexander Hamilton, who expressed their admonitions in the *Federalist Papers.*

As Professor Arthur M. Schlesinger, Jr., perceptively wrote:

> The Founding Fathers recognized . . . in the 63rd *Federalist* that "attention to the judgment of other nations" was indispensable to the American government for two reasons:
>
> . . . one is that, independently of the merits of any particular plan or measure, it is desirable, on various accounts, that it should appear to other nations as the offspring of a wise and honorable policy; the second is that, in doubtful cases, particularly where the national councils may be warped by some strong passion or momentary interest, the presumed or known opinion of the impartial world may be the best guide that can be followed.
>
> What has not America lost by her want of character with foreign nations; and how many errors and follies would she have not avoided, if the justice and propriety of her measures had, in every instance, been previously tried by the light in which they would probably appear to the unbiased part of mankind?[26]

Those words vividly reflect the situation with which our government is now presented. The vetoes America has cast in deference to Israeli sensitivities are a classic illustration of how "the national councils may be warped by some strong passion" that leads us to ignore the "known opinion of the impartial world."

The effects of our passionate attachment have spilled over to our domestic scene. They have inspired citizens "who devote themselves to the favored nation . . . to tamper with domestic factions, to practice the arts of seduction, to afford [them] opportunities to mislead public opinion, to influence or awe the public councils. . . ."

George Washington was remarkably prescient when he observed that though groups or individuals supporting the favored nation are applauded, those who may "resist the intrigues of the favorite, are likely to become suspected and odious." If a passionate attachment harms the infatuated country, it can equally injure the nation that is the object of its unrequited affection.

Apart from the fact that America's passionate attachment has been monstrously costly in financial terms, neither Israel's nor America's national interest is served by perpetual war, terrorism and bloody reprisals, arms races, nuclear, biological, and chemical weapons programs, and the increasing probability that present practices may ultimately result in an unconventional war.

Let us then be true to our own avowed principles. No country can possibly reconcile its concern for liberty and human rights with the continued abusive mistreatment of the Palestinian people, whose only crime is their desire for self-determination—the same sentiment that prompted the Founding Fathers of the United States and the founders of Israel a half century ago.

country, it can equally injure the nation that is the object of its unrequited affection.

Apart from the fact that America's passionate attachment has been monstrously costly in financial terms, neither Israel's nor America's national interest is served by perpetual war, terrorism and bloody reprisals, arms races, nuclear, biological, and chemical weapons programs, and the increasing probability that present practices may ultimately result in an unconventional war.

Let us then be true to our own avowed principles. No country can possibly reconcile its concern for liberty and human rights with the continued abusive mistreatment of the Palestinian people, whose only crime is their desire for self-determination—the same sentiment that prompted the Founding Fathers of the United States and the founders of Israel a half century ago.

# Notes

## FOREWORD

1. Albert J. Beveridge, *The Life of John Marshall,* Vol. II (Boston and New York: Houghton Mifflin, 1916), pp. 278–79.

2. Not only did Washington in his Farewell address fiercely condemn a "passionate attachment" to a foreign nation, he equally opposed "antipathy in one nation against another." That attitude, he said, would dispose "each more readily to offer insult and injury, to lay hold of slight causes of umbrage, and to be haughty and intractable when accidental or trifling occasions of dispute occur." *The Annals of America,* in *Encyclopaedia Britannica,* Vol. III, pp. 1784–96.

3. In Chapter 11 we shall say more about the key influences on Arab opinion, the meaning of conflicts between Arab states such as those now in progress, and describe how the current fragile political structure of the Arab world came into being largely through violence or the threat of violence.

## CHAPTER ONE

1. Lord Cecil's doubts as to the dangers of involving America in colonial administration in the Middle East gained support from history. In their long years of colonial endeavors, the British had become masters at the art of divide and rule, of periodically switching allies and of dealing with all nations on a pragmatic basis. At the same time they took deserved pride in fulfilling their responsibility to educate the natives. During the Victorian era, Britain ruled over one quarter of the globe. America's brief spasm of colonialist infatuation near the end of the nineteenth century, by contrast, was limited narrowly to small islands and the conquered remnants of the Spanish Empire. Moreover, in almost

every case, the Americans made clear that, preoccupied with conquering a continent of their own, they would remain colonial masters for only a brief time. America lacked the impersonal approach needed for empire. If the United States assisted another nation, the government felt it necessary to justify its action by uncritically embracing that nation as a "noble ally." In their effort to empathize with the people of that country, Americans—and their political leaders—frequently forgot the principles that had inspired their initial efforts.

But, though the Americans were capable of excessive sentimentality about other nations, such emotions were shallow and thus volatile; the same people could, from boredom and disillusionment, quickly shift from pride in their so-called "ally" to contempt for its behavior.

2. War Cabinet Eastern Committee, October 29, 1918, meeting, pp. 1–7. David Hirst, *The Gun and the Olive Branch: The Roots of Violence in the Middle East,* 2nd ed. (London: Faber and Faber, 1984), pp. 41–42. FO 371, 4183, Balfour to Curzon, 21 August 1919.

3. The U.S. State Department regarded that proposal with disfavor, since it believed that the effect would be to create two theocratic states in which their respective Jewish and Moslem minorities would receive scant consideration. William A. Eddy, an aide to Secretary of State George C. Marshall, predicted that the proposal would result in "a theocratic racial Zionist state" at marked variance with the American commitment to self-determination and to the American ideal of a "non-clerical political democracy, without prejudice to race or creed."

4. The announcement of the abandonment of the mandate electrified the American Jewish community, who immediately made their feelings known to Congress. Motivated by sympathy for Israel and domestic pressure from committed constituents, congressmen rejected President Truman's request for an emergency immigration allocation that would admit 100,000 stateless Jews to the United States. Jews, the congressmen insisted, should settle in their new "homeland." Delegates to the 1944 Democratic Convention adopted the following resolution in Section V: "We favor the opening of Palestine to unrestricted Jewish immigration and colonization and such a policy as to result in the establishment there of a free and democratic Jewish Commonwealth." The Republicans, not to be outdone, declared that "we call for the opening of Palestine to . . . unrestricted immigration and land ownership, so that in accordance with the full intent and purpose of the Balfour Declaration of 1917 and the resolution of the Republican Congress of 1922, Palestine may be constituted as a free and democratic Commonwealth. . . ."

Both platforms operated under the unflattering assumption that Palestine could be "free and democratic" only if there were a Jewish state there. The Republicans also ignored the proviso of the Balfour Declaration protecting the Arabs. No one was willing to admit that the Zionist program could be carried out only by systematically violating the Arabs' rights. In the 1946 congressional elections not only did the Republicans secure strong majorities in both houses of Congress, but, in spite of his strong efforts on behalf of the Zionists, Truman failed to receive help from the Jewish vote. As he wrote bitterly just before the election: "The Jews themselves are making it impossible to do anything for them. They seem to have the same attitude toward the 'underdog' when they are on top as they have been treated as 'underdogs' themselves. I suppose that is human frailty." The end of electoral activities did not, of course, mean an end to Zionist agitation and pressure; rather, it marked the beginning. Truman Papers, Palestine-Jewish Immigration Files, Truman to Panby, October 22, 1946.

5. RG 50, Office of Near Eastern Affairs Palestine, Box 1, Merriam, 11 December 1947. The Firestone family took it on themselves to line up Liberia. See also Senate Library, Vol. 1174 (4), 18th Cong., HR 2910, 4–27 June 1947; 2–18 July 1947.

6. Eleanor Roosevelt Papers, Box 4560, Truman to Eleanor Roosevelt, 20 May 1948, FDR Library, Hyde Park, New York. Harry S. Truman, *Memoirs,* Vol. II: *Years of Trial and Hope* (Garden City, N.Y.: Doubleday, 1956), pp. 160–64.

7. On October 6, 1947, the Joint Chiefs of Staff warned of future U.S. oil needs in the area and implied that America's pro-Zionist policies could give the Soviet Union influence with the Arabs even more effectively than it could secure through direct conquest. How the United States was to avoid this dilemma, they did not say. Joint Chiefs of Staff, Leahy Records, National Archives, Washington, D.C., Folder 56, JCS 1684/5, Strategic and Military Implications of Partition, approved 10 October 1947.

8. *Foreign Relations of the United States, 1947,* Vol. V, *The Near East and Africa* (Washington, D.C.: U.S. Government Printing Office, 1971, cited hereafter as *FRUS, 1947,* Vol. V), pp. 702–03. Secretary of State (Marshall) to the U.S. Representative at the United Nations (Austin).

9. The chief of the Planning Staff of the State Department, George Kennan, pointed out the folly of having the United States assist in the expansion of a Jewish state in Palestine. Such a U.S. policy would undermine the British, the only Western power with assets in the region. Secretary of Defense James S. Forrestal repeated the earlier warnings of the Joint Chiefs and his fear that the Marshall Plan would be ruined if oil resources were cut off. It would, he asserted, be "stupid" to prejudice our relations with the Arab states permanently or get ourselves into a position where we might "stumble into war" over the disposition of Palestine—*Policy Planning Staff,* National Archives, Washington, D.C.), PPS/23, Review of Current Trends in United States Foreign Policy, 24 February 1948; Kenneth W. Condit, *The History of the Joint Chiefs of Staff. The Joint Chiefs of Staff and National Policy,* Vol. II, *1947–1949* (Marshall Library, Lexington), Joint Secretariat Joint Chiefs of Staff, 22 April 1976, f. 93. See also *Forrestal Diaries,* Princeton University Library, Princeton, N.J., Box 4, Vol. 9, f. 2026, Cabinet, 16 January 1948; Walter Millis, ed., *The Forrestal Diaries* (New York: Viking Press, 1951), pp. 340–45, Diary, 6 Jan.–21 Jan., 1948. *Foreign Relations of the United States, 1948,* Vol. V, Parts I and II, *The Near East, South Asia, and Africa* (Washington, D.C.: U.S. Government Printing Office, 1976, cited hereafter as *FRUS, 1948,* Vol. V), pp. 573–81, Kennan to Lovett, and Annex, 29 January 1948.

10. *FRUS, 1948,* Vol. V, Part II, p. 633, Marshall to Lovett, 19 February 1948; pp. 651–54, statement of Austin to the United Nations, February 4, 1948; pp. 742–44, statement of Austin before the Security Council, March 19, 1948. See also Truman, *Years of Trial and Hope,* p. 163. Part of the reason for the Trusteeship proposal was to move the debate from the Security Council, with its veto, to the Trusteeship Council, where majority rule prevailed.

11. John Snetsinger, *Truman, the Jewish Vote, and the Creation of Israel* (Stanford, Calif.: Hoover Institution Press, 1974), pp. 107–09. Kermit Roosevelt, *Middle East Journal,* vol. II, no. 1 (1948), p. 16.

12. Truman to Niles, May 13, 1947, File of President's Secretary Palestine, 1945–1947 folder, Box 184, H. S. Truman Library, Independence, Missouri.

13. Snetsinger, *Truman,* p. 131.

14. But the final seal of approval was not provided until a Security Council resolution of May 11, 1949, admitted Israel to membership in the United Nations and all its agencies. The effect of that resolution, so Abba Eban has written, was to integrate the new state into what he referred to as "the system of interlocking agencies which enable a sovereign state to live within the evolving international community." That resolution, according to Eban, "was more powerful and decisive than the partition recommendation of 1947."

15. Simha Flapan, *The Birth of Israel: Myths and Realities* (New York: Pantheon, 1987), p. 33 (emphasis added).

16. Justified as needed to relieve the beleaguered Jews in Jerusalem.

17. *FRUS, 1948,* Vol. V, Part I, pp. 880–91, Consul at Jerusalem (Wasson) to Secretary of State, May 3, 1948. See also pp. 895–95, draft memo of Dean Rusk to Under Secretary Lovett, May 4, 1948. See also Chaim Herzog, *The Arab-Israeli Wars* (New York: Random House, 1982), pp. 16, 25, 24–44. While the People's Administration in Tel Aviv was for-

mulating by a vote of five to four the declaration of the new state without mention of its boundaries, Eliahu Epstein, the Agent of the Provisional Government of Israel, with the aid of Clark Clifford, was asking President Truman for recognition, saying that "the state of Israel has been proclaimed as an independent republic within frontiers approved by the General Assembly of the United Nations in its Resolution of November 29, 1947."

Epstein followed this up by cabling Prime Minister Sharett that he had given "unqualified assurances" that Israel would respect the November 29 lines, but "this is without prejudice to the requirement of military action." This ambiguity was immediately noted at the United Nations, where Abba Eban reported much adverse commentary. He urged that this point be clarified promptly. Flapan, *Birth of Israel,* pp. 32–36. See also *FRUS, 1948,* Vol. V, Part II, p. 989, letter from Epstein to Truman, May 14, 1948.

18. Walid Khalidi, "Plan Dalet: Master Plan for the Conquest of Palestine," *Journal of Palestine Studies,* vol. XVIII, no. 1 (autumn 1988), pp. 6–33; the text of Plan Dalet appears on pp. 34–37.

19. *FRUS, 1948,* Vol. II, Part I, pp. 761–64, memorandum of conversation by the Under Secretary of State (Lovett), Washington, D.C., March 26, 1948. See also the Consul General at Jerusalem (Macatee) to the Secretary of State, February 9, 1948, *ibid.,* pp. 609–11.

20. *Ibid.,* pp. 1047–50, especially p. 1049. the Ambassador in the United Kingdom (Douglas) to the Secretary of State, London, May 25, 1948.

21. *Ibid.,* pp. 1024–27, United Nations Representative (Austin) to the Secretary of State, May 21, 1948. The American consul general in Jerusalem estimated Haganah strength at 80,000, although he recognized that the mustering of the entire Jewish male population would leave little manpower to operate the new Jewish state's economy, *ibid.,* p. 608, the Consul General of Jerusalem (Macatee) to the Secretary of State, Jerusalem, February 9, 1948 (The Ambassador), *ibid.,* pp. 1047–50. (British Minister), *ibid.,* pp. 882–85, memorandum of conversation by the Director of the Office of Near Eastern and African Affairs (Henderson), May 2, 1948.

22. *Ibid.,* pp. 983–84, the Secretary of State to certain diplomatic offices, Washington, D.C., May 13, 1948.

23. *Ibid.,* pp. 984–85, the Consul of Jerusalem (Wasson) to the Secretary of State, May 13, 1948. This statement is important since Israel had to invade Arab-allocated territory to fight the Arab state armies, except in the case of Syria, which invaded lands allocated to the Jews in the upper Jordan Valley.

24. *Ibid.,* pp. 991–92, the Ambassador in Egypt (Tuck) to the Secretary of State, May 14, 1948. In the light of this analysis, the United States' embargo on arms shipments, subsequently copied by Resolution 50 of the Security Council, appears to have been one-sided. The Americans had initiated their embargo ostensibly to stop the fighting and achieve an arms balance in the area; yet the American government knew that arms from France, Italy, and Czechoslovakia were pouring into Israel, the stronger side, and that American arms producers and munitions brokers were flouting the embargo in favor of Israel. Still the United States continued to press Britain not to extend credit to the Arabs, because Americans knew that the Arabs lacked funds to buy arms elsewhere. *Ibid.,* pp. 640–43, memorandum of conversation by the Under Secretary of State (Lovett), February 21, 1948. The American arms embargo reminds one of the embargo of arms to Republican Spain that worked to Franco's advantage. *FRUS, 1948,* Vol. V, Part I, pp. 1143–44.

25. See Simha Flapan, *Zionism and the Palestinians* (London: Croom Helm, 1979), p. 320. Research by the late Israeli editor, Simha Flapan, has shown that, without exception, all the Arab regimes were eager to avoid a war with Israel in 1948. The big battle at Latrun came because the Israelis attempted to seize a town allocated to the Arabs and the Jordanians resisted.

26. *Ibid.,* p. 153, citing Walid Khalidi. By April 30, 1948, just two weeks before the end of the mandate, public outrage finally forced the Arab Chiefs of Staff to set to work on a plan for military intervention.

27. Note the seizure of the Golan in 1967 after a truce was adopted; the continued

Israeli advance in 1973 to surround the Egyptian Third Army; the further attacks in June 1982 to seize the Beirut-Damascus highway. In each case, alleged Arab truce violations served as the pretext for strategic offensive operations which the Israelis had already planned to carry out.

28. The story has been well told in a book by Avi Shlaim, *Collusion Across the Jordan: King Abdullah, the Zionist Movement, and the Partition of Palestine* (New York: Columbia University Press, 1988).

29. *FRUS, 1948,* Vol. V, Part I, pp. 1105–06, Vice Consul Burdette to Secretary of State, June 8, 1948. By no means were all Arab leaders irrevocably opposed to Israel. For example, Abd Al-Rahman Azzam Pasha declared that "the Arabs are ready to make far-reaching concessions toward the gratification of the Jewish desire to see Palestine established as a spiritual, or even a material home." In an interview on October 5, 1945, he told a French-language publication, "if you could assure me that the handing of Palestine to the Jews would mean peace everywhere, I should give all of it." Interview in *Le Progrès Egyptien,* reported in *Ha'aretz,* October 24, 1945. See also Flapan, *Birth of Israel,* p. 130.

30. Flapan, *Birth of Israel,* p. 140.

31. Avi Shlaim, *Collusion Across the Jordan* (New York: Columbia University Press, 1988), pp. 202–03.

32. Far from doing anything to justify its destruction, as the commander of the Haganah, David Shaltiel, noted, the village had been "quiet since the beginning of the disturbances . . . not mentioned in reports of attacks on Jews, and one of the few places which had not given a foothold to foreign bands." Larry Collins and Dominique Lapierre, *O Jerusalem!* (New York: Simon & Schuster, 1972), p. 272. See also Alfred M. Lillienthal, *The Zionist Connection: Still, What Price Israel?* (New York: Dodd, Mead, 1978), pp. 151–56. In fact, "When an Arab band tried to make its base there last month the villagers themselves repulsed them at the cost of the Mukhtar's (headman's) son." Levin, *Jerusalem Embattled,* p. 57.

33. Flapan, *Birth of Israel,* pp. 89–93. Benny Morris, *The Birth of the Palestinian Refugee Problem, 1947–1949* (New York: Cambridge University Press, 1989), pp. 111–12.

34. *Maariv,* May 6, 1973. This and other comments, coupled with indisputable Israeli actions in accordance with them, prove that Israel, throughout the 1947–49 fighting, was pursuing an expansionist policy.

35. Collins and Lapierre, *O Jerusalem!,* p. 275. The stories told by survivors were gory in the extreme. "The daughter of one of the principal families of the village has declared that she saw a man shoot a bullet in the neck of my sister Salhiyeh, who was nine months pregnant, then he cut her stomach open with a butcher's knife." A sixteen-year-old survivor, Naaneh Kalil, claims she saw a man take "a kind of sword and slash my neighbor Jamil Hish from head to toe and then do the same thing on the steps of my house to my cousin Fathi." Hirst, *The Gun and the Olive Branch,* p. 125. Most information comes from the Red Cross Representative's report, plus British Mandate reports of April 13, 15, 16, 1948, Dossier 179/110/17/65, "Secret," signed by Richard Catting, Assistant Inspector General of the Criminal Investigation.

36. There is a dispute over these figures in Eric Silver, *Begin: The Haunted Prophet* (New York: Random House, 1984), p. 95.

37. According to the account of Harry Levin, once Middle East correspondent of the *Daily Herald* and then Israeli chargé d'affaires in Australia, "the Mukhtar of Deir Yassin, his womenfolk and children were in one truck." Levin, *Jerusalem Embattled,* p. 57.

38. Menachem Begin, *The Revolt: Story of the Irgun,* 10th ed., trans. by Samuel Katz (Tel Aviv: Steimatzky, 1983), pp. 162–65. In addition, Begin persists in perpetuating the myth that the villagers were warned and that the Irgun even sacrificed the element of surprise to warn the villagers the attack was coming. But he boasts that the attack greatly contributed to the Palestinian flight, noting that the Palestinians "were seized with limitless panic and started to flee for their lives. This mass flight soon turned into a mad, uncontrollable stampede. Of about 900,000 Arabs who lived on the present territory of the state of Israel, only some 165,000 were still living there in 1949. The political and economic signifi-

cance of this development could hardly be overestimated." *Ibid.*, p. 164. To this the American journalist I. F. Stone added, "neither can Begin's cold-blooded nationalistic calculation." See also Silver, *Begin*, p. 88.

39. Ritchie Ovendale, *The Origins of the Arab-Israeli Wars* (London: Longmans, 1984), pp. 4–7.

40. Joseph B. Schechtman, *The Arab Refugee Problem* (New York: Philosophical Library, 1952), pp. 1–33.

41. Erskine B. Childers, *The Spectator,* (London), May 12, 1961, p. 253; Walid Khalidi, "Why Did the Palestinians Leave?" (London: Arab Information Paper No. 3, 1958). See also Christopher Hitchens, "Broadcasts," in Edward Said and Christopher Hitchens, eds., *Blaming the Victims: Serious Scholarship and the Palestinian Question* (New York: Verso, 1988), pp. 73–83. The tactic employed is vividly illustrated by a contemporary report: "Nearby a loud speaker burst out in Arabic. Haganah broadcasting to civilian Arabs, urged them to leave the district before 5:15 A.M. Take pity on your wives and children and get out of this bloodbath . . . Get out by the Jericho road, this is still open to you. If you stay you invite disaster." Harry Levin, *Jerusalem Embattled: A Diary of the City Under Siege, March 25, 1948 to July 18, 1948* (London: Victor Gollancz, 1950), p. 160.)

42. Childers, *The Spectator* (London), May 12, 1961.

43. Natanal Lorch, *The Edge of the Sword* (New York: G. P. Putnam's Sons, 1961), p. 103, quoted by Hirst, *The Gun and the Olive Branch,* p. 140.

44. Hirst, *The Gun and the Olive Branch,* p. 141.

45. Ian Lustick, *Arabs in the Jewish State: Israel's Control of a National Minority* (Austin, Tex.: University of Texas Press, 1982), pp. 31–32.

46. References to these figures are found in the *Christian Century* for March 16, 1949 (Jon Kimche, *Seven Fallen Pillars*). Still, some idealistic Zionists registered deep chagrin. Don Peretz described the result of Deir Yassin as a "mass fear psychosis which grasped the whole Arab community." Arthur Koestler wrote that this "blood bath . . . was a psychologically decisive factor in the spectacular exodus of Arab refugees."

47. That report, which has recently been revealed, had been produced for internal IDF consumption. It was presumably given to the director of Mapam's Arab Development by a contact in the IDF General Staff or Intelligence Branch on July 8, 1948.

48. Benny Morris, "The Causes and Character of the Arab Exodus from Palestine," *Middle Eastern Studies,* vol. XXII, no. 1 (January 1986). In *The Birth of the Palestinian Refugee Problem, 1947–1949* (New York: Cambridge University Press, 1987), Morris comes to the same conclusion.

49. While the report does not cover the flight of a similar number of Arabs in the remaining months of the war, the trend can presumably be extrapolated. The report notes the departure of the Palestinians, which thus conveniently solved a potentially embarrassing problem of how to handle a large and probably hostile minority.

The disclosure of the report in a lecture by Morris to the Shiloah Institute of Tel Aviv University evoked noisy controversy in Israel. Though some challenged its findings, Ya'acov Shimoni, who had been the acting director of the Middle East Affairs Department of the Foreign Ministry in 1948, was quoted as saying that "The thrust of Morris' paper, and the details presented in the IDF report, were 'correct and accurate' to the best of his recollection."

50. In the opinion of Morris, the IDF Intelligence Branch "was very well placed to collect and analyze data about the Palestinian exodus." And he further asserts that "there is no reason to cast doubt on the integrity of the IDF Intelligence Branch in the production of the analysis." Finally, Morris concludes that "while the report was not produced with any propagandizing intention in mind, its author seemed to have exhibited a perhaps understandable tendency to minimize the role that direct expulsion orders played in bringing about the departure of the Palestinians." Benny Morris, "The Causes and Character of

the Arab Exodus from Palestine: The Israel Defense Force Intelligence Board Analysis of June 1948," *Middle Eastern Studies,* Vol. XXII, no. 1 (January 1986). The comments in our book are taken from the material in this article, which was subsequently expanded into a book, *The Birth of the Palestinian Refugee Problem, 1947–1949* (Cambridge, England: Cambridge University Press, 1989). See also Amnon Kapeliouk, "New Light on the Israeli-Arab Conflict and the Refugee Problem and Its Origins," *Journal of Palestine Studies,* Vol. XVI, no. 3 (Spring 1987), pp. 16–42.

51. Tom Segev, *1949: The First Israelis* (New York: Free Press, 1986), p. 27. Afterwards, the demoralized troops were subjected to "prolonged propaganda activities" to mollify them and explain "why we were obliged to undertake such a harsh and cruel action." *Ibid.,* p. 25. See also *The New York Times,* October 23, 1979, p. A3, article by David K. Shipler. One is struck by the similarity of this account with that appearing in William Shirer, *The Rise and Fall of the Third Reich* (New York: Simon & Schuster, 1960), p. 664, regarding German troops in Poland. Collins and Lapierre, *O Jerusalem!,* noted that in the forced march, many elderly people and small children died in the overpowering heat.

52. *The Guardian,* June 1, 1986.

53. *Yediot Aharonot,* April 14, 1972.

54. Uri Avnery, *Israel Without Zionists: A Plea for Peace in the Middle East* (New York: Macmillan, 1968), p. 223.

55. *Ha Sepker, Ha Palmach,* Vol. 2, p. 286, cited by Walid Khalidi.

56. *Foreign Relations of the United States, 1949,* Vol. VI, *The Near East, South Asia, and Africa* (Washington, D.C.: U.S. Government Printing Office, 1977, cited hereafter as *FRUS, 1949,* Vol. VI), pp. 681–82. See also the Consul at Jerusalem (Burdett) to the Secretary of State, Jerusalem, October 29, 1949, *ibid.,* pp. 1456–57. Present Israeli efforts to annex the West Bank and Gaza are, therefore, nothing new.

57. *Ibid.,* p. 1267, Secretary of State to the United States Delegation at Lausanne, July 28, 1949.

58. The Israelis had employed similar policies during March, April, and May 1949, forcing Jordan to surrender all the Arab lands owned by the villagers of Tulkarm. *Ibid.,* pp. 946–47, memorandum of conversation by the Secretary of State, April 26, 1949. Present were Secretary Acheson, Elihu Elathe, the Israeli ambassador; Abba Eban, Israeli UN Representative; and Joseph C. Satterwhite, Director, NEA.

59. *Ibid.,* pp. 975–77, Ethridge to the Secretary of State, May 4, 1949. In addition, Eytan flatly contradicted the United States' figures; only 550,000 people, not 800,000, Eytan asserted, had been left homeless.

60. *Ibid.* Although Eytan claimed that prior to the war the Jews had been prepared to accept a large Arab minority, that claim was false; the State Department reports showed that expulsion was a key part of the Israeli leaders' program.

61. The Arabs, Eytan scornfully informed Ethridge, were too feckless to handle their own funds responsibly. Such a method of payment, though Eytan did not say so, would hide the inadequacy of the compensation paid.

62. Nor, regardless of whether the owners returned or not, would the Israeli government suspend its "requisition measures and occupation of Arab property" that the Israeli authorities defined as "abandoned." *Ibid.,* pp. 1065–67, the Minister in Switzerland (Vincent) to the Secretary of State (Byrne), May 28, 1949. Israeli officials even forced Israeli Arabs to move elsewhere at gunpoint, then seized their property as "abandoned," even though the owners were Israeli citizens resident in the country.

63. Pressed by strong opinions expressed around the table, Eytan fell back on his familiar complaint that he could not understand why the Arabs refused to make peace before discussing the refugee problem. But in the end, he agreed to ask his government for a definitive number of the refugees they would accept if the Gaza Strip were not annexed. *Ibid.,* pp. 1069–71, the Minister in Switzerland (Vincent) to the Secretary of State (Byrne), May 28, 1949.

64. *Ibid.*, pp. 1112–14, the Minister in Switzerland (Vincent) to the Secretary of State (Byrne), June 10, 1949.

65. He also demanded the present international boundary with Egypt or, at any rate, negotiations regarding the Gaza Strip. Since Israel refused to furnish guarantees that it would not expel the Arab inhabitants and refugees from that area if it acquired it, the United States dropped its efforts to get Egypt to leave Gaza.

66. *Ibid.*, pp. 980–82, Stabler (U.S. Chargé at Amman) to Secretary of State, May 7, 1949. See p. 1145 for a memorandum.

67. *Ibid.*, pp. 1051–53, the Acting Secretary of State (Webb) to the Legation in Switzerland, May 24, 1949.

68. *Ibid.* Note the echo of the French claim to Marshall.

69. *Ibid.*, pp. 1060–63, memorandum by the Acting Secretary of State (Webb) to the President, May 27, 1949.

70. *Ibid.*, pp. 1072–74, the Acting Secretary of State to the Embassy in Israel, May 28, 1949.

71. The failure to put Jordan on this interesting list of "aggressors" furnishes further proof of the Israeli-Jordanian connection and the ambiguous status which that country held in the Israeli plans.

72. It was evident to everyone with access to diplomatic cable traffic that McDonald's prime interest was in defending Israel's positions and criticizing his State Department superiors rather than in fulfilling his assigned task of effectively representing the United States. Unfortunately, in placing Israel's interests above America's, McDonald was setting a pattern all too often followed by later U.S. ambassadors. *Ibid.*, pp. 1074–75, the Ambassador in Israel (McDonald) to the Secretary of State, May 29, 1949.

73. *Ibid.*, p. 115.

74. In summing up his comments on his colleagues, the American diplomat who was a co-member with McDonald on the Anglo-American Committee of Inquiry on Palestine remarked: " . . . We understood from the outset that McDonald favored the Jewish cause. But as my colleague Crossman has put it, he was thoroughly 'enigmatic.' It was impossible to predict his final viewpoint on any topic that came up for discussion. After the report had been filed by all, McDonald was to come out strongly for a Zionist state and was to be naturally acclaimed by the Jewish communities wherever he went. Very naturally also he became the first American Minister to Israel." William Philips, *Ventures in Diplomacy* (Boston: Beacon Press, 1952), p. 448.

An insight into McDonald's bias toward Israel even against U.S. interests can be gained by considering the manner of his selection. At 4:25 P.M. on June 22, 1948, Clark Clifford, the President's political adviser, telephoned Under Secretary of State Lovett to tell him that the President had appointed McDonald to be the U.S. ambassador to Israel. The State Department should, therefore, prepare his papers and announce his nomination that very afternoon. Lovett asked who McDonald was and Clifford replied that he had been a member of the Anglo-American Committee of Inquiry on Palestine. Lovett pointed out that only zealous Zionists were members of that body and that, in view of the delicate diplomatic situation, such an appointment would be neither timely nor tactful. Lovett then asked if the State Department might at least have the opportunity to present its views to the President. Clifford replied that the decision had already been made and, therefore, no further discussion was in order. *FRUS, 1948,* Vol. V, Part II, pp. 1131–32, memorandum of telephone conversation by the Under Secretary of State (Lovett). A copy of this correspondence was sent to Secretary Acheson, who initialed it. McDonald reported the circumstances of his appointment and his discussions with President Truman and other officials before his departure for Tel Aviv in his memoirs. See James C. McDonald, *My Mission in Israel, 1948–1951* (New York: Simon & Schuster, 1951), pp. 3–19.

75. Because he believed that the United States was "coddling" the Arabs, McDonald wholeheartedly supported that view. Moreover, McDonald lectured the President that the

U.S. government should not express its views in terms of imperatives, and he warned both Truman and Webb against "extreme measures" that might have unpredictable effects. Such unprofessionalism disgusted longtime diplomats such as David Bruce, who was then the U.S. ambassador in France. *FRUS, 1949,* Vol. VI, p. 1085, Lausanne, June 2, 1949, Mark F. Ethridge to the Secretary of State. See also p. 1125, the Ambassador in France (Bruce) to the Secretary of State, June 10, 1948.

76. *Ibid.,* pp. 1102–06, Government of Israel to the Government of the United States. But this last contention overlooked the fact that Eban's position on the refugee question had been far different from the hard line Israel's representatives were then pressing at Lausanne and in the June 8 reply. Had Eban taken the line his colleagues were now pushing, Israel would probably not have been admitted to the United Nations.

77. *Ibid.,* pp. 980–82. Stabler, U.S. Chargé at Amman, to Secretary of State, May 7, 1949. See also p. 1145 memorandum.

78. George McGhee, *Envoy to the Middle World: Adventures in Diplomacy* (New York: Harper & Row, 1983) p. 37. After his experiences in June 1949, McGhee spoke with Dr. Charles Malik, the Lebanese minister to the United States, who had suggested an American-imposed settlement. McGhee replied that "We were not politically adept at this kind of action and, furthermore, we did not like the kind of responsibility which such advice necessarily entailed." McGhee also noted that Americans were not comfortable in that role and many would feel it constituted interference in other nations' affairs. In retrospect, he was inventing a rationalization for a policy based solely on domestic political considerations. *FRUS, 1949,* Vol. VI, p. 1212, memo of July 8, 1949.

79. *FRUS, 1949,* Vol. VI, pp. 1126–27, the Acting Secretary of State to the Secretary of State in Paris, June 12, 1949.

## CHAPTER TWO

1. *The New York Times,* October 25, 1953. Such a line of defense could be used to justify Iraq's invasion of Kuwait.

2. *The New York Times,* October 19, 1953, p. A8.

3. *The New York Times,* October 19, 1953.

4. The Soviet Union was not, however, prepared to leave the situation alone. On January 22, 1954, it cast its 55th veto (its first in reference to Palestine) to prevent the adoption of a mild, Western-sponsored resolution (relating to the dispute over the water operations at Banat Ya'qub in the Syrian demilitarized zone). The resolution failed to back Syria in its quarrel with Israel by condemning Israel as the aggressor. List of vetoes cast, United States Mission to the United Nations, Veto 55 of Resolution S/3151/Rev 2.

5. Hollis W. Barber, *The United States and World Affairs 1955.* (New York: Harper Brothers, 1957), pp. 176–77.

6. Donald Neff, *Warriors at Suez* (New York: Simon & Schuster, 1981), p. 374. So, when it became clear that Britain and France had attacked Egypt, Eisenhower exploded. "The White House," it was reported, "crackled with barrack-room language the like of which had not been heard since the days of General Grant." Neff quotes James Reston, *ibid.*

7. Neff, *Warriors at Suez,* p. 365. America's sense of urgency was increased by Moscow's saber rattling and American concerns that the Soviet Union might intervene. Nor were American efforts helped by the fact that the Hungarian crisis had to be dealt with at the same time. Eisenhower's first priority was to disentangle America's NATO allies from Egypt. Since a resolution in the Security Council had been vetoed by Britain and France, he took the resolution to the General Assembly, which passed it on November 2. The resolution called for a cease-fire, the withdrawal of troops, and a halt in the movement of troops to the area.

8. Neff, *Warriors at Suez,* pp. 392 and 410.

9. "Secret" record of decision, Israel memorandum for Colonel A. J. Goodpaster, the White House, from Fisher Howe, Director, Executive Secretariat Department of State, dated November 11, 1956, in the White House Central Files, confidential file, Box 82, Folder Suez-Canal crisis, Dwight Eisenhower Library, Abilene, Kansas. Neff, *Warriors at Suez,* pp. 415–16.

10. Neff, *Warriors at Suez,* pp. 432–33.

11. Kenneth Love, *Suez, The Twice-Fought War* (New York: McGraw-Hill, 1969), p. 666.

12. The Israelis retained the Auja neutral strip (95 square miles).

13. With the presence of UN forces in the Gaza Strip, it was thought that Egypt would be excluded from that area. Egyptian forces later returned when UNEF proved unable to keep order.

14. See Presidential News Conferences of February 17 and 18, 1960, in *The New York Times.*

15. See Section II, Public Law 86–472, approved May 14, 1960. See also the State Department Bulletin of May 23, 1960, pp. 832–34.

## CHAPTER THREE

1. Resolution 1604(XV), April 21, *Documents on American Foreign Relations,* no. 68. See details in the *United Nations Review* (May 1961), pp. 11, 44, and 47. In an acrimonious debate over the fate of the Arab refugees during the spring 1961 meeting of the General Assembly, the United States failed to convince either side of its impartiality.

2. At the same time, Nasser informed the American State Department that Egypt also had other problems requiring its attention and did not desire a peace conference in 1962—which effectively sidetracked any settlement. See *Documents in American Foreign Policy,* no. 67. See also Mordechai Gazit, *President Kennedy's Policy Toward the Arab States and Israel: Analysis and Documents* (Tel Aviv: Shiloah Center for Middle Eastern and African Studies, 1983), pp. 15–22.

3. I. L. Kenen, *Israel's Defense Line: Her Friends and Foes in Washington* (Buffalo, N.Y.: Prometheus Books, 1981), p. 161.

4. Rusk Memorandum for the President, 30 January 1961, P.O.F. Box 119A, John F. Kennedy Library, Boston, Massachusetts.

5. The first meeting took place in July 1962, and another was held in the autumn of 1963.

6. Gazit, *President Kennedy's Policy,* pp. 44–46.

7. At the beginning of his term, Johnson tried to finesse the established policy that America would not directly arm Israel. Instead, he attempted to persuade the West German government in 1964 to undertake this role. When that exposed the Germans to a fierce diplomatic counterattack from the irate Arabs, the Bonn government canceled the contracts made by German firms and banned any German company from selling arms to anyone in the Middle East. That put the United States under excruciating Israeli pressure to fill the void—a pressure increased by growing French coldness toward Israel. Ambassador Averell Harriman visited Tel Aviv in February 1965 to discuss arms sales with Israel on the condition that the Israelis would promise to avoid any overt actions against their Arab neighbors. "Following that visit and to emphasize America's objectivity, Washington announced the sale of arms to Saudi Arabia, Jordan, Lebanon and Iraq as well as Israel—for the purpose, it was said, of supplying limited amounts of conventional military material to meet legitimate defense needs." *New York Herald-Tribune,* April 16, 1965. See also *New York Times,* April 14 and April 29, 1965.

8. Even before his accession to the presidency, Johnson had been aware that the United States' ability to control events in the Arab world was greatly limited by the chilly relations between the United States and President Nasser, but even more by the attitude of Congress

toward the Egyptian leader. Under a $432 million grant of American surplus food promised Egypt by an agreement concluded in 1962, $37 million was still unappropriated. Although, in January 1965, Congress tried to freeze these funds, eventually, after some rigorous arm twisting, President Johnson managed to get "some freedom of action" that gave him discretion to provide the aid if he thought best and, on June 22, 1965, he sent Egypt the remaining $37 million of food aid.

President Nasser had been hoping for an additional $500 million of U.S. food shipments during the years 1966 through 1968, but Congress passed a general prohibition on aid to countries that failed to protect U.S. property against mob action (an Egyptian mob had sacked the U.S. Information Agency Library in Cairo) and expressly banned further surplus food sales to the UAR unless the President found it essential. Such commitments could only be made a year at a time. Stephen Green, *Taking Sides: America's Secret Relations with a Militant Israel* (New York: William Morrow, 1984), pp. 184–87; see also "secret" State Department telegram DEPTEL 963 from U.S. Embassy, Tel Aviv, to Secretary of State, dated May 15, 1964, in Carelton Press, declassified documents reference system, 1979/193C.

9. The Israelis challenged the UN figures and attempted to justify their acts by pointing to sixty-nine incidents of sabotage along their border during the last two years. Even though the Israelis admitted that these sabotage efforts originated not from Jordan but from Syria, they contended that the purpose of the raid was to compel the Jordanians to prevent saboteurs from getting into Israel. *The New York Times,* November 16, 1966.

10. Samie A. Mutawi, *Jordan in the 1967 War* (Cambridge: Cambridge University Press, 1987), pp. 100–04.

11. *Facts on File* (*Weekly World News Digest with Cumulative Index* [New York], cited hereafter as *Facts on File*), 1967, pp. 169–70, 175–87.

12. "Secret" memorandum for the President from Robert W. Komer, dated January 18, 1966, NSF Country File—Israel, Vol. V, memos 12/65–9/66, Lyndon Baines Johnson Library, Austin, Texas.

13. By April 1967 the Israelis were planning to display their new weaponry in an elaborate Independence Day Parade in Jerusalem, but because he deemed that gesture unnecessary and provocative, Secretary Rusk advised the U.S. ambassador in Tel Aviv, Walworth Barbour, not to attend the ceremonies. "Unclassified" State Department telephone 3419 from U.S. Embassy, Tel Aviv, to Secretary of State, dated April 28, 1967, NSF Country File—Israel, Vol. VI, memos 12/66–7/67, Lyndon Baines Johnson Library. It should be noted that despite the facts of the case, the United States joined the Israeli government in charging Nasser with having started the war (not technically true), and it also sharply criticized UN Secretary General U Thant for withdrawing UN forces. The latter charge was unfair, since UNEF was there only at the invitation of Egypt, and Israel had refused to institutionalize the UN troops' presence on Egyptian territory. Thus U Thant really had no option but to withdraw his forces at Nasser's demand. See Brian Urquhart, *A Life in Peace and War* (New York: Harper & Row, 1977), pp. 209–11.

14. "Secret" memorandum for the President from Secretary of State Dean Rusk, dated May 26, 1967, NSF Country File—Israel, Vol. XII, Lyndon Baines Johnson Library.

15. Lyndon B. Johnson, *The Vantage Point: Perspectives on the Presidency, 1963–1969* (New York: Holt, Reinhart & Winston, 1971), p. 293. In drafting the official reply to Eshkol, Walt Rostow, the President's National Security Adviser, noted in his transmittal memorandum to the President that "it may be urgent that we put this letter on record soon." The United States wanted it clear in the history books that it was opposed to an Israeli attack, when, in fact, the U.S. government was merely expressing opposition pro forma.

16. Lyndon Baines Johnson Library Oral History Project, Interview No. 3 with Nicholas Katzenbach, recorded December 11, 1968.

17. G. H. Jansen, "The Shattered Myths," *Middle East International,* February 18, 1983, p. 13.

18. James M. Ennes, Jr., *Assault on the Liberty: The True Story of the Israeli Attack on*

*an American Intelligence Ship* (New York: Random House, 1979), pp. 61–173, 209–16, 284–88.

19. On June 19, 1867, the day before the meeting of the Fifth Emergency session of the United Nations General Assembly, President Johnson laid out a program for the Middle East. It consisted of six points: *First,* every nation in that region had a fundamental right to live in peace and be respected by its neighbors. *Second,* the refugees required just treatment. *Third,* maritime rights and free passage through international waterways must be secured. *Fourth,* he pledged that "The United States, for its part, will use every counsel of reason and prudence to find a better course" to head off the Middle East arms race. *Fifth,* to give meaning to his first principle, Johnson proposed a firm peace between the parties. They needed recognized boundaries and other arrangements against terrorism, destruction, and war. *Sixth,* adequate recognition must be accorded to the common interest of the three great religions in the Jerusalem holy places.

20. Gideon Rafael, *Destination Peace: Three Decades of Israel Foreign Policy* (London: Weidenfeld & Nicolson, 1981), p. 177.

21. Citing Noring and Smith, "The Withdrawal Clause in UN Security Council Resolution 242 of 1967," pp. 12–13, "Secret." The study is widely quoted in Neff, *Warriors for Jerusalem,* pp. 342–47.

22. Neff, *Warriors for Jerusalem,* p. 342. See also Noring and Smith, "The Withdrawal Clause," pp. 12–13, 340–42.

23. Noring and Smith, "The Withdrawal Clause," p. 15.

24. Since the United States was furnishing Israel with more arms as part of its program of achieving superiority over all the Arab states, the deletion of this clause accorded with Israeli wishes.

25. As the inclusion of the definite article "the" would have required Israeli withdrawal from all the lands seized in the recent conflict, the resolution would have been in effect self-executing.

26. As late as January 1983, Secretary Shultz wrote to Hussein that "the President believes, consistent with Resolution 242, that territory should not be acquired by war. He believes, as well, however, that Resolution 242 does permit changes in the boundaries which existed prior to June 1967, but only where such changes are agreed between the parties." Significantly, Shultz added that the "United States considers Jerusalem part of the occupied territories."

Subsequent efforts by Arthur Goldberg and Eugene V. Rostow to justify extensive Israeli annexations in the West Bank by denying that any such promises were made to Hussein are refuted not only by the statements of Dean Rusk and Henry Kissinger, but by the very fact that the King supported Resolution 242. Moreover, the Russians would have vetoed it had it been represented to them in that manner. Neff, *Warriors for Jerusalem,* p. 349; Henry Kissinger, *White House Years* (Boston: Little, Brown, 1979), p. 345. See also Arthur J. Goldberg, "Withdrawal Needn't Be Total; An Interpretation of Resolution 242," *Washington Star,* December 9, 1973, p. B3.

27. The Israelis had consistently opposed this clause since it first appeared in the American draft; they referred to it as "the ominous formula of the inadmissibility of conquest of territory by war." Israel's representatives presented vigorous arguments regarding the "inadmissibility" of this "doubtful principle"—as it pertained to themselves. They were, they declared, the victims of aggression, who had fought what they regarded as a defensive action to protect their own territory and sovereignty. As a fallback, they argued that if that principle were to be applied to Israel, it should also be applied to Jordan's acquisition of the West Bank and Egypt's occupation of the Gaza Strip. But they rejected any thought that the principle might equally apply to their own conquests in 1948 of lands designated for an Arab state by the partition resolution.

28. That acceptance was shortly confirmed by Ambassador Joseph Tekoah in a speech at the direction of Prime Minister Eshkol before the United Nations. But that did not

prevent Moshe Dayan in 1970 from denying that Israel had ever agreed to it, or deter both Menachem Begin and Dayan from objecting to the resolution. Indeed, only when Gideon Rafael pointed out to Golda Meir that Israel's acknowledgment and acceptance of the resolution had been signed by Eshkol (a prudent bureaucratic precaution which Rafael had taken in 1969) was she willing to acknowledge that such an acceptance had been made, even though she did not personally agree with it—Rafael, *Destination Peace,* pp. 197–99. Her subsequent reiteration of acceptance in 1971 was simply a clarification arising from her earlier denials that had been based on her ignorance of what had actually taken place. Cheryl Rubenberg claims that the August 4, 1971, ratification was the first, which would appear to be an oversight in light of Gideon Rafael's statement in the matter. Israel's ratification was irrelevant since 242 was binding on all parties whether they accepted it or not. Rubenberg also claims Syria rejected 242, yet the authors were told in 1985 both by Vice President Khaddam and Foreign Minister Sharra that Syria had agreed to 242. See Cheryl A. Rubenberg, *Israel and the American National Interest: A Critical Examination* (Urbana, Ill.: University of Illinois Press, 1986), p. 145.

29. While these negotiations were creating a great muddle in New York, endemic warfare and the arms race were continuing in the Middle East. It was in large part America's fault for, in spite of his pious appeal to end the arms race, President Johnson, disregarding earlier policy, authorized the emergency air shipment to Israel of armored personnel carriers, tank spare parts, spare parts for the Hawk missile air defense system, bomb fuses, artillery ammunition, and gas masks in June 1967. In September 1967, the United States delivered to Israel forty-eight A-4 Skyhawk fighter bombers that had originally been promised in 1966.

In order to mute Arab criticisms, Washington further announced shipments of spare parts to Lebanon, Saudi Arabia, and Tunisia, as well as the delivery of jet fighters previously ordered by Morocco and Libya. Simultaneously, the Soviet Union responded to this development by delivering armaments to the United Arab Republic, Syria, and others with a view to improving their defense posture, but it still withheld offensive armaments to discourage aggressive Arab moves. See "Top Secret" Note—and attached table from Harold Saunders to Louis Nivens, dated May 23, 1967. See also a note from Marvin Watson to the President, dated June 5, 1967. Both are in National Security File NSC History—Middle East Crisis, May 12–June 19, 1967, Vol. I, Lyndon Baines Johnson Library.

30. Not the guerrillas, who exaggerated their role in the affair and chiefly profited thereby.

31. Wolf Blitzer, *Between Washington and Jerusalem; A Reporter's Notebook* (New York and Oxford: Oxford University Press, 1985), pp. 72–73.

32. Helen Cobban, "Israel's Nuclear Game: The U.S. Stake," *World Policy Journal,* vol. V, no. 3 (Fall 1988), p. 425.

## CHAPTER FOUR

1. Kissinger, *White House Years,* p. 370. See also *Facts on File,* 1968, p. 529, and Seymour M. Hersh, *The Price of Power. Kissinger in the Nixon White House* (New York: Summit Books, 1983), p. 214.

2. Kissinger, *White House Years,* pp. 559 and 564; see also Richard M. Nixon, *The Memoirs of Richard Nixon* (New York: Grosset & Dunlap, 1978).

3. Nixon, *Memoirs,* pp. 481–82. Nixon did not give the date of the memo, but from its context it apparently was written in early 1970.

4. In addition, he was sensitive to the fact that the supporters of Israel were so strong that a President could quickly use up his energies and political capital if he embarked on a course opposed by Israel.

5. Nixon, *Memoirs,* p. 481.

6. See, for instance, Hersh, *The Price of Power,* pp. 216–17. Both Nixon's and Kissinger's memoirs are replete with references to the global dimensions of the Arab-Israeli conflict.

7. Nixon, *Memoirs,* pp. 347–63, 477. "I did this partly because I felt that Kissinger's Jewish background would put him at a disadvantage during the delicate initial negotiations for the reopening of diplomatic relations with the Arab states," Nixon recalled in his memoirs. In explaining his decision to Kissinger, Nixon added: "You and I will have more than enough on our plate with Vietnam, SALT, the Soviets, Japan and Europe." *Ibid.,* p. 477.

8. The Egyptians had encouraged the Soviets to handle their diplomatic exchanges with the United States in the immediate years after the 1967 War. "This, it was felt," observed the journalist Mohamed Hassanein Heikal, "would not only show [the Soviets] the virtual impossibility of achieving any positive results but would also involve their interest and their prestige directly in the outcome of the conflict. . . . Greater Soviet presence in Egypt would mean greater Soviet interest in Egypt's future, and that greater Soviet interest would mean more Soviet aid." Heikal, *The Sphinx and the Commissar: The Rise and Fall of Soviet Influence in the Arab World* (New York: Harper & Row, 1978), p. 243.

9. Edward R. F. Sheehan, *The Arabs, Israelis, and Kissinger: A Secret History of American Diplomacy in the Middle East* (New York: Reader's Digest Press, 1976), p. 19.

10. Hersh, *The Price of Power,* p. 220.

11. Alvin Z. Rubinstein, *Red Star on the Nile: The Soviet-Egyptian Influence Relationship Since the June Wars* (Princeton, N.J.: Princeton University Press, 1977), p. 102; see also Yaacob Bar-Siman-Tov, *The Israeli-Egyptian War of Attrition, 1969–1970: A Case Study of Limited Local Wars* (New York: Columbia University Press, 1980), p. 138.

12. Kissinger, *White House Years,* p. 569.

13. *Ibid.* The movement surely began sometime before this, probably in late February. Nasser's speech on July 23, 1970 (as reported in Rubinstein, *Red Star on the Nile,* p. 107), confirms this chronology. He said the Soviets had promised him in late January that "the support we required would reach us in no more than 30 days. The Soviet Union kept its promise." Additionally, Saad El Shazly, Chief of Staff of the Egyptian Armed Forces, cites February as the start of the Soviet arrival, though he does not say when. See *The Crossing of the Suez* (San Francisco: American Mideast Research, 1980), p. 13. *The New York Times* reported the Soviet presence two days after Kissinger was told of it on March 17 (Kissinger, *White House Years,* p. 569). The authors incline to the view that the Russian move was directly provoked by Israel's conduct and made in response to it.

14. Bar-Siman-Tov, *The Israeli-Egyptian War of Attrition,* p. 153. As Dayan admitted, "Since Israel is dealing not only with SA-2s but with the Soviets, I want to state in all simplicity that we have no capability for an all-out confrontation with the Soviet Union. If the USSR decides to enter into the Middle East conflict 'fully' and if the USA fails to restrain it and refuses to help Israel, we shall be in a very difficult situation." *The New York Times,* March 19, 1970.

15. Kissinger, *White House Years,* p. 606.

16. The Americans, less wisely, were encouraging the growth of an Israeli arms industry.

17. Henry Kissinger, *Years of Upheaval* (Boston: Little, Brown, 1982), p. 222.

18. In May 1971, Sadat had dismissed his foreign minister, Ali Sabry, when he learned that he had been sounding out the Soviets for a possible revolt. Sabry was an advocate of aggressive war, and in part, Sadat's decision to embark on conflict was an endeavor to appease the hawks.

19. The respected military analyst Anthony Cordesman explained in a memo sent to the authors that

> Israel never was able to develop a full understanding either of the meaning of President's Sadat's ascent to power upon the death of Nasser on September 26, 1970, or the rise to power in Syria of Hafez al Assad on October 18, 1970. This lack

of understanding was to prove critical in shaping Arab success in achieving strategic surprise in October, 1973. Virtually all sources show that Israel had all the proper warning indicated, but failed either to monitor properly the meaning of the detailed changes in air force structures between 1970 and 1973, or to understand Sadat's and Assad's intention in spite of several exercises that were near rehearsals for their later attacks.

20. Kissinger, *Years of Upheaval,* p. 619.

21. *Ibid.,* p. 622.

22. *Ibid.,* p. 641.

23. *Ibid.,* p. 759. Letter dated December 13, 1973.

24. Kissinger, *Years of Upheaval,* p. 1052.

25. *Commentary,* Vol. LIX, no. 1 (January 1975).

26. "Seizing Arab Oil," *Harper's* (March 1975), pp. 45–62. (Widely attributed to Professor Edward Luttwak.)

27. Because they feared that the presence of the Syrian population would put pressure on the Israelis to yield the adjacent farms, which had once been cultivated by the city's inhabitants.

28. The authors visited the city in 1985, noting that every house had had explosive charges set off next to each supporting pillar so the cement roof fell flat onto the floor. They also noted the single 50-caliber machine-gun bullet hole in the center of each marble slab where it had once been attached to the hospital walls. Everywhere there are signs of systematic looting and destruction. Israel denies responsibility and claims that Syria is using the city (which has been left as the Syrians claim they found it) as a means to damage Israel's reputation. They also claim that Syria's failure to reconstruct the city is proof of Syria's hostile military intentions. They overlook the fact that Israel is in all probability responsible for most of the damage; the Syrians have a perfect right to cash in on the propaganda windfall Israel has furnished them. Such conduct on the part of the Israelis is prohibited by Geneva Convention IV, Article 50.

29. Matti Golan, *The Secret Conversations of Henry Kissinger* (New York: Quadrangle Books, 1976), pp. 229–30. See also *Ha'aretz,* December 17, 1974.

30. See *The New York Times,* March 28, 1975. When Foreign Minister Allon arrived in Washington on March 21, he laid out Israel's position on the Egyptian negotiations before President Ford and Secretary Kissinger. Foreseeing the rejection of the Israeli and Egyptian proposals and counterproposals, Kissinger went to Israel to see if he could speed up the process. Israel's policies would, he warned, simply result in driving Egypt and other Arab nations into alliance with the Soviets, while United States–Israeli relations would be severely strained. He also reminded the Israelis that the Egyptian leader had offered to pledge "non-use of force," which was as near as he could safely move toward a commitment to nonbelligerency.

31. *U.S. Overseas Loans and Grants and Assistance from International Organizations,* July 1, 1945–September 30, 1977, p. 19.

## CHAPTER FIVE

1. Clinton, Mass.: "Remarks on a Question and Answer Session at the Clinton Town Meeting," March 16, 1977, *Public Papers: Carter,* 1977, Vol. I, p. 387.

2. Flapan, *Zionism and the Palestinians,* p. 116.

3. Silver, *Begin: The Haunted Prophet,* pp. 71, 74–80, 88–96.

4. *Ibid.,* p. 79.

5. *Ibid.,* p. 45.

6. "A Framework for Middle East Peace: Shaping a More Stable World," *Department of State Bulletin,* vol. 77 (July 11, 1977), p. 45.

7. The Arabs, after years of experience, have since come to the conclusion that it is useless trying to back the Israelis into a corner, since the United States will avoid confrontation with the Israelis.

8. William B. Quandt, *Camp David: Peacemaking and Politics* (Washington, D.C.: Brookings Institution, 1987), p. 72.

9. "U.S. Statement on the Middle East," *The New York Times,* June 28, 1977.

10. Simultaneously, the U.S. government made substantial preparations for a revived Geneva Conference. Secretary Vance favored a single Arab delegation, despite Sadat's dubiety and Israel's well-known dislike for the idea.

11. Begin's reply was to deliver an encomium of the U.S. ambassador to Israel, Samuel W. Lewis.

12. Israeli overflights of Arab territory were routine into the 1980s, so the authors were told in 1985 during their visit to the Middle East. Only protests to the United States finally forced Israel to stop overflying Jordan in 1984. Such flights were justified by Israel on the ground of its security needs—further proof that Israel has no regard for anyone's security or feelings, except its own.

13. Quandt, *Camp David,* p. 80.

14. Ignoring Begin's known rigidities as an ideologue, Carter convinced himself that the Israeli position was simply a bargaining ploy, which would ultimately be modified in negotiations.

15. No less than $107 million in foreign military sales credits had been allowed for the Mekerva "Chariot" tank.

16. Cyrus Vance, *Hard Choices: Critical Years in America's Foreign Policy* (New York: Simon & Schuster, 1983), p. 186.

17. Quandt, *Camp David,* pp. 86–87, Letter from President Carter to Secretary of State Vance, July 30, 1977.

18. Quandt, *Camp David,* pp. 88–91.

19. This did not square with the fact that there are numerous cases of countries not at war with one another who do not have diplomatic relations.

20. See Moshe Dayan, *Breakthrough: A Personal Account of the Egypt-Israel Peace Negotiations* (New York: Alfred A. Knopf, 1981), p. 25. Also see Quandt, *Camp David,* p. 92. Dayan makes no mention in his book of Begin's autonomy or citizenship proposals.

21. Vance, *Hard Choices,* pp. 191–92.

22. "U.S., U.S.S.R. Issue Statement on the Middle East," *Department of State Bulletin,* vol. 77 (November 7, 1977), pp. 639–40. This statement was officially issued in New York City.

23. Brzezinski, *Power and Principle,* p. 110; Jimmy Carter, *Keeping Faith: Memoirs of a President* (New York: Bantam Books, 1982), p. 293; and Vance, *Hard Choices,* pp. 191–92.

24. Geneva Peace Conference on the Middle East: United States-Israel Joint Statement issued following a meeting between the President and Israeli Foreign Minister Moshe Dayan, October 5, 1977, *Public Papers: Carter,* 1977, Vol. II, p. 1728.

25. See Martin Indyk, *To the Ends of the Earth: Sadat's Jerusalem Initiative* (Cambridge, Mass.: Harvard University, Center for Middle Eastern Studies, 1984), pp. 41–43.

26. The Carter government was unwilling to invoke the principle established in 1888 when the British ambassador, Sir Lionel Sackville-West, was declared persona non grata for telling a British subject who also had American citizenship for whom he should vote in the election that year.

27. Quandt, *Camp David,* p. 157.

28. Brzezinski, *Power and Principle,* pp. 115–20.

29. Quandt, *Camp David,* pp. 164–65.

30. Carter, *Keeping Faith,* pp. 306–08.

31. "The President's news conference of March 9, 1978," *Public Papers: Carter,* 1978, Vol. I, pp. 491–94.

32. Ezer Weizman, *Battle for Peace* (New York: Bantam Books, 1981), pp. 260–62.

33. See Don Oberdorfer, "Carter's Summary of Begin's Stand Is Bleak," *The Washington Post,* March 26, 1978.

34. Shortly before the Camp David meeting, the senior author had dinner with the President. The author made his standard plea that the President at all costs avoid a bilateral deal between Israel and Egypt since that would greatly diminish the chances of ever reaching a fair settlement of the much more important Palestinian issue. The President stated with great conviction that he was well aware of the problem and that he would keep Begin and Sadat at Camp David as long as necessary, since he also recognized the paramountcy of a Palestinian settlement.

35. Quandt, *Camp David,* pp. 207–08.

36. All this fitted in with the long-term schemes of Begin's advisers, Moshe Dayan (foreign minister) and Ezer Weizman (defense minister), who were both eager to make a separate deal with Egypt with as little linkage to the other Occupied Areas as could be decently managed.

37. Quandt, *Camp David,* p. 219.

38. *Ibid.,* pp. 241–42.

39. Sadat did not help matters by telling the press on September 19 that there was to be a three-month freeze, and that Israel had also agreed not to expand settlements during this period. Since the Egyptian president had not been present during Begin and Carter's discussions, he was in no position to discuss the subject, and later Israeli efforts to cite Sadat in proof of their own position can scarcely be viewed as valid.

40. On September 27, 1978, Begin showed the American ambassador, Samuel Lewis, notes purported to have been taken by Israeli Attorney General Barak, which disclosed that Begin had not agreed to give Carter a firm commitment on a freeze, but had merely said he would "consider" such a step.

41. *Facts on File,* 1949, March 17, 1978, p. 173.

42. The Soviets and China abstained because of dissatisfaction with the particulars of the plan, as did the Soviets' satellite, Czechoslovakia.

43. The details of this incident were confirmed in a telephone call by the senior author to Ambassador Viets on April 2, 1992.

44. *Facts on File,* 1978, p. 256.

45. Cluster bombs, known as CBUs (cluster bomb units), are anti-personnel weapons consisting of a number of small bombs housed in a canister. On impact, the bombs explode individually, each scattering more than two hundred diamond-shaped pieces of shrapnel over a wide area. They are widely regarded as a particularly inhumane weapon.

46. *Facts on File,* 1978, p. 256.

47. *Ibid.* It had been reported that Israeli front-line officers had used the bombs indiscriminately on refugee camps and other civilian targets in Lebanon. In answering these charges, the Israeli military spokesman had claimed that the weapons had been used against enemy "artillery" units and field positions.

48. *Facts on File,* 1978, p. 300. As no American weapons were to be used for offensive purposes, this defense is questionable at least.

49. *Facts on File,* 1978, p. 462.

## CHAPTER SIX

1. Ronald Reagan, "Recognizing the Israeli Asset," *The Washington Post,* August 15, 1979, p. 25. "Reagan also chided the administration for attempting to sell weapons and military hardware to Israel's enemies, saying he was 'appalled' by the U.S. decision to abstain from voting on, rather than veto, a United Nations resolution condemning Israel for its declaration that all of Jerusalem was its capital." *Facts on File,* September 3, 1980, p. 681.

2. Seth Tillman, *The United States in the Middle East* (Bloomington, Ind.: Indiana University Press, 1982), pp. 36, 227.

3. Harold H. Saunders, *The Middle East Problem in the 1980's* (Washington, D.C.: American Enterprise Institute for Public Policy Research, 1981), p. 8.

4. Blitzer, *Between Washington and Jerusalem,* p. 61.

5. *U.S. Overseas Loans and Grants and Assistance from International Organizations Obligations and Loan Authorizations, July 1, 1945–September 30, 1988,* p. 18, "Israel."

6. Ronnie Dugger, *On Reagan: The Man and His Presidency* (New York: McGraw-Hill, 1983), p. 277.

7. See A. Craig Murphy, "Congressional Opposition to Arms Sales to Saudi Arabia," *American-Arab Affairs,* no. 24 (Spring 1988), p. 106.

8. Rubenberg, *Israel and the American National Interest,* p. 258. The narrow victories of Senators Symms of Idaho (1986) and Chafee of Rhode Island (1988) illustrate this point.

9. If possible Israel chooses a time when urgent events elsewhere are distracting the attention of key Western leaders. Examples of this have been the 1956 Sinai campaign during the Hungarian revolt; the annexation of the Golan in 1981 during the Polish crisis; and the 1982 Lebanese invasion during the Versailles economic summit meeting.

10. The United States does not have any principled objection to the use of military or economic pressure against other nations; indeed, it routinely uses these against nations such as Nicaragua and Libya. Pressure is a standard part of any powerful nation's diplomatic repertoire. But in this, as in all else, the deviation from standard practice in favor of Israel is based on pure political expediency.

11. Quoted in Straus, "Israel's New Superlobby in Washington: Reagan and Co.," *The Washington Post,* April 27, 1986, "Outlook." If the Americans miss their cue, the Israeli ambassador makes the same comment for them.

12. Note the Mondale speech during the Carter administration, and the statements after the various conflicts noted in Chapters 1–6.

13. Tillman, *The United States in the Middle East,* p. 170.

14. Silver, *Begin: The Haunted Prophet,* p. 254. Half the settlers were emplaced during the two years of the Reagan administration.

15. Carter's only exception to this policy came in 1980, when he allowed the sale of less advanced Kfirs to Mexico, Venezuela, and Columbia. *Facts on File,* 1980, p. 865.

16. *Facts on File,* March 13, 1981, p. 152; March 27, 1981, p. 188.

17. The French had furnished Iraq with enriched uranium, but not a reactor suitable for nuclear weapons production. Iranian planes may have raided the facility in November 1980, and there had been various acts of sabotage, probably of Israeli origin, prior to the installation of the reactor.

18. Andrew and Leslie Cockburn, *Dangerous Liaison* (New York: HarperCollins), 1991, pp. 173–74. There were stories at the time that the Soviet Union sent a ship with nuclear materials on board to Alexandria in Egypt and then recalled the vessel after the war.

19. *Facts on File,* June 12, 1981, p. 386.

20. *Facts on File,* June 12, 1981, pp. 385–87.

21. *Facts on File,* June 26, 1981, p. 436.

22. *Facts on File,* July 29, 1988, pp. 510–11.

23. *Facts on File,* August 21, 1981, p. 592.

24. *Facts on File,* September 11, 1981, p. 648.

25. *Facts on File,* November 25, 1981, p. 686.

26. *Facts on File,* December 18, 1981, p. 925.

27. *Facts on File,* December 18, 1981, p. 924.

28. Institute for Palestine Studies, International Documents on Palestine, 1981, pp. 429–31.

29. Israeli-American relations were not improved by another incident involving press exposure of an alleged Libyan plot to assassinate President Reagan. It was a sensation for a day or two, then, on investigation, was traced to an Israeli source. Besides exposing inef-

fective American intelligence operations and our nation's self-imposed dependence on Israel, it also disclosed Mossad's incompetence and the administration's credulity in failing to verify information from Israeli sources before rushing into print. (*Facts on File,* December 18, 1981, p. 926.) Begin's comment on Congress's pandering to the American Greeks' hatred for Turkey simply illustrates, in another sphere, the undesirability of American citizens backing foreign governments in their quarrels with other nations.

30. *Facts on File,* December 25, 1981, p. 949.

31. Amnon Kapeliuk, "Begin and the 'Beasts,'" *New Statesman,* June 25, 1982, reprinted in *The Israeli Invasion of Lebanon, Press Profile: June/July 1982* (New York: Claremont Research and Publications, 1982), p. 93. See also Noam Chomsky, *The Fateful Triangle: The United States, Israel and the Palestinians* (Boston: South End Press, 1983), pp. 198–201; *The Washington Post,* July 15, 1982.

32. *Ha'aretz,* June 25, 1982.

33. Henry Kamin in *The New York Times,* July 11, 1982.

34. The official Kahane Report, made after the Sabra and Shatilla killings, stated that "the subject of the Palestinian population in Lebanon, from among whom the terrorist operations sprang up and in the midst of whom their military infrastructure was entrenched, came up more than once in meetings between Phalangist leaders and Israeli representatives. The position of the Phalangist leaders . . . was, in general, that no unified and independent Lebanese state could be established without a solution being found to the problem of the Palestinian refugees who numbered half a million people. In the opinion of the Phalangists, that number of refugees, for the most part Moslems, endangered . . . the stability of the state of Lebanon and the status of the Christians in that country. Therefore, the Phalangist leaders proposed removing a large portion of the Palestinian refugees from Lebanese soil, whether by methods of persuasion or other means of pressure. They did not conceal their opinion that it would be necessary to resort to acts of violence in order to cause the exodus of many Palestinian refugees from Lebanon." The report contains no evidence that the Israeli representatives dissented from this view. Quoted in *The Israeli Invasion of Lebanon, Part II. Press Profile: August 1982/May 1983* (New York: Claremont Research and Publications, 1983), p. 205.

35. Ze'ev Schiff, *Ha'aretz,* May 23, 1982.

36. Yoel Marcus, "The War Is Inevitable," *Ha'aretz,* May 23, 1982.

37. Superseding his father "as the military and political leader of the Phalange," Bashir "enjoyed unimpeachable authority." Israel maintained close relations with the Phalange through the Israeli equivalent of the American CIA, the Mossad (the Institute for Intelligence and Special Assignments). Israel guaranteed the security of the Phalange and provided it with arms, uniforms, and training. Bashir Gemayel originally approached the Israelis for help against the Syrians. The history of the discussions that followed is contained in Ze'ev Schiff and Ehud Ya'ari, *Israel's Lebanon War,* ed. and trans. by Ina Friedman (New York: Simon & Schuster, 1984), pp. 31–61.

38. Marcus, "The War Is Inevitable."

39. Benny Morris, "Diligent Diarist" (review of David Ben-Gurion's Diaries), *The Jerusalem Post,* International Edition, April 22–28, 1984, p. 19.

40. Moshe Sharett, *Personal Diary,* p. 1024, quoted in Livia Rokach, *Israel's Sacred Terrorism* (Belmont, Mass.: Association of Arab-American University Graduates, 1980, AAUG Information Paper Series no. 23), pp. 28–29.

41. Ze'ev Schiff, "Green Light, Lebanon," *Foreign Policy,* no. 50 (Spring 1983), pp. 73–85. This plan had been hatched in discussions over a long number of years. The background is described in Jonathan C. Randal, *Going All the Way: Christian Warlords, Israeli Adventurers, and the War in Lebanon* (New York: Viking Press, 1983).

42. Alexander M. Haig, Jr., *Caveat: Realism, Reagan, and Foreign Policy* (New York: Macmillan, 1984), p. 326.

43. *Ibid.,* p. 332. Very few PLO personnel were killed on these occasions. Since the

PLO leadership had learned not to stay more than twelve hours in any one place, it was generally their innocent neighbors who were killed. PLO offices under these circumstances consisted of a telephone, a few chairs, tables, and a filing cabinet. *Facts on File,* 1982, June 11, 1982, p. 414.

44. *Ibid.,* p. 330.

45. *Ibid.*

46. Haig, *Caveat,* pp. 330–35. *Facts on File,* June 4, 1982, p. 380.

47. Schiff and Ya'ari, *Israel's Lebanon War,* p. 31. The authors report that when Begin made a trip to Washington during the second week of the war, the White House was known to be unhappy that the IDF had entered Beirut. Still Haig insisted on arranging a visit between Begin and the President, advising Begin in advance of the meeting, "Hold out for what you want." As the meeting concluded and the participants took their leave, Haig was seen to give Begin a surreptitious thumbs-up sign (p. 202).

48. *Ibid.,* p. 98.

49. A high Israeli aide later admitted in Washington that Israeli pronouncements on the invasion had been "perhaps misleading." *Facts on File,* 1982, pp. 413–14, 475.

50. Schiff, "Green Light, Lebanon," p. 79.

51. Schiff and Ya'ari, *Israel's Lebanon War,* p. 229.

52. Robert Fisk, *The Times* (London), October 7, 1982, p. 32.

53. *Newsweek,* February 20, 1984, p. 47.

54. Schiff and Ya'ari, *Israel's Lebanon War,* p. 225.

55. *Facts on File,* August 13, 1982, p. 583.

56. William Espinoza and Les Janka, *Defense or Aggression? U.S. Export Control Laws and the Israeli Invasion of Lebanon* (Washington, D.C.: American Educational Trust, n.d.), pp. 15–16.

57. T. Elaine Carrey, *Christian Science Monitor,* August 19, 1982. See also Warren Richey, *Christian Science Monitor,* November 2, 1981.

58. *Facts on File,* October 1, 1983, p. 715. One may safely assume the prohibition was for the Arab consumption.

59. *Facts on File,* December 2, 1983, p. 901.

60. *Christian Science Monitor,* July 21, 1982.

61. Prepared statement of George W. Ball before the Senate Foreign Relations Committee, July 15, 1982. The role of a peacekeeper should be to interpose its forces between the contending parties and thus stop the fighting. For obvious reasons that role is appropriate only for nations which have no special interests in the area or special relations with any of the contending parties. That, by definition, excludes the superpowers.

62. Report of the Sub-Committee of the Committee on Arms Services, House of Representatives, 98th Congress, 1st Session, entitled "Adequacy of U.S. Marine Corps Security in Beirut," p. 25.

63. Schiff and Ya'ari, *Israel's Lebanon War,* pp. 224–25. This action was taken to give the Israelis a freer hand. The Israelis believed their own propaganda that large numbers of PLO fighters had stayed behind disguised as civilians in the refugee camps. Sharon proposed to solve this problem by combing through the camps and seizing any suspects the army located. He would find this awkward if the international force were still in position.

64. *The New York Times,* September 10, 1982. See also William B. Quandt, "Reagan's Lebanon Policy: Trial and Error," *The Middle East Journal,* vol. XXXVIII, no. 2 (Spring 1984), p. 239. It has been claimed that this initiative was the result of American embarrassment over the Israeli campaign and a desire to make amends. But since no embarrassment was displayed until after the Sabra and Shatilla massacres, which took place some days later, the plan had other origins. Meron Benvenisti, *The West Bank Data Project: A Survey of Israel's Policies* (Washington, D.C.: American Enterprise Institute for Public Policy Research, 1984), p. 66.

65. Quandt, "Reagan's Lebanon Policy," p. 239.

66. *Facts on File,* September 10, 1982, p. 658.
67. *Facts on File,* September 10, 1982, pp. 657ff.
68. *Ibid.*

CHAPTER SEVEN

1. *Facts on File,* September 17, 1982, pp. 673–74.
2. Milton Viorst, "America's Broken Pledge to the PLO," *The Washington Post,* December 19, 1982; see also Chomsky, *The Fateful Triangle,* pp. 388, 389. The Reagan administration's lack of real concern about these massacres is neatly illustrated by an incident that took place in 1987. Israel appointed General Amos Yaron to Canada as its military attaché to Ottawa. Because he was among those named by the official Israeli report as responsible for these murders, the Canadian government declined to receive him on March 4. The United States, however, had already received him with open arms for the same position in Washington in 1986, only to be embarrassed when the general was targeted in a court suit asking for his arrest as a war criminal and that, in accordance with international law, he be stripped of his diplomatic immunity. Embarrassed, Israel recalled him as soon as the suit was quashed.
3. Thomas L. Friedman, *From Beirut to Jerusalem* (New York: Farrar, Straus & Giroux, 1989), p. 164.
4. *Ibid.,* pp. 166–67.
5. *Ibid.,* pp. 164–65. See also *The Commission of Inquiry into the Events at the Refugee Camps in Beirut—1983—Final Report (Kahan Chan Report).* Reprinted in *The Israeli Invasion of Lebanon: Part II, Press Profile* (August 1982–May 1983), p. 206, Col. 2. If one remembers the Israeli-Gemayel discussions in 1982 about ways to force the Palestinians out of Lebanon, one need not be paranoid to detect in these massacres an attempted repeat of Deir Yassin, which caused the Palestinians to flee into exile. The carnage at the Lebanese refugee camps failed in its desired effect only because there was now nowhere for the Palestinians to go.
6. Press Conference, September 28, 1983, *Facts on File,* p. 715.
7. Friedman, *From Beirut to Jerusalem,* pp. 503–04.
8. Patrick Seale, *Assad: The Struggle for the Middle East* (Berkeley: University of California Press, 1988), pp. 383–86, 407. Assad felt double-crossed because the Israelis had continued their attacks after the cease fire was to commence. Pagnelli was promptly fired for his unwelcome advice.
9. *Nahum Barnea Koteret Rashit,* May 11, 1983, in *The Israeli Invasion of Lebanon: Part II,* p. 352.
10. Seale, *Assad,* p. 408.
11. *Facts on File,* May 20, 1983, pp. 357–59.
12. *Facts on File,* June 10, 1983, p. 425.
13. *Facts on File,* March 18, 1983, p. 184.
14. *Facts on File,* February 10, 1984, p. 82.
15. *Facts on File,* February 27, 1984, p. 109.
16. *Facts on File,* October 28, 1983, pp. 818–19. Congressional resistance would have prevented such a scheme in any case.
17. It was subsequently reported in a book by Victor Ostrovsky, *By Way of Deception,* that Israel knew of the impending Shia attack on the Americans and provided no warning—*Newsweek,* September 24, 1990, p. 33. The Italian members of the peacekeeping force, who confined themselves to their UN mission, were left alone and departed later amid the flowers and tears of the Lebanese, whom they had honestly sought to protect.
18. *Facts on File,* October 26, 1983, pp. 809, 813–14.
19. As is described in Chapter 11, no country until then had ever been exempted from

the requirement that military aid funds be used exclusively for the purchase of American weapons. That exception set a precedent, which other nations exploited.

20. *Facts on File,* December 2, 1983, pp. 901–02.

21. *Facts on File,* March 16, 1984, p. 182.

22. See the diary of Israeli Lt. Col. Dov Yermiya, *My War Diary: Israel in Lebanon,* trans. by Hillel Schenker (London: Pluto Press, 1983), in which he vividly describes the IDF's mistreatment of the Shias, the Israelis' indifference to anyone's feelings but their own, and their persistent violation of generally accepted modes of conduct.

23. Congress, in 1985, had not only codified that constraint in statutory form but had also expanded the restriction by adding that the PLO must also formally renounce terrorism. It was intended that this would keep the PLO out of the diplomatic picture.

24. Yehoshafat Harkabi, *Israel's Fateful Hour,* trans. by Lenn Schramm (New York: Harper & Row, 1988), pp. 213–14. This scandal came to light when Von Hontig, a minor German diplomat who had served in Athens prior to the German invasion in 1941, inconsiderately published his memoirs.

25. *Facts on File,* September 7, 1990, p. 666. The case is discussed *in extenso* in Robert I. Freedman, *The False Prophet: Rabbi Meir Kahane—From FBI Informant to Knesset Member* (Brooklyn, N.Y.: Lawrence Hill Books, 1990).

26. See Kathleen Christison, "The Arab-Israeli Policy of George Shultz," *Journal of Palestine Studies,* vol. XVIII, no. 2 (Winter 1989), pp. 29–47.

27. *Facts on File,* February 24, 1988, p. 124.

28. *Facts on File,* April 8, 1988, p. 233. Not surprisingly, Israel's state-run television denied Shultz's request to include Arabic as well as Hebrew subtitles on his April 3 broadcast so he could speak to the 2.2 million Palestinians under Israeli rule. Nor was he more successful in Jordan. The Jordanian government refused to air an April 5 interview with Shultz, because they regarded as insulting his defense of Israeli security needs, his assertion that the PLO could not join in any talks, and his repudiation of the U.S. commitment to Hussein that Resolution 242 required Israel to return practically all the Occupied Territories to Jordan. The Jordanians were particularly incensed by Shultz's demands that Jordan make heavy territorial sacrifices for peace, while asking no sacrifices of any kind from Israel.

29. *The Washington Post,* March 30, 1988. Nor was the Palestinians' cause advanced when the Assistant Secretary of State for Human Rights and Humanitarian Affairs, Richard Shifter, testified on March 29 at a congressional hearing that, "in our view, Israel clearly has not only the right but the obligation to preserve or restore order in the occupied territories and to use appropriate levels of forces [*sic*] to accomplish that end."

30. *The Washington Post,* April 20, 1989.

31. *Facts on File,* April 29, 1988, p. 298.

32. *Facts on File,* December 25, 1987, p. 954. Also March 11, 1988, p. 156; April 1, 1988, p. 216; April 29, 1988, p. 298; and September 16, 1988, p. 671. The final ruling came June 29; the appeal lapsed sixty days later. While the public watched the *Intifada,* Congress moved to close the PLO Information Office in Washington and to expel the PLO Observer Mission at the UN in New York. Preempting the Congress, the State Department unilaterally imposed diplomatic status on the PLO Washington office and then closed it. Though the PLO lost its court suit, it was offered refuge as a suboffice of the Arab League, which the Congress and administration dared not attack directly.

The Justice Department then moved to expel the PLO Mission in New York. On March 2, 1988, the UN General Assembly, by a vote of 143–1, adopted two resolutions; the first provided that the closing was a breach of the 1947 agreement between the UN and the United States, while the second invoked the mandatory arbitration provisions of the agreement by seeking a ruling of the International Court of Justice. The United States initially responded that the reference was moot, since it had not yet taken any action, then discarded this defense on March 11 when it ordered the office closed. On March 22, the United

States filed suit against the PLO Observer Office, and the next day the Assembly firmly reprimanded the United States. On April 26, the International Court ruled the American proceedings unlawful, but the administration, copying Israel's contempt for international rules or opinions, announced it would ignore that decision. However, it could not ignore Federal District Judge Edmund L. Palmieri's formal ruling on April 12 that the agreement was binding and the Justice Department's suit illegal. Fearing a more definitive opinion from a higher court, and confronted by State and Justice Department wrangling on the subject, the U.S. government decided on August 29 not to appeal. Thus the PLO Observer Office at the UN continued to operate. See *Facts on File,* 1988, pp. 156, 216, 299, and 671.

33. The schemes failed primarily because the Secretary was unable—and, indeed, unwilling—to compel the Israelis to agree to any terms that the King could possibly defend to other Arab leaders.

34. From the Israeli viewpoint, this threatened a number of unsatisfactory results. Contrary to the claim advanced by Israel that the UN was ineffective, the UN was now playing a useful role. A rash of peace sickness in Angola, the Sahara, and elsewhere followed. Then the Soviets declared the intention to pay off their peacekeeping arrears to the UN, leaving the United States in the unedifying position of being chief non-dues-paying delinquent. Still worse, the long-predicted end of the Iran-Iraq War found the Israelis unprepared. They had backed Iran (which was not thankful for the aid), while in the process they had antagonized Iraq by their attack on its atomic reactor. Israelis suddenly feared that Iraq's veteran million-man army might now become available to join in the war against Israel. Fortunately, the Iraq Army proved in 1991 to be totally unready for modern warfare.

35. Since the Orthodox proposed to declare all conversions except by their own rabbis as invalid, the predominantly Reform and Conservative American Jews were mortally insulted. Yet their intervention in the affairs of Israel was resented by the Israelis, who failed to see the importance of the whole question from the American view. Since they were directly or indirectly furnishing Israel with an indispensable subsidy from their own pockets and those of the American taxpayers, the American Diaspora in turn resented Israel's resentment.

36. *Facts on File,* November 18, 1988, pp. 849–50; December 2, 1988, p. 887; December 15, 1988, p. 925.

37. Through AIPAC and sympathizers, and particularly through the efforts of Jewish members of congressional staffs led by Richard Perle, they had forced the adoption of the so-called "Jackson-Vanik Amendment." That act had the effect of making Soviet trade with America almost impossible, since it would deny most favored nation treatment to Soviet exports and therefore subject them to prohibitive tariff rates.

38. If anyone were under the impression that this negotiation was going to produce anything, they were speedily disillusioned by Secretary Baker's answer to a press question: "Mr. Secretary, why was the idea of an international peace conference dropped for the regional conference, which bypasses the international forum of the U.N.?"

> [Baker] "The primary reason is because we want to develop and create a process that will work. No one can impose peace in this situation. Peace will only come if the parties are determined to make it happen. It can't be imposed by the United Nations. It can't be imposed by the United States. It can't be imposed by the Soviet Union. It can't be imposed by a collection of all these entities, organizations and countries and a whole lot more." Foreign Broadcast Information Service, *Near East & South Asia,* April 22, 1991, NES-91-007, p. 39.

## CHAPTER EIGHT

1. Efforts in the fall of 1987 to secure a written constitution based on a draft drawn up by a distinguished group of law professors was defeated in the Knesset by a vote of 80 to

15. Most ministers were opposed because it would restrict their powers. But it is still ironic that men like Shamir, who was deported under the British rules, see nothing wrong with them now that they control the levers of power.

2. Quoted in Ze'ev Schiff, *A History of the Israeli Army, 1974 to the Present* (New York: Macmillan, 1985), p. 59.

3. *Ibid.*

4. Nathan Glazer and Daniel Patrick Moynihan, *Beyond the Melting Pot: The Negroes, Puerto Ricans, Jews, Italians and Irish of New York City* (Cambridge, Mass.: MIT Press, 1963).

5. Arthur Koestler, *The Thirteenth Tribe: The Khazar Empire and Its Heritage* (New York: Random House, 1976), pp. 223–24. Koestler denies that the absence of any biological connection with the ancient Jews constitutes a barrier to Jewish residence in modern Israel.

6. *Ibid.,* pp. 58–82, 181–200. Koestler also denies that there is any such thing as a Jewish race. The terms "Oriental" and "Sephardic" most precisely refer, respectively, to "eastern" Asian and African Jews and to Jews of the ethnic culture and Latino language rooted in fifteenth-century Spain. In this book we have used the words "Sephardic" and "Oriental" interchangeably. See Asher Arian, *Politics in Israel: The Second Generation* (Chatham, N.J.: Chatham House, 1985), p. 22.

7. Paul Johnson, *A History of the Jews* (New York: Harper & Row, 1987), p. 529. It should be noted that nearly half of these 252, 642 came from Morocco, which did not drive its Jews out. Iraq paid inadequate compensation for some property; the others none at all.

8. Sammy Smooha, *Israel: Pluralism and Conflict* (Berkeley: University of California Press, 1978), pp. 86–87, 281.

9. *Ibid.,* p. 281. Because of the disproportionate number of children, however, the voting power of the two groups remained roughly even until the 1980s. See Peter Grose, *A Changing Israel* (New York: Vintage Books, 1985), p. 24.

10. Smooha, *Israel,* p. 87.

11. Quoted in *ibid.,* p. 88. Similar sentiment was expressed by Golda Meir: "We have immigrants from Morocco, Libya, Iran, Egypt, and other countries with a Sixteenth Century level. Shall we be able to elevate these immigrants to a suitable level of civilization? If the present state of affairs continues, there will be a dangerous clash between the Ashkenazim, who will constitute an elite, and the Oriental communities of Israel. This is the most tragic thing that can befall us." Quoted in Nissam Rejwan, "The Two Israels: A Study in Europecentism," *Judaism,* vol. XVI, no. 1 (1967), pp. 97–108.

12. Arian, *Politics in Israel,* p. 24.

13. Central Bureau of Statistics, *Statistical Abstracts of Israel* (Jerusalem: Government Printer, 1985), p. 610.

14. Grose, *A Changing Israel,* pp. 36–38; Smooha, *Israel,* p. 137.

15. CBS, *Statistical Abstracts,* 1985, pp. 341–42.

16. CBS, *Statistical Abstracts,* 1985, p. 295.

17. Meron Benvenisti, *Conflicts and Contradictions* (New York: Villard, 1986), p. 151. There was a joke in Israel in 1985, which illustrates this point. A grandmother was telling her grandchildren about their grandfather's backbreaking toil to help build the new nation. "But Grandma," the grandchildren protested, "we didn't know that Grandpa was an Arab!"

While the Sephardim prefer the present system, the Ashkenazis favor Orientals filling the low-status jobs. Sammy Smooha describes the situation: "Since . . . the turn of the last century, the Jews have insisted on a Jewish society and economy and have taken various measures to avoid dependence on Arab labour, and to prevent the creation of a split labor market of unequal wages and work conditions." Smooha, *Israel,* p. 245.

18. From *The Land of Israel* as cited in Benvenisti, *Conflicts and Contradictions* p. 150. See *The Jerusalem Post,* International Edition, November 14, 1987, p. 3, regarding plans

for funds to be allocated to teach Israeli youth the merits of coexistence with the Arabs.

19. Benvenisti, *Conflicts and Contradictions,* pp. 209–10. The Black Panthers (Moroccan youths) at the lowest end of the economic ladder (many with criminal records) started in March 1971 a series of demonstrations which lasted a year. They demanded better education, standard housing, and greater public support for large families. In the end they were suppressed.

20. Arian, *Politics in Israel,* pp. 139–40.

21. There is a street in Ashdod named after Mohammed V, which caused a riot by other anti-Arab Sephardim.

22. Quoted by Smooha, *Israel,* p. 103. This suggests that the Ashkenazi also have a racist view of the Arabs, which they at least take some pains to conceal.

23. Roberta Straus Feuerlicht, *The Fate of the Jews: A People Torn Between Israeli Power and Jewish Ethics* (New York: Times Books, 1983), pp. 236–41. The American Jews, she has written, "regard their contributions to Israel as premiums on an insurance policy, guaranteeing them a home if they are ever forced to leave America" (p. 241). Israel's neglect and harassment of the Falashas casts doubt on this assumption.

24. These groups, plus the Arab minority, constitute a majority in Jerusalem. Thus, there is an anti-Zionist majority in the Zionist capital.

25. Arian, *Politics in Israel,* p. 87.

26. Quoted in *American University,* 1979, p. 74.

27. Smooha, *Israel,* p. 213. This intolerant intrusion into the daily lives of the Jewish Israelis has had two serious effects. First, Israel has no constitution. A major reason for this anomaly was that the Israeli founding fathers in 1948–49 were unable to formulate acceptable legal phraseology regarding religion to meet the diametrically opposed demands of the ultra-Orthodox and the secular Jews. The religious parties thus maintain the hope that they may ultimately have the opportunity to adopt a constitution which imposes their views.

Second, as the first step toward an intolerant, theocratic state, a bitter battle has been waged to elevate Orthodox Judaism into the status of being the only recognized form of that faith. The battle lines are drawn over a host of issues, one of which has centered on women's participation on religious boards and their voting for board members. Thus far, the Israel Supreme Court has consistently ruled in favor of female participation, despite Orthodox anti-feminist objectives. *The Jerusalem Post,* International Edition, May 28, 1988, pp. 1, 2.

28. *The New York Times,* February 8, 1987, p. E8.

29. The only Middle East countries with parallel procedures are theocratic Islamic states, such as Saudi Arabia and Iran.

30. *Middle East Times,* February 15 through 21, 1987, p. 4. This sexist remark overlooked the licentious misconduct of male soldiers.

31. The authors have seen the ultra-Orthodox in action in Jerusalem.

32. Such rules were inaugurated by the coalition government, simply because neither the Likud nor the Labor alignment risks offending the Orthodox groups.

33. William Frankel, *Israel observed: An Anatomy of the State* (London: Thames & Hudson, 1980), pp. 217–20. Noting all these trends, *The Jerusalem Post* observed that a great deal of superstitiousness and ritualism seemed to be seeping back into Judaism, with a highly undesirable impact on that faith. It called for an examination of such practices and their speedy abandonment. *The Jerusalem Post,* International Edition, "Perversions," February 4, 1987, as reported January 14, 1987, p. 24.

34. *The Jerusalem Post,* International Edition, January 11, 1986, p. 9. At a time when the ultra-Orthodox were rioting against the Mormons, ninety-six professors published an advertisement in *The Jerusalem Post* asserting that the Mormons were notorious converters of Jews; that they would solicit converts in violation of the law; and that there were many Jews whose commitment to Judaism was so fragile that they must be protected from missionaries. Indeed, the professors claimed that the Mormons constituted a clear and

present danger to the Jewish faith and demanded that they be banished from the country.

35. *Ibid.* Would-be missionaries among the Jews, but not other faiths, are liable to imprisonment and a fine. Such conduct is, of course, a continuing embarrassment to westernized Israelis. But its threat to a cohesion of Israeli society and an effective Israeli government is more significant. The new creation of Orthodox national schools and the expansion of Orthodox influence in civil law bespeak growing Orthodox influence.

36. Quoted in William Frankel, *Israel observed, an Anatomy of the State* (New York: Thames & Hudson, 1981), p. 72. If such trends continue, Israel may ultimately resemble medieval Europe with its host of religious personnel. *The Jerusalem Post,* International Edition February 28, 1987, p. 9.

37. In the long run, Israel faces the hard question as to where it is going religiously. Thus Smooha states: "The non-separation of religion from the state will preserve the monopoly of the orthodox stream of Judaism, halakhic jurisdiction of personal status and other religious legislation, public financing of religious services and the machinery of the Chief Rabbinate, Rabbinic courts and local religious councils." *Israel,* pp. 247–48.

Writing in 1988, Smooha predicted that

> The religious minority for its part, is well organized and is capable of disrupting the system if a major change were to be unilaterally imposed. It is a permanent political force whose interest must be considered. . . . Since about half of the religious vote goes to nonreligious parties, the major Labor and right wing Likud Parties cannot afford to undercut whatever votes they usually obtain from religious Jews. The ongoing process of becoming a floating coalition partner . . . will add to the negotiating power of the religious parties.
>
> On the other hand, the ineffectiveness of the secular majority to oppose Orthodox moves suggests that the Orthodox may yet get their way. Israeli law and Orthodox doctrine have never accepted the principle that one's form of worship is an individual matter, not one to be decided by group or state pressure. For underlying Israel's seeming hyperdemocratic actions . . . is a strong streak of authoritarianism and conformism, accentuated by the lack of deep democratic convictions among the Sephardim, many of whom have a limited acquaintance with self-government (p. 269).

Georges Tamarin researched Israeli grade school students' attitudes toward genocide and reported that 60 percent of the students saw nothing wrong with Joshua's massacre of the Canaanites. Tamarin was dismissed by the University of Tel Aviv for the "double speak" reason that his research had caused problems between his university department and the Ministry of Education. He thus became, in his own words, the last victim of Joshua's massacre. See Georges R. Tamarin, *The Israeli Dilemma: Essays on a Warfare State* (Rotterdam: Rotterdam University Press, 1973), pp. 9, 27–40, 53–76, 79–94.

38. In 1981 and 1984, the religious parties held twelve seats. Through internal factionalism, these groups had grown to six parties that captured a total of eighteen seats in 1988. The relative decline of the main parties and the unacceptability of the Israeli left prevented the formation of a stable majority government and led to the 1984 coalition. A grand coalition was assembled again in 1988, although just before that election a coalition was opposed by over 60 percent of the voters polled. *JPI,* August 5–11, 1984, p. 2; October 8, 1988, p. 5.

39. Ian S. Lustick, "Israel's Dangerous Fundamentalists," *Foreign Policy,* no. 68 (Fall 1987), p. 118.

40. Quoted in *ibid.,* p. 123.

41. *Ibid.,* p. 123.

42. *Ibid.,* pp. 123–124.

43. *Ibid.,* p. 124. One may note that the Jews are nowhere exempted from the observance of the Ten Commandments; that if the Ten Commandments were promulgated solely for Gentile observance, why were they *first* disclosed to the Jews from Mount Sinai? Finally, Scripture makes clear that the Ten Commandments were simply a codification of

the covenants made with the patriarchs, whose obedience to the divinely ordained rules were a condition precedent for their receipt of divine favor.

According to one Gush Emunim leader, the lamentable outcome of the 1982 Lebanon War was thus "a natural and an expected, if unfortunate, part of the redemption process," and he quotes Rabbi Eliezar Waldman, a member of the Knesset and Gush Emunim—linked to the Tehiya Party—as saying, "It is impossible to complete the Redemption by any means other than war. By fighting the Arabs, Israel carries out its mission to serve as the heart of the world, in contact with every organ, and with the world understanding that it must receive the blood of life from the heart." *(Ibid.)*

44. *Ibid.,* p. 120. The movement's ideology leaves no room for disagreement, public discussion, or the rule of law. In 1982, when the Israeli government moved to dismantle the settlements in the Sinai, rumors flew through Jerusalem of an impending Gush *putsch.* By way of precaution, reservists from left-wing Israeli military units were called up to stand guard at the president's and the prime minister's residences and other key points. Confronted by hundreds of heavily armed troops, Gush gave up any coup plans they had ever entertained—Interview with Dr. Israel Shahak by the authors in Jerusalem, April 1985. Shahak was among the reservists called up on that occasion.

45. Smooha, *Israel,* p. 68. The Arabs now control only 7 percent of Israel's land.

46. This majority may now have eroded with the Arabs having a 70 percent majority in western Galilee. *The New York Times,* October 26, 1989, p. A1.

47. *The Washington Post,* October 26, 1989, p. 33.

48. Smooha, *Israel,* p. 36.

49. Israel is among the few countries to divorce citizenship from nationality, there being Jewish, Arab, and Druse nationalities. Smooha, *Israel,* p. 48.

50. Smooha, *Israel,* pp. 78, 52. Kahane, when an MK, introduced a package of bills which, among other things, prohibited Arab-Jewish marriages. These proposals were vehemently denounced in the Knesset as copies of the Nazi Nuremberg laws.

51. *News from Within,* vol. II, no. 33 (August 26, 1986), p. 102. Of the area of 65,000 dunums seized by the British in 1944, only 12,000 are being returned, of which only 2,500 dunums are being returned to their Arab owners, the rest being given to the state or Jewish settlers (the dunum equals a quarter of an acre).

52. Supporters of Shin Bet, like Ron Ben Yishai, complained in *Yediot Aharonot* that the agency would have to work at a slower pace and with less success because of the verdict. Openly advocating the use of torture, he declared: "One of the most effective means of obtaining the vital information is exerting pressure—including physical violence and psychological manipulation—on those being interrogated. . . . Even jurists are well aware of this fact and they therefore tended until now to look the other way . . . it was very convenient for jurists that [Shin Bet] personnel did the dirty work and contended in court that no undue pressure was exerted on the defendant." *The Washington Post,* May 26, 1987. pp. A1, A8.

53. *The Jerusalem Post,* International Edition, May 2, 1987, p. 2. Yossi Sarid (Citizens Rights movement) called on the cabinet to dismiss the "nightmarish" idea. Sarid said that "the Shin Bet must conform to the law and not the law to the Shin Bet."

54. Sabri Jiryus, *Democratic Freedoms in Israel,* trans. by Meric Dobson (Beirut: Institute for Palestine Studies, 1972), pp. 61–65. This practice can be traced back to Germany and the Soviet Union in the mid-1930s.

55. *The Jerusalem Post,* International Edition, January 10, 1987, pp. 1, 3. The Attorney General's report indicates clearly that Prime Ministers Shamir and Peres were eager to sweep this matter under the rug until exposure became inevitable in February and March 1986. GSS head Avraham Shalom first claimed that the order to execute the Arabs came from Defense Minister Moshe Arens. Confronted by the irate minister, he retracted his statement and claimed general authority from the prime minister, Yitzhak Shamir. The three senior Shin Bet officers, who blew the whistle, were all dismissed from office, while the

executioners, their chief, and other associates in the cover-up were all pardoned and retained in their posts.

56. *Facts on File,* 1984, p. 315. After this incident with its severe financial losses, no Israeli paper will be tempted to be so bold again.

57. Benvenisti, *Conflict and Contradictions,* p. 104.

58. CBS, *Statistical Abstracts,* 1985, p. 69. Hence the desire for Russian Jews.

59. *The Jerusalem Post,* International Edition, "Israel and the Vacuum," . . .. . ., 1986 p. 2. The use of Arab demographic figures as a scare tactic, employed by Labor during the 1988 elections, reinforces Israeli racism or ethnocentrism.

60. Arian, *Politics in Israel,* p. 133.

61. Flapan, *Birth of Israel,* 333.

62. *The Jerusalem Post,* International Edition, November 19, 1988, p. 3.

63. *The Jerusalem Post,* International Edition, March 11, 1989, p. 3.

64. Meir Kahane, *They Must Go* (New York: Grosset & Dunlap, 1981), Rabbi Kahane advanced the view that democracy and Israel's territorial program are incompatible.

65. Harkabi, *Israel's Fateful Hour,* pp. 106–07.

66. Benvenisti, *Conflicts and Contradictions,* p. 53.

67. Amnon Rubenstein, *The Zionist Dream Revisited: From Herzl to Gush Emunim and Back* (New York: Schocken Books, 1984), p. 4. This was nicely illustrated by the 1960 series Israeli 50-pound notes. Kibbutzniks portrayed this type of Zionist *par excellence.* Though Kibbutz members over the years never constituted more than 4% of Israel's population, they long filled a disproportionate share of the available roles in government and provided the elite corps of the military. As former Prime Minister Begin put it: "The Kibbutzim are millionaires and almost every member of the cabinet had experience on a kibbutz before he became a General and then a politician." Smooha, *Israel,* p. 24.

68. Rubenstein, *The Zionist Dream Revisited,* p. 184.

69. *Facts on File,* 1991, p. 249; *Middle East International,* no. 403, June 28, 1991, p. 9.

70. Rubenstein, *The Zionist Dream Revisited,* p. 20.

71. Amos Perlmutter, *Israel: The Partitioned State* (New York: Charles Scribner's Sons, 1985), p. 293.

72. *The New York Times,* November 8, 1988, p. A6.

73. *Congressional Quarterly,* 1986, p. 153.

74. Bernard Reich, *Israel, Land of Tradition and Conflict* (Boulder, Colo.: Westview Press, 1985), pp. 123–36.

75. Earlier, in 1981, a proposal was made that the squabbling Israeli Arabs should hold a convention at Nazareth with a view to composing their differences and fielding a unified slate of candidates. Although peace reigned throughout the country, Prime Minister Begin, in his capacity as acting defense minister, banned the meeting as a danger to the state.

76. *The Jerusalem Post,* International Edition, April 2, 1988; October 15, 1988.

77. Arian, *Politics in Israel,* p. 263.

78. Nadav Safran, *Israel: The Embattled Ally* (Cambridge, Mass.: Belknap Press, Harvard University Press, 1978), pp. 151, 152.

79. For a discussion of the Israeli economy, see Robert J. Loewenberg, "Why Prop Up Israeli Socialism?" *The New York Times,* June 24, 1991. See also Shlomo Maoz, "The Economy: Shooting from the Hip," *The Jerusalem Post,* International Edition, January 7, 1989, p. 8. Maoz is the economic editor of *The Jerusalem Post.* See also Joel Bainerman, "Israel Needs Reform, Not Charity," *Newsday,* July 29, 1991, p. 29.

80. *The New York Times,* July 25, 1991, p. A9. Many of these firms have been saddled with usurious 30 percent interest rates on loans after the currency reform, which has sent many into bankruptcy.

81. *The Jerusalem Post,* International Edition, March 18, 1989 (editorial, March 6, 1989), p. 24; September 14, 1991, p. 6.

82. *Newsweek,* March 19, 1990, p. 34.

83. *The Jerusalem Post,* International Edition, July 6, 1991, p. 1.

84. Ami Doran and Eli Teicher, "Feeding the Nuclear Idol," *Maariv,* March 22, 1987, as reported in *Israel Press Brief* (March–April 1987), pp. 16–17. Israeli gangs, both in New York and Israel, are now active in drug traffic.

85. That compares with the American figure of $6,000, yet Americans have twice Israel's per capita income.

86. Robert Gilpin, *War and Change in World Politics* (New York: Cambridge University Press, 1981), pp. 189–90.

87. *Ibid.,* p. 165.

## CHAPTER NINE

1. During his brief tenure in 1968 as the U.S. Permanent Representative to the United Nations, the senior author was asked by Prime Minister Eshkol to convey to King Hussein of Jordan an offer to return almost all the West Bank. Hussein obviously felt bound by the Khartoum Declaration and also by the need not to concede Jerusalem to Israel for fear of being overthrown.

2. Meron Benvenisti, *The West Bank Data Base Project: A Survey of Israel's Policies* (Washington, D.C.: American Enterprise Institute, 1984), p. 64. What this means in translation is that Israel simply considered the 1967 War as an opportunity to fulfill its plans to take over all the land once part of the Palestinian Mandate.

3. The Labor Party also used such terminology; it was simply not anxious to show its hand. The underlying tactical assumption of this operation and the progress made in executing it are described in a recent book by Geoffrey Aronson, *Israel, Palestinians and the Intifada* (Washington, D.C.: Institute for Palestine Studies, 1990; London: Kegan Paul, 1991).

4. *The Jerusalem Post,* International Edition, June 29, 1991, p. 1.

5. Benvenisti, *West Bank Data Base Project,* p. 64.

6. Meron Benvenisti, *1986 Report: Demographic, Economic, Legal, Social and Political Developments in the West Bank* (Jerusalem: West Bank Data Base Project, 1986), pp. 48–49. In 1989, the numbers were behind schedule at 80,000.

7. *Inquiry* magazine, Washington, D.C., December 8, 1980.

8. *Department of the Army Pamphlet 27-1. Treaties Governing Land Warfare,* December 1956, p. 150. Geneva Convention Relative to the Protection of Civilian Persons in Time of War, August 12, 1949, Part III, Article 69, para. 6.

9. Other legal analyses of the Israeli settlements reach the same conclusions regarding all of the Israeli legal claims to avoid application of the Hague Regulations and the Civilians' Convention. Thomas W. and Sally V. Mallison, *The Palestine Problem in International Law and World Order* (Harlow, Essex: Longmans, 1986), pp. 240–75.

10. The relevant provisions of the Hansell opinion are the following:

> 1. As noted above, Israeli armed forces entered Gaza, the West Bank, Sinai and the Golan Heights in June, 1967, in the course of an armed conflict. Those areas had not previously been part of Israel's sovereign territory nor otherwise under its administration. By reason of such entry of its armed forces, Israel established control and began to exercise authority over these territories; and under international law, Israel thus became a belligerent occupant of these territories.
>
> Territory coming under the control of a belligerent occupant does not thereby become its sovereign territory. International law confers upon the occupying state authority to undertake interim military administration over the territory and its inhabitants; that authority is not unlimited. The governing rules are designed to permit pursuit of its military needs by the occupying power, to protect the security of the occupying forces, to provide for orderly government, to protect the rights and interests of the inhabitants and to reserve questions of territorial change and sovereignty to a later stage when the war is ended. . . .

On the basis of the available information, the civilian settlements in the territories occupied by Israel do not appear to be consistent with these limits on Israel's authority as belligerent occupant in that they do not seem intended to be of limited duration or established to provide orderly government of the territories and, though some may serve incidental security purposes, they do not appear to be required to meet military needs during the occupation.

2. Article 49 of the Fourth Geneva Convention relative to the Protection of Civilian Persons in Time of War, August 12, 1949, 6 UST 3516, provides, in paragraph 6:

> The Occupying Power shall not deport or transfer parts of its own civilian population into the territory it occupies.

Paragraph 6 appears to apply by its terms to any transfer by an occupying power of parts of its civilian population, whatever the objective and whether involuntary or voluntary. . . .

The Israeli civilian settlements thus appear to constitute a "transfer of parts of its own civilian population into the territory it occupies" within the scope of paragraph 6. . . .

4. It has been suggested that the principles of belligerent occupation, including Article 49, paragraph 6, of the Fourth Geneva Convention, may not apply in the West Bank and Gaza because Jordan and Egypt were not the respective legitimate sovereigns of these territories. However, those principles appear applicable whether or not Jordan and Egypt possessed legitimate sovereign rights in respect of those territories. Protecting the reversionary interest of an ousted sovereign is not their sole or essential purpose; the paramount purposes are protecting the civilian population of an occupied territory and reserving permanent territorial changes, if any, until settlement of the conflict. . . .

Conclusion

While Israel may undertake, in the occupied territories, actions necessary to meet its military needs and to provide for orderly government during the occupation, for the reasons indicated above the establishment of the civilian settlements in those territories is inconsistent with international law.

Still the Hansell legal opinion's logic remains irrefutable. Its basic argument consists of six points:

*First,* as a result of its conquest in the 1967 War, Israel's armed forces entered the area where it established control, thus making Israel, in the language of international law, a "belligerent occupant." *Second,* the achievement of the status of belligerent occupant did not give Israel sovereignty, but merely the right to undertake "interim military administration over the territory"—an authority that is far from unlimited. *Third,* "the civilian settlements in the territories occupied by Israel do not appear to be consistent with these limits on Israel's authority as belligerent occupant in that they do not seem intended to be of limited duration or established to provide orderly government of the territories, and, though some may serve incidental security purposes [the original justification for the settlements was that they were needed for security purposes], they do not appear to be required to meet military needs during the occupation." *Fourth,* Paragraph Six of the Fourth Geneva Convention Relative to the Protection of Civilian Persons in Time of War (August 12, 1949), provides that "The Occupying Power shall not deport or transfer parts of its own civilian population into the territory it occupies." *Fifth,* "Since paragraph Six appears to apply by its terms to any transfer by an occupying power of parts of its civilian population, whatever the objective and whether involuntary or voluntary, it seems clearly to reach such involvements of the occupying power as determining the location of settlements, making land available and financing their creation, as well as other kinds of assistance and participation in their creation." *Sixth,* the opinion concludes that the Israeli civilian settlements appear to constitute a "transfer of parts of its own civilian population into the territory it occupies within the scope of paragraph six."

On the basis of these considerations, it concludes that "While Israel may undertake, in the occupied territories, actions necessary to meet its military needs and to provide for orderly government during the occupation . . . the establishment of the civilian settlements in those territories is inconsistent with international law. It should also be noted that whether the occupying power claims that it is the rightful owner of the territory cannot be used to justify settlements in the captured area."

The Hansell opinion is important for reasons far beyond the immediate topic addressed. The Israelis have claimed that the territory is not occupied, since they regard it as part of Israel, but the Israeli government has graciously chosen to enforce the Geneva Conventions anyway as regards the Arab inhabitants. See Allan Gerson, *Israel and the West Bank and International Law* (London: Frank Cass, 1978), pp. 80–116, 131. Hansell's opinion shows, first, that the Geneva Conventions do apply to the Occupied Areas and their enforcement by Israel is not optional at its discretion. Second, the opinion also demonstrates in one important particular that the Conventions are not being enforced; in fact, they are only being violated.

The Israeli defense against the Hansell opinion raises more questions than it purports to answer. If, as stated, the West Bank and Gaza were simply illegally occupied regions of Israel from 1948 to 1967, why have not Israeli citizenship and Israeli law been uniformly applied to everyone in those regions, instead of only to the settlers? Why was East Jerusalem specifically annexed if it was always by right part of Israel? In any case, the Hansell opinion, carried to its obvious conclusion, implies not only a violation of a section of the Geneva Conventions but that the settlements themselves are illegal; that their presence, being unlawful, confers no valid title to the territories by Israel, and the settlers, as in the case of the Egyptian treaty, may be removed from the territories and are not entitled to compensation.

11. Physicians for Human Rights, *The Casualties of Conflict: Medical Care and Human Rights in the West Bank and Gaza Strip* (Somerville, Mass., 1988).

12. Ze'ev Schiff and Enud Ya'ari, *Intifada* (New York: Simon & Schuster, 1990), p. 146.

13. *Ibid.*, p. 63. The list of alleged Israeli violations enumerated earlier and the list provided by Article 51 speak for themselves.

14. Raja Shehadeh, *The West Bank and the Rule of Law* (New York: International Commission of Jurists, 1980), pp. 102–03.

15. Gaza comes under the southern commander, who issues his own regulations. What is true for the West Bank is not therefore uniformly applicable to other Occupied Areas. The hidden notice story was told to the authors by a foreign service officer assigned to the consulate general in Jerusalem.

16. Since 1947, the Israeli government and its agencies have expropriated 87 percent of Israel's surface area, the most massive uncompensated confiscation of property in history outside of the Communist states. In this regard the Israelis are simply carrying out in the Occupied Territories policies which have often cost the Arab Israelis their land and economic independence west of the Green Line. Brian Van Arkadie, *Benefits and Burdens: A Report on the West Bank and Gaza Strip Economies Since 1967* (New York: Carnegie Endowment for International Peace, 1977), p. 70.

17. Nancie L. Katz, in *Christian Science Monitor,* June 28, 1989. In 1988 there were as many demolitions of Israeli Arabs' homes as in the Occupied Territories. Indeed, Israel now proposes to demolish seventy villages built without permission and to confiscate their land.

18. The need for such peremptory haste, except as a device for destroying personal property, is not apparent. Israeli jurisprudence, so far as the Arabs are concerned, is routinely marked by Lewis Carroll's Queen of Hearts' justice: "Sentence first—verdict afterwards."

19. In one case, an Arab who protected some Jewish girls from assault during a clash with settlers was rewarded for his pains by having his home blown up. The IDF later

grudgingly apologized, but current regulations prohibited the payment of any compensation to him. *Facts on File,* April 15, 1989, p. 249.

20. *Christian Science Monitor,* June 28, 1989.

21. That sentiment is at least vaguely suggestive of the reverence of certain Oriental peoples for the bones of their ancestors, which discourages them from ever leaving the place where they have lived their lives.

22. Raja Shehadeh, *Occupier's Law: Israel and the West Bank* (Washington, D.C.: Institute of Palestine Studies, 1985), pp. 4–5. Benvenisti has said that "The Israelis [in 1984] are in the process of gaining direct control over 40 percent of the West Bank land mass and 81 percent of the Gaza Strip area." He quotes the conflicting estimates of the size of the expropriated area, "which varies between a quarter and two-thirds of the total area of the West Bank." Benvenisti, *West Bank Data Base Project,* pp. 19, 31.

23. Jeffrey D. Dillman, "Water Rights in the Occupied Territories," *Journal of Palestine Studies,* vol. XVIII, no. 4 (Autumn 1989), pp. 46–48.

24. The political party named Tsomet claims that "Approximately 60 percent of Israel's water supply is contained in geological structures (aquifers) which . . . are affected directly and indirectly by civilian and ecological activity in Judea and Samaria. . . . " *The Jerusalem Post,* International Edition, September 30, 1989, p. 6. A confidential study furnished to the authors reports that aquifers lie under Gush Katif, Nezarim, and Erez in Gaza, the waters of which are reserved for Israel or its settlers.

25. Benvenisti, *1986 Report,* pp. 18–20. Although the State of Jordan offered Jordanian citizenship to all Palestinians, very few, other than those actually resident in Jordan, have accepted this offer, except insofar as it provides them with a passport. Nevertheless, although denying that the West Bank was ever legally part of Jordan, because it finds it advantageous, Israel still applies Jordanian law (as amended by the Israeli military authorities) and declares all Palestinians resident in the West Bank to be Jordanian citizens, whether they wish to be or not. Nor has there been any change in status since Hussein's renunciation speech on July 31, 1988. The prime purpose of this Israeli charade is to establish the fiction that those living on the West Bank are not natives but merely resident enemy aliens who can be deported at will.

26. *The Karp Report: An Israeli Government Inquiry into Settler Violence Against Palestinians in the West Bank* (Washington, D.C.: Institute for Palestine Studies, 1984), pp. 1, 35–49. *The Jerusalem Post,* February 7, 1987, p. 8 editorial; February 8, 1992, pp. 1–2, "Law Enforcement Lax for Jews in West Bank."

27. Schiff and Ya'ari, *Intifada,* pp. 30, 31.

28. *Ibid.,* p. 31.

29. We have borrowed freely from pp. 25–30 of Schiff and Ya'ari's *Intifada* for this account of the early hours of the outbreak.

30. Citing *Al-Fajr,* December 27, 1987, quoted in Geoffrey Aronson, *Israel, Palestinians and the Intifada,* p. 324.

31. *The New York Times,* January 1, 1988. Shamir, on December 23, 1987, stated: "This is not the first time there is ferment. We know the Arabs of Eretz Israel do not accept or are not pleased with our rule. This, however, does not mean that we should accept their demands, some of which would put an end to the conflict between us—naturally to their advantage and to their satisfaction. A political solution is not always what puts an end to the opposition of one's enemies or one's existence. First of all, one must repel the dangers and then think about peace, if that is possible . . . let there first be tranquility and then we will sit down and talk."

32. Aronson, *Israel, Palestinians and the Intifada,* p. 329.

33. *Al-Hamishmar,* October 20, 1988, for October 19, 1998, quoted in Aronson, p. 331.

34. Aronson, *Israel, Palestinians and the Intifada,* p. 337.

35. *Ibid.,* p. 338. This was an illegal collective punishment.

36. *Ibid.* p. 341. Though that announcement was politically welcome to the leadership

of the *Intifada* as representing an acceptance of the PLO's role in the territories, their financial difficulties were compounded by Hussein's announcement on July 31 that Jordan was relinquishing administrative and political responsibilities for the West Bank.

37. Amnesty International, *Annual Report* (London, 1989), pp. 260–61.

38. *Facts on File,* 1989, p. 27, reporting statement made on January 19–20.

39. Aronson, *Israel, Palestinians and the Intifada,* p. 328.

40. *Ibid.,* p. 328.

41. *Ha'aretz,* May 4, 1989.

42. This restriction gainsaid the claim of Defense Minister Rabin, who had declared that "no demonstrators have died from being thwacked on the head."

43. *Ha'aretz,* May 4, 1989. The incident was styled "the night of broken clubs" which was presumably a parody of *"Kristallnacht"* (Night of Broken Glass) in Nazi Germany. The leaving of one victim capable of returning to the village for help reminds one of the calculated cruelty of the Byzantine emperor, Basil II, who blinded 15,000 Bulgarian captives, leaving one man in 50 with one eye so he could lead the others back to their homes. In March 1991, the colonel commanding the perpetrators of this atrocity was convicted by a military court of responsibility for his troops' actions. However, significantly, his effort to introduce evidence that this action was taken at the behest of Rabin, the defense minister, was quashed on the ground that the court could not take cognizance of ministerial actions.

44. *Facts on File,* February 19, 1988, p. 972. Had the Palestinians attempted such a crime they would have been lucky to get off with fifteen years imprisonment.

45. Israeli soldiers, disguised as Arabs, are rumored to be infiltrating into Arab towns to execute summarily those whom they fear or mistrust. There is even one case where one of the suspects turned himself in to the occupying authorities only to be told that they didn't want him in prison—they wanted him dead. Three days after being sent home, he was murdered. Similar events are recounted by Mary Boudinet, "Death Squads: Israeli Phenomenon Ignored by U.S. Media," *Middle East Times,* March 6–12, 1990, p. 5.

46. Under the governance of the British, the Palestinians were among the first Arabs to realize the importance of education and avail themselves of the opportunities offered to them. They remain, as a group, among the best educated of the Arabs.

47. *Facts on File,* 1989, p. 858. Schools were closed in January 1989 and ordered reopened July 22, 1989.

48. Jackson Diehl, *The Washington Post,* February 27, 1990, and Joel Brinkley, *The New York Times,* February 27, 1990. That action taken by the twelve governments of the EEC clearly had its effect and suggested how much more could be accomplished by the full exercise of the Community's potential for sanctions. The same is even truer of the United States' leverage. The two-way trade between Europe and Israel is reportedly $27 billion. *The Jerusalem Post,* International Edition, May 25, 1991, p. 1.

49. Comments in answer to a question as to the Israeli attitude toward the *Intifada,* the macNeil/Lehrer News Hour, Friday, December 8, 1989. Though, in fairness to Goodman, he later stated that "If Israel did not have a moral conscience, it could put up with this indefinitely. It is not an existential problem for Israel. What it is, is a constant lacquering of our legitimacy. And we realize that we cannot live as a garrison state. We have to resolve this problem. . . . "

50. Aronson, *Israel, Palestinians and the Intifada,* p. 344, citing *FBIS,* December 19, 1988. Also *The New York Times,* December 17, 1988, p. 27.

## CHAPTER TEN

1. This experience is described in several books, including Stephen D. Isaacs, *Jews and American Politics* (Garden City, N.Y.: Lee O'Brien, *American Jewish Organizations and Israel* (Washington, D.C.: Institute for Palestine Studies, 1986); and Max I. Dimont, *The*

*Jews in America* (New York: Simon & Schuster, 1978). Jews are reported to attend religious services only a third as often as Christians.

2. Art Stevens, *The Persuasion Explosion* (Washington, D.C.: Acropolis Books, 1985), pp. 104–05. Stevens notes that unhappily for Uris's pretensions to objectivity, Uris became carried away by the passion of his own propaganda. He followed *Exodus* with another book on the Middle East called *The Haj,* which an Israeli reviewer in *The Jerusalem Post* described as "a raving diatribe against Arabs, their culture and their religion," adding that it "depicts Arabs in a manner that would make Meir Kahane blush."

3. Losing in the attack eight Irgun members and suffering the capture of three others, who were later hanged.

4. Nicholas Bethell, *The Palestine Triangle: The Struggle Between the British, the Jews and the Arabs, 1935–48* (London: Andre Deutsch, 1979), pp. 308–09.

5. He had now transformed the illegal Irgun into a political party, the Herut, which was quite legal under the laws of the fledgling nation of Israel.

6. Thus a few years ago the senior author received a letter from one of the best known Jewish matriarchs in America—a woman of great detachment and courage—saying that she had been quite indifferent to the Zionist movement because it challenged assimilation, but that the Holocaust had totally changed her position.

7. Morris T. Amitay, "A Field Day for Jewish Pacs," *Congress Monthly* (June 1983), p. 11.

8. Blitzer, *Between Washington and Jerusalem: A Reporter's Notebook,* pp. 72–73.

9. Yet that reformulation of Israel's position disturbed some older leaders, still imbued with original Zionist ideals. For example, the former president of the World Zionist Organization, Nahum Goldmann, wrote that "Israel is losing its moral qualification and is becoming only a small, aggressive state . . . thus losing the respect and admiration of the larger part of world public opinion."

10. Friedman, *From Beirut to Jerusalem,* pp. 453–54.

11. *Ibid.,* p. 454.

12. *Ibid.,* p. 455.

13. *Ibid.,* p. 461.

14. *Ibid.,* p. 469.

15. Ibid., p. 486.

16. See Hal Lindsey, *The Late Great Planet Earth* (Toronto: Bantam Books, 1973), for a sample of this literature. See also Grace Halsell, *Prophecy and Politics: Militant Evangelists on the Road to Nuclear War* (Westport, Conn.: Lawrence Hill Books, 1986), pp. 96–116.

17. "No Way to Run a Spy Ring," *The Jerusalem Post,* International Edition, March 21, 1987, p. 3.

18. Lee O'Brien, *American Jewish Organizations and Israel* (Washington, D.C.: Institute for Palestine Studies, 1986), pp. 7, 15, 159. There are claims that as many as 4.5 million American Jews belong to thirty-eight major Jewish (and pro-Israel) groups. This devotion to Israel is not matched by a similar enthusiasm for the practice of the faith of their forebears. Ari L. Goldman, "Polls Show Jews Both Assimilate and Keep Tradition," *The New York Times,* June 7, 1991.

19. O'Brien, *American Jewish Organizations,* p. 8.

20. *Ibid.,* p. 9.

21. This is particularly important in major electoral vote states where the Jews are concentrated. The U.S. Census Bureau estimated that America's population at the beginning of 1987 was 242.1 million.

22. O'Brien, *American Jewish Organizations,* p. 155.

23. Indeed, Israel today would be a far less impressive country without the array of parks, museums, and hospitals, all generously furnished by Diaspora Jews and their organizations.

24. Jewish American gifts have from time to time given rise to controversy. Arab organizations in the United States have challenged the deductibility of gifts to Jewish charities on the ground that some money ends up part of Israel's operating budget. (In at least one case, a couple found that their gift for a recreation facility had been inadvertently diverted to cover a deficit in the Israeli Defense budget. The Israeli government hurriedly corrected the situation by naming a government-built playground in their honor.) In other cases, funds supposedly solicited for Israel have been used in the United States. On the other hand, the United Jewish Appeal has been sued by American ultra-Zionists, who demand that UJA funds be spent in the Occupied Areas, which the Fund declares would be illegal, as they are not part of Israel. Only in the heterogeneous United States could such profuse support avoid challenge. *The Jerusalem Post,* International Edition, March 28, 1987, p. 10.

25. *The Jerusalem Post,* International Edition, March 21, 1987.

26. Philip Roth, *The Counterlife* (New York: Farrar, Straus & Giroux, 1986), pp. 73–74.

27. See, e.g., Rabbi Jacob Neusner, *The Washington Post,* March 8, 1987, "Outlook," p. B1. For an angry pro-Israeli attack on this attitude, see Edward Alexander, "Where Is Zion?", *Commentary,* vol. VIII, no. 3 (September 1988), pp. 47–50.

28. *The Jerusalem Post,* International Edition, November 18, December 31, 1988.

29. *The New York Times,* July 22, 1989.

30. See *The New York Times,* September 10, 1985, p. A20. During the Reagan administration, the influence of pro-Israeli apologists became so powerful that its leaders and lobbyists were routinely consulted by America's highest officials about any major initiative that might even remotely affect Israel. For example, Secretary of State George Shultz and other officials regularly met with Thomas Dine, head of AIPAC, to discuss Middle East policies before presenting them to Congress, and President Reagan personally called Dine to thank him for his help in influencing Congress.

31. Kenen, *Israel's Defense Line: Her Friends and Foes in Washington,* p. 66.

32. Smith, *The Power Game,* p. 229. The senior author and others in 1989 filed a complaint against AIPAC, pointing out that because of these connections, AIPAC was indeed a PAC within the meaning of the law. The Federal Elections Commission, after over a year's delay and without investigating the charges, dismissed them (without notifying the complainants)—another clear example of AIPAC's political clout.

33. *U.S. News and World Report,* March 27, 1978, p. 25. When Representative Thomas J. Downey of New York, a supporter of Israel, expressed doubts about the size of aid to Israel, he was swamped with letters. Downey, despite earlier mail opposing foreign aid, got 3,000 telegrams in two days supporting a "yes" vote.

34. O'Brien, *American Jewish Organizations,* p. 177.

35. This success is related by former Representative Paul Findley in his excellent book, *They Dare to Speak Out* (Westport, Conn.: Lawrence Hill Books, 1985): "One day I whispered to a colleague in the Foreign Affairs Committee I might offer an amendment to a pending bill cutting aid to Israel. Within 30 minutes two other Congressmen came to me with worried looks, reporting they had just had calls from citizens in their home districts who were concerned about my amendment" (pp. 35–36).

The distinguished former senator from Maryland, Charles Mathias, described the mechanics of AIPAC's operations: "When an issue of importance to Israel comes before Congress, AIPAC promptly and unfailingly provides all members with data and documentation, supplemented, as circumstances dictate, with telephone calls and personal visits. Beyond that, signs of hesitation or opposition on the part of a Senator or Representative can usually be relied on to call forth large numbers of letters and telegrams, or visits and phone calls from influential constituents." See Charles McC. Mathias, Jr., "Ethnic Groups and Foreign Policy," *Foreign Affairs,* vol. LIX, no. 5 (Summer 1981), p. 993.

36. *Near East Report,* May 1, 1989, p. 69, also spreads stories that Syria is the sole

source of Lebanon's troubles; nowhere is it acknowledged that Israel plays a role or that the 60-plus percent Moslem majority is fighting for a share in the Lebanese government commensurate with its numbers. See Chapter 1 for the real facts regarding the Palestinian flight.

37. Quoted in Findley, *They Dare to Speak Out,* p. 36.

38. In 1986, the ambassador told his audience that Saudi Arabia gave the PLO $250 million when the real number was $85 million.

39. O'Brien, *American Jewish Organizations,* pp. 172–74.

40. Findley, *They Dare to Speak Out,* p. 33.

41. International Edition, July 8–14, 1984.

42. Robert G. Kaiser, "The U.S. Risks Suffocating Israel with Kindness," *The Washington Post,* May 27, 1984.

43. Findley, *They Dare to Speak Out,* pp. 25–26.

44. O'Brien, *American Jewish Organizations,* p. 159. Obviously, there are a fair amount of overlapping members.

45. Rubenberg, *Israel and the American Interest,* pp. 354–55.

46. Feuerlicht, *The Fate of the Jews,* p. 271.

47. *Ibid.*

48. O'Brien, *American Jewish Organizations,* p. 177. The invocation of the Holocaust on every possible occasion serves the dual purpose of playing upon any available guilt feelings while simultaneously making the subject that is opposed the equivalent of that cataclysmic event.

49. Tillman, *The United States in the Middle East,* p. 120.

50. *Ibid.,* p. 121.

51. Findley, *They Dare to Speak Out,* pp. 66–67.

52. Tillman, *The United States in the Middle East,* p. 121.

53. Professor Cheryl A. Rubenberg, an authority on U.S.-Israeli relations, has noted: " . . . thereafter how a senator voted on this issue became the most important factor in the lobby's determination of an individual's 'friendship' toward Israel. Those who were labeled 'unfriendly' faced difficulties over reelection." Rubenberg, *Israel and the American National Interest,* p. 258.

54. *Ibid.,* p. 358. All opponents of Israel, according to this line of reasoning, are either anti-Semitic or bought with Arab oil money. We have even heard the term "Arab lover" employed, which odiously parallels the racist epitaph "nigger lover" used in the American South during the civil rights struggle of the 1950s and 1960s.

55. Richard B. Straus, *The Washington Post,* April 27, 1986, "Outlook."

56. *The Washington Report on Middle East Affairs* (February 1989), pp. 15–16.

57. Tillman, *The United States in the Middle East,* p. 66. Many legislators are too busy to inform themselves fully on matters outside their committee assignments. They therefore have to depend on the judgment of their aides.

58. O'Brien, *American Jewish Organizations,* pp. 167–68; *The Washington Post,* February 13, 1983.

59. Findley, *They Dare to Speak Out,* p. 35. No protest was sent to Israel regarding this proposed action, though an Arab government acting in that manner would have received plenty of complaints.

60. O'Brien, *American Jewish Organizations,* p. 169. Hecht and Lautenberg are both reported contributors to AIPAC. In 1988, a Jewish senator (Hecht, R-NV) lost; but Lieberman (D) was elected in Connecticut.

61. Senator Inouye was chairman of the Select Committee established to investigate the Iran-Contra affair, in which Israel played a significant role, and was a candidate for the Democratic leadership in 1989. Significantly, Israel's role in the Iran-Contra affair was not deemed important enough for public airing. Senator Inouye was also the recipient of $57,000 in Jewish PAC funds in 1986. See *The Almanac of American Politics, 1988* (Washington, D.C.: National Journal, 1987), p. 319.

62. *Ibid.,* pp. 168–69.

63. Jonathan S. Kessler and Jeff Schwaber, *The AIPAC College Guide: Exposing the Anti-Israel Campaign on Campus* (Washington, D.C.: AIPAC, 1984). The list would doubtless be longer today as opposition to Israel's policies grows on campus.

64. Findley, *They Dare to Speak Out,* p. 35. The list can be found in Amy Kaufman Goott and Steven J. Rosen, eds., *The Campaign to Discredit Israel* (Washington, D.C.: AIPAC, 1983).

65. Edward Tivnan, *The Lobby: Jewish Political Power and American Foreign Policy* (New York: Simon & Schuster, 1987), p. 183. George Ball, one of the authors of this book, is cited in Amy Kaufman Gooth and Steven J. Rosen, eds., *The Campaign to Discredit Israel* (Washington, D.C.: American-Jewish Public Affairs Committee, 1983), pp. 98–99, where the reader may learn that he is a former Under Secretary of State and UN Representative, and author of a "best-known" article in the April 1977 edition of *Foreign Affairs,* entitled "How to Save Israel in Spite of Herself." The reader would also learn that Ball argues that " 'sympathy should be felt for the Jewish need for a homeland,' but he believes the United States should put 'disciplinary restraint' (Ball's phrase) on Israel."

Tivnan then continues: "Ball is also for imposing peace in the Middle East. It's all true, and Ball wouldn't question the facts. But does dissent from the Begin government's policies make one an 'enemy of Israel'? Why does a former top American official have less right than a top Israeli official to criticize Israeli policy?"

66. Tivnan, *The Lobby,* p. 53.

67. One further point should be made with regard to the trivialization of the term "anti-Semitism"; it practically invites retaliation by suggestions on the part of Israel's critics that its conduct toward the Palestinians resembles the Nazi treatment of minorities in occupied Europe (Jim Muir, " 'Terrorism' Under the Microscope," *Middle East International,* no. 346, March 17, 1989, p. 8). On March 7, 1989, the Israelis smashed through a UNIFIL barrier manned by the Norwegians and raided a village, expelling the inhabitants. In protesting, the Norwegian colonel in command commented *inter alia* that such behavior reminded him of the Nazis in occupied Norway. This set off a bitter altercation between the UN and Israel. The enraged reaction of the American Jewish community to this nasty comparison is quite understandable (*Israeli Mirror,* 1988, no. 773, February 21, 1988, pp. 4–6). Because both parties are busy heaping Nazi epithets on one another, neither makes a contribution to reasoned or civil discourse.

How far this process has gone is illustrated by a bizarre incident that occurred in the second term of Reagan's presidency. The Reagan administration was about to announce a decision to sell arms to an Arab country when it was discovered that the announcement would coincide with Yom Kippur. Rather than make an arms sale announcement during the holy days, the administration, to avoid an affront to Israel, delayed the request.

68. Isaacs, *Jews and American Politics,* p. 133. Isaacs was quoting Herbert E. Alexander, of the Citizens Research Foundation.

69. Richard H. Curtiss, "What's Special About Pro-Israel PACs," *The Washington Report on Middle East Affairs* (October 1988), pp. 7–8.

70. Smith, *The Power Game,* p. 229.

71. *Wall Street Journal,* February 26, 1985.

72. Isaacs, *Jews and American Politics,* p. 121. Unless, like John D. Rockefeller IV or Herb Kohler, you are affluent enough to pay for your own campaign.

73. *Ibid.*, pp. 4–5.

74. Interview with Abourezk, Washington, D.C., December 30, 1986. He won, however, without their aid.

75. *The New York Times,* December 30, 1986, p. 14.

76. Findley, *They Dare to Speak Out,* pp. 133–35.

77. *Ibid.*, p. 135.

78. *Ibid.*, p. 113.

79. John P. Egan, "Michael Goland Active in Cranston-Zschau Senate Race," *The Washington Report on Middle East Affairs* (December 1986), p. 10. (Egan quotes Shields.) Goland was later indicted and subsequently convicted for funneling funds illegally to a

third-party candidate in the California race—with a view to drawing off votes from the Republican candidate and then reelecting Senator Cranston, one of Israel's most ardent supporters. *Facts on File,* 1988, p. 934.

80. *The Almanac of American Politics, 1988,* p. 1100. Daschle's expenses reached $3,485,870, about $75,000 more than Abdnor's.

81. *Ibid.,* p. 17.

82. *Ibid.,* p. 117.

83. Findley, *They Dare to Speak Out,* p. 54.

84. These included the races in Alabama, California, Colorado, Georgia, Louisiana, Nevada, North Carolina, Pennsylvania, South Dakota, and Wisconsin.

## CHAPTER ELEVEN

1. Algebra, chemistry, Arabic numerals and the zero, the giant water wheel, underground water channels, improvements in shipbuilding, and the weaving of textiles are all example of Arab contributions to our culture. Arabs were early steelmakers and pioneers in brass work. The Arab American Anti-Defamation Association has had to work hard with the media to induce them to stop using unflattering anti-Arab stereotypes.

2. "The American Perception of the Arab World," in George Atiyeh, ed., *Arab and American Cultures* (Washington, D.C.: American Enterprise Institute, 1976), pp. 15–25.

3. Michael W. Suleimen, *The Arabs in the Mind of America* (Brattleboro, Vt.: Amana Books, 1988), p. 11.

4. A later incident further exemplified America's penchant for ill-considered actions toward the Arabs. In 1904, a Moroccan bandit named Raisuli abducted an American citizen named Perdicaris. Asserting that America would not deal with kidnappers, Theodore Roosevelt drew loud applause from the Republican National Convention by his declared vow to defend American citizens wherever they might be. The applause reached a crescendo when he dispatched a memorable telegram: "Perdicaris alive or Raisuli dead." We landed the Marines in Morocco to chastise Raisuli, while ultimately paying him a ransom to free Perdicaris. Not until 1933 did a scholar accidentally discover that at the time Roosevelt made his stirring declarations, he had already been warned that Perdicaris was not in fact an American, having reverted in 1863 to Greek nationality to protect property held in the South.

5. It should not be forgotten that at a time when there was supposed to be an Arab boycott of land sales to Jews, the Shuqari family secretly sold property to Jewish organizations. Official British reports also indicate that the Abdul Hadis, the Tajis, and other members of the Arab Higher Committee were surreptitiously selling land, usually through intermediaries. Indeed, the Banu Sakhr, the Mejlis of the Trans-Jordan, and the Amir Abdullah helped out the Jews by leasing them 70,000 dunums (1 dunum = ¼ acre) in the Ghos al Kald. *Reports on Agricultural Development Land Settlement in Palestine,* Louis French. First Report, Jerusalem, December 1931; Supplementary Report Jerusalem, April 1932. See also Yehovshva Perath, *The Emergence of the Palestinian Arab National Movement,* Vol. 1, *1918–1929;* Vol. 2, *1929–1939* (London: Frank Cass, 1974, 1977), Vol. 2, pp. 72–73.

6. See Pamela Ann Smith, *Palestine and the Palestinians, 1876–1983* (London: Croom Helm, 1984), pp. 60–62. Palestinian efforts to meet the Jewish challenge were further hampered by the division between Christian and Moslem groups. This was startlingly revealed as recently as 1985 when the Tadmor Center, outside Jerusalem, invited Palestinian Moslem and Christian leaders from the Bethlehem area to a conference to promote interreligious harmony. It presently transpired that these leaders, though living in neighboring villages and having the same problems, did not know one another and only reluctantly attended the meeting, at which, for the first time, a real dialogue was opened between them.

7. Similar futility was displayed by those Palestinians with Israeli citizenship in the November 1, 1988, election. Not only did a quarter of the Arab electorate stay away from the polls at the mullahs' behest (costing the Arabs four seats in the Knesset), but each Arab party that did contest the election refused, out of hatred for one another, to allow their extra votes to be given to another Arab party, thereby guaranteeing the loss of a further seat. Five additional Arab seats could have played a key role in the late 1988 and early 1990 government crises in Israel.

8. A good example of this was the private deal made by the inhabitants of Deir Yassin that they would not oppose the Israelis in their attacks on other Arabs if the Israelis would leave them alone. Their reward was to be massacred by Menachem Begin.

9. Then, in 1990–91, following the Gulf War, President Bush has declared that it is U.S. policy to overthrow Saddam Hussein, as though America had a divine right to determine who Iraq's ruler should be. Nor is this the end of the matter. The United States opposed the republican regime in San'a until 1968; backed, through the help of the Shah, the suppression of a republican rebellion in Dofar province in Oman (1975); and tacitly approved of Israel's 1982 scheme to impose a Quisling regime in Beirut. More recently, the U.S. Air Force sought to kill Colonel Kadafi in his home outside Tripoli.

The dependence of the Gulf monarchies on the United States offers benefits and serious problems to those governments. As the protecting power, the government in Washington is urging these absolute monarchs to adopt representative government institutions, though everyone knows that that is the last thing the rulers of these nations want.

10. The reason for this is that the Gulf states desire to retain these funds in safe havens, far from the dangers lurking in their own neighborhood. There is reality to those dangers. In practically every case, *Gastarbeiters* in the Gulf states constitute a large minority, or in the case of Kuwait, Qatar, and the UAE, a large majority of the resident population. Most of the Kuwaiti ministries were staffed with foreigners, with a handful of Kuwaitis occupying the top jobs. The discriminatory treatment accorded these noncitizen workers exacerbates the bad feeling between the natives and the resident foreigners who are frequently needed to make such societies work.

11. Moreover, many army personnel have a detached view of the societies they are supposed to be defending. This separation is neatly illustrated in Egypt, where the Cairo skyline is dominated by the Officers' Club.

12. Morocco, Kuwait, and Saudi Arabia have all committed brigades at one time or another, but neither Morocco nor Saudi Arabia has made a military effort in any way commensurate with its potential. Iraq was the only nonconfrontation state to participate effectively. Iraqi forces played an important role in holding the West Bank in 1948, but, because of Arab blunders in 1967, they arrived too late to help the Jordanians.

13. By that time, Assad was well aware that the Arabs had not recovered an acre of territory, except by fighting for it. He insisted, therefore, that the Arabs should not negotiate with Israel except from a position of military equality, if not superiority. With the assistance of the Soviet Union, Assad promptly undertook a massive military buildup.

14. So far as the other Arab states are concerned, their arms programs reflect their parochial concerns, not membership in an anti-Israeli coalition. And while eager to have the confrontation, states at war with Israel, Algeria, Libya, and Yemen have notably failed to send troops to the front or provide any substantive assistance to their overmatched fellow Arabs.

15. This impression was strengthened at the Battle of Karameh on March 21, 1968. Each side gave a confused and contradictory report of the outcome of this engagement. The guerrillas claimed sole credit for the enforced retirement of the Israelis, although the heavy Jordanian Army casualties and the destruction and capture of Israeli heavy equipment suggests that the brunt of the fighting was borne by the Royal Army. *Facts on File,* March 21–27, 1968, p. 183.

16. See Malcolm Kerr, *The Arab Cold War, 1958–1967: A Study of Ideology in Politics,*

2nd ed. (London: Oxford University Press, 1969), pp. 129–30.

17. Fuad Jabber, "The Palestinian Resistance and Inter-Arab Politics," in William B. Quandt, Fuad Jabber, and Ann Moseby Lesch, eds., *The Politics of Palestinian Nationalism* (Berkeley: University of California Press, 1973), p. 160.

18. In fact, the first Palestinian fatality was a guerrilla shot dead by the Jordanian Army as he returned from a raid into Israel. Fatah's raids into Israel were all launched from Jordan. This tactic was calculated to protect Syria, which was behind these operations, from reprisal.

19. See Jabber, "The Palestinian Resistance," p. 184. Fuad Jabber explained the subsidies as their attempt to buy acceptance in the Arab world of their friendly relations with the West; he attributes their bellicose statements about Israel to the same reason.

20. Quoted in Helena Cobban, *The Palestinian Liberation Organization: People, Power, and Politics* (New York: Cambridge University Press, 1984), p. 245.

21. See *ibid.,* pp. 16–17. The percentages of persons favoring a Palestinian state have fluctuated from 38 percent to 13 percent in recent polls, suggesting a very volatile state of public opinion or defective methods of polling respondents.

22. Council on Foreign Relations, *United States Policy and the Middle East,* 1983, p. 5. See also *Washington Report on the Middle East,* October 1989, p. 24.

23. The poisonous fruit of America's contradictory policies ripened with the embarrassing disclosure of the U.S. arms shipments through Israel to Iran at a time when Iran, as a terrorist center, was on an American boycott list. Since Saudi Arabia was actively backing Iraq in its war with Iran, the Saudi Arabian ambassador, Prince Bandar Bin Sultan, on November 7 called on Admiral John M. Poindexter, the President's National Security Adviser, to complain about the "lack of candor" in the United States-Saudi Arabian relationship. Although the admiral pleaded with the ambassador to "trust us," the Prince's tart comment was, "You've already proven that we can't trust you." *The Washington Post,* November 15, 1986. America's position was further undermined when the American ambassador in Amman lectured the Jordanians about not selling arms to Iran. When the Iraqi ambassador was falsely assured that America was selling no arms to Iran, he pointed out the patent falsity of that assurance and cited newspaper reports that Israel was selling arms to Iran by the shipload.

## CHAPTER TWELVE

1. In suggesting this examination, we necessarily reject the current faddish contention that one cannot seek the causes of terrorism without appearing to condone it. Only by isolating its underlying causes can one find the source of the trouble and so move politically to eliminate it.

2. See Avner Yaniv, *Deterrence Without the Bomb: The Politics of Israeli Strategy* (Lexington, Mass.: D. C. Heath, 1987), pp. 225–27.

3. The bourgeois nationalist Fatah differs from both the PFLP and the PDFLP in its attitude toward the Arab regimes. Both the PFLP and the PDFLP are interventionist, meaning that they involve themselves in inter-Arab struggles, in part because of their belief that the liberation of Palestine can come about only through a regionwide revolution which will allow for a unified, popular struggle against Israel. The current regimes, in their estimate, are too corrupt and too preoccupied with their own concerns to be of any use to the Palestinians. Fatah insists that the liberation of Palestine should be the first concern. It is strictly noninterventionist, in the hope that it can exchange neutrality in Arab quarrels for Arab government protection and support.

4. That was fortunate for Israel, since there were many targets that by systematic attack might have given real meaning to terrorism. The panicky American reaction to two attacks in Berlin and Vienna (helped along by the Reagan administration's hysteria) fright-

ened hundreds of thousands of Americans into staying at home at a cost to Israel thought to be in excess of $500 million. Rumors spread in the 1970s about poisoned Israeli fruit (only one actual incident is recorded) occasioned a short-lived boycott of Israeli citrus products. To curb even random terrorism, the Israelis were put to great expense to protect the national airline, El Al. They installed electronic detection equipment, as well as elaborate hand-baggage inspection procedures, large numbers of security guards, and other protective means to prevent attacks on El Al's planes and customers. During the same period, gangsters in the greater New York metropolitan area murdered more people without the benefit of the PLO's nominal 20,000 gunmen and $3.4 billion of subsidies.

5. Yet, as shall be seen, the Israeli Cabinet routinely ordered the bombing of PLO headquarters in Tunis (with a view to killing Yasser Arafat), and on December 12, 1988, Israel's forces also attacked the PFLP-GC headquarters south of Beirut. On April 14, 1988, it dispatched commandos to assassinate Khalil Wasseir (Abu Jihad), whose primary fault was that he was supervising the PLO support of the *Intifada.* This action was ordered by the Israeli Cabinet, where only one person, Ezer Weizman, persistently opposed it. Evidently, the Israelis imagined that Abu Jihad's death would end the resistance. Their intelligence proved defective.

6. *Facts on File,* January 28, 1989, p. 80.

7. The historical precedent of Saladin's unification of the Fertile Crescent before he attacked the Kingdom of Jerusalem lends theoretical plausibility to such radicals as Dr. George Habash and Abu Nidal, who contend that only overthrowing all the present governments and replacing them with a unified radical regime will create the power base needed to destroy Israel. See Matti Steinberg, "The Radical Worldview of the Abu Nidal Faction," *The Jerusalem Quarterly,* no. 48 (Fall 1988), pp. 88–104, especially pp. 89–90. Abu Nidal supports a greater Syria and opposes Palestinian nationalism.

8. *Middle East International,* September 26, 1986, p. 14.

9. *Ibid.* He then recalled an incident in Israel some months before when Mohammad Mi'ari, III, who had been arrested for expressing sympathy toward the PLO, declared that he deplored all terrorism. When asked what other agents of terrorism he had in mind he cited, for example, an Israeli Air Force raid on a school in Lebanon. Peled then continues: "His critics replied that the state of Israel does not commit acts of terrorism since its military actions are legitimate measures of self defense." This argument, Peled notes, is based on the assumption that violent acts can only be described as terrorism when committed by forces other than those of an established state. Under this tendentious definition, even clandestine acts of murder or kidnapping carried out by secret agents of a state would not be regarded as acts of terror. Such a statement is morally reprehensible on its face. The argument Peled cites is also an ethnocentric formulation, which simply declares that Israel cannot, by definition, commit certain crimes.

10. Quoted in Nicholas Bethell, *The Palestine Triangle,* pp. 277–78 (emphasis added).

11. The lack of precise definitions of terrorism and counterterrorism (reprisals) offers the opportunity for political sophists to make subtle distinctions blaming other countries for practices in which their country also indulges. The hard policy line of the Reagan administration is illustrated by a State Department bulletin for June 1986, which states: "The U.S. Government will make no concessions to terrorists holding official or private U.S. citizens hostage. It will not pay ransom, release prisoners, change its policies, or agree to other acts that might encourage additional terrorism." (Bureau of Public Affairs, U.S. State Department, "International Terrorism: U.S. Policy on Taking Americans Hostage.") It does no good for America's credibility to note that that declaration was issued at a time (June 1986) when Secretary Shultz knew that America and Israel were engaged in arms deals with Iran—deals that had been in progress since the previous August.

Secretary Shultz's role model, Israel, has never pursued the policy of the United States against dealing with terrorists. In May 1985, Israel swapped *1,150* Arab prisoners for *three* Israeli soldiers held by the PFLP general command. In June 1985, hijackers of a TWA jet demanded that Israel release hundreds of Lebanese prisoners; and, once the passengers were freed, Israel allowed 300 Lebanese to go home. On July 28, 1989, it kidnapped Sheik Obeid on Lebanese soil in the hope of using him as a trading counter for three Israeli soldiers who had been captured by the Hizbullah. "Palestine Chronology, June–August, 1985," *Journal of Palestine Studies,* vol. XV, no. 1 (August 1985), p. 225. Israel's leaders have regularly portrayed their Palestinian opponents as a low form of animal life. Taking the opposite side, Article 22 of the Palestinian National Covenant declares unflatteringly that Zionism "is a racist and fanatical movement in its formation; aggressive, expansionist and colonialist in its aims; and fascist and Nazi in its means."

Such comments are obviously not the language of reconciliation. They prolong and deepen the struggle. The late Jewish American journalist I. F. Stone wrote some years ago of a more humane and enlightened approach. "I feel honor bound to report the Arab side . . . the essence of tragedy is a struggle of right against right. Its catharsis is the cleaning piety of seeing how good men do evil despite themselves out of unavoidable circumstances and irresistible compulsion. . . . For me the Arab problem is also the No. 1 Jewish problem. How we act toward the Arab will determine what kind of people we become; either oppressors and racists in our turn like those from whom we have suffered, or a nobler race able to transcend the tribal xenophobia that afflict mankind." Article in *New York Review of Books,* August 1, 1967, reprinted in *The Israel-Arab Reader* (pamphlet), I. F. Stone, "Holy War," pp. 323–24.

12. Noam Chomsky, *Pirates and Emperors: International Terrorism in the Real World* (New York: Claremont Research, 1986), p. 1.

13. Quoted in Maurice Edelman, *Ben Gurion: A Political Biography* (London: Hodder & Stoughton, 1984), p. 109. Later, as prime minister, Ben-Gurion was a staunch advocate of violent reprisals.

14. *Facts on File,* March 17, 1989, p. 178.

15. Having served during World War II as a director of the U.S. Strategic Bombing Survey, the senior author never believed Air Force claims that they are capable of "surgical strikes." Even the Gulf War, with its "smart boms," inflicted plenty of civilian casualties, some from mistaken targeting.

16. Begin, *The Revolt: Story of the Irgun,* pp. 213–14. It has also been argued by Kaplan and Katzenbach that Israeli-style reprisals are not in violation of the UN Charter because "Forcible sanctions to guarantee rights are not aggression . . . and are not . . . threats to the peace—*provided* the force employed is moderate and limited to the vindication of legal rights. . . . " (emphasis added). Morton A. Kaplan and Nicholas de B. Katzenbach, *The Political Foundations of International Law* (New York: John Wiley, 1961), p. 199.

17. Abram Leon Sachar, *A History of the Jews* (New York: Knopf, 1968), pp. 19–20, cited in Barry M. Blechman, "The Consequences of Israeli Reprisals: An Assessment" (Ph.D. dissertation, Georgetown University, 1971), p. 253.

18. Blechman, "Consequences," p. 284.

19. *Ibid.,* pp. 286–87.

20. *Ibid.,* p. 288.

21. Moshe Dayan, "Why Israel Strikes Back," in Donald Robinson, ed., *Under Fire: Israel's Twenty Year Struggle for Survival* (New York: Norton, 1968), pp. 122–23. See also *The Jerusalem Post,* September 1, 1955, p. 1.

22. Blechman, "Consequences," pp. 48–49.

23. *Ibid.,* p. 289.

24. *Discussion of Methodology.* Obviously the figures are not complete, but the sample is large enough to indicate a believable proportion.

25. Brian Urquhart, *Hammarskjold* (New York: Harper Colophon Books, 1972), p. 157.

26. "Reagan's Irresolute Mid-East Policy Keeping Region Drift," *Middle East Times,* July 19–25, 1987, p. 11.

27. One has only to go to the Middle East and compare the U.S. embassies with those

of the Western European powers. The American Embassy looks like a fortress, without windows and surrounded by guards; the European buildings are open, with windows. The difference demonstrates the acute unpopularity of the United States in that region.

## CHAPTER THIRTEEN

1. Department of State, *Background Notes* (Washington, D.C.: Bureau of Public Affairs, Government Printing Office), Belgium, December 1989, p. 1; Israel, January 1991, p. 1; and Spain, April 1991, p. 1. All are reports for the year 1989. See also World Bank, *World Development Report 1990* (New York: Oxford University Press, 1990).

2. *Newsweek,* March 19, 1990, p. 34. Although the United States opposes the use of our aid for establishing new Jewish settlements, we have, as we shall later point out, relinquished any means of tracing the use of our aid funds. The $35 billion figure certainly seems high and could not be paid by the United States.

3. *Congressional Record,* Senate discussion of S.5426, May 1, 1990.

4. *Ibid.*

5. The nominal amount comes to $66.95 billion, but from that one must deduct $13.6 billion of interest and principal repayments. For a full discussion of this point, see Richard H. Curtiss, *A Changing Image: American Perceptions of the Arab-Israeli Dispute* (Washington, D.C.: American Educational Trust, 1986), p. 2; Mohammed El-Khawas and Samir Abed-Rabbo, *American Aid to Israel: Nature and Impact* (Brattleboro, Brattleboro, Amana Books, 1984), pp. 27 and 19; and Clyde R. Mark, *Israel: U.S. Foreign Assistance Facts* (Washington, D.C.: Congressional Research Service, May 7, 1990, cited hereafter as Mark, *CSR*), pp. 4–5. Total aid for fiscal 1991 is as follows:

CONGRESSIONAL AID

$1.8 billion in military aid, $475 million of which could be spent in Israel, and $1.2 billion in economic aid. Both economic and military aid were all grants, and the economic aid was paid in cash for direct deposit in Israel's treasury without restrictions on its use. In addition, the aid was paid within thirty days of the beginning of the fiscal year instead of in quarterly installments, meaning Israel earned $86.1 million in interest.

ADDITIONAL MILITARY AID

*Surplus military equipment:* $700 million worth of materiel from U.S. stockpiles in Europe.

*Excess military equipment:* $500 million, including $200 from U.S. stockpiles and $300 million from U.S. stockpiles in Israel.

*Interest subsidy:* $150 million in debt reduction resulting from restructuring of Israel's military loans.

*Pricing revisions:* $60 million decrease in Israeli payments resulting from revisions of costs by the Defense Department.

*Extra military aid:* $43 million in equipment given Israel during the Gulf War.

*Arrow project:* $42 million for Israel's anti-missile missile program.

ADDITIONAL ECONOMIC AID

*Supplemental aid:* $850 million for Israel's economic loss during the Gulf War.

*Refugees:* $45 million for resettlement of Soviet Jews.

*Third World countries:* $7.5 million for Israeli aid programs in Africa.

*Cooperative programs:* $7 million for Israeli-Arab cooperative programs.

In addition, there was granted a $400 million housing loan guarantee for housing for Soviet immigrants (the aggregate United States to Israel in 1991 alone).

From the House Committee on Foreign Affairs, June 1991, cited in George Moses, "1991 U.S. Government Outlays for Israel," *The Washington Report on Middle East Affairs,* March 1992.

6. In addition to the costs that will be mentioned in the following pages, some additional minor costs may be cited: (1) The 1990 State Department appropriation (PL101-162) moves $183.5 million for the construction of radio transmitters in the Negev to be used by the United States for Radio Free Europe and Radio Liberty. The utility of these in light of the end of the Cold War is doubtful. (2) The 1990 foreign aid bill included $25 million for resettling Jews in Israel. Senator Inouye (D-HI) proposed to increase this to $400 million. Since President Bush put a cap on the number of Jews to be admitted from the Soviet Union (50,000 per year) on the grounds of expense and budgetary stringency, this would amount to the claim that we cannot afford to settle Soviet Jews here, but we can afford to pay their bills in Israel. (3) About $87 million a year is appropriated for joining Egyptian-Israeli agricultural and scientific projects. (4) Israel gets $10 million out of $35 million a year spent for foreign schools and hospitals. This program has become widely political in Israel and is the target of congressional reform or abolition. (5) Israel has received $7.5 million a year to help it buy recognition from various African states by launching projects of various sorts.

7. *The Jerusalem Post,* International Edition, June 29, 1991, p. 8.

8. *The Washington Post,* July 9, 1990.

9. *Congressional Record,* Senate, May 1, 1990, p. S-5417.

10. Sec. 4 of P.L. 93-199, December 26, 1973; repeated in subsequent years.

11. The inadequacy of the revised procedures was demonstrated in January 1985 when U.S. officials questioned Israel about reports that America's refugee resettlement funds were being illegally used to settle Ethiopian Jews in the West Bank near Hebron, in violation of Sec. 532(b)(2) of P.L. 95-384 (92 Stat. 734), September 26, 1978, repeated in subsequent years. Israeli officials evasively replied that those funds were being used only for a processing center (*The New York Times,* January 18, 1985; Mark, *CSR,* May 7, 1990, p. 9). Yet *The Jerusalem Post* on March 12, 1985, reported that the Ethiopians of Hebron were not recent immigrants.

12. Preventing the United States from monitoring aid funds has amounted to putting blinders on both America's executive branch and Congress. That was clearly demonstrated during Israel's invasion of Lebanon in 1982. Although that war cost Israel at least $1.2 billion (*U.S. Assistance to the State of Israel* [uncensored], p. 35), the Israelis insisted at the time that such outlays would require no additional U.S. government aid. Yet, U.S. military aid rose from $1.4 billion in FY 1982 to $1.7 billion in FY 1983 and 1984, while our government also "forgave" an increasing percentage of old debt aid. Similarly, U.S. economic aid increased $100 million between 1982 and 1984. Then, in FY 1985, the United States enacted an "emergency" $1.5 billion economic aid package for Israel, to be spread over two years. Thus the Security Supporting Assistance Program, which included the Commodity Import Program (CIP), required that all aid recipients buy commodities in the United States and submit vouchers for reimbursements. But when, in 1978, the Israeli government complained that it found it a nuisance to furnish such documentation, our government gave up even that shallow pretense of accountability.

13. Sec. 531 of P.L. 98-473 (98 Stat. 1901), October 12, 1984; repeated in subsequent years.

14. *Congressional Record,* Senate, May 1, 1990, p. S-5421.

15. Mark, *CSR,* March 8, 1988, p. 5.

16. Sec. 101(b)(3) of P.L. 98-151 (97 Stat. 969), November 14, 1983; repeated in subsequent years.

17. Mark, *CSR,* March 8, 1988, p. 6. The loans are paid in inflated dollars of reduced purchasing power. In 1987, Congress authorized the recipients of military aid loans to refinance all such debt bearing interest at more than 10%. To enable such countries, including Israel, to sell their debt at 9%, Israel got the United States to guarantee its new bonds so that if there were a default, the U.S. Treasury would have to pay. So far, Israel has refinanced approximately $5.5 billion of such debt. Under normal congressional practice no appropriation can be voted without Congress first passing an authorizing bill. Since that involves the participation of two separate committees and substantial time delay, the Con-

gress has made an exception for Israel, by passing an authorization bill not limited in duration with respect to aircraft. Thus, in the words of the CRS Report, "The President was authorized to transfer to Israel aircraft and equipment to maintain and protect the aircraft as may be necessary." Sec. 501 of P.L. 91-441 (84 Stat. 909), October 7, 1970; extended by Sec. 807 of P.L. 95-79 (91 Stat. 323), July 30, 1977; expired 1979.

18. Title IV of P.L. 98-573 (98 Stat. 2948), October 30, 1984, authorized the President to negotiate the agreement, and P.L. 99-47 (99 Stat. 82), June 11, 1985, implemented the agreement. See 19 U.S.C. 2112, and 19 U.S.C. 2518.

19. Sec. 1103(a)(2)(D) of P.L. 99-661 (100 Stat. 3816), November 14, 1986, added subsection (j)(1) to Section 27 of the AECA: Section 1105(F) of P.L. 99-661 called for an annual report from the Secretaries of State and Defense naming non-NATO allies: on February 2, 1987, the Secretary of State informed the House Foreign Affairs Committee by letter that Israel was designated a non-NATO ally.

20. Israel and the United States signed a Memorandum of Understanding on May 6, 1986, providing for Israeli involvement in SDI. According to the Washington *Jewish Week* of November 1986, Israel and the United States signed contracts in November 1986, providing for Israeli research on an anti-tactical ballistic missile (ATBM) as part of the SDI research.

21. Rowan Scarborough, "Israelis Set to Acquire 75 New F-16s," *Defense Week,* March 14, 1988, p. 5.

22. United States General Accounting Office, *Foreign Assistance Analysis Cost Estimates for Israel's Lavi Aircraft* (Washington, D.C.: U.S. National Security and International Affairs Division, January 31, 1987), p. 19. This was an extremely accurate prediction, for the precedent of providing Israel with loans up to thirty years was ultimately extended, at their demand, to Egypt, Greece, Turkey, Somalia, and the Sudan, while the extension to Israel of the privilege of cash flow financing was also exacted on the basis of precedent by both Egypt and Turkey. Finally, when America's aid to Israel was first transformed solely to grants, Egypt and other Third World nations clamored for similar treatment and, to some degree, got it, at an additional charge to the U.S. Treasury.

23. GAO, p. 37.

24. Lawrence W. Whetten, *The Canal War: Four Power Conflict in the Middle East* (Cambridge, Mass.: MIT Press, 1974) pp. 205–06.

25. GAO, p. 38.

26. Israel recently signed a $1 billion contract to make heavy mortars for the U.S. Army. Helena Cobban, "Baker Draws a Line in the Sand,"

27. GAO, p. 45.

28. In May 1982, Israeli Defense Minister Ariel Sharon requested a further $250 million per annum for the in-country use of FMS credits for Merkava tank production and other projects—an idea that lapsed in the uproar over Israel's Lebanese invasion.

29. The Lockheed bailout vividly illustrates this point.

30. *The Washington Post,* August 6, 1986, p. A1.

31. GAO, pp. 1, 9.

32. *Facts on File,* 1987, pp. 649–50. As will be indicated in Chapter 14, the Israelis have learned nothing from this affair and Moshe Arens is talking once more of reviving his pet project.

33. Donald Neff, "Tale of Two Planes," unpublished article, August 23, 1987, pp. 3–5.

34. U.S. Assistance to the State of Israel, Washington, D.C., GAO, June 24, 1983. Some assiduous representatives of either the Departments of Defense, or State, or of the Treasury deleted the quoted language from the finally published version, but an uncensored version has long been obtainable.

35. El-Khawas and Abed-Rabbo, *American Aid,* p. 35. It increased from $30 million in 1970 to $545 million in 1971.

36. Robert Lacey, *The Kingdom: Arabia & The House of Sa'ud* (New York: Harcourt Brace Jovanovich, 1981), pp. 398–99.

37. *Ibid.,* p. 400. The chairman of the board of the Standard Oil Company of Califor-

nia, Otto N. Miller, urged in a company letter to the firm's nearly 300,000 shareholders and employees that America should foster "the aspirations of the Arab people [and] their efforts toward peace in the Middle East. There is now a feeling in much of the Arab World that the United States has turned its back on the Arab people. . . . " Although his statement made no direct mention of Israel, Jewish groups exploded in protest, urging a boycott of Standard Oil products. To calm the waters, Miller later issued a statement saying that peace of course had to be based "on the legitimate interests of Israel and its people as well as the interests of all other states in the area."

38. *Ibid.*, pp. 401–02.

39. *Ibid.*, pp. 403–12.

40. *Facts on File,* 1978, p. 97. The sale was announced February 14, 1978.

41. On October 19, 1973, Kadafi had announced that Libya was immediately cutting off all oil shipments to the United States and raising the price of its premium oil to other countries from $4.90 to $8.25 a barrel, an additional 70 percent price hike from the price imposed by OPEC only three days earlier.

42. copy tk

43. Kissinger, *Years of Upheaval,* pp. 885–86.

44. GAO, p. 53.

45. Lillienthal, *The Zionist Connection,* p. 764.

46. Anthony Cordesman, *The Gulf and the Search for Strategic Stability: Saudi Arabia, the Military Balance in the Gulf, and Trends in the Arab-Israeli Military Balance)* (Boulder, Colo.: Westview, 1984), pp. 124–25.

47. *Facts on File,* February 17, 1978, p. 97. Israel demanded 150 F-16s, worth $6.25 billion, in compensation.

48. *Financial Times,* February 19, 1986. The planes were worth $9 billion, which together with the side and collateral contracts running until the 1990s, brought the total deal to an estimated $28 billion.

49. Dennis J. Wamsted, "Election Year Politics," *Washington Report,* January 27, 1986, p. 5.

50. Dennis J. Wamsted, "Saudi Arms and Election Year Woes," *Washington Report,* June 16, 1986, p. 4.

51. *Facts on File,* 1986, pp. 185, 408. Senator Cranston, a heavy recipient of Jewish PAC money, subsequently got into trouble for taking large contributions from Charles Keating of the failed Lincoln Savings and Loan Company.

52. See also *Facts on File,* June 15, 1988, pp. 506–07. France also sold Saudi Arabia a large quantity of arms.

53. *Council for the Advancement of Arab-British Understanding (CAABU) Bulletin,* vol. 5, no. 6, April 1, 1989.

54. Andy Pasztor, *Wall Street Journal,* March 18, 1991, p. 113.

55. *The Washington Post,* David Ottaway articles, March 23, 1988, March 25, 1988, and May 23, 1988. This issue resurfaced in 1992 when reports of illegal technology transfers by Israel to other countries again came to the fore. See Edward T. Pound, "U.S. Sees New Signs Israel Resells Its Arms to China, South Africa," *Wall Street Journal*, March 13, 1992, p. 1.

56. Since the Bradley frequently sinks when crossing rivers (fortunately not plentiful in Saudi Arabia), the senator may have concluded that this weapon was more dangerous to its user than its enemies.

57. March 31, 1988; *Facts on File,* June 10, 1988, p. 411. Congress forbade the sale of any Stinger missiles to any Gulf state (except Bahrain) during 1988–89. Secretary Murphy told the junior author in May 1991 that there may only have been one missile which was returned after its battery wore out. Iran offered to sell the Gulf states some Stingers its supporters in Afghanistan had acquired.

58. Robert Hazo, "A Turning Point: British-Saudi Arms Deal," *Washington Report,*

August 1988, pp. 7–9. Israelis prefer U.S. sales with strings attached. *Washington Report,* July 15, 1985, p. 4.

59. *Facts on File,* October 25, 1985, p. 800.

60. America's passionate attachment handicaps our industry even when specific sales are not blocked. Thus, Boeing lost the sale of a civilian Kuwaiti aircraft to Europe's Airbus consortium despite our escorting of Kuwaiti vessels in the Gulf. By that gesture the Kuwaiti government sought to emphasize its disapproval of our passionate attachment to Israel and our indifference toward the Palestinians. Saudia (the official airline of Saudi Arabia) and Lebanon's Middle East Airways promptly followed suit. If there is unemployment in our aircraft industry, American unions can readily pinpoint the cause. *Middle East Economic Digest,* February 13, 1988, p. 12.

61. *Near East Report,* vol. XXXII, no. 29, July 18, 1988, p. 1.

62. Dennis J. Wamsted, "The Facts Don't Matter: A Year End Review," *Washington Report,* December 30, 1985, pp. 4–6.

## CHAPTER FOURTEEN

1. Aaron Klieman, *Israeli Arms Sales: Perspectives and Prospects* (Jerusalem: Jaffee Center for Strategic Studies, Paper No. 24, 1984), pp. 21–25. To keep up with Israel's military sales operations, see Jane Hunter, *Israeli Foreign Affairs,* December 1984 and on.

2. Patrick Martin, "Israel's War Machine," *Toronto Globe and Mail,* March 30, 1985. See also Jane Hunter, *No Simple Proxy: Israel in Central America* (Washington, D.C.: Washington Middle East Associates, 1987).

3. Klieman, *Israeli Arms Sales,* pp. 40–41.

4. Benjamin Beit-Hallahmi, *The Israeli Connection: Who Israel Arms and Why* (New York: Pantheon, 1987), p. 78, citing B. Debusmann, "After Embassy Flap, a Look at Israel's Latin Arms Role," *Philadelphia Inquirer* (Reuters), April 24, 1984.

5. Beit-Hallahmi, *The Israeli Connection,* p. 248.

6. Although the Israeli government invariably denies any connection between shady characters and its own official activities, there is substantial evidence that at least semi-official Israelis have been involved in dubious operations.

7. It is generally believed that he was engaged by Colombia's Medellín drug merchants to train their death squads. His arrest was sought by Colombia in 1989, but Israel refused to cooperate, limiting itself to prosecuting Klein for mainly local offenses.

8. David Halevy and Neil C. Livingstone, "Noriega's Pet Spy," *The Washington Post,* January 7, 1990, pp. B1–2. American troops have also captured another Israeli citizen, Ben Gaitan, who is said to have been the civilian supervisor of Noriega's security detail.

9. The Israeli press reported that Harari arranged for General Noriega's protection on foreign trips, that he masterminded Noriega's first official visit to Israel in June 1984, and that Noriega subsequently bought a seaside house in Israel.

10. See *Israeli Foreign Affairs,* vol. VI, no. 1 (January 1990), pp. 1–2.

11. Ever since then, the Guatemalan government has relied exclusively on Israel for weapons, military intelligence, and advice on handling discontented Maya Indians demanding land reform.

12. Guatemalan leaders openly boast that their pacification program is based on Israeli models in Lebanon, and they resent the U.S. refusal to approve $300 million for their "anti-Communist" program. Congress's unwillingness to subsidize genocide directly while ostentatiously refusing to bring Israel to account has left Israel in a particularly strong position of influence.

Israeli agents smuggled former President Rios Montt (again a candidate for President in 1990) to safety in Miami after his overthrow in 1984. Montt is one of the growing band of fundamentalist Protestants in Guatemala with important ties to right-wing, pro-Zionist

Christian groups in the United States. In the past, these groups have produced large donations to support the Guatemalan regime's concentration camp policies. Guatemala is one of only five countries that diplomatically accepts Israel's unilateral annexation of East Jerusalem, a position the United States has avoided. Guatemala usually supports Israel in the United Nations and has tried to use Israel's influence in Washington for its own purposes—so far with no success.

13. Israeli services to the outcast Guatemalan regimes have been many and varied. Israeli computer operatives set up an intelligence system under the auspices of Tadiran, a Histadrut-owned firm, which assembled data on at least 80 percent of the country's adult population. These lists have enabled the regime up to the present day to pinpoint would-be enemies and have them quietly murdered by provincial death squads (Debusmann, "After Embassy Flap . . . " [Reuters], *Philadelphia Inquirer,* April 24, 1984).

Israeli advisers have also assisted the Guatemalan Secret Police (G-2) and trained the army in counterinsurgency. At least three hundred native-born Israelis are helping Guatemala. They teach the locals how to torture victims and still keep them alive for continued interrogation. Israeli operatives may also intervene directly; in February 1986, Israeli nationals kidnapped and severely beat the secretary of the municipal workers union (SCTM) (Israel Shahak Papers, December 1, 1981). The Shahak papers are memorandums prepared by Shahak over the years on various aspects of Israeli life and policy. Shahak is one of the earliest opponents of Israel's treatment of the Arabs and the absence of civil rights.

14. Experts on security trained the Salvadorean secret police, ANSENAL. Among their pupils was the late Robert d'Aubuisson, head of the right-wing death squads for many years. The list of his victims included the archbishop of San Salvador, Oscar Arnulfo Romero. Another alumnus was Colonel Sigimudo Ochon Perez, who in 1984–85 launched a brutally repressive operation in Morozon and Choletenengo provinces. He declared the inhabited areas of his district to be free-fire zones, enforced a food blockade to starve the villagers into submission, and forced those in his thrall to enroll in "civil defense patrols," which were little more than local murder gangs.

Ochon, d'Aubuisson, and the current president, Christiani, have declared their admiration for Israel and applauded its 1982 invasion of Lebanon. They dismiss with contempt the Americans who, they remind everyone, lost the war in Vietnam. They would like to end American moderation, land reform, and other unwanted innovations. They believe that brute force is the solution to every problem. (The fact that Israel has not been successful in crushing Arab civilian population resistance is either unknown to or ignored by those who hire its experts.) In consequence, the Salvadorean regime stepped up its systematic bombardment of villages, torpedoed peace talks until 1992, and pressed Israeli-trained computer personnel into service to help identify and liquidate suspected guerrillas. Concentration camps in the form of villages have been set up, and 500,000 people forced into them.

15. Edy Kaufman, Yoram Shapira, and Joel Brinkley, *Israel-Latin American Relations* (New Brunswick, N.J.: Transaction, 1979), pp. 187–205.

16. *The Jerusalem Post,* April 26, 1984, p. 10. See also Ilana Debora, "Dilemma in Central America," *The Jerusalem Post,* April 27, 1984, p. 7.

17. Disturbed by Israel's reluctance to get too openly involved, the Reagan administration tried to encourage greater zeal in Jerusalem by floating anti-Semitic charges against the Sandinista regime. These accusations were designed to persuade Israel to back the administration and induce AIPAC to pressure Congress and public opinion, both of which were rebelling against the Reagan administration's stand. It was, in a curious way, a repetition of the tactics both Johnson and Nixon had used to rally Israel's support for the Vietnam War. And it, too, failed. Pressure on Israel to get further involved in the Nicaraguan affair proved futile, largely because Prime Minister Shamir did not want to irritate Congress.

As 1984 advanced, Israel wearied of Washington's constant importunings. Iranian arms sales offered a possible way around this problem. Robert McFarlane and Oliver

North each claimed later that David Kimche, the civil service head of the Israeli Foreign Ministry, had suggested the use of Iranian arms sales profits for the Contras (*The New York Times,* December 30, 1986)—which Kimche promptly denied (*Jerusalem Post,* January 4, 1987). Attorney General Edwin Meese's interrogation further revealed that North had discussed the matter with the late Amiram Nir, Prime Minister Peres's "terrorism" adviser, who suggested using the profits for the Contras and taking "funds from a residual account and transferring them to a Nicaraguan account" (*The Times* [London], January 12, 1987, Report on Preliminary Inquiry, p. 43).

Israeli aid to the Contras before the 1986 exposure of the Iran-Contra affair ran to about $5 million, consisting of arms captured in Lebanon and a little cash. Arms shipments to the Contras greatly increased as the money from Iran was received. Private Israeli arms dealers, such as Ya'acov Nimrodi, shipped arms to the Contras at the request of CIA Director William Casey. Since the arms had been captured, Israel's out-of-pocket expense was minimal (*The Washington Post,* December 12, 1986). Other private sales included RPG-7 grenade launchers and SA-7 surface-to-air missiles, used to shoot down Soviet-supplied helicopters. Also, there were rumors that arms had been stolen from U.S. arsenals and, through the good offices of the Israelis, made available to the Contras (*Milwaukee Journal,* January 19, 1987). Israel vehemently denied any official role in this business, blaming the private arms dealers, whom it professed to be unable to control (*Los Angeles Times,* September 18, 1986).

18. Faced by a large Costa Rican debt and the need for fresh loans, President Monge had promised during his campaign to relocate the Costa Rican Embassy to Jerusalem if Israel would help out with a $7 million loan and use its influence in Washington to refinance Costa Rica's debts. Israel also agreed to help promote tourism among the American Jewish community. Once Israel had complied, the Costa Rican Embassy was indeed moved to Jerusalem in violation of UN Assembly Resolution 478.

19. Jane Hunter, *No Simple Proxy,* pp. 49–55. See also Jonathan Marshall, Peter Dale Scott, and Jane Hunter, *The Iran Contra Connection: Secret Terms and Covert Operations in the Reagan Era* (Boston: South End Press, 1987), pp. 136–37.

20. Beit-Hallahmi, *The Israeli Connection,* pp. 101–04. In justification, Israel has claimed that its cozy relationship with the junta was part of a plan to protect the Jewish community in Argentina. Inconveniently, one of the junta's victims, Jacobo Timerman, demonstrated that Israel had done nothing to protect the local Jews. He then published *The Longest War,* criticizing the 1982 Lebanese War. For this act Timerman was harassed into leaving Israel. Israeli dignitaries like General Mordechai Gur, Yitzhak Rabin, *et al.,* visited Argentina, and it is rumored that the Israelis tried to prevent the junta's overthrow after its Falkland Islands debacle.

21. *Israeli Foreign Affairs,* vol. vI, No. 1 (January 1990), p. 6. See also *The New York Times,* November 5, 1989, for reports of three thousand Israeli personnel in country helping out at the Debra Zeit Air Base south of Addis Ababa and elsewhere.

22. The weapons involved included thirty-six Kfir jets, hundreds of Gabriel missiles, howitzers, communications equipment, radar systems, intelligence technology, airplane parts and ammunition, jets, and artillery.

Israel has also helped the South Africans to procure needed communication, detection, and night-vision equipment, including ground radar stations and anti-guerrilla alarm systems; and to copy the Israeli border defense system, complete with fencing and detection arrangements.

23. Although it signed an agreement with Israel in 1972 to co-produce the Merkava main battle tank, South Africa canceled that arrangement a year later when it realized that it did not need such weapons. The South African Iron and Steel Corporation (ISCOR) has, however, continued to supply the special armor plate that Israel still needs for the manufacture of this tank, as well as the special chemical steel mixes used at the Urdan plant near Netanya. Israel has, in turn, helped South Africa to modernize all of its British Centurion

tanks and Panhard armored cars with that same new armor plating. Moreover, the Israelis have supplied hundreds of Israeli military personnel to train South African troops, including the elite South African Reconnaissance Commandos.

24. Quoted in Jane Hunter, *Israeli Foreign Policy, South Africa and Central America* (Boston: South End Press, 1987), p. 54.

25. Beit-Hallahmi, *The Israeli Connection,* pp. 108–65. See *Newsweek,* November 6, 1989. The U.S. government, despite widespread discussion of these matters, continues to deny their existence.

26. *Facts on File,* July 4, 1991, p. 514. Reportedly, South Africa denied having tested a weapon of its own, but the indications were that it was capable of making such weapons.

27. *The Washington Post,* October 24, 1989. The department refused to answer any inquiries that Israel and South Africa were working on an intermediate missile. See also *Middle East International,* no. 362, November 3, 1989, pp. 11–12.

28. See the *Boston Globe,* July 27, 1983; see also *The New York Times,* March 7, 1982. On April 15, 1991, Gary Sick in *The New York Times* reported that representatives of the Reagan campaign (most likely William Casey) met with Iranian officials to prevent the freeing of American Embassy hostages prior to the November 1980 election, and promised arms sales for such cooperation. While Casey, who was managing Reagan's campaign, is dead and cannot answer back, it is fair comment to note that Casey's subsequent actions during the Iran-Contra affair appear consistent with such a story.

29. *Facts on File,* June 18, 1982, p. 435. On April 16, 1991, Alexander Haig, the Secretary of State during this era, was questioned on television about Israel's claims for American authority in such trades. Haig admits giving Israel limited permission to trade in some items, but then the Israelis went beyond this authority and General Sharon lied about it. Far from being indignant about this shabby treatment accorded him by his friend, Haig, with smiling cynicism, wrote such behavior off as the usual small change of international relations.

30. Seymour M. Hersh, *The New York Times,* December 8, 1991, p. A1. Again, the Hersh article notes there is some dispute as to whether Haig continued to authorize U.S. equipment by Israel to Iran, as some Israeli Defense Ministry officials report.

31. *Ibid.* Danish sailors blew the whistle on this operation in 1986, but no action was taken.

32. Why should Pakistan refrain from building nuclear weapons when Israel is not even urged to sign the Non-Proliferation Treaty? And why should the United States be concerned solely with the chemical weapons production of Iraq, Syria, and Libya when Israel openly admits its own chemical capabilities?

33. David Ottaway, "Israelis Aided China on Missiles," *The Washington Post,* May 23, 1988, pp. A1, A27.

## CHAPTER FIFTEEN

1. *The Jerusalem Post,* International Edition, April 25, 1992, p. 1. Shamir's attempt to justify a new strategic role for Israel by substituting Moslem fundamentalism for the Soviet Union is, on its face, an act of desperation rather than reason.

2. The Israelis regarded America's obedience as so automatic that they inserted the first installment of the guarantees in their budget without clearance from Washington.

3. FBIS-NES 92-030, February 13, 1992, p. 33.

4. Several of Israel's most prominent economists have proposed from time to time that America reduce its aid. Assaf Razin, an economist at Tel Aviv University and former economic adviser to the government, was both emphatic and specific: "The best thing the United States could do for Israel is to force it to take the medicine the politicians here cannot give . . . they ought to condition aid on economic policies. Without certain pres-

sures, the politicians here cannot do anything on their own initiative." Mr. Fisher, the senior economist at the Bank of Israel, added: "I don't want to accuse the United States of overgenerosity, but there is always the tendency here to fall back on Uncle Sam. I am not saying, 'Don't give us aid.' Give us aid, but it has to be tied to some economic conditions." (*The New York Times,* October 29, 1984, p. D6.)

The Minister of Finance, Yitzhak Modai, admitted that part of Israel's problem was that "we definitely lived beyond our means." There was general agreement that the new national unity government had taken only "token" steps, while Histadrut, the labor monopoly, had rejected even these governmental proposals.

5. As American aid spiraled upward and inflation skyrocketed in the early 1970s, the Israeli pound, which had been at par with the British pound in 1948 at $2.80, by 1973 was worth only 24 cents. This inflationary spiral was, to a considerable degree, cushioned for the Israeli people by the retention of the old price index system, carried over from the days of the British Palestinian Mandate; it protected savings and wages from inflationary attrition.

6. Koor, a large conglomerate corporation owned by the trade union, Histadrut, lost $250 million in 1988; after it had defaulted on $30 million of notes to the Banker's Trust Company of New York, the Israeli government bailed it out.

7. Donlan quotes an Israeli Holocaust survivor who first lived in Israel, then "fled from its economy" to Australia, as saying: "Israel has been committing economic suicide from the very establishment of the state. If Israel had adopted a tax system similar to Hong Kong's, it would not be facing the existing problems, as it is reasonable to assume that Israel's Jewish population would have been twice as large as it is now and that the country's gross national product would have been four times larger than now."

8. Israel's military effort also disrupts the functioning of the economy by compelling large elements of its work force to undergo annual military service and frequent special call-ups. Such interruptions penalize efficiency by periodically draining off productive workers and breaking the rhythm of efficient production. To be sure, Israel receives gratis from America the highly sophisticated military equipment in which it takes great pride, but that only multiplies the pressures on Israel's economy. In Israeli defense circles it is commonly assumed that every dollar's worth of military equipment America provides costs Israel four dollars of its own defense budget to man and maintain.

9. Stein and Fischer's comments were first contained in an article in *The New York Times* (October 12, 1991) entitled "Overhaul the Israeli Economy." They were then repeated in the testimony each gave before the Subcommittee for Foreign Operations of the House Committee on Appropriations on February 21, 1992.

10. Arnon Gafny, who served as governor of the Israeli Central Bank from 1977 to 1982, suggests that Israel has suffered from what is commonly called the "Dutch Disease." He means by that that a temporary "gift of nature" like the Dutch natural gas fields, or Israel's external aid, may confer benefits for a limited period, but in the long run will impair a country's competitiveness by encouraging it to spend beyond its people's own means.

Among other things, this steadily increasing influx of funds encourages Israel to press forward with the expansionist ambitions of its right wing, and to waste money profligately in such fatuous programs as its fiasco in trying to build the Lavi and in such irrational military adventures as its brutal and misbegotten invasion of Lebanon in 1982.

11. By 1987, aid had jumped to 76% of the value of Israel's trade deficit, from 24% in 1970. Loewenberg has pointed out that if Israel's economy were reformed (largely, he implies, by pruning its socialist vestiges), Israel might resume its pre-1973 growth rate, double its GNP in just ten years, and, by the year 2002, generate the equivalent of ten years of aid and philanthropy every year, thus eliminating the need for outside subsidization.

For a further discussion of the Israeli economy, see Robert J. Loewenberg, "Why Prop Up Israeli Socialism?" *The New York Times,* June 24, 1991. See also *The Jerusalem Post,* International Edition, January 7, 1989, p. 8, for an article by Shlomo Maoz entitled "The

Economy: Shooting from the Hip." Maoz is the Economic Editor of *The Jerusalem Post.*

12. Joel Bainerman, "Israel Needs Reform, Not Charity," *Newsday,* July 19, 1991, p. 29. There are conflicting numbers on the firms owned by the government, mergers and sales of the companies making it difficult to get current data.

13. These statistics were first provided by Professor Richard C. Wade of the Graduate School, University Center, City University of New York, in his testimony before the New York Governor's Commission on Libraries. They were reprinted in the *Congressional Record* for April 17, 1992, p. 18.

14. Lester C. Thurow, "Money Wars: Why Europe will 'Own' the 21st Century," *The Washington Post,* April 19, 1992, p. C1.

15. Howard M. Sachar, *Diaspora* (New York: Harper & Row, 1985). The Diaspora's sense of being shut out is intensified by the knowledge that many Israelis fiercely resent any American nuance of phrase that might be interpreted as doubting their total competence. So, made conscious of their status as a privileged aid recipient, most Jewish Americans wish to avoid any implication that America is buying Israeli cooperation. They fear also that any collaborative effort by Jewish American leaders with their Israeli counterparts might be attacked by Israeli extremists as a device to enable America to dictate Israel's internal policies.

16. Francis Plimpton (who had earlier served as U.S. ambassador with special responsibilities for the Security Council) observed that with that decision, America's "virginity was lost." Any reader of eighteenth-century novels knows that the loss of virginity is the prelude to a slippery slide toward promiscuity—and that is what happened to America in its relations with Israel.

17. The Israelis complain that the Security Council more often censures Israel (or would, were it not for America's veto) for violating Security Council resolutions, the UN Charter, or various treaties such as the Geneva Conventions than it does the Arab nations when they violate human rights. Many, for example, have censured Kuwait for its expulsion of the Palestinians. However, the deportation of aliens from Kuwait is an internal affair of that country, beyond the authority of the United Nations, while Israel's expulsion of Palestinians from the Occupied Territories is a violation of the Geneva Conventions and therefore not an internal matter. Israel commits its most blatant offenses outside its own territory. Its violations are therefore unequivocally under UN jurisdiction.

18. In addition, the United States has supported General Assembly Resolutions 181(II), 191, and 3236, which (though not legally binding) have declared in favor of the Palestinian right of self-determination and the creation of a Palestinian state. In the preamble to Security Council Resolution 242, the Security Council referred to the "inadmissibility of the acquisition of territory by war," thus invalidating Israel's continued occupation of the territories it had seized in 1967. The most recent instance in which the United States has voted to approve a resolution critical of Israel was when it approved Resolution 726, which saved the ongoing peace negotiations by censuring Israel for the deportation of twelve Palestinians.

19. Donald Neff, *Warriors at Suez* (New York: Simon & Schuster, 1981), p. 68.

20. Opponents of the resolution would no doubt remind us that the United States originally rejected self-determination at the Lausanne Conference in a desire to please the British, who were anxious to punish the Mufti of Jerusalem for his pro-Nazi activities. Today, the British are wholeheartedly in favor of self-determination for the Palestinians and have made their views well known in the Security Council. Jordan is no longer a player, in view of King Hussein's decision to withdraw from the game. Thus, the only nations that oppose application of the principle to the Palestinians are the United States and Israel, for reasons which, in our view, are wholly discreditable. There is a Palestinian people, and the UN settlement must reflect that reality if it is to keep the peace.

21. Testimony before the Subcommittee for Foreign Operations of the House Committee on Appropriations, February 21, 1992.

22. In part, no doubt, Israel's expansionist actions have acquired a theological overlay. With fantasies of a reconstructed Kingdom of David and of a covenant with God, Israel has been prepared to make few if any compromises to advance the march toward peace. Nor have the Arabs been much more forthcoming. They forfeited by inaction what might well have been a propitious moment for settlement after the failure of the Lausanne Conference. Immediately following the 1967 War they reacted with shame and nihilism when they issued the Khartoum Declaration.

23. If one needs any confirmation for the suggestion that Israel would use a temporary delay to produce an irrevocable expansionism, one need only observe what has happened since the Bush administration deferred the curtailment of American aid for new settlements but reserved grandfather rights for existing settlements. That resulted in frenzied building as well as large-scale government promotion for moving Jews to the West Bank.

24. The disposal of the colonies in the Sinai was a major contentious issue at Camp David, but the Israeli citizens resident in the Sinai were only a small number compared with those in the Occupied Territories. Although there was some violence in connection with the Sinai withdrawal, Egypt and America stuck to their guns and the settlers were carried off kicking and screaming.

Today, the Israel settlers in the Occupied Territories are far better entrenched than were those in the Sinai. Thus, many even predict that the settlers could not be removed without an intensity of violence approaching a civil war. That may become a breaking issue without some concession—either an international fund to assist the reestablishment of the settlements, or an offer that they may remain providing they choose to live in the West Bank under the same laws and regulations as the other Palestinian residents.

25. One encouraging item of news is that world developments have significantly reduced the power of AIPAC to dominate the American Congress. When the issue of the loan guarantees was first raised in September 1991, Congress was deterred only by the threat of a presidential veto from granting Israel's unqualified request. But when congressmen went home during the Labor Day recess, they found their constituents strongly opposed to foreign aid, including loan guarantees to Israel. Public hostility to spending—particularly to help foreign governments—continues to mount. These findings have been confirmed by a nationwide poll taken by the *Wall Street Journal* and NBC News in March 1992. Only 13% of American voters in that poll favored an unconditional loan guarantee; 32% backed the President's position of putting conditions on the deal; and 49% opposed the guarantees however qualified.

Still worse from Israel's view, its powerful political engine—the American Jewish community—is riven by disagreement. With the commencement of the peace negotiations, many concluded that Israel's long-hoped-for goal of peace with its neighbors was at last at hand. Then followed their distress and disgust with the Shamir regime's efforts to sabotage the negotiations. The result is a visible split within this hitherto united group. Within families, older members have remained committed to expansion, while the younger members strongly prefer efforts for peace.

26. Arthur M. Schlesinger, Jr., *The Cycles of American History* (Boston: Houghton Mifflin, 1986), p. 68.

# Index